Classrooms & Staffrooms

Classrooms

&

Staffrooms

THE SOCIOLOGY OF
TEACHERS & TEACHING

Edited by
Andy Hargreaves and Peter Woods

Open University Press
Milton Keynes

Open University Press
Celtic Court
22 Ballmoor
Buckingham
MK18 1XW

and
1900 Frost Road, Suite 101,
Bristol, PA 19007, USA

First published 1984
Reprinted 1987, 1989, 1993

This selection and editorial matter © 1984 Open University Press

British Library Cataloguing in Publication Data

Classrooms and Staffrooms.
  1. Techers   2. Educational sociology
  I. Hargreaves, Andy   2. Woods, Peter, 1934–
305.9'372   LB1775

ISBN 0-335-10583-1

Text design by W. A. P.
Cover design by Paul Clark.

Typeset by Mathematical Composition Setters Ltd,
Ivy Street, Salisbury, Wilts.
Printed in Great Britain by St Edmundsbury Press Ltd,
Bury St Edmunds, Suffolk.

Contents

Acknowledgements

The Open University Press would like to thank the following for permission to reproduce copyright material. All possible care has been taken to trace ownership of the selections included, and to make full acknowledgement for their use.

Reading 1: M. Hammersley and *Sociological Review*, Vol. 22, No. 3, August 1974; pp. 355–368.

Reading 2: D.H. Hargreaves, S.K. Hester and F.J. Mellor, *Deviance in Classrooms*, Routledge and Kegan Paul, 1975; pp. 67–89.

Reading 3: P. Atkinson and S. Delamont, in P. Woods and M. Hammersley (eds.) *School Experience*, Croom Helm, 1977; pp. 87–108.

Reading 4: P. Woods in P. Woods and M. Hammersley (eds.) op. cit.; pp. 271–293.

Reading 5: A. Hargreaves in L. Barton and R. Meighan (eds.) *Sociological Interpretations of Schooling and Classrooms: A Reappraisal*, Nafferton, 1978; pp. 73–96.

Reading 6: A.C. Berlak, H. Berlak, N.T. Bagenstos, E.R. Mikel and *School Review*, 83(2), 1975; pp 215–243. By permission of A.C. Berlak *et al.* and University of Chicago Press.

Reading 7: H.S. Becker and *Journal of Educational Sociology*, 25(4), 1952; pp. 451–65. By permission of H.S. Becker and the American Sociological Association.

Reading 8: N. Keddie in M.F.D. Young (ed.) *Knowledge and Control*, Collier-Macmillan, 1971; pp. 133–158.

Reading 9: R. Sharp and A. Green, *Education and Social Control*, Routledge and Kegan Paul, 1975; pp. 114–127.

Reading 10: L. Tickle in A. Hargreaves and M. Hammersley (eds.) *Curriculum in Practice*, Falmer Press, 1983; pp. 107–125.

Reading 11: M. Stanworth, *Gender and Schooling: A Study of Sexual Divisions in the Classroom*, Hutchinson, 1982; pp. 21–29, 48–53.

Reading 12: W. Waller, *The Sociology of Teaching*, Wiley, 1932; pp. 375–398. Reprinted by permission of John Wiley and Sons Ltd.

Reading 13: D. Lortie, *Schoolteacher*, University of Chicago Press, 1975; pp. 83–89, 91–106, 269–274.

Reading 14: P. Woods, *The Divided School*, Routledge and Kegan Paul, 1979; pp. 210–212, 216–236.

Reading 15: M. Hammersley, 'Staffroom News'. © Martyn Hammersley, 1984 (this volume).

Reading 16: A. Hargreaves in L. Barton and S. Walker (eds.) *Schools, Teachers and Teaching*, Falmer Press, 1981; pp. 303–329.

Reading 17: S. Ball and C. Lacey in P. Woods (ed.) *Teacher Strategies*, Croom Helm, 1980; pp. 157–177.

Reading 18: G.F. Riseborough and *Sociology*, Vol. 15, No. 3, 1981; pp. 355–381. By permission of G.F. Riseborough and the British Sociological Association.

Introduction

Some fifty years ago, Willard Waller published his classic text on *The Sociology of Teaching* (1932). It is both a compliment to his skill and insights and indicative of the enduring themes of his study, that it remains as relevant and popular today as ever (see Reading 12). In this book, we aim to show how the most central concerns of his pioneering work have been built on more recently through the upsurge of interest in school processes.

The themes which Waller was concerned with and which grew from his work were to do with how teachers maintain order in the classroom; what strategies they use to maintain their authority; how they cope with the pressures that bear down on them; how they manage the teacher role; their treatment of pupils; the implications of these classroom involvements for teachers' relations with their colleagues; what goes on in staffrooms; how teachers engage in educational debate; what ambitions teachers have for themselves; and how their perceptions of their careers are affected by changing socio-economic circumstances and educational policies.

These matters require detailed understanding of the nature of school life and of the perspectives on it of teachers and pupils. Pupils are considered in the companion volume to this reader, *Life in School; The Sociology of Pupil Culture* (Hammersley and Woods, 1984). The articles presented here try to get to grips with what it is like to be a teacher, to make sense of the moment-by-moment trials and tribulations of the job, the rewards and the penalties, the opportunities and the constraints.

This is the hallmark of what is known as the *ethnographic* method of educational inquiry. It aims to bring to life by close observation and/or depth interview the internal workings of an institution or culture, to reveal the perspectives of its members, to highlight the constraints that they work under, the kinds of adaptations they make as a result, and to make explicit the routine and taken-for-granted features of institutional life on which orderly management may depend. All the papers in the volume are to one degree or another located within this tradition. But they all begin with detailed observations of what life is actually like in schools for those who work within them. This is not to say that they lose sight of the wider constraints that bear down on the school from society as a whole, such as the impact of divisions of class, race, and gender, the effects of economic crisis on educational policy, or the consequence of demographic changes for falling rolls and teacher careers.

The ethnographic approach has only become established within the last ten years or so. Until the 1970s, sociologists of education were largely preoccupied with the effects of home background (parents' attitudes, incomes, provisions for homework etc.) as a set of 'inputs' which children brought with them to school, on their ultimate achievement in the 11 plus examination, university entrance or whatever—on their educational *outputs* as it were. What went on inside schools and classrooms was largely left out of account.

Waller's book (from a previous age) and its concern with the cultural life of the school was perhaps the outstanding exception to this. But there were other influences at work too. In the rest of this introduction we shall trace briefly the traditions and trends that lay behind the awakening of interest in ethnography in British sociology of education during the 1970s, and the insights these afforded to the study of teachers teaching.

The Chicago School

One set of studies which has had a long standing and pervasive influence has been that of a group of American sociologists who worked at the University of Chicago. *Theoretically*, much of their inspiration was derived from the symbolic interactionist writings of George Herbert Mead which placed the self at the centre of social interaction, looked at the active role that the self played in constructing the making sense of the world, and examined how the self changed and adapted as situations demanded. For symbolic interactionists, people do not respond automatically and unthinkingly to any stimulus or pressure they are subjected to, but they make sense of these pressures in terms of frameworks of meaning they have built up through their lives and come to share with others. *Substantively*, the interests of the Chicago School were broad too, but in practice much of their writing was concerned with deviant and underprivileged groups, and with the study of occupations and their effects on the person (Becker, 1970). The work of Howard Becker in the 1950s and 1960s included the lives of students and teachers among such studies. One such study (Becker 1952a, 1952b, 1953) charted the career and the occupational circumstances of Chicago public schoolteachers (see Reading 7). A number of important points were highlighted in this work. In the classroom, Becker noted, teachers treated pupils differently according to how close to or distant from the teacher's *ideal* those pupils were. With less able, usually 'working class' and ethnic minority pupils for instance, teachers would often lower their expectations, concentrate on discipline not learning, and teach more slowly. The result of this was that already disadvantaged pupils were disadvantaged still further by the way the teacher treated them. The type of classroom adaptation that Chicago public schoolteachers made to the problems their pupils presented for them had implications for their careers too. The aim of most new entrants to teaching in Chicago was to move out of the inner city slum schools of their first appointments at the earliest opportunity, and gain a posting in a more attractive, higher status, suburban school where the discipline was easier and the children better motivated. But, Becker noted, if this move was not achieved in the first few years, teachers adjusted their career ambitions. They became reconciled to their inner city fate. Moreover, as they gained competence in discipline and control, they found reward in the authority this gave them, and, being used to a rather slow pace of learning involving little preparation of their part, they became fearful of the demands on their time outside school that a change of job to a desirable suburb would make. Becker's analysis is in this sense an excellent illustration of the close connection between what happens in the classroom and the broader aspects of a teacher's work.

Dan Lortie (1975), a later member of the Chicago school took the study of these interconnections between different parts of the teacher's job still further. The central feature of teaching, he argued, was the isolation of teachers into tight little egg-crate-like compartments where they interacted with pupils. This gave them a much valued sense of autonomy, and they rated these rewards of contact with their pupils highly; but, lacking feedback from colleagues on the effectiveness of their teaching, this also made them continually anxious about their competence. As a result of these classroom conditions the culture and thinking of elementary schoolteachers became dominated by what Lortie (see Reading 13) called *presentism* (avoidance of long-term planning and the concentration of efforts on short-term projects which might make a difference), *conservatism* (resistance to radical change), and *individualism* (unwillingness to collaborate with colleagues).

Similar comments on the nature of teacher thinking and its origins in the condition of the job were made by Philip Jackson (1968) in his *Life in Classrooms* where he pointed to the *immediacy* of the classroom, the pressing necessity for elementary teachers to make innumerable instantaneous decisions which allowed little time for reflection or critical thought. One consequence of this, Jackson pointed out, was that teachers lacked a technical vocabulary, their talk having a disconcerting 'conceptual simplicity' about it. Jackson himself was not an interactionist, but like Louis Smith (see Smith and Geoffrey, 1968), a psychologist by initial training, who abandoned traditional psychological methods for ethnography in order to get closer to what was happening in schools. Smith's intent, for example, was to 'describe the silent language of a culture, a classroom in a slum school, so that those who have not lived in it will appreciate its subtleties and complexities' (p. 2). The two books were notable landmarks in that they helped to legitimate and popularize the hidden curriculum as an area of study.

As a group, the Chicago School writers and the interactionist concerns that underpinned their work have had an enormous impact on later studies in the ethnography of teaching. In particular, along with Waller's classic text, they still provide one of the major sets of insights into teacher cultures, insights which are clearly traceable through to some of the most recent work on this theme in Britain (e.g. D. Hargreaves, 1980, 1982; and see Readings 4, 6, 14, 15 and 17).

Ethnomethodology

A rather different set of explanations of the internal processes of schooling has been provided by a group of writers known as ethnomethodologists. As Harold Garfinkel (1967), the coiner of the term puts it, ethnomethodology means little more than the charting of the methods ('methodology') that people ('ethno') use to make sense of one another, and construct a social order together in everyday life.

Ethnomethodologists ask, what are the basic rules—the sense-making practices—by which we understand one another, and which make conversation possible and prevent order dissolving into chaos? When somebody asks 'How are you?', why is that instead of simply saying 'Fine' we don't challenge them to be more specific and say whether they mean 'How are you physically?' or 'How are you mentally?'. The answer, ethnomethodologists argue, is that it is what we do *not* say in interaction that matters most: the competences we assume of one another, the working assumptions we make that we all see the world and interpret our words the same way, the way we *trust* one another to 'fill in' the gaps between our words and treat what is said as obvious. This is what makes order possible.

Thus, Hargreaves, Hestor and Mellor (1975; and see Reading 2) point out that when a teacher shouts out 'Jones!' to a pupil, it is assumed that Jones will know, for instance, that there is a rule (copying) which he is breaking (by being out of his seat) and that he must remedy this (by returning to his seat immediately). Indeed, so taken for granted is this ability to interpret what is *not* said in classroom interaction, that if Jones replies 'What?', the teacher will assume him not to be incompetent but knowingly awkward. It is the assumptions of this kind, the tacit rules that are laid down in the first few days with a new school or teacher, and which quickly become taken-for-granted, along with the shared competence of teachers and pupils to interpret them in the same way, that make classroom order possible.

In America, the study of these basic rules and competences has tended to focus on the abilities of young pupils, to recognize what teachers want, and the teachers' reciprocal ability to recognize the competences that these pupils already have (Cicourel *et al.*, 1974; Mehan, 1976, 1979; MacKay, 1973). To a lesser extent, ethnomethodologists have also looked at the commonsense assumptions teachers draw on when they assign pupils to different ability groups (Leiter, 1974; Cicourel and Kitsuse, 1963). In Britain, though, ethnomethodologists have been concerned more with how teachers maintain classroom order as in the study by Hargreaves *et al.* (1975) mentioned above; or with how they defined knowledge (see Readings 1 and 3).

Such studies, it has been argued, have important implications for teacher training. As Payne and Hustler (1980, p. 49) put it, while 'experienced teachers may well arrange their classes in such taken-for-granted ways that they are not consciously aware of the nature of their accomplishment', the important thing is to make this tacit knowledge, this routine behaviour explicit to new teachers so that they too can become competent classroom managers.

The Chicago interactionist and ethnomethodological traditions with their respective emphases on control as against order, strategies as against rules, provide two of the most powerful influences on contemporary ethnographic work. In practice, most current work does not fall clearly into one type or the other. The two approaches are often combined in the recognition, sometimes explicit, sometimes less so, that strategies involve manipulations of existing rule systems, and that equally, these rule systems are nothing more than the residues of previously successful teaching strategies which have become routinized over the years (Hammersley, 1980). Strategy and rule are in this sense interdependent, an acknowledgement that is implicit in the contribution of Hammersley in this volume (Readings 1 and 3).

Non-sociological influences

Not all American influences on the ethnography of teaching are strictly sociological in nature, though. As Delamont and Atkinson (1980) point out, most American research on schools and classrooms has not been conducted from a sociological angle at all, but within the field of applied *anthropology*. In part, this results from continuing concern in American society with the problems of cultural minorities, a concern which has been reflected in studies of culture class between teachers and black pupils (Rist, 1973), and in studies of the cultural misunderstandings that occur between teachers and American Indian pupils (Dumont and Wax, 1969).

Another influence has been the *social-psychological* investigation of teachers' expectations of their pupils and of the self-fulfilling prophecies which often result. Much of this work was initially experimental in nature as in Rosenthal and Jacobson's (1968) study of *Pygmalion in the Classroom*, where 'false' predictions of pupil improvement were fed to teachers who then, so it turned out, treated those pupils in such a way as to confirm that initial prediction of 'academic blooming' (see also Beez, 1970). Despite the serious methodological problems with this work (see, for example, Thorndike 1968), it pioneered the way for investigations of the same phenomenon on the lines of labelling theory in interactionism (D. Hargreaves, 1976), personal construct theory (Nash, 1976), and typification theory within ethnomethodology/phenomenology (D. Hargreaves *et al.*, 1975; Sharp and

Green 1975—see Reading 9), or the *actual* processes by which and conditions under which such self-fulfilling prophecies operated. (For a review see D. Hargreaves, 1977.)

Last, but by no means least, in the late 1960s and early 1970s, a number of writers known as the 'Deschoolers' produced a number of critiques of the schooling process and its effects upon children. The very titles of their books—for example *Compulsory Miseducation* (Goodman, 1961), *Deschooling Society* (Illich, 1971) and *School is Dead* (Reimer, 1971)—summed up the savage nature of the attacks their authors mounted. Among them were some highly insightful if rather journalistic accounts written 'from the inside', as it were, of what it was like to be a teacher or pupil in a school. Kozol (1968) provided an engaging autobiographical account of his own early experiences as a teacher in a slum school trying to educate rather than merely control his pupils. Most influential of all, perhaps, were John Holt's (1969, 1971) perceptive accounts of teacher–pupil interaction in elementary school classrooms, and of teachers' inability to recognize how they dominated classroom talk, how they inculcated an intense sense of failure amongst those pupils, and how all this was deeply antithetical to learning.

To sum up, there have been a number of different traditions within American studies of teachers and teaching which have highlighted different facets of the world of the classroom:

1 Chicago-school interactionism: with its emphasis on strategy and control.
2 Ethnomethodology: with its stress on competence and order.
3 Anthropology: with its insistence on viewing classroom life through the eyes of its participants.
4 Social psychology: with its pioneering work on teacher typifications and self-fulfilling prophecies.
5 Deschooling: with its emphasis on the gaps in classroom understanding, and the ironies and consequences of this for teachers' ability to educate.

The more the study of teachers and teaching has developed, the more these influences have cross-cut and overlapped. But there are indigenous antecedents to the ethnographic study of teaching in Britain too.

British influences: early developments

Early British influences fall into two areas—sociolinguistics, and studies of the internal organization of primary and secondary schools:

1 *Sociolinguistics.* As early as 1958, Basil Bernstein in his work on sociolinguistic codes was arguing that teachers use and approve of an 'elaborated' code of speech, to which the working class child is not accustomed (see Bernstein, 1973). As a result, Bernstein argued, teachers consistently devalued working class forms of expression in its typically 'restricted' code. Douglas Barnes (1968) took this point further in his analysis of the language used in classrooms by secondary school teachers. These teachers, Barnes argued, were prone to using a technical, high-flown *language of secondary education* in their lessons which mystified and bemused students and created a distance, a power gap, between students and teachers. In this sense, Barnes was offering one particular educational example of a more general point appreciated by sociolinguists as a whole that in social terms, language use can realise and express relationships of

formality and informality on the one hand, or those of equality or power imbalance on the other. Thus, the greater the degree of formality and/or power imbalance, the more likely one will find such things as the use of received pronunciation as against local dialect, and so on. Such variations of language use with social context even in the same speaker, have taxed the minds and energies of sociolinguists for years. And in the classroom with its forms of discourse that are so far removed from everyday conversation, they have found a fascinating laboratory for their work. Here, sociolinguists have noted not only that the formality and asymmetry of the teacher–pupil relationship is confirmed by the language of secondary education, but that the teacher's customary right to evaluate the worth and correctness of what pupils have to say (Sinclair and Couthard, 1974) and indeed the appropriateness of *how* they say it ('speak up', 'don't mutter', 'Now—in a proper sentence please!') (Stubbs, 1976) also have the same effect. Pupils have no such rights. Pupil evaluation of teacher talk is, in consequence, a rare event. If such routine reaffirmations of the basic asymmetry of interpersonal relations in the classroom ever look in doubt, teachers can always abandon subtlety and go back to the old-fashioned imperative, the direct command. In this sense, as Cooper (1976) points out it is curiously ironic that by Bernstein's definition, much teacher talk belongs much more to the restricted rather than to the elaborated form.

Organizational studies. If this push to look more closely at the nature of classroom teaching came from outside the sociology of education, another followed from the inner logic of the problems facing the sub-discipline itself in the late 1960s. By this point, all the statistical studies of the relationship between home background and pupil achievement were turning up very similiar findings— little 'news' was being created (Bernstein, 1975). Yet there were just the smallest of hints that schools and teachers might be making some contribution of their own to pupil failure. J.W.B. Douglas (1964) for example, in his massive national survey of primary schoolchildren, pointed out that once pupils had been allocated to different streams, the attainment gap between them actually *widened* during their primary school careers. Brian Jackson (1968) took up this point in his critique of streaming in primary schools. But Joan Barker Lunn's (1970) study of the streaming phenomenon turned up what were possibly the most interesting findings. It did not matter, she concluded, whether classes were streamed or unstreamed. This, of itself, made little difference to pupil achievement. What *did* matter was the attitude of the teacher involved. For if pro-streaming teachers ran what were, on paper, unstreamed classes, they still effectively operated them as streamed ones—with pupils being grouped *within* the classroom rather than between them. A mere organizational change, it seems could not legislate for changes in teacher perspectives—the new organizational framework was simply redefined by the teacher and reinserted into his/her existing frame of reference. The existence of similar processes was beginning to be appreciated at the secondary level too. Lacey (1970) and Hargreaves (1967) pointed to the way in which pupils were first *differentiated* by streaming, and then because of the different treatments accorded each group of pupils by their teachers, subsequently *polarized* into separate sub-cultures with opposing values. Moreover, not only were the pupils streamed, but so too were the teachers, deriving their status from the kinds of classes they were given. Although much of the Manchester work was not ethnographic—most of the data being collected from pupils' essays, sentence completion tests, and sociometric tests—they did help persuade the sociological and teaching communities that the internal processes of schooling were worth further investigation. Indeed, while the thrust of research then turned, as we shall see, to more purely ethnographic forms of inquiry, large remnants of the Manchester tradition with its mixture of statistical and ethnographic data survived into certain later studies. The best example of these came from a student of Lacey's, Stephen Ball (1981),. in an analysis of broad ability banding and mixed ability grouping in a comprehensive school.

The New Sociology of Education

At the beginning of the 1970s, these various influences, together with a certain despair at the failure of traditional approaches to make much impact upon educational inequalities, a new climate of cultural radicalism, and a massive expansion of sociology of education within colleges and departments of education where lecturers were searching for 'relevant' classroom material that would engage the interest of their intending teachers (Gorbutt, 1972)—all these things led to the emergence of what came to be known as the *new sociology of education*. This turned the theoretical focus of the sociology of education to the internal processes of schooling. It drew widely on fashionable theoretical developments within the parent discipline of sociology to do this, and appealed to both the immediate classroom concerns *and* the radical ideals of intending teachers, many of whom hoped to change the world by transforming the nature of their own classroom relationships. With the dissemination of its ideas in the Open University course *School and Society* (1972) and the adoption of one of the definitive texts, M.F.D. Young's (1971) *Knowledge and Control*, as a set book for that course, the new sociology of education despite its theoretical difficulty achieved great popularity among intending and inservice teachers.

Theoretically, the new sociology of education was a curious mixture. In *Knowledge and Control*, for instance, Nell Keddie's paper (see Reading 8) drew widely on cultural anthropology, Howard Becker's notion of the ideal pupil, and Alfred Schutz's concept of typification. And the papers by Young and Esland, cited writers as different as Marx, Mead, Weber and Schutz, as theoretical forbears. *Substantively*, while there was a great deal of talk at the level of theory about *knowledge*, its organization and selection, and its availability to different kinds of pupils (Young, 1971; Bernstein 1971), this led to virtually no empirical studies of the school curriculum or school subjects in the broader sense. In practice, empirical work settled down to classroom analyses of teachers as agents of differentiation and of the hidden forms of control that underlay versions of teaching which were, so it was claimed, only *ostensibly* 'progressive' and 'democratic' (e.g., Keddie, 1971; Sharp and Green, 1975).

The classroom, then, with its forms of pupil differentiation, and its modes of teacher control was the major focus of the new sociology of education. Yet while Keddie (1971) in her seminal paper on 'Classroom knowledge', made an important distinction between the *teacher context* of the classroom and the *educationist context* of educational discussion and staffroom debate, empirical studies of the educationist context, of subject and staffroom cultures and of teachers' involvement in school decision making did not follow until much later. It is interesting to observe, perhaps, that this delayed growth of sociological interest in teacher cultures, along with empirical studies of teacher careers and the organization of the curriculum, has coincided with two other things: a shift in the balance of teacher education from the initial training of young classroom-centred teachers to the in-service education of more mature members of the profession with their greater interest in career and organizational matters; and a developing appreciation that resistance to classroom and curriculum innnovation is often located in the cultural context of teaching, in the overt and subtle pressures that teachers exert on their colleagues.

Lately, the self-conscious preoccupation with theory which frequently tended to outrun empirical documentation has subsided a little among school ethnographers. Without abandoning theory altogether, school ethnography in line with the recommendations of Woods (1984), Pollard (1984), and D. Hargreaves (1981), is becoming increasingly problem-centred and policy-focussed in its concerns. Ethnographers are drawing judiciously on theory, or even competing theories where relevant, to clarify problems and issues associated with such things as crisis points in teacher careers (Measor, 1984; Sikes, 1984), the effects of examinations on teaching and learning in secondary schools (Scarth, 1983), and the variations in curriculum practice between different subjects (see the collection in Hammersley and Hargreaves, 1983). Theoretical bearings remain important, as does the development and modification of any such theory. Indeed some have explicitly addressed themselves to the theoretical possibilities within ethnography, and have urged that they not be lost sight of (Hammersley, 1980; A. Hargreaves, 1980; D. Hargreaves; 1981, Woods, 1984). However, it is the issues, not the theories which are increasingly coming to dominate the research agenda. The current economics and politics of the financing of research, which puts a premium on matters of immediate practical application, might accelerate this trend.

Yet despite all these more recent developments, there remains one set of theoretical approaches which has added a particularly distinctive dimension to the ethnography of teaching in the 1970s and 1980s—Marxism.

Marxism

One problem with the ethnography of teaching is that it is prone to treating the school or the classroom as if it existed in a social or cultural vacuum, unaffected by the economic demands, political pressures and social influences of the wider society. This preference for 'splendid isolation' in much school ethnography sometimes leads not only to incomplete accounts of school processes but to *distorted* ones too (A. Hargreaves, 1980). There is sometimes a tendency to exaggerate the latitude and freedom engaged by the teacher and to underestimate the constraints bearing down on the teacher from the wider society.

In trying to rectify this collective bias within the ethnography of schooling, Marxist sociology of education has offered extensive explanations of 'the system' (in this case a capitalist one), in which the actions and perspectives of teachers (and indeed pupils) play only a small part. Where they are taken into account, they tend to be derived more from the theory or from 'commonsense' than from close-up observations of classroom and staffroom life (Bowles and Gintis, 1976; Althusser, 1971; Sharp, 1980; Harris, 1982).

Where Marxists *have* endeavoured to apply the ethnographic method, this has almost always been in the service of analyses of pupil rather than teacher cultures and adaptations (e.g., Willis, 1977). This perhaps reflects their concern to outline the conditions of the most obviously exploited group in the school—the pupils (especially working-class ones) and to reveal patterns of resistance among them which might later be used as a platform for transformative pedagogy and revolutionary socialism (Anyon, 1981). One important exception, though, is a fairly extensive Marxist analysis by Sharp and Green (1975) of the perspectives and actions of three 'progressive' infant school teachers.

Sharp and Green's study (Reading 9) points to the way in which infant school teachers have to adopt strategies like 'busyness' (ensuring most pupils are 'busy' while giving disproportionate attention to a selected few) in order to deal with material constraints deriving from the nature of capitalism (like high teacher–pupil ratios, low resources, public expectations for emphasis to be placed on basic skills) while still maintaining the 'progressive' appearance of pupil choice and child-centred education. Moreover, they argue, the necessity to resolve these contradictory demands leads to inconsistencies in the teachers' thinking when they attempt to explain their practice.

Now the adequacy of this analysis of the effects of capitalism on the teacher has been heavily criticized, on the grounds that the constraints are asserted rather than demonstrated, that teachers are never asked about them, and that apparent inconsistencies in teacher accounts of their practice may well be due to other factors instead, or as well as, capitalism (D. Hargreaves, 1978; Hammersley, 1976). Some of these might be due to micro, situational elements, such as changes in context, some to macro elements other than capitalism, such as *bureaucracy* (e.g., Cicourel and Kitsuse, 1963; Kanter, 1973; Gracey, 1972) or patriarchy (Arnot, 1983). However, the need to link the closely observed world of teaching to changes in society and educational policy as a whole, forms some of the most important unfinished business for the sociology of education.

Summary

The theoretical underpinnings of the ethnographic study of teaching are remarkably diverse—interactionist, ethnomethodological, sociolinguistic, anthropological, social psychological and Marxist, to name but a few. The range of topics covered is now impressively large too. In this volume, we have sought to bring together examples of some of the most important and influential pieces of work which illustrate that range and which have hitherto been spread widely among different research reports, academic journals, and collections of conference papers. Brought together in this way and organized into coherent areas of interest we hope that they will encourage comparison and assessment, broaden the overall understanding of the nature, determinants and consequences of teaching, and promote further work within the field.

References

Althusser, L. (1971) 'Ideology and the state', in Althusser L. (ed.) *Lenin and Philosophy and Other Essays*, New Left Books, London.

Anyon, J. (1981) 'Social class and school knowledge', *Curriculum Inquiry*, Vol. 11, No. 1.

Arnot, M. (1982) 'Male hegemony, social class and women's education', *Journal of Education*, Vol. 164, No. 1.

Ball, S. (1981) *Beachside Comprehensive*, Cambridge University Press.

Barnes, D. (1969) 'Language in the secondary school classroom', in Barnes D., Britton, J. and Rosen, H. (eds) *Language, the Learner and the School*, Penguin, Harmondsworth.

Becker, H. (1952a) 'The career of the Chicago public schoolteacher', *American Journal of Sociology*, Vol. 57, March.

Becker, H. (1952b) 'Social class variation in the teacher–pupil relationship', *Journal of Educational Sociology*, Vol. 25, No. 4.

Becker, H. (1953) 'The teacher in the authority system of the public school', *Journal of Educational Sociology*, Vol. 27, November.

Becker, H. (1970) *Sociological Work*, Aldine, Chicago.

Beez, W. V. (1970) 'Influence of biased psychological reports on teacher behaviour and pupil performance', in Miles, W.V.R. and Charters, W.W. (eds) *Learning in Social Settings*, Allyn and Bacon, New York.

Bernstein, B. (1971) 'On the classification and framing of educational knowledge', in Young M.F.D. (ed.), *Knowledge and Control*, Collier-MacMillan, London.

Bernstein, B. (1973) *Class, Codes and Control:* Vol. 1, Paladin, St. Albans.

Bernstein, B. (1975) 'The sociology of education: a brief account', in Bernstein B. (ed.) *Class, Codes and Control: Volume III*, Routledge and Kegan Paul, London.

Bowles, S. and Gintis, H. (1976) *Schooling in Capitalist America*, Routledge and Kegan Paul, London.

Cicourel, A.V. and Kitsuse, J.I. (1963) *The Educational Decision-Makers*, Bobbs-Merrill, New York.

Cicourel, A.V. *et al.* (1974) *Language Use and School Performance*, Academic Press, New York.

Cooper, B. (1976) *Bernstein's Codes: A Classroom Study*, University of Sussex Education Area Occasional Paper 6.

Delamont, S. and Atkinson, P. (1980) 'The two traditions in educational ethnography: sociology and anthropology compared', *British Journal of Sociology of Education*, Vol. 1, No. 2.

Douglas, J.W.B. (1964) *The Home and The School*, Panther, St. Albans.

Dumont, R.V. and Wax, M.L. (1971) 'Cherokee school society and the intercultural classroom', in Cosin, B.R. *et al.* (eds) *School and Society*, Routledge and Kegan Paul, London.

Garfinkel, H. (1967) *Studies in Ethnomethodology*, Prentice-Hall, Englewood Cliffs.

Goodman, P. (1961) *Compulsory Miseducation*, Penguin, Harmondsworth.

Gorbutt, D. (1972) 'The new sociology of education', *Education for Teaching*, Vol. 89.

Gracey, H. (1972) *Curriculum or Craftsmanship: Elementary School Teachers in a Bureaucratic System*, University of Chicago Press.

Hammersley, M. (1976) *E202 Schooling and Society*, Unit 9 Teacher Perspectives, The Open University Press, Milton Keynes.

Hammersley, M. (1980) 'Classroom ethnography', *Education Analysis*, Vol. 2, No. 2 (Winter).

Hammersley, M. and Hargreaves, A. (1983) *Curriculum Practice* Falmer Press, Lewes.

Hammersley, M. and Woods, P. (eds) (1984) *Life in School: The Sociology of Pupil Culture*, The Open University Press, Milton Keynes.

Hargreaves, A. (1980) 'Synthesis and the study of strategies: a project for the sociological imagination', in Woods, P. (ed.), *Pupil Strategies*, Croom Helm, London.

Hargreaves, D.H. (1967) *Social Relations in a Secondary School*, Routledge and Kegan Paul, London.

Hargreaves, D.H. (1976) 'Reactions to labelling', in Hammersley, M. and Woods, P. (eds) *The Process of Schooling*, Routledge and Kegan Paul, London.

Hargreaves, D.H. (1977) 'The process of typification in the classroom: models and methods', *British Journal of Educational Psychology*, November.

Hargreaves, D.H. (1978) 'Whatever happened to symbolic interactionism?' in Barton, L. and Meighan, R. (eds) *Sociological Interpretations of Schooling and Classrooms: a Reappraisal*, Nafferton Books, Driffield.

Hargreaves, D.H. (1980) 'The occupational culture of teachers', in Woods, P. (ed.) *Teacher Strategies*, Croom Helm, London.

Hargreaves, D.H. (1981) 'Schooling for delinquency', in Barton, L. and Walker, S. (eds) *Schools, Teachers and Teaching*, Falmer Press, Lewes.

Hargreaves, D.H. (1982) *The Challenge for the Comprehensive School*, Routledge and Kegan Paul, London.

Hargreaves, D.H., Hester, S.K. and Mellor, F.J. (1975) *Deviance in Classrooms*, Routledge and Kegan Paul, London.

Harris, K. (1982) *Teachers and Classes*, Routledge and Kegan Paul, London.

Holt, J. (1969) *How Children Fail*, Penguin, Harmondsworth.

Holt, J. (1971) *The Underachieving School*, Penguin, Harmondsworth.

Illich, I. (1971) *Deschooling Society*, Harper and Row, New York.

Jackson, B. (1968) *Streaming: An Educational System in Miniature*, Routledge and Kegan Paul, London.

Jackson, P.W. (1968) *Life in Classrooms*, Holt, Rinehart and Winston, New York.

Kanter, R.M. (1974) 'Commitment and social organization', in Field, D. (ed.), *Social Psychology for Sociologists*, Nelson, London.
Keddie, N. (1971) 'Classroom knowledge', in Young, M.F.D. (ed.), *Knowledge and Control*, Collier-MacMillan, London.
Kozol, J. (1968) *Death at an Early Age*, Penguin, Harmondsworth.
Lacey, C. (1970) *Hightown Grammar*, Manchester University Press.
Leiter, K.C.W. (1976) 'Ad hocing in the schools: a study of placement practices in the kindergartens of two schools', in Hammersley, M. and Woods P. (eds) *The Process of Schooling*, Routledge and Kegan Paul, London.
Lortie, D. (1975) *Schoolteacher*, University of Chicago Press.
Lunn, J.B. (1970) *Streaming in the Primary School*, NFER, Slough.
Mackay, H. (1973) 'Conception of children and modules of socialization', in Dreitzel, H.P. (ed.) *Recent Sociology*, No. 5, *Childhood and Socialization*, Collier-MacMillan, London.
Mead, G.H. (1934) *Mind, Self and Society*, University of Chicago Press.
Mead, G.H. (1936) *Works of George Herbert Mead: Movements of Thought in the 19th Century*, Merritt H. Moore (ed.) University of Chicago Press.
Measor, L. (1984) 'Critical periods in teacher careers', in Ball, S. and Goodson, I. (eds) *Life Histories and Teacher Careers*, Falmer Press, Lewes.
Measor, L. and Woods, P. (1984) *Adapting to Comprehensive School: The Sociology of Pupil Transfer*, The Open University Press, Milton Keynes.
Mehan, H. (1976) 'Assessing children's school performance', in Hammersley, M. and Woods, P. (eds) *The Process of Schooling*, Routledge and Kegan Paul, London.
Mehan, H. (1979) *Learning Lessons*, Harvard University Press, New York.
Nash, R. (1976) 'Pupils' expectations of their teachers', in Stubbs, M. and Delamont, S. (eds) *Explorations in Classroom Observation*, Wiley, Chichester.
Open University, The (1972) *E 282 School and Society*, The Open University Press, Milton Keynes.
Payne, G. and Hustler, D. (1980) 'Teaching the class: the practical management of a cohort', *British Journal of Sociology of Education*, Vol. 1, No. 1.
Pollard, A. (1984) 'Ethnography and social policy for classroom practice', in Barton, L. and Walker, S. *Social Crisis and Educational Research*, Croom Helm, London.
Reimer, E. (1971) *School is Dead: An Essay on Alternatives in Education*, Penguin, Harmondsworth.
Rist, R. (1973) *The Urban School: a Factory for Failure*, MIT Press, Cambridge, Mass.
Rosenthal, R. and Jacobson, L. (1968) *Pygmalion in the Classroom*, Holt, Rinehart and Winston, New York.
Scarth, J. (1983) 'Teachers' school-based experiences of examining', in Hammersley, M. and Hargreaves, A. (eds) *Curriculum Practice: Some Sociological Case Studies*, Falmer Press, Lewes.
Sharp, R. (1980) *Knowledge, Ideology and the Politics of Schooling*, Routledge and Kegan Paul, London.
Sharp, R. and Green, A. (1975) *Education and Social Control*, Routledge and Kegan Paul, London.
Sikes, P. (1984) 'The life cycle of the teacher', in Ball, S. and Goodson, I. (eds) *Life Histories and Teacher Careers*, Falmer Press, Lewes.
Sinclair, J.M. and Coulthard, R.M. (1974) *Towards an Analysis of Discourse: The English Used by Teachers and Pupils*, Oxford University Press.
Smith, L.H. and Geoffrey, W. (1968) *The Complexities of an Urban Classroom*, Holt, Rinehart and Winston, New York.
Stubbs, M. (1976) *Language, Schools and Classrooms*, Methuen, London.
Thorndike, R.L. (1968) 'Review of *Pygmalion in the Classroom*', *AERA Journal*, Vol. 5, No. 4.
Torode, B. (1977) 'Interrupting intersubjectivity', in Woods, P. and Hammersley, M. (eds) *School Experience*, Croom Helm, London.
Waller, W. (1932) *The Sociology of Teaching*, Wiley, New York.
Willis, P. (1977) *Learning to Labour*, Saxon House, Farnborough.
Woods, P. (1984) 'Ethnography and theory construction in education', in Burgess, R. (ed.) *The Ethnography of Educational Settings*, Falmer Press, Lewes.
Young, M.F.D. (ed.) (1971) *Knowledge and Control*, Collier-MacMillan, London.

PART ONE

Teachers and
Classroom Management

1   The Organization of Pupil Participation

M. HAMMERSLEY

In this article Martyn Hammersley examines some ways in which teachers maintain classroom order in conventional 'chalk and talk' teaching in secondary school classrooms. He draws particular attention to the ways in which teachers organize pupil participation in class as a way of transmitting knowledge which also secures their attention to the task in hand.

The purpose of this paper is largely descriptive: to give an account of an aspect of the order that the teachers in one school seek to impose on classroom interaction.[1] Analysis of that order is essential for any satisfactory account of pupil actions. The explanation of pupil orientations in terms of 'background' or even 'subculture' is premature without detailed attention to the organisation of the school and particularly to the nature of the 'teaching' in classrooms.

Attention to teachers' classroom activities is also important for any account of schools as 'socialising' agencies seeking to mould pupils in terms of a particular version of cultural competence. It is in relation to some such notions of competence and achievement that pupils are judged by teachers to be 'bright', 'stupid' etc. Assessments of a person's intelligence are based on evaluations of his performances at particular activities and in particular circumstances. Whatever the claims of those doing the assessment, it is essential to investigate the conditions under which those who are being evaluated must act if they are to be seen as 'intelligent', and the conception of intelligence in terms of which they are being judged—the activities that are taken as crucial and the criteria of 'success' or 'intelligent attempt' that are applied. Schools are agencies assigning particular importance to certain activities and able to a considerable degree to impose a particular definition of achievement on pupils.

My focus in the present paper is the way in which the teachers in a particular school work to organise pupil participation in classrooms and the relevance of that organisation for the 'intelligence' pupils are required to show. The nature of the knowledge which the teachers present, in terms of which pupils must display their 'intelligence', is an equally important topic, but, like the overall organisation of the school, will have to be left to another paper.

The teachers set out to establish and maintain the 'proper attention' of pupils to official proceedings in the classroom.[2] Pupils are to watch and listen to the teacher when he is at the front talking and to 'follow' what he says. When written work is set they are to get on with it 'sensibly', 'carefully' and at a 'reasonable' speed. The teacher monitors pupil behaviour and sometimes when he detects inattention he will look up from working at his desk or interrupt his discourse in order to demand attention.

However, the establishment and maintenance of attention is only one element of the teachers' concern with 'discipline' in the classroom. They do not merely require pupils to pay attention but also to participate. Pupil participation, though, should conform to certain rules: the teacher tries to reduce classroom interaction to a two-party format, with himself as one speaker and one or another pupil acting as the other.

Furthermore, he reserves for himself the right to talk to the whole class and to produce extended utterances, often ruling pupil initiatives out of order. He is therefore faced with the problem of making pupils behave as one, subordinate, participant.

The teacher provides for pupil participation by asking questions. However, even if pupils were not to make initiatives when the teacher asked a question, problems would necessarily arise since only one slot is provided for the participation of a large number of pupils. Potentially some seventeen speakers are competing for one answer slot.

From the point of view of the teachers, the classroom encounter as an interaction system, focused on and co-ordinated from the front, can just as easily disintegrate as a result of 'non-participation' by pupils as it can by escalating inattention. The teachers seek a solution to this problem by insisting that they select answerers, either directly or indirectly. Direct selection involves tagging a question with a name or 'One of you four', 'You', combined with pointing, etc.

(a) T: First of all let's. have a, little bit of revision on what we've done so far since Christmas. Our friend Leach can tell us what we *need*, to make iron?

P: Iron?

T: Yes iron

P: Sir is it carbon sir?

P: Sir   Sir
             (

T: Dear me, tell us
     Richardson in a clear voice
                    (
                  Sir

P: Sir y'use iron ore sir an' put it in a blast furnace y'need coke, iron-coke

P: Limestone

P: Limestone and iron ore sir

T: Good, in what kind of furnace Short?

P: Blast

P: Ehr blast furnace

T: In a *blast* furnace. Good. What type of temperature do we need?
     (H)

More frequently teachers enforce indirect selection: the teacher asks a question, calls for 'hands up' or waits for hands to go up automatically, and then appoints an answerer by naming, pointing, nodding, loking, or whatever, from among those with raised hands.

(b) T: If you listened carefully to that story yesterday you'll have noticed that two things in the story created terror, anybody remember what they were?

P: Sir

T: Don't sir just put your hand up.
     Campbell?

P: Head-headless horse, headless horses pulling a wagon sir
                                   (
                  Headless horses pulling a carriage yes that's one very
     good
        (
       Sir
     ((Pause, then the teacher appoints))

P: The castle

T: The castle, I don't think so may 'ave done but may alright we'll
                accept the castle
P: (Laughing) sir
P: ((appointed)) When he saw the knight
T: When he saw the knight yes but there was something before then
                (
P: Sir
T: I think there was the headless horseman which is something that
                he *saw*
P: Sir
P: Sir
                (
P: Sir
P: ((appointed)) When he heard that laughing sound
T: Yes the noise, the laughter (W)

Selection of answerers is backed up with demands that pupils 'don't "sir"',
'don't shout out', speak 'one at a time', etc. As with the maintenance of
'attention', the preservation of 'one speaker at a time' is a continuous concern, the
teacher issuing demands for 'disciplined' participation when he judges things to be
getting out of hand. At times, however, the teachers seem to worsen the problem
of 'over-particicaption' by refusing to ask those with their hands up, clamouring
to answer:

(c)   T: What, in what way Crick in what way was the river a bit of a prob-
                lem to them a problem or a
                                     (
P: (Washing)
T: nuisance
                (
P: Sir
P: Sir
P: Sir
P: Sir
P: Sir
P: Sir
                (
T: It had its good things but it also
                                     (
P: Sir
                                     (
P: Sir
T: had its bad side
P: Sir (   )
                (
P: Sir
                     (
P: Sir
                          (
T: Just a minute hands down
Pn: Augh::
T: Look at this side of the class what's the matter with them
Pn: Sir Sir
T: Numbskulls c'mon
Pn: Sir Sir
T: Wha-what-where d'you think a river can be a nuisance?
P: Yes sir
P: Sir

T:	If you lived in a village an' there was a river running right past it, in what way would the river be a nuisance
P:	Sir Sir
T:	a problem?
Pn:	Sir Sir
T:	Now look, I can see you, I don't need to have a silly chorus, y'sound like a lot of little sparrows bumbling away in the hedgebottom
Pn:	((Mimics of sparrows))
T:	It's somebody over this side I'd like to hear from. What way could a river be said to be a nuisance yes? (D)

On such occasions the teacher is attempting to maximise the attention of all members of the class by demonstrating the potential built into directly selective questions for the embarrassment of pupils who have not been 'following' the lesson. The problems of participation control that this kind of action causes point to a conflict of purpose facing the teacher: the more successful he is in generating pupil motivation to attend and participate, the greater may be his problems in controlling participation. However, this is not just a problem for teachers but one which also faces pupils. Pupils' 'failure' to conform fully to the participation rules is not to be explained in terms of their perversity or on the grounds that they are operating on the basis of values opposite to those of the school. If these explanations were correct, it could be expected that there would be a refusal to answer questions rather than the clamour that generally occurs.[3] The teachers demand participation and differentiate pupils on the basis of the 'quality' of that participation, yet the form which official participation must take is highly restricted and there are only limited opportunities, given the number of pupils in a class.[4] It is not surprising, therefore, that considerable unofficial participation occurs.[5]

However, there is no need to assume that clamour to answer the teachers' questions is simply the product of successful mobilisation by the teachers. On many occasions pupils seemed to be pursuing their own rather different purposes. They seemed to be using the teacher as a quizmaster, turning teacher questions into a contest. Acclaim from other pupils appeared to be desired as much as praise from the teacher, and the aim to be not the building of an academic career but the acquisition of a reputation for smartness.[6]

To be successful in demonstrating 'intelligence' to the teacher or in the quiz, a pupil must get his answers heard and if possible accepted by the teacher as 'the right answer'. But a pupil is only one among many, a good number of whom may be equally anxious to provide the answer. It is known that the teacher very rarely asks all those offering answers and sometimes does not ask any of them. Even if the teacher does start an answer-round, there is always the danger that another pupil will come up with 'the right answer' and thus stop the round (unless the question asked for the members of a list); that someone-else will suggest the answer which the pupil is seeking to present and thus make it difficult for him to claim it as his own; or that the teacher may stop the round to reformulate or drop the question before the pupil has had chance to get his answer in.

These contingencies explain why pupils are not content merely to put their hands up and wait to be selected. Pupils use two main strategies in trying to win the competition. They may try inserting 'answers' as soon as or just before the teacher has apparently finished the question. It is important to get in first for the reasons I have mentioned and because if the answer is 'right' the teacher may, or may be forced to, accept it despite the fact that it was 'shouted out'. The insertion of answers maximises the possibility of success if the answer turns out to be adequate. Identifying the point of question completion, however, is no easy matter since teachers often repeat, elaborate, or reformulate questions before they actually begin to select answerers. Hence pupils often find themselves talking simultaneously with each other and with the teacher, and this reduces, even if it does not eliminate, the chances of getting an answer heard and accepted.

Instead of 'shouting out' his answer, a pupil may seek explicitly to summon the teacher by the use of 'sir'. 'Sir' has the obverse advantages to answer insertion, being of short duration and immediate impact; it is easily insertible into what turns out to have been a minor pause, and requires little work at understanding. Indeed 'sir' is often inserted into what must be recognised as non-terminal pauses in teacher or official pupil talk in the hope of turning them into terminal pauses and securing the floor—a strategy which trades on both the features mentioned above. 'Sir' works, if it works, like all summonses: if the teacher replies and replies with an invitation to speak not a deferral (with 'yes' not 'hold on a minute'), the pupil is then virtually guaranteed a hearing. The aim of a summons is not just to attract attention but to gain the floor and the deferential character of 'sir' is important in this. While something like 'Hey you' would be doubly effective in attracting the teachers' attention and quieting competitors, it would be unlikely to result in the speaker being able to present his answer. This highlights the problem pupils face in answering teachers' questions. To obey the rules by not 'shouting out' or even trying to summon the teacher with 'sir', involves the danger of losing the chance of the floor to other less conforming answers. On the other hand, to be the most effective competitor opens a pupil up to charges of 'bad manners'. To the extent that pupils are quiz-motivated they will care little about being labelled 'bad mannered', but there is always the danger that the teacher may ignore or rule out an answer simply on the grounds that it was inappropriately presented or that he will not appoint an answerer who tries to summon him with 'sir'. Pupils have to make some trade-off between the two sources of possible failure on every answering occasion.

The point of the above analysis of pupil answering is to suggest that, first, there are reasons for pupil deviance built into the organisation the teachers seek to impose on classroom interaction; and secondly, that pupils' orientations are not usually simply for or against school but generally involve using or attempting to adapt its organisation to make something 'valuable', 'bearable', 'enjoyable', and/or functional for certain purposes. There are of course limitations to pupils doing this, but then there are equally limitations to teachers' power to prevent such making out.

Pupils are not wholly restricted to offering answers to teacher questions; they do make initiatives, again sometimes inserting them in gaps they hope are adequate, sometimes trying to summon the teacher. In making initiatives pupils operate under the same constraints as in the presentation of answers. The teachers do not totally proscribe pupil initiatives but they frequently ignore 'shouted out' initiatives and 'sirs' and demand that pupils 'do not talk while I'm talking' and speak 'one at a time', though even raised hands are sometimes ignored or waved down by teachers.

The teachers insist on their control of pupil initiatives, as on their control of pupil answers, in order to control the setting and maintenance of topic. The teacher 'starts the lesson' by embarking on the topic he has decided to deal with in the lesson.

(d)   ((Noise of class entering and talking))
       P: ((appointed)) Sir can we read those short stories?

((Movement noise and talking continues, apparently no answer from the teacher))

T:	Right a'right close your books look this way. Now, you boys at the back, no reason why you shouldn't have books, are there any more left?
P:	No sir
T:	Right then eh will you share with him please, ( ) you share with him. All you need to do is... ((Much shuffling of chairs)) All you need to do is to sit... ((Noise continues)) Oh dear me can we have the noise stopped as soon as possible. Now look this way, closed book and look this way. Anybody tell me, keep your feet still, and everything else, anybody tell me what a legend is?
P:	It's a story
T:	Sh: : what is a legend?
P:	Sir it's a story that's been told thousands and thousands of years ago and people still believe in it. (W)

The teacher always starts the topic talk and his right to do so is never challenged, although the first utterance in (d) above seems to be an attempt to influence the lesson by suggestion. Note, however, that the suggestion is framed as a request, tagged with 'sir', and that the pupil does not insist on an answer. Not only are pupils given no rights in topic establishment, the teacher only rarely provides pupils with any initial indication of what the topic he has decided on is, or what he intends to teach them in this lesson. He launches straight into the lesson and they are required to pick up the pieces as he goes along. The expectation that they correctly construct 'what this lesson is about' from what he says as the lesson goes on may well be intended as and certainly operates as an attention maintaining device, relying on the relevance of 'what this lesson is about' to the provision of answers to the teacher's questions.

Having set the topic by starting out on it, the teacher controls and develops it himself by speaking for extended periods and controlling pupil participation:

(a)	T:	A little while ago there was a general election, that is a time when everybody who can *vote* that's most people over the age of?
	Pn:	Eighteen
	T:	Over eighteen that's right when the people who can vote vote for the persons that they would like to represent them in parliament, and to *try an' make* people vote for them, the men who are trying to get into parliament often go and *visit* people whose votes they are trying to catch. Our M.P. did that, he came round in an open sports car with one of his helpers driving with himself not sitting on the back seat but sitting on the back of the car with his feet on the back seat so that he was raised up a little bit, in shirt sleeves, it was a sunny evening and he
		(
		Blah blah blah
	P:	That's right, saying things like that through a megaphone saying vote for me I am a good bloke I have been in parliament for umpteen years y'can't go far wrong with me. His name is Sir — —. What do we call someone who is allowed to put 'sir' before their name?
	P:	Knight
	T:	What?
	P:	(Lord)
	T:	He's a knight, that's right. Now there are lots of *knights about*, people called Sir something or other some of them become Sir 'cos their dads were called Sir and some of them are called Sir because the Queen decides to reward them for something that they've

	done. Can you think of any recent people who've been made a Sir for something that they've done?
P:	Sir Alf Ramsey
P:	Sir Alf Ramsey
T:	Alf Ramsey. When England won the World Cup in sixty-six he was just plain Mr. Alf Ramsey and he became Sir
P:	Sir Stan Matthews
P:	Francis Chichester
T:	Francis Chichester because he was a lone yachtsman he sailed round the world
P:	Stanley Matthews
T:	Stanley Matthews is an earlier footballer
P:	Sir Walter Raleigh
T:	Sir Walter Raleigh, now there's one going back a bit isn't it, which Queen made him a knight?
P:	Victoria
P:	Elizabeth
T:	The first Elizabeth that's right, all the others that we've mentioned were made knights by?
P:	( )
T:	The present Elizabeth, Raleigh was made a knight by the first Elizabeth, well he was a knight in her reign
P:	Sir Francis Drake
T:	Sir Francis Drake was another of the knights of the first Queen Elizabeth's reign
P:	Alexander Fleming
T:	Erh yes he was rewarded for his work on a famous drug which can cure people, can you see what it is by looking around?
P:	Penicillin
T:	Penicillin, oh there now, it used to be just there ((pointing to wall)) didn't it, Alexander Fleming one of those little people, it used to be there. Penicillin is a famous drug which is used in just about every hospital in the world to cure diseases and Alexander Fleming was a scientist who discovered what it could be used for, not that's obviously important and he was knighted for it. Now a little while ago when we were talking about the set-up in Norman England with the King at the top and the serfs the ordinary people down at the bottom we mentioned knights then. Now if you could imagine a ladder with four rungs on it the King was on the top on his own, the serfs were right at the bottom and the other groups were knights and lords and barons now which of those two groups would come higher up the Ladder?
P:	Barons
T:	The barons. The knights were very often ordinary skilled fighting men who ended up being employed by a moire important baron or lord. Remember also in Norman times each person *including* the barons and the knights each person *owed* his land to somebody else, he had his land thanks to somebody else above him (B)

Teacher questions form the major opportunity for pupils officially to participate in the lesson. But these questions differ from questions in other settings in two respects. First, the teacher demands and is accorded the right routinely to command, interpret and openly judge answers. Secondly, they are not usually requests for information, opinions, experiences, etc. unknown to the questioner. The teacher knows the answer he wants and although he may occasionally be surprised by an unanticipated answer which is 'right' in some respect, it is always *he* who decides the status of any 'answer'. These two features result in question rounds aimed at forcing 'clarification':

(f) T: In a *blast* furnace. Good. What type of temperature do we need, ahm Calder, what type of temperature do we need?

P: Sir very high temperature

T: Yes that's pretty obvious but what *type* of *range* are we talking about? Three candle power?

Pn: ((Laughs))

P: A thousand degrees

T: A thousand degrees

P: Right

T: Any advance on a thousand?

P: (
                Sir

P: Fo-fourteen hundred
         (

P: Sir   fourteen hundred

T: Really

P: 'Bout eight 'undred
             (

P: 'Bout fifteen 'undred sir, 'bout fifteen 'undred

T: Now let's get this straight we're not talking about the melting point *of iron* we're talking about the melting po-or the, the maximum needed or the minimum needed in a blast furnace to release the iron from the iron ore

P: About eight hundred sir

P: Eight thousand sir, eight hundred and fifty

P: Sixteen hundred sir
              (

T: Now look we-we've really got confused with this. We need   a *minimum* of
        (

P: Seven thousand (   )

T: two thousand degrees *centigrade*. Once you've got the iron out then yer fourteen fifteen hundred degrees centigrade was about right (H)

(g) T: Anybody tell me what a legend is?

P: It's a story

T: Sh: : what is a legend?

P: Sir its a story that's been told thousands and thousands of years ago and people still believe in it

T: A story that's been told thousands and thousands of years and people still believe in it. Can anyone improve on that answer?

Pn: Sir Sir

P: Sir it's a story that's been made about something that's happened and er people-everbody knows about it (nearly everybody) sir

T: Yes. Yes Campbell?

P: Sir it's half-true and half not true sir

T: It's?

P: Sir sort of made up sir, half true

T: It's half true, yes. The actual definition, that means the meaning, of a legend is a story that is, probably true but not absolutely true. . Can anybody tell me a legend they know? (W)

The teacher knows the answer he wants because he knows the point he is trying to make; the question he asks is designed to get pupils to make that point. He asks questions to which he wants a particular answer and he will work until he gets that answer or some substitute or until he decides to provide it himself.

The teacher's framing of his questions and his treatment of pupil answers and initiatives are lesson-planning decisions—decisions about the topical organisation of the lesson; what the topic is, what points will be made, in what order and detail, with what slant, in order to carry on from and lead on to what, etc. It is the teacher who makes all these decisions; he continuously organises his talk as a lesson-long phenomenon and it is *his* talk which officially constitutes the lesson. Pupils are officially limited to making or trying to make contributions to his talk, their participation is not on their own terms but on his; they are expected to listen to what he says and follow his development of the topic in order to 'learn'.

The underlying image is of the transmission of knowledge from teacher to pupils. What is to be learned is pre-ordained: pupil contributions must either reproduce something already known by the teacher or be judged correct in terms of his criteria. There is no question of pupils exploring or discovering in an open-ended kind of way; 'what has to be learned' would not be learned in that fashion. The teachers set out to teach a body of knowledge, but this knowledge is not seen as something which simply might be useful to pupils but rather as something anyone *should* know; it constitutes a definition of cultural competence. Hence, pupils are not accorded the ability to judge the education they are receiving, they must subordinate themselves to the teacher and be taught. The function of the teacher is not seen as to entertain them or to minister to their 'psychological needs' or 'social problems', but to render them 'culturally competent' up to the level of their 'capacities'. The teacher is the source of 'knowledge' and therefore his communications must dominate proceedings, he must be free to direct pupils so as to maximise their 'learning' and he must be allowed to present the curriculum in an 'orderly' fashion.

The teachers in this school seek to organise classroom interaction on a two-party basis, reserving for themselves the rights to extended speech, speaker selection, evaluation of pupil contributions, and thus the control of lesson-topic. There are reasons for pupils not to conform fully to the participation rules built into this organisation itself, besides those deriving from particular pupil orientations to school activities. But, by one means or another, the teachers to a large extent successfully impose an order on classroom interaction which enables them to set the topic, expound at length on it, and make pupil answers and initiatives contribute to it.

In order consistently to display their 'intelligence' to the teachers and to their fellows, pupils must command the necessary cultural resources both to work out what the teacher is getting at in questions and to construct answers which meet his requirements. They must also, for one reason or another, be prepared to adopt the teacher's topical interests. Similarly with initiatives, since the teacher decides what the lesson-topic is to be and continuously defines its proper bounds and inner structure, to display 'intelligence' a pupil must orient to that topic and either add something 'valuable' or anticipate what the teacher is about to say. Thus, in order to 'learn', to develop the cultural resources required to answer questions or produce 'acceptable' initiatives in the future, pupils must have been attending to and 'correctly' processing teachers' talk in the past, and in the present must follow at the pace the teacher sets, covering the ground he deems relevant, and going by the route he decides is appropriate.

To demonstrate 'intelligence' also requires accepting the teacher's claims legitimately to speak for long periods, to ask questions to which he knows the answers, and to be the ultimate arbiter of candidate answers. This is true whether the pupil's aim is to impress the teacher or other pupils. Thus, an even more basic requirement for the display of 'intelligence' is 'recognition', at least for working purposes, of the teacher's 'right' to organise classroom interaction, of the authority the teacher claims.[7] Every time a pupil answers a teacher's questions, allows him to control the topic, or accepts his evaluations of answers or initiatives, even by default, that interaction can be seen by the pupil, other pupils and the teacher as symbolising and reinforcing the teacher-pupil, superordinate-subordinate relationship. There were signs on many occasions in the lessons I observed that the interaction was being seen in that way by the participants.

These two conditions of 'intelligent' answering indicate the importance of the way in which the teachers organise classroom interaction. Furthermore they apply not only to the pupils' oral contributions, with which I have been concerned here, but also to the written work that is set. The teachers stress the importance of 'proper presentation' of written work; they formulate the task, which usually derives from the oral lesson-topic; and they mark the work in relation to 'what was wanted'. The investigation of what constitutes 'school achievement' is essential both for sense to be made of pupils' actions and for the analysis of schools as socialising agencies.

Key to Transcriptions

T:	—	Teacher speaks.
P:	—	Pupil speaks.
Pn:	—	Two or more pupils speaking at once.
(( ))	—	Observer descriptions.
( )	—	Uncertain/guessed materials.
(H), (W), (B), (D)	—	The four teachers whose lessons have been quoted from.

Sir   Sir
(—
Dear me

                                                    Speech overlap.
need   — Raised voice.
Sh: :   — Sound prolonged.
All you...   — Speech tails oil.

Acknowledgements

I would like to thank Isabel Emmet, Phil Harris and Joan Hammersley for comments on an earlier version of this paper. Above all, I am grateful to the pupils and staff of the school for their friendly co-operation.

Notes

[1] This paper forms part of a larger research report still in the process of being written. The research focuses on teacher–pupil interaction in the classrooms of a secondary modern school, though the concern is more with the activities of teachers than those of pupils. Comments made about teachers and pupils in this paper are intended to apply only to this school. Though my aim is not to depict the school in its uniqueness, further generalisation will require careful comparison with the work of other teachers in other schools. Little can be said about methods of fieldwork here other than that, while I have provided extracts from tape transcripts to give some indication of the kind of evidence I've used and the way I've used it, the reader is inevitably reliant on my observation and reporting.

² I cannot provide conclusive evidence for the reader that my description of teacher activities is applicable to all the teachers in the school. Even full reproduction of all the transcriptions would be inadequate since, while I observed most of the teachers at work at one time or another, my observation and tape-recordings were largely focused on four of them. There were differences between even these four, but the differences between all the teachers seemed to be in technique rather than in basic concerns—for instance some of them used speaker selection far more strictly than others.

³ The enthusiasm to answer questions was less among the older than the younger pupils in the school, but even pupils towards the end of the third year still competed to answer questons, 'shouting out' answers simultaneously. (My data on fourth year pupils is inadequate for a judgement on this issue.) There was no streaming in the school, though in the third year 'those willing to work' had been creamed into a separate class and in the second year there was setting for maths. and English. There seemed to be little difference in clamour to answer questions between classes in the same year that I observed. However, I must stress that the way in which pupils' orientations in the classroom change as they progress through the school was not a central research topic and therefore this footnote is tentative and superficial.

⁴ Mean average class size for the lessons I observed was 17 and the range was from 7 to 30. This is on the low side for any school, never mind a secondary modern, though the task which the teachers set themselves of making seventeen pupils behave as one party to the interaction is probably not much less difficult than making even more behave in the same way.

⁵ Besides unofficial answers and initiatives directed at the teacher, there is always some pupil to pupil communication in any lesson, varying considerably between lessons and teachers, but this is usually at a low volume level and is directed to someone sitting close by. Shouts across the room are relatively infrequent while the teacher is present and unofficial pupil address of the whole class even rarer.

⁶ My evidence for this orientation is difficult to specify but basically lies in the following observation: pupils often laughed at what they regarded as 'silly answers' or laughed themselves while providing an answer, presumably to distance themselves from it in case it turned out to be 'silly'; yet they appeared to invest written work with much less importance, whereas that seemed to be regarded as, if anything, more important by the teachers. Of course this orientation was not adopted by all the pupils or by any pupil all the time.

⁷ I am not suggesting by implication that this claimed authority is illegitimate—that is not my concern *here*—nor is it a question to which I find any easy answers. Rather what I am arguing is that if for any reason and at any point in his school career a pupil sees teacher authority as illegitimate and acts on that belief, he will tend to be seen as lacking in 'intelligence' by the teachers in this school. Even if the teachers decide that a pupil is 'more intelligent' than his school work would imply, that does not in itself alter the 'standard' of his school work.

2   Rules in Play

D.H. HARGREAVES, S.K. HESTOR and F.J. MELLOR

The rules of classroom order are not universally the same. They vary between teachers and indeed between different parts of the lesson. In this excerpt from their study of *Deviance in Classrooms* Hargreaves, Hestor and Mellor identify different *phases* of the lesson in which very different sets of rules appear to apply.

[...] There are five principal phases which are common to virtually all lessons. These phases are:

1 The 'entry' phase.
2 The 'settling down' or preparation phase.
3 The 'lesson proper' phase.
4 The 'clearing up' phase.
5 The 'exit' phase.

The lesson proper [...] typically [...] occupies most of the time, being sandwiched between the first two phases ('getting started') and the last two phases ('finishing up'), though with some teachers these initiatory and terminatory phases were sometimes fairly lengthy [...]
[...]The entry phase[...] is concerned with the task of ensuring that the teacher and pupils are assembled in the physical boundaries of the classroom. Accordingly, there exists a set of rules for accomplishing this task of entering the room. Because the precise rules of entry are at the teacher's discretion, there is considerable variation between teachers in the nature of these rules and the emphasis placed upon conformity to them. Typically there are three rules in play in this phase: (1) Pupils must line up outside the room in the corridor. (2) Pupils must not enter the room until the teacher gives them permission to do so. (3) Pupils must enter the room 'in an orderly fashion', i.e. without running or pushing.

(1) *I*: They were lining up outside, then you said, 'Come in', and then you had to repeat it, 'I said come in', because they didn't come. Is that a kind of school rule that the pupils don't come in unless you give instructions?
    T: Well, I don't know whether it's a general school rule but it applies to me because often I'm not quite ready and perhaps I'm speaking to my own form, but it may not be the same with every teacher, but I do it. Often I'm not quite ready for them to come in or I'm speaking to someone and I don't want an interruption. But normally I call, 'Come in' regularly and they don't hear me and I have got to say again, 'Come in', you see. Often they don't hear me but I do say it and have to repeat it.
    I: Do you expect all forms to wait?
    T: Yes.

(2) *I*: Sorry, can I just take you to a bit earlier, are there any rules of procedure for actually entering the room?
    T: I require them to enter quietly. On occasions they barge in in a disorderly rabble and in that case I sometimes send them out and ask them to return in a proper

manner. They go to their places—depending on the class. If it's a junior class, they know to sit down and look towards the board.

Many teachers did not apply these rules in the case of senior pupils, or small classes, or in other special situations. The pupils soon learn what each teacher expects of them in the entry phase.

(1)   I: Yes, well, they all come along, this one girl came along, she waited outside the door. . .

T: Christine, that's right.

I: And you said, 'Right, come on, Christine, come in.' I mean is this a general sort of thing? Is it a rule that they have to wait?

T: Generally speaking yes. But I don't enforce it with 3E because they are such a small group and it doesn't matter to me whether they wait or not, and in fact it's rather awkward waiting outside my door because Mr— and I are right next door to each other and if he gets a form lining up, girls on one side, boys another, well one of us is a space short for one line, so with small forms I tend to let them in as soon as they come.

I: It was as if Christine expected to wait—

T: That's right.

I: Now, with other forms then, is this—with other forms you take—you take the fifth form and you take some fourth years—

T: Yes, I don't make them line up ever.

I: Is it the same with all forms you take?

T: No, any others, especially the large forms, they do need, you know 2A and 3A, do need to be made to come in in an orderly fashion.

I: So they have to line up outside?

T: Yes, because they tend to push you see, and crowd through the doorway and there are so many of them that you have to have some sort of rule.

(2)   I: I'm sorry, shall we presume that you are sitting there or you're standing there perhaps and the pupils come in. Do you expect them to be, do you tolerate in fact a certain amount of behaviour at that time or perhaps misbehaviour, noise and disturbance, this sort of thing? Do you think it is a common characteristic of the start of the lesson?

T: Yes, I think it is to some extent, unfortunately. I don't agree that it is a good thing. Well, I think it is a very bad thing but I think there often is—the more you are prepared then the less you get this, if you like, this upset at the beginning because the quicker you get them started. On the other hand, I don't like them to come in in a too regimented fashion because for me it doesn't create the right atmosphere at the beginning of the lesson to have to come in and stand there like zombies. It rather takes me back to sitting with your hands on your head, that sort of attitude and I think it differs with the age of the child. I mean, I don't like the fourth years, particularly a fourth year group, I don't want them to line up outside because this would create again, for me anyway, the wrong atmosphere, the wrong atmosphere between us.

I: So you make a distinction on that? On lining up outside you make a distinction on a sort of age basis?

T: Yes, I think I would, I think at that point there ought to be enough self-discipline. I know it isn't always there but I suppose it's a form of trust and respect between teacher and pupil because they're older. When all's said and done, they ought to be able to come into a classroom. There would be at least a semi-relaxed atmosphere. [. . .]

[. . .] For most teachers, the entry phase ends as the pupils enter the room and move towards their seats. In rare cases, there is an additional rule that pupils must proceed to their seats and wait for the teacher to tell them to sit down.

I: When they came in you said, as they were standing about in the class, 'Good morning, 3C', and they said, 'Morning, Miss', and they all sat down. Would they not have sat down if you did not say, 'Good morning, 3C'?

T: They are supposed to stand until I have said, 'Good morning' to them and if they forget they soon get to realize they have got to stand up. It is one of my rules.

In these cases it is the teacher's statement of 'Good morning' or 'Sit down' which serves as a switch-signal to end the entry phase and usher in the preparation phase.

During this settling down or preparation phase, the following rules are typically in play: (1) Pupils most go to their seats and sit down or remain in close proximity to the seat. (2) Pupils are free to talk to other pupils on any matter, but they must not shout or scream. (3) Pupils must co-operate in the distribution of equipment, if this takes place. There are, of course, considerable variations in the noise-level of the talk permitted under the second rule.

(1) I: When the kids come into the lesson, do you expect them to come in and sit down straight away and stop talking?

T: I don't expect them to. As a teacher I ought to, I could make it so. I could keep sending them out until they came in—the only thing is, I remember at school it was a good thing because it meant wasting a bit more time of the lesson to keep charging out and coming back in again. I don't think they get bored with doing it. The thing is I don't insist on it because most of them come in and they make a noise and then eventually I say 'Quiet' and then I talk. These lot are the worst I have in that respect because this morning they just did not keep quiet any of the time. I could not really explain anything or do anything.

(2) I: Once they came in there were various acts going on—talking, shouting out, and moving about, and even some whistling; now, during this warm-up period, you might say, you are prepared to accept this sort of—

T: Oh yes, I don't expect them to be quiet until I tell them to, it's just too much to expect with 3E that they will come in and say, 'What are we doing? Can we get anything ready?' which an A form might do, you know, 2A might do that but not 3E. [...]

[...] The preparation phase is terminated and the lesson proper phase is initiated by a verbal switch-signal. Although occasionally non-verbal switch-signals are used, such as banging on the desk with a blackboard duster or standing silently at the front of the class with arms akimbo, the verbal form is much more common. Sometimes the switch-signal is a statement of the teacher's readiness to begin the lesson, i.e. the lesson proper.

'Right, I'm ready, 3B.'
'Right, are we ready to begin?'

If equipment has been distributed, the switch-signal can take the form of a check that this task of the preparation phase has been completed.

'Right, have we got everything out now?'
'Right, have we got what we're supposed to have?'

Alternatively, the teacher may indicate that silence is required.

'Right, quiet now.'
'Right, let's have quiet now.'
'Right, pay attention now.'

The switch-signal terminates the preparation phase, and its rules are no longer in play. Instead, the pay attention rule is brought into play: pupils must stop talking, listen to and look at the teacher. On most occasions, it is also understood that pupils will be sitting at their desks unless other spatial locations are required for pupils.

(1) I: When they come into lessons, at the start of the lesson, do you expect them to come in and sit down and be quiet?

T: Oh, no, I don't expect 3E to be quiet. I know whether they are making more noise than I want or not. I'm going to have to say something but if they haven't been making such a terrific row as they were this morning I would simply say, 'Right are we ready to begin?' or something like that.

(2) I: In this period, when you were writing on the blackboard and giving the books out, are you prepared to tolerate the chatter and noise?

T: Yes, provided it keeps at a decent level and provided it doesn't interrupt me at the blackboard because I'm very susceptible to noise. I cannot do with a great amount and they know that. I don't mind them talking quietly because after all I'm not giving them anything to do at that moment only get ready, so I feel I can't impose on them a great restriction. But when I'm ready, that is when I start to put my foot down.

I: When you say that you're ready, do you mean by that that at the same time it's time to start work?

T: Yes, I'm ready as soon as I've completed the blackboard. I'm ready for them to start and they know they have not to talk.

I: Later on you said, 'Right, no talking now.'

T: Exactly, that's the reason. [. . .]

[. . .] From this point any pupil talk is defined as deviant, since it breaches the pay attention rule which is now in play. Often the pupil talk does not cease immediately or pupils do not look at the teacher, so the teacher reiterates the switch-signal, which now has the force of a deviance-imputation, or gives a specific instruction about paying attention, or makes a deviance-imputation against a target pupil.

I: Can I ask you a more specific thing about the beginning of your lesson with 3E? You said, 'Right, the lesson has started.'

T: Because they were talking. Sheila was nattering and Andrew never shut his mouth for the last three months. I don't know what's wrong with him. They all just carried on talking. Sheila was talking with Andrew, and I was trying— well, I was just waiting to tell them what we were going to do. Actually, I explained that and just let them talk and see if they would all talk for the whole lesson [. . .]

[. . .] Occasionally, it is the pupils themselves who initiate the lesson proper.

T: They usually ask me. They come in and tell me what they feel like doing very often. 'Can we write today, Miss?' And they want to do some writing and if I can see that they are in that mood then I abandon whatever I have prepared, because you have to catch them in the right mood. . .

Once the pupils are paying attention, the lesson proper can commence. For the most part it is more adequate to conceive of the lesson proper not as a single phase but as a sequence of subphases, each of which is concerned with one dominant task. There is considerable variation between lessons in the number of subphases in the lesson proper as well as in the order in which they occur. We shall try to simplify this complexity by referring to three types of subphase.

The first type of subphase is one in which the teacher is highly active, usually in the form of talking, whilst the pupils are relatively passive. He is working examples on the blackboard; giving a verbal exposition or explanation; demonstrating at the front (especially in science, handicraft and domestic science); reading to the class. In all these subphases, the dominant rule in play is the pay attention rule, i.e. pupils must sit quietly, watching and listening to the teacher. Any pupil activity which conflicts with conformity to this rule is defined as deviant, especially talk, movement and auto-involvements.[1]

(1) *I*: During the lesson [...] where you identified two kinds of phases, this blackboard demonstration and then copying from the blackboard. [...] what sort of things do you expect the pupils to do whilst you're giving the blackboard demonstration?

T: Well, I expect them obviously to be observing what I'm doing, the writing I'm doing on the board and also I would hope—I don't say this is always the case because one can't be writing on the board and watching the class at the same time—but I would hope that they would be following everything I was doing on the board, and take, for example, the rough working I did on the side of the board to support the general run of the solution, I would hope they would be following those details. Now I don't say they always do. I don't say everyone does that, but I would hope that.

I: Can I look from the other side now? What shouldn't they do whilst you're demonstrating at the blackboard?

T: Well, for example, talking to the next-door neighbour, that's an obvious one, or if I caught anyone drawing the image of a football or something like that when he's supposed to be watching. To my mind I can't say that they can be taking sufficient interest if they're fiddling about with other things that are outside the classroom, thoughts which take them outside the classroom. I think whilst a lesson is on, concentration is necessary... I do think that anything that is detrimental to concentrating should be stopped.

(2) *I*: Next one. 'Aitken, will you stop playing with your money.'

T: Well, again it's inattention if he is playing with his money. He's not listening to me. [...]

[...] A second important rule in play in this first type of subphase is that pupils must not interrupt the teacher with superfluous or irrelevant comments or questions. The teacher should not be interrupted 'in mid-flight', unless the situation is urgent, for instance when the pupil cannot see the teacher's demonstration. Otherwise, comments and questions should be left until the end of the teacher's exposition, explanation or demonstration.

(1) *I*:: You said after a while, 'Will you let me get my words out!'

T: Yes, that's a typical 3E trick. You get half of what you are saying out and the others start asking questions or tell you they can't do it, or 'I haven't got a pen', you know, in the middle of explaining what to do and then hearing half the story, 'We can't do that because...', and they will give you a list of reasons and you have not finished telling them how you are going to do it or why or anything and it is very irritating sometimes, but it is a thing I accept. They can't help it. They can't wait, I think that's the thing, they are impatient. [...]

(2) *I*: 'We don't need any comments, thank you.'

T: It's just that every time you're trying to explain something you say the first half of the sentence and immediately they are sort of shouting things out. I think this is more to do with their minds than in the discipline thing. I don't think it's intentional misbehaviour. It's immaturity that they can't sit and listen and concentrate, they have to shout something out as a reaction. I just have to keep saying, 'Wait until I have finished speaking.' You get a few there who were saying, 'Be quiet', because I had started and they wanted to listen even if they weren't going to do it.

I: You said, 'Will you please let me finish', at the same time.

T: There was someone who was going to ask me about what they were going to do. I think that they are so sort of self-centred they don't see it as a sort of thing you are directing at people and they should wait and ask afterwards. They think of it immediately and shout it out.

In the second type of subphase in the lesson proper, it is the pupils who take the active role and the teacher no longer plays such a dominant verbal part in activities. Typically, pupils are assigned to a piece of work which does not involve directing their attention to the teacher. Common examples are: writing an essay; solving written problems; copying from the blackboard; reading on one's own; conducting experiments; doing practical work; group work; project work. The dominant rule in play in this type of subphase is that the pupils should involve themselves in the set task and carry it out according to the teacher's instructions. In contrast to the first type of subphase, pupil–pupil talk is permitted, provided that (1) there is no loud talking or shouting, (2) the talk is work-related or relevant to the task, except for the occasional irrelevant talk. Further, pupils must not interfere with, distract, or disturb other pupils in their work by excessive irrelevant talk or by any other kind of action. On some occasions movement is permitted (e.g. project work), when a certain amount of movement between groups or the collection of needed equipment is necessary to the accomplishment of the task. In other situations (e.g. reading alone) movement is forbidden.

(1) I: And if they're working in groups you're prepared to accept that then there is a bit of nattering?

     T: Oh yes. The thing is I say to them, 'Look, I'm not having this nattering. If it's constructive natter I don't care. If it's got something to do with the lesson, yes, but I'm not having nattering about United's chances on Saturday.' [. . .]

(2) I: When you change from working at the blackboard to where they're working by themselves, what do you permit then that you wouldn't permit when you were talking at the blackboard?

     T: Well, if they're working, I don't mind them sort of saying, 'What are nine times seven?' and the answer will come back from somebody else because they pick one another's brains, you know. It doesn't matter if they are nattering about something else and it doesn't go on for long and they don't raise their voices to disturb anybody else, so this is the thing. I don't mind when a child's finished or in the middle of something, something might cross his mind about— you know, house matches or something that's going on—it might suddenly dawn on him, something that he should have done or wants somebody else to know. I don't mind as long as they get the work done, this is the thing. I don't want a noise that disturbs other people, you know, this is the thing, I don't mind quite frankly. Same with 3D and I separated them into halves, one that would work and one that wouldn't work, and I said to them one day, 'Look, you can please yourselves whether you work or not, but I will not have you disturbing the rest of the class. It doesn't matter to me if you don't want to learn anything, this is up to you, but you will not disturb others.' Now this is my sort of policy, that you like to think you're teaching everybody and you'd like to think that you give a perfect lesson where everybody will learn something, but you don't. You can't hope for this, not in this type of school. Not in the lower streams. Really, as long as a child is not worrying other children, not stopping him from working, then quite frankly I don't care what he does.

     I: So you permit a fairly wide range of things that they could do, provided you were sure they were working?

     T: Yes, as long as they stay where they are. I'm not having them wandering around the room because they are disturbing other people once they start to wander, because other kids get up and wonder where they're going to for a start or what they're doing. But if they stay where they are or lean over to somebody's desk or even get up to the desk next door well that is all right, but I don't want them wandering all the way across the room. [...]

[...] The third type of subphase in the lesson proper is a mixture of the other two types. Both teacher and pupils are actively involved in the task. Examples are question-and-answer sessions, discussions and tests (where the teacher poses the questions orally). Question-and-answer sessions are more common than discussions, but the two have similar rules. The main rules of question-and-answer sessions are:

1. On the whole it is the teacher who asks the questions and the pupils who contribute the answers.
2. Pupils should be willing to volunteer answers.
3. That a pupil is willing to volunteer an answer should normally be signalled to the teacher by hand-raising.
4. Pupils must answer when called upon to do so, and normally should not 'shout out' an answer on their own initiative.

OR

5. If the teacher does allow the pupils to take the initiative, several pupils must not call out their answer simultaneously.
6. Pupils must not offer an answer whilst another pupil is stating his answer.
7. Pupils must not talk to one another whilst (1) the teacher is talking, or (2) a pupil is answering the question.

   (1) *I*:   Then when you move on to the next stage, the discussion?
       T: This is different, I find this different. Very rarely do you get just one child who has a comment to make by himself. You generally get three or four wanting to have a comment after what I've said, because sometimes I can be provocative to the children generally and say, 'No wonder!' and I would say to them that, 'You're in 4D and you're so thick you don't know what day it is!' and this stimulates some of them when I've given my talk on the revision on the book itself, and, 'None of you are articulate enough to get up!' Well, then you get, 'We are! we are!' you see, and sometimes you get a response and you get four or five talking at once. Now I would try then to calm them down. Now I allow some laxity in this kind of thing, because I say, 'OK, well, will you be quiet while he says this?' and if they're eager to get up I accept a more tolerant attitude. I take a more tolerant view of the kid when he's trying to say something and someone else is speaking, than I would do if I was reading or talking myself, because I want all of them to say something and I don't want to shout and frighten him off from what he's saying. I'll say, 'Hold on what you've got until he's finished', and that kind of thing. I allow them to talk to themselves if I feel that it's relevant to what we are discussing.
       I: How strongly do you feel about somebody who just didn't answer, didn't attempt anything?
       T: Well, again I'm very tolerant. Very rarely do I get a good discussion going ... I don't get angry with them all for not making a contribution, but I do tend to get annoyed with kids I know have a contribution to make but yet don't even bother putting it forward ... and maybe when we're writing the essay, they may pop up and say, 'Well, what about such a thing?' and I'll say, 'You ought to have said that in the discussion stage!'

   (2) *T*: I come down like a ton of bricks if they call out when I'm asking for answers, because it doesn't give the child a chance who I wish to answer. So they have got the habit now that they must not call out in my class; they must put their hands up.

I: Is this always true?

T: I think most teachers ask for hands rather than calling out for that reason, if I ask a child and am not sure that the child knows the answer, I want to know, and if they call out it spoils it. So it is a general principle that they must put up their hands and not call out. [. . .]

[. . .] In tests the principal rule is that each pupil must work independently. This means that pupils are not allowed to talk at all; they must not look at or copy from the work of a neighbouring pupil.

'We'll have a test to see how much hasn't sunk in,' says the teacher, as the kids settle into their places.
'What does it mean when I say we're going to have a test? Does it mean turning to your neighbour?'
'No, Miss', answer the class.
'Does it mean copying from your partner?'
'No, Miss.'
(Observation notes)

T: I don't object to boys looking over the work of their colleagues. I don't want them to wander from one corner to the other corner. I don't mind them looking over the work of another boy in the vicinity. Of course, if it were a test it would be different. Everybody would be rooted to their chair . . .

The lesson proper, then, typically consists of a sequence of subphases of these three types. Only on rare occasions is only one type of subphase involved; more typically several of them occur. Some combinations are particularly common, for example, teacher exposition (type 1) + question-and-answer session (type 3) + group work or working from books (type 2). Every transition from one subphase to another is effected by means of a switch-signal. There is an infinite variety of these, even though most individual teachers betray particular preferences.

I: One more question, how do you get the pupils to switch from either listening to you to doing work by themselves, or from doing work by themselves to listening to you?

T: Fairly difficult. I've had many ways of doing this. One way is if I want them to stop work I say, 'Stop work please', and perhaps, even though I've raised my voice only three-quarters they will stop and then I'll pick out those who have not stopped and shout further to them and even after that there might be one boy who is determined to carry on and finish what he was doing. I've put this down to no fear of the consequences and perhaps in the old days a boy could be punished physically or in any other way. I, of course, don't punish physically these days and I don't give them any punishment in any other way. Sometimes I bang on the blackboard with a ruler. I find that a sharp noise will stop them better than even my voice. I think that perhaps it is familiarity . . . . At one time in my career I even tried a whistle. I said to myself that they immediately respond on a football field, so I got my whistle out and gave a quiet whistle and lo and behold everybody stopped. I tried this for a week or two and then I thought, well, it's not done so I'd better discontinue the practice, but it certainly works, just like any sudden shock will stop people and, of course, as I said my voice is too familiar to them and some of them don't stop for it. Very often I've gone right up to a boy who has deliberately kept on, and just banged a ruler in front of his face to give him a shock and that's stopped him of course.

If the pay attention rule is in play, as is the case if a type 1 subphase is ending, the teacher can proceed to give the task indicator directly.

'Now what I want you to do is to answer the question on the board.'
'Right, now form a circle round the desk.'

Sometimes the teacher is able to assume that the pupils know the subphase that is to follow, in which case the switch-signal can be reduced to:

'Right, carry on.'
'OK, get on with it.'

If the pay attention rule is not in play, then such statements will be preceded by an instruction to stop the activity of the preceding phase and to put the attention rule into play.

'Right leave what you're doing, put your pens down and face me.
'Stop work now and look this way.'
'Right, look this way now.'

The last of the subphases of the lesson proper is followed by the fourth phase, the clearing up phase. In those lessons where the pupils are not using equipment of any kind, this phase may be very brief, but in most cases the pupils do have some kind of equipment. Usually, the transition to the clearing up phase is marked by a clear switch-signal, which directs them to stop work and to clear up whatever equipment has been in use during the last subphase according to the rules operated by the teacher in charge. Examples are:

'Right, it's time to stop work for break.'
'Close your books, now.'
'Put the rulers and pencils away please.'
'Now can I have all the papers in?'
'It's time to stop now. Pass your books forward.'
'Right, everybody pack up and put the equipment straight.'

Most teachers permit talking during this phase, and frequently the clearing up requires considerable movement.

(1) *I:* How do you end a lesson?
   T: Well, about five minutes before the end I'll say, 'Right, 2C, that's it', and it's finished like that, the lesson comes to an end abruptly, you know. 'Let me have your books in. Jeffrey, can you collect the rulers? Peter, will you collect the pencils? Anyone else had a pen of mine can you bring it back now? Let me have the books on the side table.' And they just go and sit.

(2) *T:* If the room is needed for another class I don't have the equipment collected. I ask them to spread out the equipment on the drawing board in a set pattern and I have this set pattern so I can quickly check. I don't just say all your equipment on the board, I have the equipment in a set pattern . . . . I then ask the boy nearest to the remainder of the equipment in the racks to check the remainders, so he knows how many are out in the room [. . .]

[. . .] The switch-signal that is used to usher in the clearing up phase does not need to be very explicit, since the pupils know that the lesson is near its end from their own watches. As one teacher said:

Well, some pupils will have been watching the clock. They'll be aware of the time. They know when the bell goes, so towards the end of the lesson they'll be looking towards me like spectators at a football match blowing their imaginary whistles.

Pupils are thus able to fill in that a statement, such as 'Right, stop now' is fact in the clearing up phase switch-signal.

> T: Before the end of the lesson, perhaps five minutes before the bell is due to go, 'It's time to collect up.' Having said it's time to collect up I'd probably detail one or two boys to collect specific items from the groups so I'll say, 'You collect all the . . . . You go and get all the watch glasses. You go and get all the forceps and count them.' At this stage if I find any lads doing nothing at all, I usually try to remind them that they too should be putting things away, tidying up, picking up odd things that may be lying about. The aim of that is to have everything away so that I can have them back in their places before the bell goes. This is an ideal of course, usually they are moving about, but I would hope to get them together. Often it will be necessary for me to say something. I might even have to point out why we have done the thing if I thought it needed emphasizing and why we had done the lesson at all. I might emphasize that this case of an organism what looks like nasty slime in a pond, when in fact it's delightful, you know, and they can apply this sort of thing to other things . . . .

The exit phase is complementary to the entry phase and is concerned with the accomplishment of leaving the classroom. The main rule is that pupils may not leave the room until the teacher indicates that they have his permission to do so. And the teacher will not grant this permission until the bell has rung, for this is one of the rules that the teachers must follow.

> (1) I: Do you always wait for the bell before you say that?
>   T.   Oh yes. I would be in trouble if I let them out. [The headteacher] does not want to see any child outside the classroom before the bell goes.
>
> (2) I: Are they allowed to just leave the room?
>   T: I don't let anybody leave before the bell. I don't let anybody go before my say, even though the bell has gone.

But the sound of the bell does not in itself permit the children to leave, even though it signals the official end of the lesson.

> I: At the end . . . you turned round and said, because they started moving, 'Somebody say leave?' and they said, 'But, sir, the bell's gone', and you said, 'That's for me not for you.'
> T: Yes. I honestly feel that this is slackness if teachers let them get up and wander off without either looking for some sort of expression from the teacher that it is the correct thing to get up and go. I think it is impolite, really, for behaviour in school. Nothing to do with teaching a subject, but I think they should say, 'May we go?' I don't mean that they should stand on their hands or anything silly, but at least look towards the teacher and get some sort of acceptance from the teacher that it is time to go . . . .

Permission to leave is signalled by phrases such as:

> 'Right, away you go.'
> 'Off you go then.'
> 'Right' ('you can go' being filled in by the pupils).

With older children, teachers generally do not impose any further rules for the exit phase, except that the pupils are not expected to push or run during the exit. Typically in these cases the teacher will say, if the bell has gone, 'You can go when you're ready', or, if the bell has not yet rung, 'You can go when the bell goes.' But with the younger pupils, there are many more rules governing the exit.

> (1) 'Right, get in line,' says the teacher. Pupils get up from the seats and line

up by the door waiting to go out. Bell goes. 'Right, you can go.' Teacher follows them out into corridor and dismisses them.
(Observation notes)

(2) 'I'm waiting for everyone to be quiet.'
'I've some pencils and rubbers missing, so we'll just wait for those to be found before we think about going out.' This is done.
'Stuart, will you shut up.'
'Now we'll have everybody sat straight, arms folded and we'll have a period of silence.' There is still some talking.
'We still have some person in the room who doesn't understand the word silence.'
When this occurs, the teacher lets them go. They later line up in the corridor, and then off.
(Observation notes)

[...] This material illustrates the variations in, and the complexity of, the exit phase rules. For some teachers, especially those with younger pupils in large classes, the exit phase may extend well beyond the physical exit through the door and sometimes almost runs into the entry phase of the pupils' next lesson.

I: So you say you have to see them down the stairs, you get them all together [...]

T: Yes, at the door, they line up at the door going down and then they go down, supposed to go down the stairs in single file because by the time they've got to the first landing there's half a dozen of them collected and then you've got to try and get them going down the corridor in single file so that they're not interfering with people coming the other way. I always ask where they're going next so that I know where they're going when they get to the bottom of the stairs, either up or down. It's confusing if you don't, and then that's the end of the lesson. [...]

[...] The analysis of lessons in terms of these five phases is essentially a structural analysis. As such it is perhaps of interest in its own right, and makes an interesting comparison with the way in which a curriculum developer or a classroom interaction analyst might seek to analyse a lesson. Our analysis stems directly from our need to understand classroom rules and proposes that every phase or subphrase brings into play a distinctive combination of rules. Pupils know which rules are in play because they know which phase they are in, though they would describe a phase in terms of the activity of that phase. Phases—and their rules—are changed by switch-signals, which are usually verbal statements made by the teacher. All this constitutes part of teachers' and pupils' common-sense knowledge of classrooms, and it is on this basis that members can make some deviance-imputations which invoke unstated rules which are known to be in play at particular points of time in the lesson.

Notes

[1] This is Goffman's (1963) term, and refers to picking one's nose, cleaning one's finger-nails, various forms of 'fidgeting', daydreaming and dozing. In an auto-involvement a person is excessively self-absorbed at the expense of the attention that should be paid to other persons present.

Bibliography

Goffman, E. (1963), *Behaviour in Public Places*, London, Free Press.

3 Mock-ups and Cock-ups: The Stage-management of Guided Discovery Instruction

P. ATKINSON and S. DELAMONT

'Progressive' classrooms, be they in primary or secondary schools, often appear disorderly to the outsider. Yet, as Atkinson and Delamont show in this study of Nuffield Science teaching in a Scottish girls' independent school, even so-called 'discovery' methods are strongly stage-managed by the teacher. Making comparisons with bedside teaching in hospitals, they show that 'guided discovery' is treated by teacher and pupil alike as only a 'mock up' of real life.

Part I

We propose to discuss two varieties of educational practice which, in rather similar ways, stress the first-hand 'experience' of the student in the process of learning. We wish to strike a recondite harmony between two learning situations which at first glance may appear quite diverse. The two situations we consider are guided-discovery science at secondary school level, and the bedside teaching of medicine in medical school. The examination of these two areas derives from our own 'experience' as researchers. The paper is based upon research in an independent Scottish girls' school 'St Luke's' (Delamont, 1973) and in the Edinburgh medical school (Atkinson, 1975). In discussing these two, apparently disparate, types of educational experience, we have been struck by a number of parallels; here we shall attempt to draw out some of these common themes, and to set them in a theoretical framework.

The curriculum development movement of the 1960s produced what purported to be a new way of learning at secondary level. Instead of the pupils being the passive recipients of lectures, or participating in drill-and-practice sessions, the new curricula posited a different relationship between teacher and taught, and a different mode of learning. Such new curricula as the Nuffield Science developments, or the Schools Council Humanities Curriculum Project attempted to take away from the teacher what had hitherto been her primary role—imparting knowledge. Rather than the teacher delivering *ex cathedra* statements of fact, the new curricula envisaged that the pupils should retrieve information from a range of resources provided for them. The teacher's role was to be modified to a cross between just one more resource, a 'counsellor-and-friend', or a neutral chairperson.

Such an approach was central to the ideology which informed changes in science curricula. In the development and implementation of 'Nuffield Science', it was a major principle that pupils should conduct experiments, analyse the results and draw conclusions from them. Whilst teachers would still demonstrate experiments and so on, far greater stress was to be placed on the pupil's *discovery* of the nature of things. The rationale of the new approaches had been articulated by Henry Armstrong at the turn of the century, with his advocacy of 'heuristic' approaches to science eduction:

> Heuristic methods of teaching are methods which involve our placing students as far as possible in the attitude of the discoverer—methods which involve their *finding out*, instead of being merely told about things. It should not be necessary to justify such a policy in education. . . Discovery and invention are divine prerogatives, in some degree granted to all, meet for daily usage. . . it is consequently of importance that we be taught the rules of the game of discovery and learn to play it skilfully. The value of mere knowledge is immensely over-rated, and its possession over-praised and over-rewarded.
> (Armstrong, 1898)

The new approaches should therefore stress pupils' engagement in 'real' experimentation and 'real' discovery, rather than the empty, unrealistic recapitulation of classic demonstrations. It was, therefore, hoped that such a new curricula would involve the teachers and pupils in the joint production of something that was taken to be more like the work of 'real' science. The authors of the Science Teacher Education Project (Hayson and Sutton, 1974) make this orientation explicit:

> For many of the teachers who were involved in the curriculum projects of the 'sixties and 'seventies it was in the hope of giving pupils an experience of the process of being a scientist. (p.63)

Thus the activities of science education were to become more like the real-world activities of professional scientists (or rather, what were *taken to be* their activities). In this way the natural phenomena with which students worked would also become more 'real'. This aspect of the new science was encapsulated in the survey of teaching practices undertaken by Kerr *et al.* (1963). Although this study was done before the new curricula were in full swing, it does touch on important aspects of the emergent style of thought. The researchers produced a series of statements about practical work in school science, one of which was:

> To make biological, chemical and physical phenomena more real through actual experience. Practical work can improve appreciation of basic phenomena by providing opportunities for contact with actual equipment and processes. It is the reality of the experience with the actual thing that influences so much the level of understanding.

By virtue of these developments, pupils should learn to 'think scientifically'—that is, to design experiments, perform them and draw appropriate conclusions from their observations. Emphasis was to be placed on 'ways of knowing' rather than on the retention of 'facts'. This approach comes across clearly in the Scottish Integrated Science Scheme discussed by Hamilton (1975). The official documentation associated with the scheme—known as Curriculum Paper Seven—recommends, *inter alia*, that:

> The discovery method should be used wherever possible.
> (Recommendation 5)

> A much reduced emphasis on the retention of the factual content of the syllabus. Instead. . . pupils should be exposed to many other aspects of the work of the scientist:. . . the experimental processes of thought by which he arrives at his conclusions and the language which he uses to communicate these conclusions to others.
> (Paragraph 8)

These recommendations and the ideology of the 'new' science were therefore shot through with these related themes: the importance of pupils' personal experience; the methods of discovery; the reality of science: the reality of natural phenomena. We shall go on to examine some aspects of how such approaches are worked out in classroom practice. At this point, we turn aside to consider our second type of instructional system.

While the science teaching we have outlined was innovatory, the system of medical teaching we discuss is a time-honoured one. But just as the science teaching was to bring 'learning' and 'practice' more into line, so it can be seen as analogous to the traditional methods of 'on-the-job' training characteristic of the 'clinical' phase of professional education. Such educational practices as clinical teaching on the hospital wards also stress the student's exposure to the 'real' work of the hospital: emphasis is placed on the student's own first-hand 'experience' in accumulating practical knowledge. This is emphasised in the classic study of the University of Kansas Medical School (Becker et al., 1961), where the notion of 'clinical experience' is used by staff and students alike to justify the importance of the student's first-hand involvement in work with the patients in the teaching hospital. Just as the science curricula we commented on contrasted pupils' experience and discovery with the rote-learning of 'facts', so the medical approach contrasts clinical experience with the pronouncements of textbooks (to the detriment of the latter). Whilst students chafe at learning the preclinical sciences (such as Anatomy, Physiology and Biochemistry), they greet their entry into the teaching hospitals as marking a move towards the 'real work' of medicine. They are taught by practising clinicians and come into contact with real patients. Just as the science curricula are predicated on 'discovery', a similar concern informs much of the medical teaching: in this context, the students are often required to 'discover' the correct diagnosis by questioning the patient (taking a history) and examining his body. Indeed, this is the basic objective of clinical teaching in its early stages; considerations of management and treatment of patients tend to come in a little later.

We shall go on to discuss the nature of the 'reality' which is produced and reproduced in the two educational contexts.

Part II

Although it has changed somewhat in recent years, the underlying rationale of clinical teaching in medicine has remained largely unaltered since the eighteenth century. At root, the method stems from the apprenticeship approach to medical training whereby students learn 'on the job'. Students who are in the clinical phase of their course of study are attached to clinical units ('firms') and receive instruction from the doctors in the hospital wards, out-patient clinics, operating theatres and so on. The traditional view of this activity is that presented in Richard Gordon's Doctor in the House—where students tag along behind the entourage of junior doctors, ward sister, nurses and senior students. The doctor examines his patients, occasionally throwing scraps of information to the students or pausing to fire questions at them. Such a popular view is not entirely inaccurate: as Cramond (1973) remarks, the most notable aspect of Doctor in the House is its universality. However, the contemporary approach is somewhat different. Whereas in the past, students were often attached to working rounds in this way, the Edinburgh teaching rounds described here were specifically scheduled as teaching rounds, pure and simple and consisted of just one clinician and a group of students, without any other courtiers or hangers-on. Thus the bedside teaching sessions did not form part of the management of the patient by the hospital staff: it was not a therapeutic situation. Thus the routine patient-care done by hospital personnel and the teaching or junior students did not overlap.

This *bedside teaching* is in sharp contrast to another situation to which students are exposed in the hospital. These occasions are known as *waiting nights*. The hospital wards receive emergency patients on a rota basis, and on their weekly 'waiting night' (or 'receiving night'), students who are attached to the ward are expected to come in and attend for at least part of the evening. On such occasions the students can observe the patients as they are admitted in acute conditions. They see people come in with 'acute abdomens', or in the critical phase of a heart attack: they see hospital cases when they are 'fresh'. If the patients are up to it, students may go and take a history from those newly admitted and examine them. Alternatively they may merely observe while the admitting clinician works on the patient himself, and offers a running commentary on what he is doing. In surgical units these occasions provide the student with much-prized opportunities to go into the operating theatres where they can observe things like emergency appendicectomies—or even assist at such operations. Thus waiting nights—and the sort of experience they provide for the students—can be contrasted with the teaching rounds that are routinely conducted during the day. In the former context, the students are present while the 'real' work of the hospital is going on (and it would go on even if they were not present). Teaching rounds, on the other hand, are clearly separate from the hospital's routine work with the patients—and the students are their sole *raison d'être*.

The students recognise the distinction between these two varieties of teaching situation. Whilst they do not always employ the vocabulary, they occasionally label the distinction as one between 'hot' and 'cold' medicine. It is often applied to types of surgery: 'hot' surgery is that concerned with intervention in life-threatening crises, whereas 'cold' surgery covers the elective surgery for conditions like hernias, haemarrhoids and the like. It has also been employed in the arena of medical education by the authors of the Royal College of General Practitioners' report, *The Future General Practitioner*. They distinguish between two settings:

(1) that this occurs at the time of the consultation, including discussion and observation immediately before, during and immediately after it.

(2) that which takes place at a time remote from the consultation, but employs material taken from it, based on memory or on written or on audio-visual recordings. (p. 228)

They go on to employ the vocabulary of 'hot' and 'cold' to evaluate these as effective educational occasions, e.g.:

> The effective teaching of any objective often depends on a 'hot' situation: this focal point in the consultation develops as a result of an unpredictable reaction between patient, doctor and teacher.

Whilst the vocabulary in this context is applied rather differently again it carries implications of actuality, and of a reality which is experienced at first hand, rather than through a *post hoc* reconstruction. For the medical students and their clinical experiences the contrast between 'hot' and 'cold' medicine was an important one and it concerned the nature of the 'reality' that they were experiencing.

One normal difference between the two contexts lies in the fact that the waiting night marks the beginning of a patient's hospital stay. By the time that students see them in the course of ward rounds, on the other hand, their 'career' as a hospital patient will be starting to take shape, or will be well under way. As a result of this, it is usually the case that when students see patients in the course of ward-work and bedside teaching, their trouble will routinely have been managed and/or diagnosed by the hospital personnel. Very often the patients' acute symptoms will have been treated—and things like severe pain, high fever and so on will have been controlled (if possible) and may have disappeared altogether. Waiting nights provide the students with an exposure to patients whose illness is fresh. In this situation diagnosis will not yet have been done—and the students and the doctors are in a similar state of relative ignorance concerning the precise nature of the patient's presenting complaint. But when students see patients in the course of ward rounds, unless they happen to have seen them on a waiting night, then the distribution of knowledge is rather different. Whilst the students are in a state of relative ignorance concerning the patient, now the doctor who is conducting the teaching round will already be acquainted with the patient's history and present complaint—either from his own work with the patient, or via the documentary evidence assembled in the case-notes folder.

From the point of view of the distribution of knowledge, then, the two teaching contexts differ. Yet the latter situation—that of bedside teaching—is designed to produce something which approximates to the sort of medical reality that is accomplished in the acute 'hot' situation. As we have said, it is a primary purpose of bedside teaching to provide students with practical opportunities to take histories, perform examinations and formulate diagnoses. The exercise may proceed upon the assumption that the patient's diagnosis is *not* already agreed upon by the clinical staff, or that management of the illness has not been initiated. The students may be (and often are) required to take the patient's history 'from scratch', as if the patient had not already given it—sometimes repeatedly—to the hospital doctors. This previous work that has been done by the hospital staff may, therefore, be discounted and the participants proceed as if it had not in fact been done. (This is generally possible because rather few of the patients will have been seen by students during the waiting night, as the students take turns to come in each week in twos or threes.)

This state of affairs can be illustrated in the following student's description of what happens when a student *has* seen a patient previously:

> After waiting nights, Mr Michael [the consultant surgeon] takes all students to see the new admissions. If you've already seen the patient, you keep quiet while Mr Michael plays games with the others, and sees how well they can make a diagnosis. Then you fill in the details—and try desperately to remember which abdomen it was when you've only seen a little bit of it in theatre.

This same student went on to develop his point about 'playing games'. He instanced a patient with jaundice. They could see she was yellow, he said; and they had been told already that she had cancer: they had had to take what he described as a 'very fake history', since they knew the answers to the questions anyway. He thought that the doctor who was teaching the group might just as well have said: 'There's a patient in that bed, she's got jaundice but she's got secondaries in her liver.' Here the student draws attention vividly to the way in which bedside teaching may be conducted 'as if' diagnosis of the patient's condition were starting afresh rather than being already established by the doctors.

What we have been sketching here, in describing this aspect of bedside teaching, is a situation which is contrived in order to parallel some of the features of another situation. Clearly, it is not designed to reproduce *all* the possible features of 'real' or 'hot' medicine. The participants do not pretend that this 'really is' an admission on a waiting night: they do not feign rushing about, coping with emergencies, working against the clock and so on. (In fact this is one of the contrasts that students draw between the two types of situation—that the *pace* of the work is very different: 'cold' encounters can proceed at a much more leisurely pace.) In other words, the reproduction of 'hot' medicine in clinical teaching should not be confused with 'acting out' the situation (it is not a 'dress rehearsal' in that sense). It is designed to achieve a reconstruction of selected features, in order to produce a plausible account of the supposedly 'real' situation for specific, practical purposes. We shall develop our comments on these lines subsequently.

Recalling our initial comments on the nature and practice of 'guided discovery' science teaching, it will be apparent that it shares some important features with 'cold' medical teaching; indeed, we might stretch the medical students' term and refer to it as 'cold science'. Of course, the school pupils do not have access to 'hot' science as do the medical students, but the parallel holds in so far as their school science is conducted in such a way as to replicate features of 'real' science. We concentrate on one particular area of school science—physics and biology, as taught to the fifteen-year-old girls at St Luke's. The O grade syllabuses in these subjects last for two years, and at the time of the field work the girls had completed one and a half terms of work. St Luke's was relatively unusual for a girls' school in that it had a strong science department, which was run by enthusiastic, well-qualified teachers. The biology teacher (whom we shall call Mrs Linnaeus) and the physicist (Dr Cavendish) were both firmly committed to the 'guided discovery' ideology embodied in the O grade syllabuses, and it is their classes particularly which exemplify the nature of such 'cold' science.

A typical biology lesson would run as follows: Twenty-odd girls assemble in the laboratory (described in Delamont, 1976). Mrs Linnaeus asks someone to summarise the experiment(s) completed the previous lesson. She then asks for further hypotheses relating to, and following on from, that conclusion, which now need to be tested. The girls then suggest experimental designs to test these hypotheses. Methods are discussed and written up on the board. Then the class divides into pairs and all perform the same experiment(s). Practical work occupies some forty minutes, with the girls unprompted, writing up in the lulls between bursts of work. When all, or most, of the pairs have completed the experiment, Mrs Linnaeus calls everyone's attention and asks each pair for their results. These are listed on the board, no comments being passed on their 'correctness'. When the list is complete, she asks what can be deduced from them. Pupils scan the results, comment on any that appear aberrant, and decide what the common, overall result is. They then consider whether or not the hypothesis is supported, and, often prompted or guided, produce a conclusion. Once this stage has been reached the formal part of the lesson is over, and the time remaining until the end of the double period is spent in tidying away apparatus, writing up the day's work, with the results and conclusions, and for those who still have time, starting the homework assignment.

During the field work, the classes were 'doing' photosynthesis—working through a series of controlled experiments to display the relative effects of light, chlorophyl etc. We see this as paralleling 'cold' medicine. Just as the patient's condition has been diagnosed, so the biochemical processes of photosynthesis are well known. Just as the medical students are aware that a diagnosis exists, though they do not normally have prior access to it, so too the pupils are aware that biologists know about photosynthesis, though they do not normally have access to that knowledge themselves. The students operate a 'proper' procedure (taking a history, performing a physical examination and so on)—so too the girls go through the motions of stating hypotheses, designing rigorously controlled experiments and deducing conclusions. Neither situation is 'real', but both are parallels of 'real' processes. In both cases, it is important that the appropriate techniques be learned.

The problems faced by Mrs Linnaeus and Dr Cavendish in sustaining 'cold' science came mainly from the girls' 'failure' to perform experiments correctly. On the whole, they were able to steer the discussion into the right channels: the right hypotheses were usually formulated. Difficulties arose in the performance of the experiments themselves. Mrs Linnaeus taught two parallel biology classes. The girls in one group generally produced a set of results, but in the other, the same experiments burned, boiled dry, boiled over or just failed to get finished inside lesson time. Thus, in the first class. Mrs Linnaeus usually had eight to ten sets of results to draw on; in the second, only two or three sets were generally available, or 'correct', and the ideal of scanning a *range* of results as a basis for the conclusion was rarely achieved. In this group, Mrs Linnaeus was always falling back on statements such as, 'If the experiment had worked, you would have been able to see...', 'Actually...'Given these two classes, it was possible to see Mrs Linnaeus's cold science' succeeding and failing. Mrs Linnaeus believed strongly in guided discovery methods, but, for her, the 'guiding' was extremely important. She steered the pupils' discussion firmly towards the right answers and 'stage-managed' her classes with brisk efficiency. However, her strategy was not proof against pupils' potential failure to perform the physical manipulations necessary in the experiments.

The case of physics was rather different. Dr Cavendish also believed in a discovery-based approach to science teaching. However, she did not (or could not) do any 'guiding'. She provided a context in which discovery could take place—a laboratory full of apparatus and a textbook—and left the pupils to play at science as they would. While this may be closer to the situation of 'real' scientific discovery, it produced a high degree of anxiety and confusion among the pupils, to the extent that observation was an embarrassing, even distressing, occupation. The field notes taken at the time reflect some of this confusion:

> Dr Cavendish sums up last week's experiments—in answer to queries from Fleur. Tessa and Lorraine write down this summary—tho' they were present at the lesson (Fleur was not). Tessa moves to check summary with Jackie on next bench. Dr C asks simple question on basics—Eleanor answers right—Dr C gives longish explanation of calculating acceleration. Girls then get out equipment to re-do experiment. Tessa, Mary and Fleur work near me—they discuss [lacrosse] teams—Mary says she's left the next table (where she's supposed to work) 'cos they're trying to muddle me up.'
>
> I move to next table where Charmian and Henrietta are explaining acceleration to Karen—then Angela comes to Karen for help and is passed to Charmian for a repeat performance.

Throughout the field notes similar episodes—characterised by muddle, confusion and anxiety—are recorded. For example, the next week it was noted:

> Dr C starts lesson by announcing 'Last week you discovered an important relationship.' Greeted by ironic laughs. Ignores this and gives explanations of relationship between force and mass...(Later) Getting out equipment for an experiment started last time. Chorus of 'It didn't work!' After two experiments (on force, mass and acceleration) the class are still unsure of what they are doing and why. She gives detailed explanation again. Then says 'A time will come (when they will understand it).' A chorus of ironic echoes of her sentiment.

> Tessa, Lorraine and Fleur muddle around for some time with apparatus—eventually work out what they are doing from book and common sense. Henrietta, Charmian and Michelle—much more together—have actually got some figures out of it!

Every lesson Dr Cavendish's attempt at summarising previous work would be greeted with dismay—the girls had always failed. The experiment had failed, or the mathematics were too hard, or the conclusions had simply not emerged. Dr Cavendish would be forced to re-explain, or would do the experiment herself, or rework the maths. Many of the lessons only 'worked' because of a pupil, Charmian, who conducted tutorials at the back of the room using the textbook and her group's results!

This is clearly an extreme example of the problematic nature of such 'cold' science. But we would argue that such types of encounter are always precarious: they require a degree of careful creation and maintenance and the borderline between bringing them off and spoiling them is narrow. Even the usually well-managed bedside teaching can easily be spoiled.

As we have pointed out already, patients may not be seen by the students until some time after the initial admission to the hospital ward. Now, although the teaching situation may be steered towards the diagnosis of the patient's trouble, by the time that bedside teaching takes place, the nature and the appearance of the illness may have changed. It is a normal trouble associated with 'cold' medicine that, with the passage of time, the initial signs and symptoms of the presenting complaint may abate or disappear altogether. Hence, when a teacher wishes to demonstrate a point of diagnostic observation and inference, the signs he wishes to show the students may well elude him. This contingency can be illustrated in the following field-note extract:

> Dr Muir reminded us that anaemic patients often have a dry, red, swollen tongue. He asked Miss Miniver to put out her tongue: it looked quite normal. 'I'm terribly disappointed', the doctor said, 'on Saturday she had a red swollen tongue.'

There was no doubt that the patient was still to be considered 'anaemic', but the doctor had expected to provide a further example of diagnostic signs, as well as 'clinching' the diagnosis already arrived at. In the face of such events, the clinical teachers were observed to resort to 'repair' devices of various sorts. The two commonest variants were 'In fact . . .' and 'retrospective' clauses, both of which accomplish the same thing. In the example given above, the doctor uses a 'retrospective' appeal to a previous state of affairs that 'fitted' the order of things that he is putting forward to the students. Similarly, just as Mrs Linnaeus would attempt to repair the students' failings in their experiments and findings with her 'Well, actually . . .', the doctor would fill in what 'In fact . . .' should have appeared in the patient as a reflection of the underlying pathology. For example:

> [In response to questioning from one of the students] the patient reported that he had not been having to pass water many times during the day. But Dr Massie commented, 'In fact, he reported frequency during the day as well . . .'

By means of such repair work, 'cold' medicine and science are once more brought into line with what is known about the phenomena of the 'real' world. The rationality and efficacy of scientific and medical enquiry are reaffirmed and demonstrated by the invocation of such appeals by the teachers concerned.

The successful accomplishment of 'cold' medicine and 'cold' school science depends upon the observation of context-specific conventions. In particular, sustaining the reality depends upon the participants acting 'as if' the answer to the puzzle were not already established. In the medical school, the teaching session may be threatened if a patient orients to the fact that the answer is available to the doctor. Such a patient may protest about the students' enquiries, point out that the questions are irrelevant to his or her own care, and that the doctor himself can readily provide the answers (and more). Such a patient's 'grumbling' may not only spoil the 'bedside manner' of the doctor and students—it may also threaten the encounter by laying bare the nature of its contrivance.

Such disruption is also a consequence if the patient goes even further in this direction. Some patients will not only be aware that the doctor knows what is wrong with them—they may also know the diagnosis themselves. Failure to act in accordance with the tacit rules of 'cold' medical teaching may therefore lead them to divulge this information. In other words, they may treat a student's initial question as a direct request for this diagnosis, rather than an opening move in a sequence of questions and answers from which the diagnosis may be inferred by the students. For example:

Student: What brought you into hospital . . .?
Patient: Ulcerative colitis, the doctor called it . . .

In other words, if the bedside session is to come off as a successful recapitulation of 'real' diagnosis, then the work that has been done on the patient must be set aside by those 'in the know' (cf. Atkinson, 1975). Therefore, in conducting and 'stage-managing' such bedside encounters, the teaching clinicians may need to guard against such untimely disclosure of information. This can be illustrated from our field notes:

> A girl student was exploring whether the patient [an elderly woman] had any signs of anaemia. As she was examining her eyes, the inside of her mouth, the creases in her palms etc., the old lady chipped in, 'I've had a blood transfusion since I came in . . .' The doctor interrupted, 'Don't tell them too much! You're giving the whole show away—giving away the whole shooting-match!'

Giving away too much involves revealing the stage-management of 'cold' medicine by making explicit the information which would otherwise remain unspoken.

A further field-note extract also demonstrates how the clinician may guard against such an eventuality. In this case he invents a 'mega-game' in which to locate the rule that the patient is not to divulge data to the students.

> The consultant began the teaching session by telling the students, 'Imagine that Mr— is an Eskimo, who's deaf and dumb and mentally deficient . . .' In other words they were not to take a history, but were to proceed straight to the physical examination. As the various students took the patient's pulse, examined him for *oedema*, tested his eye movements, examined his thyroid etc., the consultant commented to the patient that he was 'doing fine', and that he was using him as a 'male model'. The consultant then asked one of the students to examine the patient's *precordium*. When the student opened the patient's pyjama jacket, he exposed an operation scar on the left side of his chest.
> Patient: 'Do I tell them about that?'
> Consultant: 'No . . . as far as they're concerned that's a shark's tooth that tore you apart.'

In much the same way, trouble can occur in school science if the particular conventions of cold science are not respected. This can be illustrated in the following observation from a biology lesson, made during the girls' work on photosynthesis. (The experiment under discussion involved covering growing leaves with silver foil with several holes cut in it. After a few days the leaves are picked and tested for starch, which should only be present in the uncovered patches).

> *Michelle:* Mrs Linnaeus, I don't see how that will prove it—it could be all sorts of things we don't know anything about.
> *Mrs L.:* (Comes down the lab. to stand near Michelle, asks her to expand her problem—to explain what she doesn't see.)
> *Michelle:* Well, you said if there was starch in the bare patches it would mean there was—it would be because of the light. But it could be the chemicals in the foil, or something we know nothing about.
> *Sharon:* Of course it'll prove it—we wouldn't be wasting our time doing it if it didn't.
> *Mrs L.:* I don't think that's a very good reason, Sharon! (She laughs, then goes on into a long and detailed vindication of the experimental structure. This involves discussing the molecular structure of carbohydrates, and other phenomena. Few other girls bother to listen—Henrietta does.)

We can note how both girls' exchanges are problematic, given the nature of 'cold' science. Michelle treats it as 'hot' science—that the process really is one of scientific discovery in which the phenomenon under consideration is genuinely not understood. From the point of view of her learning the logic of science the teaching may be regarded as successful—but it causes problems in the here-and-now situation of the classroom, since the teacher's smooth production of a lesson depends upon treating the 'experiment' at its face value. Sharon's interjection can be read as an attempt at a remedial exchange: she attempts to reaffirm the nature of 'cold' science as really doing what is claimed for it. However, in doing so, she lays bare the stage machinery of the exercise—shows that it is a 'put-up job'. She explicitly orients to the teacher's prior knowledge: they would not be wasting their time. She sees that the enterprise has been managed in such a way as to produce an outcome in line with Mrs Linnaeus's intended result—the right answer. Sharon threatens the mock-up as a plausible situation. Mrs Linnaeus therefore denies that Sharon's approach is a 'reasonable' one and reaffirms the rationality of discovery methods. (Note, however, that she does not deny Sharon is right.)

As a teaching strategy, 'guided discovery' in one of its forms is difficult to sustain. There are many points at which it can go wrong. Teachers using it need to engage in artful stage-management if they are to bring it off successfully. If the nature of this management is not respected by any of the parties, then trouble can ensue. By the same token, the interaction can become problematic if the 'stage machinery' becomes too visible in the course of the encounter. In either event, it becomes difficult for the participants to create and maintain the 'reality-like' nature of the exercise. [...]

Part III

As we have shown, the successful conduct of these teaching encounters depends upon the successful discounting of already established knowledge. In medicine, bedside teaching proceeds on the basis that previously acquired knowledge about the patient's illness should be set aside so that the diagnostic exercise can proceed as it would under the 'normal' circumstances of 'hot' medicine. In the same way, school science proceeds on the tacit assumption that the pupils are engaged in the 'discovery' of phenomena which are already well-known, and which the teacher has already set up as the end point of their endeavours. In other words, what is at stake in teaching situations of this sort is not so much that the relevant conclusions should *remain* undisclosed, but rather, that they should appear in the appropriate manner and at the appropriate time. It is necessary that the parties should 'go through the motions' of correct medical or experimental procedure. The conduct of the information-games serves to ensure that an *orderly* production of knowledge should occur in accordance with the rules of appropriate 'discovery' methods.

In this regard, the sort of management of knowledge that we are describing is a regular feature of teacher-student interactions. Information-games of various sorts are normal features of classroom discourse. It is by no means the case that all 'teaching' implies the didactic *presentation* of knowledge. In various ways, the accomplishment of teaching may depend on the teacher's knowledge and information being temporarily kept back from the students. This has been noted by Sinclair and Coulthard (1974) and by Stubbs (1975). Stubbs, for example, suggests that many teachers' questions can usefully be described as 'pseudo-questions': that is, what pass as questions in the classroom are rather different from those usually encountered in other social contexts. Teachers' questions are not rhetorical, in so far as they do require an answer of some sort, but they do not indicate ignorance on the teacher's part. For most of the time, when a school teacher asks her class: 'Who won the battle of Waterloo?', we would be wrong in assuming that the teacher herself does not know, and is expecting her pupils to instruct her in elementary history. Whereas most questioners' utterances will normally be treated as displays of their ignorance, teachers' questions will normally be grounds for the display of their knowledge—either in correcting pupils' answers or in acknowledging their correctness. Similarly, when a teaching doctor asks a student to produce a diagnosis about a patient, he is normally checking to see if he can do it successfully, rather than seeking the 'second opinion' of a colleague. In other words, the production of certain varieties of pedagogical device depend upon the suppression of the teacher's own prior knowledge of the 'correct' answer, so that students themselves may display it or elicit it for themselves, whilst the teacher may prompt the students towards the right answer. From this point of view, then, the devices of 'cold' medicine and science can be seen as such elementary gambits 'writ large', so as to provide the grounds for extended educational encounters.

References

Armstrong, H.E. (1898), 'The heuristic method of teaching or the art of making children discover things for themselves. A chapter in the history of English schools'. Reprinted in W.H. Brock (ed.) *H.E. Armstrong and the Teaching of Science*, Cambridge University Press, Cambridge, 1973.

Atkinson, P.A. (1975) 'In cold blood: bedside teaching in a medical school', in G. Chanan and S. Delamont (eds) *Frontiers of Classroom Research*, National Foundation for Educational Research, Slough.

Becker, H.S., Geer, B., Hughes, E.C. and Strauss, A.L. (1961) *Boys in White*, Chicago University Press, Chicago.

Cramond, W.A. (1973) *Prescription for a Doctor*, Leicester University Press, Leicester.

Delamont, S (1973) *Academic Conformity Observed*, Unpublished Ph.D. thesis, University of Edinburgh.

Delamont, S. (1976), 'Beyond Flanders Fields' in M. Stubbs and S. Delamont (eds) *Explorations in Classroom Observation*, Wiley, Chichester.

Hamilton, D. (1975) 'Handling innovation in the classroom: two Scottish examples' in W.A. Reid and D.F. Walker (eds), *Case Studies in Curriculum Change*, Routledge and Kegan Paul, London.

Hayson, J. and Sutton, C. (1974) *Science Teacher Education Project: Theory and Practice*, McGraw Hill, London.

Kerr, J.F. *et al.* (1963) *Practical Work in School Science*, Leicester University Press, Leicester.

Sinclair, J. McH. and Coulthard, M. (1974) *Towards an Analysis of Discourse*, Oxford University Press, Oxford.

Stubbs, M. (1975) 'Teaching and talking: a sociolinguistic approach to classroom interaction' in G. Chanan and S. Delamont (eds) *Frontiers of Classroom Research*, National Foundation for Educational Research, Slough.

4   Teaching for Survival

P. WOODS

Strategies are ways of achieving goals and of adapting to constraints. They are a basic concern within interactionist studies of teaching, for they focus attention upon teachers' interests and their construction of action within the constraints imposed by the context of teaching. In the following article it is argued that teacher behaviour in the Midlands secondary school where the research was carried out is better explained by the exigencies of classroom survival rather than by any interests in 'teaching'.

An interactionist model of teaching

[...] Institutions, once established, generate a certain momentum and inter-dependence. The establishment, development and gradual expansion of com-pulsory education and the drive since the last war for equality of educational opportunity created an ethos of beneficence about the education system, which has only been seriously disputed within the last decade. This disputation was the product of developments in society which were to bring into question the struc-tures on which the education systems of industrialized societies rested—the changes accompanying advanced technology, the nature of work, upheavals of class and community cultures, the extension of the media, 'affluence', shifting definitions of morality, changes in child-rearing patterns and the growth of the social sciences. However, at the same time that the system was coming under attack, it was still, of course, receiving substantial support from within. Changes in structure, such as comprehensive education, and new developments in educa-tional theory, notably child-centredness, were adaptations to the changing social scene, which carried an air of healthy reformism to those within, though it was rhetoric and reification to those without.

Now, one way to explain the resistance of the system to radical change is to see it as the agent of the capitalist state. It is then dependent on economic forces and structures in society, and only changes in those structures can bring about any real changes in the education system. Another way to explain it is to view it as the product of institutional momentum. We can secure a more interactional viewpoint which would allow the actors more autonomy and furthermore enable us to make distinctions among the actors, by introducing the notion of commitment. I refer to the term as used by Kanter:[1]

> Commitment is a consideration which arises at the intersection of organizational requisites and personal experience. On the one hand, social systems organize to meet systemic 'needs'; and on the other hand, people orient themselves positively and negatively, emotionally and intellectually, to situations. Since social orders are supported by people, one problem of collectivities is to meet organizational requisites in such a way that participants at the same time become positively involved with the system—loyal, loving, dedicated, and obedient. This requires solutions to organizational or systemic problems that are simultaneously mechanisms for ensuring commitment through their effects on individuals—their

experience and orientations. Commitment, then, refers to the willingness of social actors to give their energy and loyalty to social systems, the attachment of personality systems to social relations which are seen as self-expressive.

This is particularly useful in my analysis, for, as Kanter has observed, it links maintenance of the self with maintenance of the system. We might regard institutional momentum as the collective sum of commitment of all the actors within the institution.

One of the major social system problems involving the commitment of actors is its continuance as an action system. This involves cognitive orientations bearing on profits and costs, and generally implies commitment to a social system role. 'The individual who makes a cognitive-continuance commitment finds that what is profitable to him is bound up with his position in the organisation, is contingent on his participating in the system.'[2] There is a profit in his remaining there and a deficit associated with leaving. Continuance is accompanied by 'sacrifice' and 'investment' processes. As a price of membership, members give up something, make sacrifices, which in turn *increases* commitment. So does investment, which promises future gain in the organization. The member takes out shares in the proceeds of the organization and thus has a stake in its future. He channels his expectations along the organization's path, and the more he does so, the more he increases the distance between this and other possibilities. They grow more remote as his commitment grows larger. In this way the process is self-validating, self-reinforcing and frequently irreversible. The member goes on further to lay down what Becker calls 'side-bets' as other, unanticipated, sources of reward appear, once the line of action has been chosen.[3]

Another process accompanying commitment is what I will term *accommodation*. This refers to the solving or riding of problems thrown up by the organization so as effectively to neutralize the threat to the actor's continuance in it. One of the most common techniques of accommodation is rationalization, which frequently follows decision-making. What previously might have been perceived as problems are explained away once a course of action has been chosen, and often reappear as benefits.

Continuance commitment among teachers is strong. It's their job—they are not trained for any other. Investment takes the form of career-bound choices—doing certain jobs, such as the timetable, accepting certain roles, taking courses. Also, the sorts of trials a teacher goes through in his first one or two years of teaching are a kind of initiation rite, a matter of pride to those who have successfully negotiated them. Sacrifice is considerable—alternative careers and the pleasures and profits associated with them. Once embarked on teaching, few turn back or alter course. Perhaps the large demands in commitment that teaching makes help to explain why so many opt out at training stage.[4]

Contributing towards institutional momentum is institutional development, reformist educational theory and much teaching tradition. A great deal of the latter already involves much 'accommodation' to perennial constraints and difficulties thrown up by such matters as the teacher–pupil ratio, the length of the teaching day, week and year, resources, such as book provision, buildings, compulsory education and examinations. While we cannot deny that generally conditions in schools have improved over the last hundred years, it is equally true that in some respects, in terms of demand on teachers' accommodation capacity, they have worsened in recent years. The leaving age has been raised, and though the 11+ has largely disappeared, 16+ examinations have become even more the yardstick by which secondary schools shall be judged, and, since CSE was begun, many more pupils have become involved. Further, it seems likely that in the foreseeable future the teacher–pupil ratio will increase and resources in general diminish.

Concerning reformist educational theory and institutional development, the teacher operates within a climate of dynamic change. The growth of departments, institutes and colleges of education, of the social sciences and their application to education, of in-service training, of general interest in and recognition of the importance of education have contributed to this. While theories about comprehensive education, mixed-ability teaching, the integrated day, Newsom courses, child-centred education, progressivism and so on also pressurize him to adapt further. Support of, and attachment to, these theories is itself, of course, a product of societal developments but all, or nearly all, are framed within the same institutional context and assume its continuance.

With regard to the trend of societal developments such as I spoke of earlier, the social consequences of technological growth are manifested for the teacher most prominently in the nature of his clientele. Musgrove has likened the school system to a 'network of bear pits'.[5] Webb found the teachers of Black School distinguished by fatigue, and hence motivated by the avoidance of circumstances that might add to it, and *fear*—fear that 'playground chaos' would spill over into the classroom.[6] That picture has become much more common today and the problems deeper and more diverse. Every week there is talk in the educational press of growing rates of violence and truancy in the schools. And there is much teacher disillusionment. One rank-and-file member told Musgrove, for example, 'because of the pressures teachers work under, because of the system, they find they have no real control over how they teach and how they carry out the job. And this is a very degrading experience.'[7]

I conclude, therefore, that the pressures on the teacher's accommodation capacities have increased, are increasing, and are likely to go on increasing. But, of course the pressures differ according to (a) type of school—there are enormous differences among secondary schools as well as between secondary and primary, and (b) teacher commitment—the less the commitment, the less the accommodation problem. If we envisage for a moment a teacher in the most besieged situation—strongly committed, but having to cope with a number of difficult classes—his problem might be construed as a crisis wherein the whole basis of his commitment may be called into question. The investments and sacrifices he has made, the side-bets he has laid down, are all at risk. He faces career bankruptcy. It is, in short, *a survival* problem. What is at risk is not only his physical, mental and nervous safety and well-being, but also his continuance in professional life, his future prospects, his professional identity, his way of life, his status, his self-esteem, all of which are the product of an accumulating investment process. Because of the concomitant sacrifices, for most people there is no second chance, no closing down and investing in another career. Teachers are stuck, and must do as best they can. They cannot leave their positions, they cannot change the social order, they therefore must adapt. They must accommodate these problems. Where the problems are numerous and intense, accommodation will prevail over teaching. In easier circumstances, the teacher can concentrate more on educational interests. However, it is not quite as clear cut as that. The problems are of such a nature, the teacher's commitment so complete, his position so circumscribed, that accommodation requires considerable ingenuity. It can, as I shall demonstrate, 'double' or masquerade as 'education'. I should make clear that I am talking of 'education' here as 'the transmission of knowledge', the model overwhelmingly subscribed to by all the teachers at Lowfield.

Survival strategies

Teachers accommodate by developing and using survival strategies. Normative means of control enshrined in the punishment structure are quite inadequate. They are after all devised for normative children. It is the kind of control one needs in order to teach. And survival, of course, involves more than simply control, though that is an important part of it. I define control in this instance as successfully dealing with incident which fractures the teacher's peace, or establishing one's power in a situation which pre-empts such an occurrence. We can illustrate this by the techniques Waller observed teachers using to secure control: (1) command; (2) punishment; (3) management or manipulation of personal and group relationships; (4) temper; (5) appeal.[8] These can be subsumed under more general strategies; for example, command, punishment and temper are all features of the general survival strategy which I term 'domination'; the others, of the general survival strategy of 'negotiation'. But these are only two out of eight survival strategies that I have observed in our secondary schools. The other six are socialization, fraternization, absence or removal, ritual and routine, occupational therapy, and morale-boosting. If control is conceived of as the handling of incident, survival includes that, but also involves the avoidance of incident, the masking or diguising of incident, the weathering of incident and the neutralizing of incident.

A feature of successful survival strategies is their permanence and ongoing refinement. They contain the seeds of their own continuance and growth, often outliving their usefulness, and festering, causing another problem for which another survival strategy must be devised. They do not take a problem out of the arena, as it were, leaving more room for teaching. Rather, they expand into teaching and around it, like some parasitic plant, and eventually in some cases the host might be completely killed off. However, like parasites, if they kill off the host, they are a failure and they must die too, for they stand starkly revealed for what they are. The best strategies are those that allow a modicum of education to seep through. Alternatively, they will appear as teaching, their survival value having a higher premium than their educational value. Theoretically, it is not difficult to point up the difference:[9]

> the intention of all teaching activities is that of bringing about learning ... If therefore a teacher spends the whole afternoon in activities the concern of which is not that the pupils should learn ... he cannot have been teaching at all. In these terms, it could be the case that quite a large number of professional teachers are in fact frauds most of their lives because their intentions are never clear ... [they] may be lost in a welter of secondary intentions.

The term 'frauds', though technically correct, carries unfortunate moral connotations. My analysis shifts responsibility largely from the teacher to the situation in which he finds himself. The factors of which I have spoken have led to teachers suffering from 'a crippling sense of uncertainty about what they are for'.[10] This is how I would conceive of many of the paradoxes in the teachers' situation in Sharp and Green's study school. Only their commitment with its capacity for accommodation keeps them going. And the immediacy of the survival problem, as Jackson has noted, determines the action.[11] I want to emphasize this situationist point. Deutscher has stated the extreme case:[12]

> The social situation is a notion which is different in kind from the constructs culture, social structure and personality. These gross abstract forces not only

provide little understanding of why people behave as they do in everyday life, but, unlike the social situation they are fictions constructed by the social scientist; none of them, in fact, exists ... These concepts are all inventions, myths, fantasies, which often blind the analyst to the very real constraints imposed by the immediate situation in which the actor finds himself.

Becker also stresses the importance of the situation with regard to personal change in his notion of 'situational adjustment', whereby the individual turns himself into the kind of person the situation demands.[13]

If we view situation adjustment as a major process of personal development, we must look to the character of the situation for the explanation of why people change as they do. We ask what there is in the situation that requires the person to act in a certain way or to hold certain beliefs. We do not ask what there is in him that requires the action or belief. All we need to know of the person is that for some reason or another he desires to continue his participation in the situation, or to do well in it.

Clearly I would not want to write off 'structure' as completely as Deutscher seems to do, since I am concerned to account for the situation in wider forces. But if we are to understand behaviour we must examine thoroughly the circumstances a person finds himself.

One work which illustrates how teachers' perceptions of pupils contribute to this is that by Jenks.[14] The teachers in the primary school that he studied characterized most of their pupils as 'difficult'. Consequently they distinguished among them according to their 'controllability'. 'Thus the strategy of coping with the present situation involves a central notion of control, usually exercised as silence: this is what is sought often, and against this success in the classroom is measured.' Control became an important part of the curriculum. Instead of a curriculum of writing, spelling and maths, it became writing and control; spelling and control; maths and control. 'Child-centred' methods were considered inappropriate by the older teachers for *that* type of child. Similarly, Denscombe noticed in two London comprehensive schools that 'the aim of motivating the unmotivated appeared to owe as much to the practical attempt to avoid disruption in the classroom as to any pedagogic "ideology".'[15] On teachers' own accounts, 'pupil motivation in the practical context of teaching was of concern in a manner which transcended and was analytically distinct from "progressive" or "traditional" perspectives on education.'[16] Their competence as teachers was accordingly judged by their 'capacity to secure for themselves quiet orderliness in "their" classroom', the actual task structure of teaching involving 'the prevention of noise emanating from the classroom without recourse to help from other members of staff.'[17]

Sharp and Green also suggest that the 'notion of "child directed learning" is related to the categorization of the pupils via the control problems presented to the teacher in [an] open fluid context.' There are 'bright' pupils who are easily 'biddable' and dull ones, who are difficult to motivate. The teacher's solution to this problem of engaging all the pupils in work is 'busyness', where[18]

children do something which they have chosen and are thus engaged in activity without requiring the constant attention which the teacher is unable to give them. To the teacher there is a logical relationship between the notion of busyness, her educational philosophy and her actions. However, there is also a contingent relation in that the situation is objectively given in the sense of the limitation of her time-space resources.

It is these contingencies that threaten to predominate in many schools Westbury has observed:[19]

> The interaction between the demands on the classroom and the constraints within it cause it to be a social setting that has only limited potentiality for manipulation by teachers. The recitation is a teaching strategy that permits teachers to deal, in at least a minimally satisfactory way, with the tensions that this interaction between demands and constraints creates; it has persisted through the fifty years that Hoetker and Ahlbrand have explored because the fundamental characteristic of the classroom that have made the recitation adaptive to the needs of teachers have persisted through these fifty years.

Westbury, however, concludes that 'the classroom does not alter the essential character of these teaching tasks, but it makes their execution more complex.' This provides us with a more humane view of traditional pedagogical processes such as formal teaching, question and answer and so on, whose inadequacies as educational vehicles are more usually simply exposed. It is what Westbury calls a *coping strategy*. However, survival entails more than coping, and I would contend that it does quite often alter the essential character of teaching tasks. Significantly, Westbury only takes into account rather mechanical or demographic constraints, such as rooms, desks, resources, *numbers* of pupils, within a general context of these other constraints. What we have to inject into this model is a more dynamic factor, namely the nature of the pupils, within the general context of these other constraints, which materially represents the pull of societal forces; together with an element of teacher creativity.[20]

I want now to give some illustrations of survival strategies that I noted during my year at Lowfield [...]

Negotiation

'You play ball with me, and I'll play ball with you'

The principle of this strategy is exchange. Commonly used are appeals, apologies, cajolery, flattery, promises, bribes, exchanges and threats:

'I'm sorry I'm talking a lot this morning but bear with me, please. I do want to get this finished.'

'We'll call it a day after this one, you've worked hard this morning, well done!'

'I thought in the second period we'd have a film, then I thought next week we'd do the nature trail in Aspley Forest, but first I want us to make up those notes.'

'You can go when you've finished, and not until.'

Often the commodity the teacher offers in exchange for good order and a representation of 'work' is escape from or relaxation of institutional constraint—films, records, visits, outings, breaks, an 'easy time'. In the pupils' reckoning, these are not 'work'. Nor are they always such in the teachers'. Thus on one occasion when a teacher found he had the wrong film, not even remotely to do with the subject in question, he felt he had to honour the bargain and offer the class the film regardless. Otherwise he might have had a survival problem. They accepted, for otherwise they might have had to do 'work'. 'Community Service' also comes under this rubric. Most pupils I spoke to 'had a good time' while doing it. Many did all that was required of them—gardening, shopping, making tea, etc.—but it was not that obnoxious commodity, 'work'.[21] Neither were 'projects', whether connected to CSE or not. One can hide somewhere, have a smoke, and fill in the worksheet later from somebody else's. The CSE, in fact, is the biggest aid to teacher survival introduced into schools since the war. It draws many more pupils into the mainstream culture of the school, and still allows pupils their secondary adjustments. Thus if you fall behind on your essays in English, you can always copy somebody else's, merely changing a few words; or you can submit your brother's or a friend's specimen in woodwork—and so on. The CSE has been a success because it has allowed for this—unlike many other innovations. These examples all support Bernstein's theory that[22]

> when [the pedagogical] frame is relaxed . . . to include everyday realities, it is often, and sometimes validly, not simply for the transmission of educational knowledge, but for purposes of social control of forms of deviancy. The weakening of this frame occurs usually with the less 'able' children whom we have given up educating.

All this adds to the teacher's resources. There are various types of admonitions teachers use. These include appeals to civilization and society in general, and the individual's fitting in to it. 'Right' conduct and attitude thus will provide access to the promised land. Waller mentions appeals to the parents' ideals, fair play, honesty, chivalry or self-esteem.[23] There are appeals against the fracturing of peer-group norms ('spoiling it for others', group punishments for individual offences), and appeals against the fracturing of a common bond between teacher and class. Of course, the particular strategies a teacher employs will depend on other factors—his conception of children, his view of teaching, his ideological make-up. Great contrasts can be found within one school. One teacher might be essentially dominative and to keep an edge on her techniques cultivate 'social distance' from her pupils; another might be predominantly negotiative, and aim for social nearness. Of particular interest here is the development of a sense of 'we-ness' between a teacher and a retrograde class of school 'failures'. These constitute the biggest potential menace to the school, and hence require a special security arrangement. This frequently involves assigning one teacher to the class full time, so that a notion of separateness develops between the backward class *and* their own teacher from the rest of the school. Strong identification is made within the unit, with feelings of loyalty, comradeship and regard, so that it acts as its own survival agent. Appeals, if made by their own teacher, rarely fail. Other teachers, however, are invariably driven to other techniques with these forms. [. . .]

Fraternization

[. . .] A prominent survival strategy is to work for good relations with the pupils, thus mellowing the inherent conflict, increasing the pupils' sense of obligation, and reducing their desire to cause trouble. It might be thought that this is fairly central to 'progressivist' forms of teaching. But the teachers at Lowfield strongly opposed 'progressivism'. It is taking place therefore within more traditionalist styles.

Fraternization takes many forms. Young teachers, especially, by their appearance, style of dress, manner, speech and interests frequently identify strongly with the pupils. They are often very popular. Implicit alliances can form against the main structure of the school, but, as with teachers of 'backward classes', it can ultimately work in the school's interests, since much bad feeling is defused through this bond with members of staff. On the other hand, of course, pupils with their own survival problem might try to increase their benefits by playing off one teacher against another ('so and so lets us chew in *his* lesson'), so it can promote instability. Older teachers can assume parts of this role. For example, they can display signs of alienation from the official culture, especially where it seeks to dominate. Explicit or implicit disapproval before pupils of a rule or action, especially if perpetrated by the upper hierarchy, is common. In fact it has been suggested that a major function of the head and his deputies is to soak up a lot of the bad feeling in the school, leaving a pleasanter field for front-line teachers and pupils to work in. Some identify with the pupils against outside aspects of the establishment:

> 'I loathe the vicar, who goes up, takes his watch off—and you know you're going to get your twenty minutes'worth—and he says "I've got four points to make"— and he's only done two of them after fifteen minutes . . .'

(Interestingly, this teacher betrays himself before typical secondary modern pupils by identifying with the establishment at all!)

Many teachers share in cultural influences which cross generations. Thus some have recourse to an earthy humour which marks them not as 'a teacher, a man apart', but as 'a man of the people'. Dirty jokes are not excluded, and seem to be particulary appreciated by rebellious male elements in the school. Another shared cultural influence is television. Some lessons I observed abounded in references to popular television programmes, advertisements included. While this might have a pedagogical value, it also has important survival repercussions for the pupils' perceptions of the teacher's identity. Sport also can form a bridge. For example, gangs of adolescent boys follow a football cult. Their discourse consists of jocular abuse directed at others' chosen teams and vigorous championing of one's own at all costs. This aggressive banter is typical of their lifestyle and is indulged in as a form of play. On these terms it is open to teachers, and sometimes they take advantage of it.

Much survival teaching takes the form of entertainment. It is quite often reflected in styles of speech and associated with culture-identification. Thus one teacher I observed employed a local, chatty, pubby style of speech in his teaching, which he indulged to good effect from the control point of view. Another had a cosmopolitan, youthful, 'with-it' style which reinforced his identification with the pupils. Another related almost everything he said to television programmes, making liberal use of standard phrases, and copying situation and character comedy. Less 'identification' associated are forms of teacher wit and humour. A stage manner helps, and the fun is often directed good-naturedly and matily towards the inmates. The displacement of reality in humour neutralizes any potential conflict.

> 'Oh, my God, that smell. Is that that "Brut" again? Open a window, stand back.' (*Hangs out of window, gasping. Returns to desk.*)

> 'Oh, my God, those socks!' (*Covers eyes with hand, puts on sunglasses.*)

> 'Now who saw *Maxim Gorky* last night? That's the programme you tune into between Mickey Mouse and Long John Silver.'

By this form of humour the teacher retains control and reinforces status. It is a kind of humorous, rather than aggressive, domination technique, but the aggression lurks in the background.

Sometimes, however, a teacher directs laughter upon himself, frequently belittling his formal role. These divergences from the mainstream expected behaviour place him in a wider context and invalidate the narrowness of the immediate scene. Impersonation is a favourite vehicle:
[. . .]

> A pupil comes into the room and requests the 'German helmet and gas mask'. Teacher goes into cupboard and comes out wearing them: 'Mein Gott in Himmel: Ve haf ways of making you talk!', and gives a five minute impersonation of Hitler.

Many aspects of modern 'progressive' teaching embrace the entertainment principle. The use of film, television, radio and records, and devising the projects, fieldwork and so on, have control as a major aim. Interesting, most general courses, particularly ROSLA, depend almost entirely on film and television. Teachers also devise their own little tactics. Many of these, for example, took the form of quizzes of one sort or another. One teacher punctuated a formal question-and-answer technique with 'hangman' games when no one knew an answer. Class involvement and hence control was always greater during the games. [. . .]

In co-educational schools flirting is a widely used technique, especially by male teachers with female pupils. Since sex is one of the most prominent interests of the more rebellious girl pupils, it can be a great aid in securing their goodwill and co-operation. [. . .] Many of these pupils see school in purely 'social' terms, as compared with instrumental or vocational, and their idea of 'social' differs a great deal from the school's 'social training' or 'education for citizenship', so topical with ROSLA. It is much concerned with the basic elements of interaction, and is rooted in their own culture. Some teachers spend their careers fighting this, others capitalize on it, while perhaps denying it:

> *Teacher:* Don't flash your eyes at me, Susan. It might work with your dad, but it won't work with me! (*However, his expression and tone indicate that it is working.*)
> *Susan* (faking embarrassment): Oh! Oh!
> *Teacher* (mimicking): Oh! Oh! (*He carries on up the row, flashing his eyes at the girls, who smile and giggle in mock confusion.*)

The sex element is strong in games. I noticed during a mixed game of volleyball that occasionally, when serving or receiving, an individual would be the centre of attraction, but that one's failings in this arena are laughed at and experienced in a different way from lessons, when they might have felt embarrassment. In the role of 'female' as opposed to pupil, all seemed to recognize that it was quite acceptable, even perhaps desirable, to be incompetent at games. The girls responded with such feminine wiles as ogling, putting out the tongue, pretending to hide confusion and so on. Thus their participation in the game was sublimated, and they found salvation in the sexual front. This technique was more used by 'incidental' games teachers. Full-time games staff were much more dominative and aroused far more resentment, especially among teenage girls. This was because they were permitted only the role of 'sportswoman', and their failure at games was of prime importance.

Here is an extract from my observation notes of an incidental games male teacher and a group of teenage girls round the trampoline:

> *Teacher:* Who wants a double bounce? (*Pet puts her hand up.*) Right oh, give us a push up. (*Two girls help push teacher up by the backside.*)

Hey, watch it! (*good humouredly*)(Teacher and Pet have a double
bounce, teacher working Pet to state of collapse and confusion.
As he gets off, he pulls another girl on, and she collapses,
bouncing and laughing, in the middle of the trampoline.)

Absence or removal

'Teaching would be all right if it wasn't for the pupils'. (Teacher folklore)

One certain way of ensuring survival is to absent oneself from the scene of potential conflict. Some teachers achieve this by upward mobility at one end, or by never
starting at the other.[24]

However, few achieve such absolute absence. Most have to make do with
partial absence, some official, some unoffical. Because it is the most efficacious and
the most relative (i.e. one usually gains only at the expense of others) of survival
techniques, it is the cause of intense and sometimes bitter struggles. This is why
the timetable is of such critical importance. 'Survival features prominently in its
construction. 'Weak' teachers have to be protected, 'good' ones rewarded. 'Weak'
ones can be given fewer lessons, none of the hard classes and the most favourable
rooms (a good example of how incompetence might be rewarded in our educational system). Whence then come the rewards? Fortunately for the hierarchy there
are some 'in-between' teachers consisting of a faceless group of those who have
not yet 'arrived' at the school, a 'disloyal' group consisting of those who are
leaving or applying for other jobs, and a 'rebellious' group who for some reason
have got in bad favour with the hierarchy. These take up the slack of 'bad' forms,
poor rooms and overloaded timetables.

Manipulation of the timetable protects the weak, rewards the good and
penalizes the unknown and unworthy. The same applies to time-table adjustments
that have to be made in the day-to-day running of the school. One of the 'rewards'
is free periods. The importance of survival as an organizing principle in the
teacher's day is evidenced by the neuroticism attending this topic. Losing free
periods can be quite traumatic, for survival becomes that bit harder; it can be very
much harder if, in exchange for an idyllic 'free', one is confronted by somebody
else's extreme survival problem—a 'bad' form in 'bad' circumstances.

Failing the legitimate acquisition of 'free periods', one can absent oneself in
other ways. Unloading the worst troublemakers onto others is a common device,
and is legitimated in schools where certain teachers have been given financial and
status compensation in return for a 'counselling' function. One can take days off
school, though the folklore regards this as defeatist. It also saddles equally hard-
pressed colleagues with extra responsibilities. Thus it is more customary to steal
extra minutes at the beginning and end of 'breaks', use delaying or deferring
tactics during lessons or work absences into one's teaching. Many new courses and
styles of teaching that have come into vogue since the Newsom Report are
characterized by a large amount of absence. Link courses, work-based courses,
Community Service, field-work, individual and group projects, all aid teacher
survival by virtue of separating the combatants for much of the time. Techniques
such as pupils taking assemblies, running parts of lessons or initiating and controlling work on their own cleverly turns the opposition back on itself and neatly fits
into fashionable educational philosophy, while the teacher sits on the sidelines.

If teachers choose to maximize their survival programme, they will follow a
policy of non-volunteering, 'keeping out of the way', and 'keeping one's nose
clean'. Some teachers have their 'secret places'. Some feel the need to go out—

often to a local pub—during the mid-day break. Some are strictly 'nine-to-four' teachers, often for survival reasons rather than lack of interest or sense of vocation. Teachers can be absent in spirit. They can 'be away' and have their 'removal activities' as well as the pupils.[25] Teachers occasionally daydream, fall asleep, look out of windows, fail to pay attention, defer or ignore problems, pass or waste time, pretend something is happening which is not and otherwise evade the head-on conflict with reality.

Ritual and routine

'You'll be all right once you get into the hang of things'

[...] In pluralistic, industrialized societies the value systems are various or ambiguous, and because of other societal developments which I spoke of earlier,[26]

> the social basis for the ritualization of the expressive order of the school will be considerably weakened and the rituals may come to have the character of social routines.

Perhaps the best example of this is morning assembly. Morning after morning the school where I did my research went through the formula of mustering, saying a prayer, singing a hymn, and listening to a peroration and exhortation from the headmaster. I described [elsewhere] the survival problem this created for the pupils, and how they coped with it. It is another example of a survival strategy that has outlived its usefulness and degenerated into yet another problem.

However, teachers would find it difficult to do without routine. Musgrove points up the problem:[27]

> The computer will take much of the routine out of teaching in schools, and will make possible far more learning which is not school-based. Although most people complain about the routine in their jobs, they would probably go mad without it. Without routine we are constantly dealing with unique, unprecedented, non-recurrent and non-standard events. This may be exhilarating; it is also exhausting. We can expect teachers to be in a state of constant exhaustion.

That prophecy for the future is for all too many teachers ancient history: routine, systematization, drill, have provided a safeguard. Black School provides a vivid example. Because of the boys' 'irrepressibility, rule-breaking and spontaneity' and the teacher's fatigue and fear of playground chaos spreading into the classroom, he insists rigidly on good behaviour and adopts a rigid style of teaching. Consequently, only rather mechanical skills can be taught:[28]

> Only certain rigid work and conduct standards can be conveyed by drilling. And these make or maintain dislike and therefore the need for drilling.

Teachers become addicted to routine and ritual. Once instituted, they are extremely difficult to get rid of. Rituals become associated with 'tradition' and 'ethos' and to change them means discontinuity and disjuncture. Routine is a narcotic, taken to soothe the nerve and mellow the situation. Once established, to do without it would involve the teacher in severe withdrawal symptoms.

Routine imposes a structure on school life which pupils and teachers almost automatically come to accept, and serves as a basis for establishing control. Registration, form periods, assemblies, timetables, lesson structures and so forth are the bones of the school day. Within this overall structure, individual teachers establish their own routines. We are all familiar with the archetypical teacher of fiction, middle-aged, soberly dressed, extremely mannered and eminently predictable in all his movements.

As Webb noted, this carries implications for what and how one teaches. Gump has shown that self-paced activities involve more difficult pupil management problems than in externally paced activities.[29] Westbury has portrayed recitations and textbook teaching as coping mechanisms.[30] Furlong has noticed, from the pupils' point of view, that 'work' and 'learning' is a desiccated, skeletal, structured and measurable form of knowledge. [31] To them, learning is 'measured accomplishment'. A recent report found that a large percentage of the writing done in school is done for the 'teacher-as-examiner', and not for the purposes which might do more to foster pupils' learning and development.[32] 'Teacher-as-examiner', it must be realized, is masking 'teacher-as-survivor'.

Many a teacher who has tried an experiment, and felt it has not been working and disorder threatening, has reverted in mid-stream to more formal techniques. The best example is the dictating of notes. This is an extremely useful device from the survival point of view for it gives pupils to believe they are being spared doing their own 'work', and thus secures their co-operation, involving quiet application, for considerable periods at a time. This is not to say that much activity associated with 'new' teaching techniques does not have a strong 'routine' component. Work cards, structured exercises, group activities, programmed learning, audio-visual techniques all provide for it, and perhaps their persistence is to be explained by it.

Occupational therapy

'It passes the time'

The principle of pupil therapy is bodily involvement accompanied frequently by dulling of the senses. The aim is to take the edge off boredom or fractiousness, and thus prevent incident arising. Pupils sometimes try to provide their own therapy such as playing cards, carving on desks, doodling on paper, reading comics. But though therapeutic, these activities are counter-official. Education must be seen to be going on. This is the purport of the 'busyness' that Sharp and Green talk of. The injunction to 'be busy' is legitimated by the philosophy of child-centred education.

Within the secondary schools of my knowledge I have encountered many therapeutic techniques. Drawing maps, pictures, patterns is good therapy. This is one of the reasons why art is a popular subject, particularly among bored and rebellious pupils. History, geography and science teachers make good use of the knowledge. 'Play' is also useful. The simple experimental kits provided for pupils' tinkering in science lessons allow for this, and for this reason the practical subjects—woodwork, metalwork, cooking, needlework, etc.—have strong therapeutic value. De-inhibiting activities such as free, unstructured swimming are wonderful therapy, and can spread their beneficial effect over several classroom periods before and after.

Pupils often fill in time with 'jobs'. 'Have you any jobs, sir?' is a common refrain from bored, inactive pupils. So teachers request blackboards cleaned, drawers tidied, corners cleaned up, pencils sharpened, files ordered and so on. It can be the major 'official' activity of older pupils outside the mainstream of the school, especially in their final year when there is common acceptance of the failure of the special 'official' programme designed for them. The girls can make tea and wash up for the staff, the boys can repair gates or glasshouses, paint sheds and so on. They are usually glad to do these jobs, for therapy is a more lasting and satisfying antidote to boredom than 'mucking about'.

A teacher can engage in therapy unilaterally. Busying oneself can help, when all around is chaos and threatening. Marking books, setting up equipment, giving individual guidance can occupy one's mind and cut out the general scene. Sometimes a teacher's whole programme is little more than therapy, like a series of science lessons I observed. Here the teacher carefully constructed the equipment for his experiment, and went dutifully through the procedure from beginning to end, explaining as he went, and elaborating on the application to the modern world of what he was doing. It was a model lesson in many respects, but none of the pupils in these classes listened. Moreover, they obviously were not listening, but clearly divided into their own groups and devised their own entertainment, often quite noisily. The two elements, teacher and pupil, though in the same room, seemed totally oblivious of each other. The only time when they came together was in the last ten minutes of the two-hour period when they were dictated the results of the experiment, and they recorded them in their exercise books. This teacher neutralized the control problem by concentrating exclusively on the 'stimulus' aspect of teaching and totally ignoring 'response'.

Another form of therapy takes the form of 'spinning-out' exercises. One example that came my way involved non-examination, non-scientific subjects allocated half-day slots because of their parallel grouping with science subjects which were reckoned to need that kind of block provision. I observed some of these sessions, and always enormous time-wasting and time-passing was resorted to as a survival technique. It was taken up with arriving late, finishing early, chatting with pupils before and after, preparation of lesson and materials for it (during it), interruptions (which seemed to be welcomed and capitalized upon), peripheral story-telling and general nonchalant pace.

Morale-boosting

'We have to believe' (deputy headmaster)

Just as socialization is an anticipatory strategy, morale-boosting is a retrospective one. For teachers need a survival strategy to 'account for' their other survival strategies. They mentally neutralize the survival problem, and they do it in two ways—by rhetoric and by laughter. I am speaking of rhetoric here as Green has done, i.e. 'it explains and constructs the necessity of the conjuncture within the disjuncture. It constructs the paradox in the teacher's actions and perspectives as itself a conjuncture.[33]

Aiding this is another aspect of commitment, group cohesiveness. Kanter defines this not in terms of sociability and mutual attraction but rather in terms of the ability to withstand disruptive forces and threats from outside the group ('sticking together'). This sort of commitment involves primarily 'forming positive cathectic orientations; affective ties bind members to the community, and gratifications stem from involvement with all the members of the group. Solidarity is high, and infighting and jealousy low.[34] Group cohesiveness among teachers is high, though it frequently pertains to sub-groups within a staff. Friction between these is only another feature of the internal cohesiveness of the groups.

The deeper the commitment, both in terms of continuance and group cohesiveness, the more extensive the rhetoric, and attachment to it. Sharp and Green give a good example in their discussion of 'busyness' as already noted. To the teacher 'there is a logical relationship between her notion of busyness, her educational philosophy and her actions'.[35] If the children are 'busy' and 'getting on with it on their own' or 'finding something to do', this is well within the spirit of child-centredness.

Well-established rhetorics attend many of the techniques discussed here in relation to secondary schools. I have touched on the legitimation of certain forms of absence and removal. Pupils running lessons, taking assemblies, going on projects are in line with progressive philosophy, as are certain aspects of therapy ('more involvement') and fraternization ('treating the pupils like people'). There is now a vast thesaurus of 'progressive' vocabulary and idioms, from which the teacher might draw to construct his own vocabulary of motives (free expression, integrated learning, activity-based learning, project work, free choice . . .).

All of the specific instances I have mentioned have a rhetoric closely attending them. Young teachers, for example, are best 'thrown in at the deep end', it is 'good experience', and better known sooner than later whether they are going to last. School uniform is championed in the interests of 'equality', preventing the poor being exposed by the sartorial elegance of the rich, of school 'ethos' and the qualities of pride and loyalty, and of 'utility', for identification purposes. Mortification procedures and dominating techniques are represented as socializing devices in the interest of the individual, whose naturally savage and uncouth character must be tamed and channelled along the 'right' paths to a civilized society. The latent survival function of the separated form of potential trouble-makers with their teacher is occluded by a rhetoric which asserts the peculiar characteristics of these pupils—personal, environmental, mental—which 'entitle' them to special preferential treatment; and the relationship they develop with the teacher concerned, which ensures the success of the survival manoeuvre, is presented as evidence of the justification of the rhetoric. Thus the problem is collapsed back into the situation and contained within a solution that masquerades, very powerfully and convincingly, as education. Even the 'jobs' that they do as therapy are justified as 'education'. In one case, for example, the boys in 5th year had to decide 'how much paint was needed', 'who was going to do which job', 'how they were going to order the materials', 'how much they were going to cost', 'how long it was going to take' and so on. This was the view of the teacher in charge of the educational value of one particular job the boys did. In essence though this is not far removed from Mr Squeers's technique:[36]

> We go upon the practical mode of teaching Nickleby—the regular education system. C-l-e-a-n, clean, verb active, to make bright, to scour. W-i-n, win, d-e-r. winder, a casement. When the boy knows this out of book, he goes and does it.

The growth of the counselling function in schools has legitimated the 'removal' technique, as mentioned above. Moral crusades and deviance amplification in the service of Parkinson's Law have provided a vast amount of rhetoric to support the counsellor's position, function and raw material.

In the struggle for survival, detection and celebration of the enemy's weakness is an enormous morale-booster. Hence the teacher's insistent representations of pupils in psychological terms as 'thick', 'idle', and the prevailing 'norm of cynicism' to be found in staffrooms.[37] One of the two beliefs on which the ideology of Black School staff was based was that the boys were rather hateful.[38] From this, the individual teacher might draw renewed strength, after flagging perhaps, towards the end of a double period and allowing the pupils to gain the upper hand. The greatest danger is that teachers should doubt what they are doing. Usually the supportive voice of colleagues available at key points of the day provides sufficient reassurance of his beliefs and reinforcement of status. Thus pupils invariably come to be held fully accountable for failings. They are responsible and free agents. Thus, with regard to the segregation that occurred in the school as the result of the subject-choice process, I was told by some that 'they had the choice'. There was no acknowledgment by these teachers of factors such as pre-conditioning, group perspectives and channelling procedures which constrain and direct these choices (though, [. . .] *some* were well aware of them). Most of such factors are so completely beyond the control of the school that knowledge of them could possibly undermine commitment and hence powers of accommodation. As I have elaborated it, commitment provides for its own defence. Teachers, therefore, would resist such knowledge.

For teachers to 'get on' in their careers, they must 'believe' in these ways; and the more they get on, the more they must believe. The firmer the commitment, the greater the accommodation. This applies particularly to belief. There are several other reasons for this. Sharp and Green point out that the deputy head in their school had to 'contend more directly with the general crisis in school-parent relations than the other staff. The ideology of domestic pathology has become more sharply articulated for her as a device for understanding and handling her situation.[39]

Webb imputed *guilt* to the upper hierarchy in Black School, though not to the teacher, whose drill-sergeant role was too narrow for him to have enough freedom to be held accountable. The headmaster eases his guilt by busying himself in administration, or exaggerating the school's achievements.[40] Perhaps also, guilt helps the upper hierarchy to invent and sustain a higher level of rhetoric.

However, it need not necessarily be a product of guilt. It is the responsibility of the head and his deputies to facilitate the teaching task for his staff. The provision or reinforcement of a rationale to support their survival strategies is a service to them, while, of course, his own responsibility for the school in general, as opposed to the teachers' classroom problems, causes him to have survival problems of a different order. He is supposed to lead and guide. Policy is his business, and where there is no scope for educational policy, he should be an expert in accommodation policy.

Less committed teachers who have less of an accommodation problem often see through this rhetoric and boost their own morale by merciless teasing and baiting of the upper hierarchy during their absence. [. . .]

Notes

[1] Kanter R.M. (1974) 'Commitment and social organization', in D. Field, (ed.). *Social Psychology for Sociologists*, Nelson, London, p. 126.

[2] Kanter, R.M. (1974) ibid., p. 132.

[3] Becker, H. (1960) 'Notes on the concept of commitment', *American Journal of Sociology*, Vol. 66, July, pp. 32-40.

[4] Lister, I. (1974) 'Drifting into more and more trouble', *The Times Educational Supplement*, 1 November 1974.

[5] Musgrove F. 'Education of teachers for a changing role', in J. D. Turner and J. Rushton, (eds) *The Teacher in a Changing Society*, Manchester University Press, p.46.

[6] Webb J. (1962) 'The sociology of a school', *British Journal of Sociology*, Vol. 13, No 3, pp. 264-72.

[7] Musgrove, F. (1974) *Ecstasy and Holiness*, Methuen, London, p.165.
[8] Waller, W. (1932) *The Sociology of Teaching*, Wiley, New York, p. 198.
[9] Hirst, P.H. (1971) 'What is Teaching?', *Journal of Curriculum Studies*, Vol. 3, No. 1, pp. 9–10.
[10] Judge, H. (1976) *School is not yet Dead*, Longmans, Harlow, p. 21.
[11] Jackson, P.W. (1968) *Life in Classrooms*, Holt, Rinehart & Winston, New York
[12] Deutscher, (1969) 'Evil-companions and naughty behavior: some thoughts and evidence bearing on a folk hypothesis', duplicated, Case Western Reserve University, pp. 28–9.
[13] Becker, H.S. (1964) 'Personal change in adult life', *Sociometry*, Vol. 27, No. 1, pp. 40–53.
[14] Jenks, C. 'A question of control: case-study of interaction in a junior school', upublished M.Sc.(Econ.) thesis, London University Institute of Education, (1971) p. 28.
[15] Denscombe, M. (1977) 'The social organization of teaching: a study of teaching as a practical activity in two London comprehensive schools', unpublished Ph.D. thesis, University of Leicester, p. 252.
[16] Denscombe, M. (1977) *ibid.*, p. 253.
[17] Denscombe, M. (1977) *ibid.*, p. 385.
[18] Sharp, R. and Green, A. (1976) *Education and Social Control*, Routledge & Kegan Paul, London, p. 121.
[19] Westbury, I. (1973) 'Coventional classrooms, "open" classrooms and the technology of teaching', *Journal of Curriculum Studies*, Vol. 5, No. 2, p. 100.
[20] A similar model of coping is expounded by Hargreaves, A. (1977) 'Progressivism and pupil autonomy', *Sociological Review*, Vol. 25, No. 3, p. 593. Hargreaves suggests that 'the response of teachers to structural pressures is a creative one. In this sense, progressive educational practice embodies a set of coping strategies which have been created in the sense of the forging of *new* roles which have the capcaity to resolve the conflictual demands contained within liberal-progressive ideology'.
[21] See Furlong, V. (1977) 'Anancy goes to school: a case study of pupils' knowledge of their teachers', in P.E. Woods and M. Hammersley (eds) *School Experience*, Croom Helm, London.
[22] Bernstein, B. (1971) 'On the classification and framing of educational knowledge', in M.F.D. Young (ed.) *Knowledge and Control*, Collier-Macmillan, London.
[23] Waller, W. (1932) *op. cit.*, p.207.
[24] Lister, I. (1974) *op. cit.*
[25] Goffman, (1968) *Asylums*, Penguin Books, p. 67.
[26] Bernstein, B. (1966) 'Ritual in education', *Phil. Trans B*, vol. 251, p. 60.
[27] Musgrove, F. (1974) 'Education of Teachers', p. 45.
[28] Webb, J. (1962) *op. cit.*, p. 265.
[29] Gump, P. (1971) 'What's happening in the elementary school classroom', in I. Westbury and A.A. Bellack, *Research into Classroom Processes*, Teachers College Press, New York, pp. 155–65.
[30] Westbury, I. (1973) *op. cit.*
[33] Furlong, V. (1977(*op. cit.* 'Anancy goes to school'.
[32] Britton, J. *et al.*, (1975) 'The development of writing abilities, 11–18', *Schools Council Research*, Macmillan, Basingstoke.
[33] Green, A. (1977) 'Structural Features of the Classroom', in P.E. Woods and M. Hammersley, (eds) *School Experience*, Croom Helm, London.
[34] Kanter, R.M. (1974) *op. cit.*, p. 128.
[35] Sharp, R. and Green, A. (1976) *op. cit.*, p. 121.
[36] Dickens, C. (1839) *Nicholas Nickleby*, Nelson, London.
[37] Hargreaves, D.H. (1972) *Interpersonal Relations and Education*, Routledge & Kegan Paul, London.
[38] Webb, J. (1962) *op. cit.*
[39] Sharp, R. and Green, A. (1976) *op. cit.*, p. 121.
[40] Webb, J. (1962) *op. cit.*

5 The Significance of Classroom Strategies

A. HARGREAVES

'Survival' represents an extreme form of adaptation in beleaguered situations. In other circumstances, it is more appropriate, perhaps, to conceive of teachers 'coping' with various pressures and constraints that may restrict their opportunities to achieve their aims. In this article, drawn from a case study of two English middle schools, Andy Hargreaves argues that the concept of coping strategies helps us consider both the wider forces in society as a whole which determine the constraints, and teachers' own resources and creativity in dealing with them.

Much of what has passed for sociology of education has either failed to grasp the consciousness of those about whom it claims to theorise, or else it has over-optimistically celebrated the seemingly limitless power of individuals to define, make and remake their own world. In taking the first line, the old sociology of education failed to treat people seriously. In taking the second, the 'new' sociology of education and the studies of classroom interaction which it spawned, insulated the classroom encounter from wider and extremely urgent social, economic and political concerns. If the 'Great Debate' *was* little more than carefully directed political drama (or farce—depending on your perspective!) it did at least teach one important lesson; that education and society cannot be so studied in isolated realms.

The message for sociologists of education should be clear. 'Structural' questions and 'interactionist' questions should no longer be dealt with as separate 'issues', each to be covered in their respective fields. Such a false separation will only lead to a continuation of what has been a sad trend in the sociology of education; that of a wild oscillation between two poles of sociological explanation. From systems theories to interpretive brands of sociology and back again to a structurally-based Marxism; almost no time has been spent in taking the opportunity to analyse how classroom matters may relate to the nature of the socio-economic and political structure and the functions which the educational system performs within that structure. Like the gymnast on the trampoline, movement has tended to be up and down between ground level and the dizzy structural heights and has rarely provided any degree of forward momentum.

We certainly need to know what goes on in classrooms. But at the same time we need to question, not just in passing but with commitment and with rigour, just what sort of society it is in which we live. We cannot assume that our society is characterised by democratic pluralism even though this might 'fit' nicely with the view that classroom realities are the product of a democratically-based negotiation process.[1] Rather, in a society where wealth is socially produced yet privately appropriated, where increased economic prosperity is paralleled by decreased humanity,[2] and where increased levels of qualification are accompanied by greater opportunities for unemployment,[3] there are grounds for seriously considering or at least confronting a Marxist analysis of contemporary British society, and for exploring how such an analysis might be linked with, an interactionally informed investigation of classroom processes.

The remainder of the paper constitutes an attempt to provide a framework which might link structural questions to interactionist concerns. The concept of coping strategy will be the important bridging point here.[4] Some empirical support for such an approach will be provided through drawing upon data gathered in a case study of two middle schools which I shall call Riverdale and Moorhead.[5] These neighbouring schools are situated some two miles apart on the commuter fringe of a large northern conurbation. Both schools contain a large proportion of parents of professional and managerial status, though each is not without its children of working class council tenants, even though these are somewhat underrepresented.

At first glance, Moorhead is a traditional school and Riverdale a progressive one; indeed these features were of major importance in their selection for case study. Moorhead School is a 10–13 middle school housed in converted post-war secondary modern premises. Its staff comprises ex-primary and ex-secondary school teachers who were drawn into Moorhead on reorganisation without necessarily having any definite commitment to the aims and purposes of middle school education in general. These staff have been supplemented and are increasingly being replaced by teachers drawn from other schools and direct from training (a few having followed some course which was organised explicitly on middle-school lines). Moorhead is relatively traditional in character. Much of the teaching is class teaching in isolated classrooms dotted along floor-tiled corridors, though this pattern holds less true for the 10–11 age group.

Riverdale school is a smaller 9–13 school, with only a two-and-a-half form entry, though this too creates problems in terms of lack of career opportunities for staff *within* the school. The school is also newer, being of a purpose-built, open plan design. There are few corridors here, only class spaces and work areas. There are also very few doors, though this is something which staff and pupils do not always appreciate, frequently finding that curtains serve as a poor screen when noise and activity threaten to penetrate their own work. In general the atmosphere at Riverdale appears much more informal, there being much pupil movement and activity in an open-plan environment.

Coping strategies—A conceptual framework

In linking features of the social structure to issues in the classroom, and in noting how the former impinge upon or even shape the latter, there are good reasons for selecting the teacher as the starting point of investigation.[6] [...] Teachers are the immediate processors of the curriculum for the child. They are the evaluators of pupils' academic work and the assessors of their overall ability. Teachers are the immediate adjudicators of childrens' moral worth and the direct arbiters of the 'appropriateness' of their everyday behaviour. It is teachers most immediately and perhaps most significantly who therefore create, transmit and attempt to impose definitions of children as successes or failures, ideal pupils or deviants.[7]

How teachers organise pupil learning experiences and evaluate them would seem to be an important topic for investigation. *Why* teachers organise and evaluate pupil learning and behaviour in one way rather than another would also seem to qualify as a question worth asking. If we pursue this latter question then we need to explore how the pedagogical strategies which teachers employ are meaningful responses to experienced problems, constraints and dilemmas. We need to consider the possibility that teachers construct the world of the classroom through the employment of different teaching styles but that this process of construction occurs perhaps in situations not of their own choosing and that there are a set of constraints in play which require some sort of resolution through the decisions that teachers are daily and repeatedly called upon to make.

The teacher is thus a crucial linch pin in the wheel of causality that connects structural features of the society to interactional patterns in the classroom and back again, thereby helping to reproduce those structural arrangements. Coping with society in its institutionally mediated forms as a set of ongoing and perplexing 'problems' provides teachers with the important yet frequently taken-for-granted challenge to devise and enact, creatively and constructively a set of teaching strategies which will make life bearable, possible and even rewarding as an educational practitioner. By focussing on teachers, the dilemmas they face and their attempts to resolve them, we might be able to connect within one framework, the *how* and the *what* questions (previously the major preserve of 'interpretive' sociology) with the *'why'* questions (over which Marxists and functionalists have thus far exercised a considerable monopoly).

In summary form, the salient characteristics of coping strategies can be itemised as follows:

1 *Coping strategies are the product of constructive and creative activity on the part of teachers.* The concept of coping strategy thus lends weight to the view that teachers respond to the 'demands' of their world not in the 'thoughtless' manner of Skinnerian rats or programmed role-players but as constructive meaning-makers. Consequently the use of the concept of coping strategy involves the recognition of people's essential humanity as creatures of consciousness. A basic and important principle of symbolic interactionism is that such constructiveness is a universal feature of human action. It is a core element of a person's being-in-the-world. This point has not always been appreciated by those who observe and document the everyday world of the school. Some researchers [. . .] have tended to give a privileged purchase on creativity to selected protagonists in the educational arena, whether these are the traditional pupil elite or the subcultural underdogs. For example, although Nell Keddie (1973) has argued cogently that much 'conventional' educational research has treated disadvantaged children as if they were deficit systems, thin cultural shadows of their rational and articulate middle class counterparts; elsewhere (Keddie, 1971) she herself has committed a very similar error [. . .] by portraying working class lower stream pupils as *more* rational and accurate interpreters of the absurd requirements placed upon them by middle class teachers, than the conformist middle class 'cultural dopes' of the 'A' stream. [. . .]

[. . .] If a model is to be developed which sensitively appreciates the meanings that different groups (pupils and teachers, working-class pupils and middle class pupils etc.) attach to their experience and situation, then it is necessary temporarily to abandon theoretical attachments to the cultural superiority of any one group over another. A good model should be like a cubist painting and present different perspectives simultaneously, equally and appreciatively. If, as researchers, we fail to do this then we will deride the perspectives of those whom we should instead be seeking to understand.

The essence of a model organised around the concept of strategy is thus that all actors whether working-class or middle-class, pupil or teacher, act meaningfully and creatively in response to their experienced world. In one very important sense, therefore, as Antonio Gramsci recognised, we are *all* intellectuals.

2 The addition of the word 'coping' to that of 'strategy' implies that there are limits

to the variety of styles which teachers may adopt in the classroom. Styles are generated and sustained only insofar as they enable successful coping with experienced constraints. *Coping strategies are therefore not only constructive but also adaptive.* They are creatively articulated solutions to recurring daily problems. The more these solutions 'work', the more they become institutionalised, routinised and hence, ultimately, taken for granted as the definition not of a version of teaching but of teaching itself. It is at this point, where coping strategies become institutionally and professionally embedded as accepted, legitimate ways of teaching, that they can come to resist demands for innovation generated by new constraints. The 'persistence of the recitation' in the face of pressures for progressive educational reform, is just one example of this process.[8]

3 Following from (2), it should be clear that *coping strategies refer to very generalised definitions of teaching behaviour which cannot be reduced to a simple set of alternative teaching and control techniques.* The latter belong more to a Goffmanesque model of strategic interaction where the actor tries to gain and maintain advantage over his or her rival. Disciplinary techniques and the second-by-second decisions which they imply can be included in this lower-level category, which I have elsewhere called 'negotiative strategies'.[9] Coping strategies subsume and establish the parameters within which negotiative strategies are deployed in any instance, though clearly, at their inception they are themselves partly the outcome of those detailed classroom negotiations and to some extent depend on the successful daily accomplishment of such negotiations for their continued existence i.e. once they fail to 'work' then the time is ripe for change.

4 The view that teachers seek to cope or 'survive' is not a particularly novel one. Howard Becker (1952) pointed out that the behaviour of the slum school teacher is a response to the 'problems' presented by the slum school child. It has also been argued at different levels by Westbury (1973) and by Sharp and Green (1975) for example, that in part, teaching strategies such as the 'recitation' or 'busyness' emerge in response to immediate material pressures such as large class sizes and building restrictions. As Sharp and Green (1975, pp. 22–23) put it,

> 'we need to develop some conceptualisations of the situations that individuals find themselves in, in terms of the structure of opportunities the situations make available to them and the kinds of constraints they impose. The actors may be conscious of these constraints but need not necessarily be so. They may be subconsciously taken for granted or unrecognised, but the situation will present them with contingencies which affect what they do irrespective of how they define it'[10]

The concept of coping strategy becomes a truly radical one only when one re-poses the question of what it is that teachers have to cope with. Such a view involves awareness of the fact that constraints like class-sizes, building limitations or the problems of teaching slum-school children are themselves the immediate institutional expression of wider social-structural and historical forces which also require investigation and analysis. It is in their failure to articulate connections between these levels that the promise of Sharp and Green's Marxist synthesis is unfulfilled. They do not make the vital link between the presence of material constraints at the institutional level and the generation of structural constraints within the wider society. How, then, might these different levels be connected?

5 At the most general level, the nature of the constraints which produce institutional problems that the teacher must resolve would appear to fall into at least three broad categories:

(a) Following Bowles & Gintis (1976) it can be argued that *in contemporary capitalist society the goals of the educational system are fundamentally contradictory.* Liberals and reformers frequently seek to promote egalitarianism and to foster personal development (the education of the 'whole' child) whilst at the same time recognising the need to prepare the child for the position he or she will be expected to occupy in the social, occupational and political order. At the classroom level, this contradiction often comes to present itself as a wish to educate and relate to children in the spirit of liberal individualism, counter-balanced by a necessity to select and socialise children for a class-stratified society [. . .]

Managing the pedagogical paradox known as 'guided discovery' is one common solution which teachers have devised here [. . .]. Guided choice as a somewhat wider pedagogic principle than 'guided discovery' tends to permeate all levels of the education system, even through to the point of occupational choice.[11] It is perhaps this principle which most broadly encapsulates the dilemmas and tensions contained in processes of 'democratic' participation and decision-making in educational and other institutions. The aptness and wider applicability of this notion is well summarised by a group of Riverdale teachers discussing the organisation of the curriculum for the following academic year:

> Mr. Button   In particular I notice (name of school) do CSE work with children and they had to choose topic work. Well very often they . . . they would choose any old thing and very soon they . . . would realise that what they've chosen is beyond them or is . . . not interesting enough for them.
> Mr. Kitchen   (Headmaster). So it's got to be guided.
> Mrs. Arrow   Yes,
> Mr. Kitchen   It's like choosing a career, isn't it?
> Mr. Button   Yeah (sharp).
> Mr. Kitchen   In . . . exactly the same things apply in this case.

It would seem that the existence of any nominal democracy at the entry point to work where channelling of the individual into the occupational structure occurs on lines very different from official conceptions of open and free choice in an equal contest for work opportunities in the job market, is therefore recognised by teachers of middle school children; children who have still some years of schooling to complete before they become directly and explicitly involved in the process of occupational choice. The one-dimensional manner in which participation is conventionally conceived as token participation and the nominal forms which 'democracy' usually takes are pervasive features of economic and political life in advanced capitalist society.[12] Choice as 'guided' choice is a definition available and taken for granted within the dominant social democratic hegemony, and is also a practice which helps resolve the dilemmas that teachers confront. These dilemmas take the form of reconciling a desire to give pupils a measure of choice and freedom in the interests of their personal development, with the necessity to impose work requirements in order to fulfil the integrative demands of required sets of knowledge, skills and competences derived externally from the wider society and internally (within the education system) from the secondary or upper school. 'Guided' choice' is thus the outcome of both pragmatic response and available ideology. [. . .][13]

At other age levels, the strategy varies from that of 'busyness' in the infant school to the employment of a Dalton-plan-like block timetable approach in some progressively organised middle schools, like Riverdale,[14] both of which reconcile to some extent the contradictory forces generated in advanced capitalist society [. . .]

(b) *The second general area of constraints upon teaching activity can be given the broad label 'material'.*

In this sense, material constraints such as school buildings, resources and class sizes are not the result of randomness in educational planning nor of administrative and political short sightedness and incompetence. There is instead a definite connection between the magnitude and variety of these constraints, and a characteristic pattern and orientation of educational and social change, which one might call both reformist and centripetal. The story of educational and social reform in British society is one of *ad hoc* adjustment and piecemeal change. Ever since the State included the large-scale provision and organisation of education within its orbit of influence, educational change has been characterised not by a radical reform of contemporary arrangements in the light of a rigorous analysis of the educational and social whole but, in the words of Forster at the time of the 1870 Act, by an inclination to 'fill up the gaps' which could be identified in the existing range of provision using the minimum possible amount of expenditure.[15] Gradualism, pragmatism and economy are the characteristic stamp of the British approach, an approach which accepts unquestioningly the legitimacy of a capitalist society based on the private appropriation of socially produced wealth, and which assumes that an educational system which selects and socialises for such a class-divided society is both desirable and necessary.

Such pragmatic underpinnings of educational reform have usually resulted in a style of policy making based on administrative convenience and economic expediency. In recent times, comprehensive reorganisation has frequently taken place within tight budgetary restrictions and where a three-tier middle school system has been chosen, for example, this has invariably been 'because the buildings fitted'.[16] As a result, teachers now work within widely variant architectural constraints; some in old 1870 buildings and others, who are fortunate enough to be working in areas of expanding population, in modern open-plan units. It is this pragmatic tradition which is as much responsible for the wide and bewildering variety of educational provision as is the devolution of considerable decision-making power to local authorities. That many teachers, especially those middle school teachers who subscribe to the central tenets of 'progressive' Plowden ideology, find themselves teaching in buildings totally unsuited to such an educational approach (many middle schools have been set up in old secondary-modern school buildings), can also be traced to the pragmatic orientations of educational reformers.

The assumption that current provision is adequate, in the main, coupled with the fact that available expenditure for education is maintained at an 'acceptable' level can also be held jointly responsible for the failure to reduce class-sizes significantly when the opportunity has presented itself in the form of falling birth rates. In consequence, no progress has been made in relieving the 'immediacy' of the teacher's role: the necessity to make a large number of decisions with a large number of pupils in a short space of time.

The most interesting case, though, is not where idealistic teachers become frustrated by material restrictions but where building constraints combine with a set of other factors to produce and shape a generalised type of coping strategy which admits of some but only a limited amount of internal variation from teacher to teacher. An example of the range of styles produced by this combinatory effect is the teaching in the upper years of Moorhead School.

Moorhead is one of many middle schools sited in converted secondary modern school premises. The architecture of the post-war secondary school is hardly conducive to the growth of non-specialist co-operatively based teaching so often advocated in documents prescribing curriculum change for 'the middle years'. The presence of corridors with classrooms leading off as a set of disparate, physically autonomous units offers few opportunities for innovatory progressive teaching practice. The very nature of the building, then, suggests a style of teaching practice which is directed more to secondary than the primary school tradition. Where adaptations have been made to the building in the provision of an open-plan wing, it is hardly surprising and perfectly reasonable that this should be allocated to the lower age groups in the school. Even architecturally then, there is the suggestion of a split at the 11 + dividing line, the conventional watershed between primary and secondary education.

These architectural restrictions are exacerbated by overcrowding. Philip Jackson has emphasised how 'crowds' are a pervasive feature of all classroom life though his stress, perhaps, is on the consequences this has for pupils rather than for teachers. The lack of sufficient expenditure for extra school building and the tardiness of the local authority in providing a new school at Millbeck which would considerably relieve the pressures on Moorhead have meant that Moorhead is an overcrowded institution. So many additional 'temporary' classrooms have been installed that from the air, the main building would no doubt appear as an island stranded in a sea of terrapins. The large pupil roll and the shortage and unsuit-ability of existing accommodation also mean that several valued educational activities cannot be provided for large groups of children. One example of this is that heavy craft and science facilities are confined within the same room such that, in any one period, the pursuit of one activity automatically excludes anyone from engaging in the other.[17]

That such constraints hinder the achievement of educational goals and elicit a consciously adaptive response, at least on the part of the headmaster, is illustrated by the comments of the head, Mr. Butcher, in interview:

> Mr. Butcher   The timetable ought not to be regarded in the middle school as it is in the secondary school and which unfortunately it sometimes is this year for all sorts of other reasons which aren't necessarily educational ... organisa-tional and which is dependent on the buildings available and so on ... There are factors which are restricting. In fact, there are many factors which have made it impossible for me to put my educational philosophy which I ... uh ... had when we were established, into practice ... um ... Those are mainly areas of accommodation, overcrowding, desperate shortage of specialist facilities. I'm not suggesting dual purpose rooms are not suitable in other schools. I *am* saying that in this situation which we find ourselves in, they are certainly most unsuitable ...[18]

In time, it is conceivable that a short term pragmatic response of the realist to a set of overwhelming and frustrating constraints, shifts to an acceptance of those very constraints such that *ad hoc* measures become accepted and defined as educational goals. That constraints not only determine possible educational policy as a set of mere pragmatic responses with which the practitioner need not necessarily agree in principle, but that they also lead to a broader shaping of educational goals and desirable definitions of teaching itself, is the essence of coping strategies and their institutionalisation. Mr. Butcher seems to be partly aware of this in his own case.

> Mr. Butcher   I suppose ... um ... I might have modified my philosophy to some extent after five years of operation in that ... um ... there is a greater need for structure than I had originally anticipated there would be ... and ... since the system itself has demanded; the situation itself has demanded, that I should structure things—obviously to cope with these large numbers of children that we have and the inadequate facilities—to some extent perhaps, that's made me realise that ... uh ... there may well be

something to be said for structure—and it isn't the dirty word that I originally thought it was.

A.H.   So you find yourself having to operate in certain ways out of necessity and, sort of, have come to appreciate their value . . . having carried them out?

Mr. Butcher Yes! Undoubtedly! So that it was necessity which . . . uh . . . it was necessity in the first place which was the reason why we introduced things . . . but after five years of operation now we've decided that these are desirable as educational aims anyway.

Experience is a great teacher. Where constraints persist, the unwilling adaptation becomes the unwitting educational goal. Practitioners 'discover' that a way of coping might be educationally desirable after all. Necessity can indeed be the mother of both invention and intention.

A further effect of the organisation of educational reform on economic and expediential grounds has been upon the organisation of staffing in middle schools. Many middle schools utilise not only existing buildings but also existing local pools of teaching labour. In this sense the evolution of a new educational concept is fettered by the legacy of inherited buildings and staff. Many staff work in middle schools not to implement educational goals as 'middle years' teachers but because employment in such a school is a marginally better prospect than employment in any other of the institutions created on reorganisation. Mr. Butcher articulately encapsulates the extent and effects of such difficulties.

Mr. Butcher Staff, I think can teach most efficiently when they are teaching the way with which they themselves are most familiar and it's nonsense to think that you can . . . uh . . . change a teacher who has been teaching for many years in a particular way into an entirely different way of teaching without allowing him or her time to develop. And therefore, initially, I think, we had one year or so of the primary school and two years in the secondary school here . . . (he goes on to argue that with some redeployment of staff the situation has changed somewhat since) . . . We inherited staffs who . . . uh . . . almost entirely were either primary trained and experienced or secondary trained and experienced and uh . . . since the introduction of comprehensive education in this area, they've not really evolved . . . uh . . . apart from marginally, the need for more teachers . . . We simply had to use the teachers who were available. So those who opted to come to the middle school either opted to do so from the primary school on the one hand or from the secondary schools on the other and eighty-per-cent of our staff were recruited in this way. They didn't necessarily have a burning desire to teach in middle schools, the burning desire being in fact to remain in Moorhead (the town) . . . uh . . . and it may well have been and certainly was the case that these . . . um . . . in some cases they just wanted a job and they found themselves becoming redundant in the primary schools . . . or else they found themselves unable to get the sort of jobs which they wanted in the upper schools and so they had no alternative . . . and certainly there were members of staff who came here . . . uh . . . not out of choice but out of necessity. [Then he states that there are some exceptions] [19]

This extract is worth quoting at some length since it expresses very clearly the problems of which the headmaster was aware on re-organisation and renders intelligible his tendencies to deploy ex-secondary teachers in the upper years and ex-primary teachers in the lower school thus reinforcing the traditional split between primary and secondary stages of schooling. In consequence without any clear intentions or manipulations to perpetuate 'valued' educational traditions, staffing and material constraints and the headmaster's response to these tend to produce and reproduce the schizoid identity of the middle school which diverges somewhat from the notion of a unique identity of the middle school which has been ideologically propounded elsewhere[20]. Although these constraints produce *generational* effects in terms of a separation between primary and secondary stages, they are nevertheless rooted in a pragmatic style of educational policy making characteristic of and acceptant of the dominant assumptions of a class-divided capitalist society. The immediate material constraints of architecture and class sizes can therefore be connected to deeper issues embedded in a pragmatic approach to educational reform which rests on the premise that fundamental change in educational arrangements and in the society which such arrangements serve, are neither necessary nor desirable.

Partly through the mediating influence of Mr. Butcher's emergent but stabilising educational philosophy and partly through the direct effect which material constraints exert in shaping, facilitating or inhibiting different patterns of teaching, Moorhead's siting in a converted secondary modern school has led to a limited range of variation in fourth-year teaching styles. Athough there are real and considerable differences between, say, Mr. Bird whom his headmaster regarded as 'a bit of a tartar' and Mrs. Close who views herself as 'firm but approachable', these differences are, even for teachers at the extremes of the continuum of teaching styles constructed and enacted in the fourth-year at Moorhead, differences of degree rather than of kind. The styles of fourth-year Moorhead teachers are all contained within a dominant model of secondary-orientated teaching. This also includes those teachers such as Mr. Bird and Mrs. Close who are not themselves secondary trained and experienced but whose conceptions of teaching and learning are nevertheless skewed in a 'secondary' direction. Mr. Bird, for example, was a teacher in one of the reorganised primary schools but his at least partial attachment to a tradition other than primary is revealed by his statement that he enjoyed teaching the 'A' class most of all and that 'the years that I was interested in were the top end'. Similarly, Mrs. Close, though specifically and recently middle-school trained, holds a firm subject identity which she sums up through a rather coy admission that 'here you've got what might be termed specialist teaching which I have to confess I enjoy because I am still interested in English as a subject'. There is thus no necessity that middle schools will blur or dissolve existing educational categories. In the case of Moorhead for instance, reorganisation has facilitated a pattern of teacher redeployment to upper and lower years which in many ways has purified the separate primary and secondary stages of education by reallotting teachers who were previously 'misplaced' to more appropriate niches in the educational system.[21] Variations in fourth year teaching styles are thus variations on a theme—a predominantly 'secondary' one reinforced by the constraints of building, crowding and headteacher policy.

Two examples must suffice. On the one hand, there is Mr. Bird, a teacher nearing retirement, who operates a typical 'recitation' style of teaching where he throws out a stream of questions and demands immediate, sharp and correct responses. Although, as Westbury (1973) has pointed out, this interactional structure maintains the attention and participation of the pupils and although it achieves the simultaneous transmission of any given content, this occurs at the expense of the growth of conceptual understanding for which is substituted a stock of 'right' answers. Such a situation arises in Mr. Bird's 'B' set where pupils experience some difficulty in producing the answers he requires.

T: There's no difference, just bigger numbers that's all. We'll be all day if we do it like this (child using long method). Read the first number. Two . . .

P: Thousand (quietly).
T: *Again.*
P: Two thousand.
T: Yeah. Read the second number.
P: Five thousand.
T: What is the common factor?
P: (No reply).
T: You've just told me? Read them again and put the accent on the last word.
P: Two thousand.
T: Two ...
P.)
T.) Thousand.
T: That's putting the accent on, yes? Read the second number.
P: Five thousand.
T: Yes. So what's the common factor?
P: (inaudible).
T: What was the word you said both times? You didn't say two both times. You didn't say five both times. What did you say both times?
P: A thousand.
T. That's the common factor isn't it? (raised voice) Eh? If it happens that it's common to both it's the common factor. A thousand is a number, isn't it? Isn't it? (louder). Divide by a thousand is just the same as divide by two. We've done it before, you know.
P. (Nods).

Mr. Bird and his class here engage in an uneasy collusion to produce the 'right' answer irrespective of the methods used. Hence it is possible for pupils and teacher to exchange mathematical comprehension for an exercise in word-repetition and still produce the required response.

The fall of reasoning and the decline of conceptual understanding which such a 'direct' teacher here produces, would be something to be abhorred by many education researchers who would instead prefer the approach of a more 'indirect' teacher like Mrs. Close.[22] Mrs. Close organises some of her lessons on discussion principles. In these lessons, pupils submit topics of interest which are then randomly selected from a hat and discussed by the class as a whole, the teacher taking on the role of neutral chairperson who guides and assists pupils in their pursuit of solutions to *their own* problems. Yet Mrs. Close's strong 'subject' attachment and her formal control over the interaction process, even as chairperson, provides her with the opportunity and the temptation to convert pupil concerns into teacher concerns. As a result a 'right-answer' structure is reinserted into a 'democratic' discussion lesson. For example, in a discussion of whether a fee should be charged for the loan of library books in order to provide income for authors, when a pupil raises the intriguing 'economic' point that certain popular writers like Enid Blyton would 'make a bomb', Mrs. Close exploits this opportunity to substitute her own problem of how far and why, many pupils *still* read Enid Blyton books.

T: In fact, of course, the sale of Enid Blyton's books do run into millions and are there any of you who still read Enid Blyton? Let's have a look. Don't be ashamed. You're usually very honest... Put your hands down. Yes, Richard, do you read any other author as well?
P: Not ... uh ... I read some of them. I look at a book and ... uh ...
T: What appeals to you about Enid Blyton's books? Why do you like them? Those of you who in fact ... Let's just have hands up again 'cos this is actually an interesting sideline. Hands up again. Just put your hands up. Now, why Richard, why are you still reading Enid Blyton?

In consequence, the exploratory talk of discussion centred around pupil concerns is transformed into a series of verbally defensive attempts by pupils to parry the teacher's thrusting inquiry as to why they *still* read Enid Blyton. Such responses range from the pragmatic and apologetic.

> P: I don't really know ... I mean ... well ... my younger brother's always reading them ... and they're really the only books we ever have in the house.

to the cultural critic's more comic response of

> P: I don't like her very much but a lot of my books are by her and I like criticising (giggles).

'Direct' and 'indirect' teaching in this context are alternatives within a set of limits which define the core of secondary-oriented teaching as explicitly teacher-dominant in a way which is directly expressed through the asymmetric structure of the interactional exchange.[23] In this scheme of classroom life, pupil participation is nominal and passive, for it is the teacher who controls and evaluates both the quality and quantity of contributions.[24]

The circumscribing factors which define the limits of alternative teacher coping strategies as a set of teaching styles can thus be partly identified in material terms as the pressures exerted by buildings and crowding and the way in which these shape at the same time as they are mediated by headteacher policy and his engineering of a 'fit' between a teacher's orientation and the year-group with which that teacher will work. However, such an analysis, though correct at one level, is somewhat incomplete. For it should also be remembered that these factors are themselves the immediate expression at the institutional level of much deeper forces at work in the wider society. Classroom and society are in this case inextricably bound together in a tangled web which *ad hoc* reformism weaves around the enduring centre of hierarchical social relations in British capitalist society. [...]

(c) *One important constraint which appears to exert some considerable influence on the emergence, maintenance and eclipse of different coping strategies is the generation and proliferation of differing educational ideologies.*

At any point in time, certain ideologies in education gain popularity and receive support from key personnel in the education system. Insofar as these ideologies, such as the progressive Plowden ideology or the Great Debate, contain definitions of 'correct' practice and provide routes for career advancement for those who attach themselves to such a body of ideas and approaches, then they can provide a clear-cut constraint to which teachers feel they must respond through their construction and maintenance of appropriate displays of educational imagery. The reasons for the emergence of particular ideologies about education are complex though it is usually possible to identify a set of socio-economic factors which appear to be of some importance—progressivism and the cult of the individual, for example, seem to flourish in times of economic prosperity when new kinds of 'adaptable' men and women are felt to be required in the workplace under new conditions of supervision, (as was the case for the United States in the 1920s and for Britain in the 1960s).[25] Whatever their origin, the important point is that such ideologies and those who support them stand as constraints to which teachers and headmasters respond. It is therefore possible for teachers to create an image of individualistically-based teaching for the benefit of interested 'outsiders' whilst maintaining either a rigid system of setting or streaming, or a carefully monitored scheme of individual learning programmes.

An illustration is provided by Riverdale which, in contrast to Moorhead, is situated within and circumscribed by the ideological constraints of Plowden as they are borne by their messengers and friends in the inspectorate, the advisory service etc. In this context, the progressive image as a public one, must be displayed consistently for all interested 'outsiders' who may pass comment and judgement upon the school. One such group of outsiders is the governing body.

In the headteacher's report presented to the joint governing body of Moorhead and Riverdale, for example, Mr. Kitchen (Riverdale) makes no mention of the extensive setting practices which are implemented in the third and fourth years of his school. By contrast, Mr. Butcher (Moorhead) in a separate report at a separate meeting explicitly refers to the existence of setting in his school when he states that 'In previous years we have deliberately inflated the numbers in the *more able sets* in order to create a small group of remedial children'. According to one informant, the governing body were unaware that setting took place at Riverdale. This view would be considerably enhanced by the photographic display of the school and its activities which confronted governors when they convened there one evening to hold a meeting. Some photographs in this display portrayed the school as an idyllic rural enclave, surrounded by trees and bathed in sunlight; a paradise for the educational romantic. The remaining photographs of indoor and outdoor educational activity reinforced this romanticism with their images of individuals or small groups of children working in creative and expressive arts; of teachers crouching with pupils as they engage in seemingly cooperative and egalitarian discussion etc. Through these photographs, nature and human nature are symbolically brought together in the portrayal of the individual child at one with a supportive, nurturant environment which he constantly seeks to explore and discover with the teacher's helpful support, guidance and co-operation.

The idyll is at once appealing and convincing yet also one-sided and partial. There are no photographs of other facets of school life in Riverdale; of formal French being taught to different ability sets, or of science 'lectures' where pupils take down dictated notes as a way of digesting not only 'scientific knowledge' but also 'appropriate' terminology as in the following extract from a lesson on plant cells.

> e.g. 'It couldn't divide like an animal cell because of the rigid cell wall. Use the word *rigid* because it really is the operative one'.

In this sense the refraction of educational reality occurs through a photographic reflection of institutional assumptions about what counts as good and favoured educational practice.[26] In reflecting, communicating and reinforcing these assumptions, the messages communicated by photographic displays are at one with messages communicated through the open-plan architecture of the school, through its internal organisation in the form of 'shared areas' and desks organised in groups rather than rows, and through the patterns of pupil movement and activity in that part of the curriculum devoted to the block-timetable which these arrangements facilitate. Openness, movement and diversity and the dissolution of curricular and pedagogic boundaries are the 'progressive' messages conveyed by these institutional features. For the educational voyeur who looks upon the school and its activity for a day or even less, the plausibility of such an appealing representation is difficult to refute and extremely tempting to accept. In consequence, it is hardly surprising if groups and individuals other than the governing body are also largely unaware of practices such as setting and tend to define the middle school in terms of its public image.[27]

At Riverdale the contradictions of progressivism and the constraints of ideology and architecture serve to produce a range of coping strategies which lock together in the form of a juxtaposition of block-timetable teaching with more formal teaching in ability sets. At Moorhead, since the architectural and staffing constraints are of a different kind and since, partly because of this, the progressive ideology has been somewhat less influential in patterns of teaching and learning, the dominant theme of teaching in the upper years is an explicitly 'secondary' one. In the sense of contradictory demands, of material constraints and of ideological constraints, teachers are thus presented with a series of problems and dilemmas with which they must attempt to cope. The outcomes, even in the limited case of Moorhead and Riverdale, are varied and depend upon the manner in which such constraints combine and exert themselves in any particular situation. But these constraints, it has been argued, originate not within the school itself but within the wider society, though they are usually experienced in a way which renders their societal origin obscure.

6 *Societal constraints are institutionally mediated.* In other words, the same societal constraint will be expressed differently in different kinds of educational institutions according to factors such as the age-level being taught and the social-class background of the school intake. The further away any group of children is from the *formal* point of selection and examination (which has become increasingly delayed in British society), the less specific are the knowledge demands made upon the children and the more diffuse are the criteria for achievement. At the middle school level, for example, the use of the block timetable for part of the schoolday enables teachers to sustain an image of progressivism and pupil choice whilst in the remainder of the curriculum they can transmit a required curriculum as a basis for 'O' level work in the upper school. In contrast, within the infant school, knowledge demands take the more diffuse form of literacy and numeracy levels which some children are expected to attain. The reconciliation of these with the child-centred approach [. . .] of the infant school is achieved through the coping strategy of 'busyness' (Sharp and Green, 1975).

In addition to the mediating factor of age-level, the social-class background of pupils would also seem to be of some importance. Schools below the secondary level frequently draw upon a relatively homogenous catchment area. Under these circumstances, where working-class children are concerned, there may be some difficulty in meshing the 'new' modes of control characteristic of progressive education with the socialisation practices that the child experiences in the home. Such a child may be unused to subtle and indirect forms of speech and social control, and find it difficult to respond as a reuslt. Maintaining a progressive image with large numbers of pupils often in unsuitable buildings whilst retaining control over learning and behaviour might then be achieved through rigidly organised and carefully broken down work programmes which are evaluated systematically and at regular intervals under a bureaucratised system of individual supervision.[28]

The age and social class background of pupils would thus seem to be two mediating factors which might lead to a variety of responses by teachers to the same general constraint.

7 *The notion of institutional mediations prevents the concept of coping stategy from being employed in an over-simplistic manner.* It enables a bridge to be built between features of the society and issues in the classroom without *reducing* statements about structure to statements about action. The minimal requirement is only that observations of interaction can and must be explained within this framework.[29] Furthermore the creation of such a bridging point in explanation leads to an understanding of the fact that teaching styles are a response, albeit a creative and personal one, to a set of institutional and societal constraints. In consequence,

injunctions to teachers to change their style or to cease engaging pupils in 'mere' busyness[30] are unlikely to be heeded unless due attention is paid to the *reasons* why teachers employ such styles and to the *pressures* which necessitate their use. 8 *Whether coping strategies persist and become institutionalised depends, in part, on the response of pupils.* The personal effort and social costs of management and control in some 'progressive' coping strategies, for example, are great. In this respect, Antonio Gramsci once offered some interesting observations on the difficulty of administering a Dalton Plan block-timetable approach to the curriculum:

> the pupils are free to attend whichever lessons (whether practical or theoretical) they please, provided that by the end of each month they have completed the programme set for them: discipline is entrusted to the pupils themselves. The system has a serious defect: the pupils generally postpone doing their work until the last days of the month, and this detracts from the seriousness of the education and represents a major difficulty for the teachers who are supposed to help them but are overwhelmed with work. (Gramsci, 1971, p. 32)

At a Riverdale curriculum meeting, Mr. Button provides some concrete grounding for Gramsci's rather generalised comments, though Mr. Kitchen then guides the discussion away from what appears to be a central staff concern—

Mr. Button   One of the things which I think are . . . One of the things that we fall down very badly is having the children organise their own time during the day when they have choices. We are . . . I mean . . . we do give them choice now in . . . in . . . what work they do and when they do it . . . well not so much what work but when they do the work. They're given a lot of free time and there are many, many children who cannot organise themselves well enough to appreciate . . . well they can't see more than a little time ahead and I think this is something that we . . . we've really got to work at . . . is how they organise their time. I mean, there's some children . . . I know when I was in the third year, we literally had to write out timetables for one or two because they just couldn't do it.

Mr. Banks: Umhum . . . And some in the fourth year can't do it either.

Mr. Button   Yeah and . . . and they are the problem children because even . . . even within that situation, if other children see them doing nothing, there . . . there is a certain . . . um . . .

Mr. Kitchen   Yes. Well can we take, what steps do we take in the first year for example that leads on to an improvement throughout the school. There's this way of looking at it . . .

The situation which third and fourth year Riverdale pupils encounter and which they themselves partly construct is a rich and complex one. A few extracts and quotations from informal discussions with different pupils during lesson time will provide at least a sense of some of the difficulties.

Firstly, although it is recognised by teachers such as Mr. Button that the opportunity for pupils to make choices is largely in the realm of how they organise their time, even this appreciation of the rather limited nature of pupil choice is not shared by the pupils themselves. For them, school time is teachers' time, not pupils' time and as one pupil complained, teachers 'are always dragging us off to do something'. Another pupil expressed it as follows:

P: 'You're just getting in your flow, then you get dragged off somewhere. It's better not to start anything at all . . . just to play noughts and crosses (which he had been doing) ready for when anybody comes'.

At this point, with an immaculate sense of timing, a teacher walked across to the pupil and his group and asked them to clear up the neighbouring Art area. With a shrug of the shoulders and a 'knowing' look the pupil muttered resignedly 'See what I mean?'

Given their recognition that school time is teachers' time but that there is a low predictability of how this time will be apportioned by teachers, some pupils express a desire for a more rigidly compartmentalised timetable which will maximise the predictability of imposed schedules. Two third year pupils stated a preference for this kind of organisation.

> P1:   You think, "I'll leave that till tomorrow", and then when tomorrow comes you find you have a film and you don't know about it, then you . . . you can't get it done. But if your work's . . . um . . . you know . . . you have set periods to do everything . . .
> P2:   Yeah.
> P1:   . . . you do get it done'.

In addition to the unpredictable nature of time allocation, some pupils also suggested that the amount of blocked time made available to complete set tasks was insufficient. Rather melodramatically, one pupil estimated that 'we get three months work a week'. Time is thus experienced by pupils as externally controlled by the teaching staff who manipulate it, extend it or contract it at their will.

It is not only time that pupils experience as an imposition, however. As Mr. Button himself recognised, such imposition also applies to the *content* of school work. Occasionally, this is described explicitly by pupils in terms of lessons being boring,[31] but more usually it is the taken-for-granted style of their speech which betrays the fact that work is imposed work and that knowledge is produced for others rather than for themselves. Thus, when pupils discuss any work in which they are currently engaged, their remarks are almost always prefaced with phrases such as 'We've got to . . .', 'We have to . . .' 'She said we had to . . .' etc.

Other constraints make the completion of imposed work an especially arduous task for many pupils. The level of noise is a pervasive problem and many believe that 'There's too much racket in here'. For some the burden of blame for the generation of noise is placed upon other pupils i.e. 'It's people like *them* being silly', but for others the open-plan architecture of the school creates a situation where noise and even odour can be either an unpleasant obstructive barrier or an appealing distraction. Three comments illustrate the range of perceptions here:

> 'They should have doors on the classrooms'.

> 'In the cookery area you have woodshavings from the craft area and also in the library you get smells from the cookery area'.

> 'I mean, they've got the woodwork area next to the library area. You can't think'.

Open-plan design allows movement and flexibility but where work is imposed and perceived as alien and where pupils engage in the inevitable side-activities as a result, the facilitating effects of such architecture are transferred into a perceived oppressive constraint. Noise is not only generated but also more effectively transmitted within such an environment.

Tensions like these may threaten the stability of the system as a whole, for there is a very real danger that at the end of the week, teachers will be confronted by a long queue of children holding out their uncompleted assignments. An emphasis on individual direction and cajoling, as Mr Button suggests, may partly resolve these tensions, but, as Gramsci pointed out, because teachers are overwhelmed with work, individual direction can only be given to a few. How then is the survival of the block-timetable system guaranteed?

Under such alienating conditions for the production of knowledge where work is imposed but time is allowed for avoiding it, (as a means of reconciling the contradictory demands for integration in the form of fulfilling given knowledge requirements, and personal development in the form of allowing some space for the existence and visibility of freedom of choice), the maintenance of any kind of managerial equilibrium and the teacher coping strategies which constitute it, are together heavily dependent upon the creative ingenuity of pupils in coping with the dilemmas *they* face, and upon the ability of teachers to create spaces where such pupil ingenuity will be allowed to develop. 'Homework', defined as 'taking work home' because it is presented as a freely chosen extension of schoolwork (i.e. it can be justified ideologically), frequently provides such a safety valve. The persistence of complex coping strategies depends upon the efficiency of such safety valve mechanisms.

These mechanisms might be viewed as engendering a peculiar form of compensatory education where the home compensates for the 'deficient' experiences which the child receives in school. The reasons for coping in this way, through homework, are clearly stated by some pupils:

P: 'I prefer working at home. It's quiet and I've got my own room'.
AH: Do you usually finish all your working during the week?
P1:   Sometimes.
P2:   But I always take my English home and do it on a Tuesday night.
(Many pupils have mentioned that since English requires high levels of concentration, it is best completed at home where there is no noise and general interference).
AH: So is that the only thing you take home then? English?
P2:   Sometime you take topic home.
AH: Um hum. That's when you're getting really keen, is it? Really interested?
P1:   Or when we've got too much to do!

In a third-year class, a small group of pupils attempted to define for me the very fine distinctions between having homework set and having its existence recognised.

AH: How do you go on for taking work home? Do you take it home?
(P: Yes.
(P: I do.
(P: I do sometimes.
P: You're allowed to. You don't have to.
P: Mrs. Speaker won't set homework.
AH: Well, do you want her to?
P: No. (laughing).
P: We take a lot home, though.
P: You take homework if you haven't finished anything . . . like . . . you take it home over the weekend or something and then if it's done on Monday morning, you're O.K.

The collusion that exists on homework is revealed somewhat unintentionally in the following pupil's remark:

AH: Is it easy to avoid working?
(P: Oh yeah.
(P: Oh yeah. Yeah, it's easy to avoid it because *you can keep saying you left it at home.* (my emphasis).
P: Yeah.

In summary, there is a mutual recognition on the part of both teacher and pupil of the existence and necessity of homework, though its specification as an official category of 'set' work is avoided, presumably because it would run counter to the expected practices of a relatively 'progressive' institution. Instead of set *homework*, there is instead, the available legitimation that in progressive forms of teaching pupils can *take work home* if they choose, as a way of breaking down the barriers between home and school. As Riverdale's headmaster puts it:

> Mr. Kitchen   Quite frankly, I think that children have had enough at this age with school alone, but I would encourage children if they wish to take work home . . .

'Homework', for the upper-middle school teacher, is as central an organising category for structuring the teaching role as is 'busyness' for the infant school teacher. For this very reason, it is just as difficult to eliminate or 'take the steam out of' (in Mr. Kitchen's words). In each case, the respective principle serves as an organising category for teachers' responses to organisational and societal constraints and cannot be readily removed unless the institutional conditions which make such coping strategies necessary are themselves transformed. It is upon these material supports and also upon the creative response of pupils in themselves coping with *their* experienced constraints that the persistence of teacher coping strategies depends. If these material supports were to be removed or if pupil responses were to prove inadequate and inefficient, then some degree of change, no matter how limited, would be expected.

9   *The claimed effectiveness of coping strategies (and hence the grounds for their institutionalisation) are ultimately validated in teacher 'experience'.* Experience should be viewed not as a basis of judgement superior to all others (as with Saville's rigid and authoritarian headmaster in David Storey's (1976) novel of that title), nor as an obstructive force to the achievement of rational decision-making (which Philip Jackson (1968) implies that *his* 'experienced' teachers are incapable of making).

Instead, in a tightly constraining environment where few opportunities are provided for individual or collective reflection, experience should be viewed as an organising mechanism for proceeding routinely yet accountably within the work situation. It is 'experience' that tells teachers which particular teaching styles have proved 'effective'. In interview, for example, when asked about the source of their ideas on various educational matters, the majority of both Riverdale and Moorhead teachers cited 'experience' as their mentor. When experience is used as the yardstick, effectiveness and efficiency are determined and assessed with reference to the teacher's explicit and tacit subscription to personal and institutional goals and to a set of mediated constraints. Rarely is the problem of efficiency translated into one of what efficiency might be for. The use of 'experience' as the dominant organising category of teachers' thought and everyday actions thus ensures that coping strategies are essentially adaptive in character, that their institutionalisation fosters the perpetuation of structures rather than their transformation and that they serve to produce stability regarding the major functions of education, rather than radical social change.

10   Following from the previous point, it should be stressed that *although coping strategies are constructive and creative in character, nevertheless they are also based upon a set of tacitly accepted and taken for granted assumptions* about schooling, children and learning. In other words, it should be emphasised that coping strategies are not created in a vacuum but are constructed within a set of definite parameters so that the scope for creativity is limited. These assumptions about, for instance, the 'needs' of working class children and the deficiency of their home backgrounds;

about the distribution of natural, hierarchically ranked ability; about the compulsory nature of education and the benevolent role of the State in providing for this; about the role of the teacher as the controller and evaluator of the acquisition of knowledge by pupils; about the compatibility of individual needs with the requirements of the society; all of these constitute a range of taken-for-granted ideas which form the building blocks out of which 'experience' is constructed and validated but only insofar as such ideas provide a plausible interpretation of everyday practice. Such assumptions also serve as parameters within which coping strategies are constructed. Furthermore as constituent features of a dominant social democratic hegemony which stresses individualism, gradualism, reasonable balance and State benevolence, they also guarantee the non-radical character of teacher coping strategies.

Conclusion

In this paper, I have attempted to provide a rather sketchy model of classroom and school based coping strategies in order to provide a bridge not only between classroom and society but also between interpretive and Marxist approaches in the study of education. Some illustrative material has been drawn from the middle school which holds a central position not only chronologically in the hierarchy of educational institutions but also sociologically as a focal point for studying the dilemmas which teachers face and the constraints with which they must cope in the schooling system of British society. If teaching styles *do* take the form of coping strategies as in the model presented here, then, given the present goals and functions of education in a society which can be called capitalist, the prospects for fundamental change are not great. As the diagram representing the model shows (Fig. 5.1), change would presently seem to occur at only two points. Firstly, if coping strategies prove inefficient then new ones will be devised. This allows for some variation in the degree of adaptive capacity which coping strategies contain, but leaves the *principle* of adaptation intact. This does mean, however, that adaptation is never complete and that the cycle of coping is never closed and static. Under these conditions the cycle itself contains an internal dynamic and, like a bicycle wheel, advances as it rotates. Secondly, new structural constraints may produce new responses on the part of teachers. Changing social relations in the workplace, for example, may produce a shift from the employment of coping strategies such as the 'recitation' to ones more characteristic of a more progressively organised system of education. Under these circumstances the degree and type of change in the educational system is dependent upon the character of changes in the wider social structure.

Neither of these current possibilities allows for fundamental social and educational change (unless, of course, change within the wider society is of a radical nature), but only for adaptation and amelioration. The crucial axis which might provide the possibility for radical alteration and humanisation of our educational and social structures would seem to be that which connects teacher 'experience' to structural constraints. Change of such a magnitude demands the active involvement of teachers in particular and men and women in general, in the collective criticism of existing practices, structural arrangements and institutional goals. Furthermore, the possibility of change is contingent upon the provision of institutional conditions under which such collective criticism could take place and be reflexively integrated with ongoing practice. Paradoxically this requires the fulfilment of 'gradualist' policies such as smaller class-sizes and the creation of more

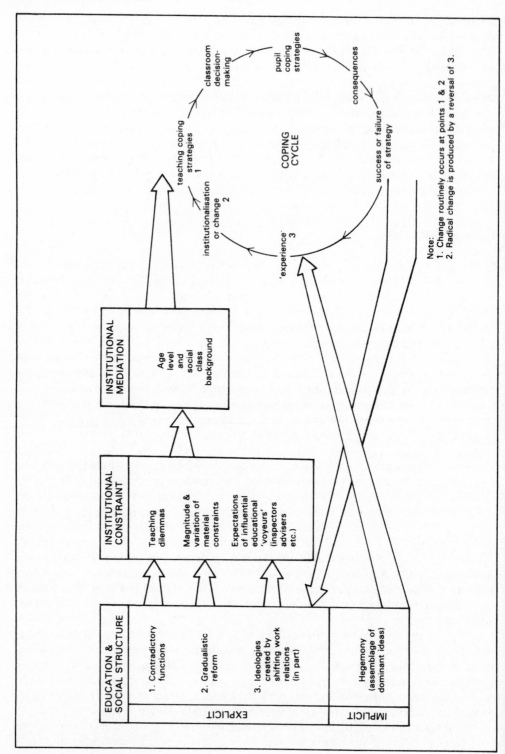

Figure 5.1 Coping strategies—a model

'free-time' so that a meaningful integration between theory and practice might arise and thus produce a reconstruction of teacher 'experience' on radical lines, infusing it with the power of transformation. Teachers might then become active and ongoing critics and producers of their educational practice and their whole social and political world, becoming one group of agents who might begin to produce basic and meaningful alternatives to the existing dominant hegemony. This would not mean that coping strategies would then become a redundant category. Coping would persist, but the constraints and goals would be democratically and collectively produced, not imposed in a seemingly arbitrary fashion from above. One cannot credibly foresee a society free from constraint, but it *is* possible to imagine a state of affairs where constraints are the democratic and rational production of peoples' collective activity. Under these circumstances, it is unlikely that coping strategies will ever approximate to the techniques which some have suggested that prisoners and teachers currently employ in the grim business of psychological survival.[32]

As a rather crude diagrammatic summary, the model of coping strategies may be expressed as in figure 5.1.

Acknowledgement

I would like to thank the SSRC for funding the research from which this article has arisen.

Notes

[1] This is not to suggest that all researchers who have focussed upon classroom processes assume that negotiations between teachers and pupils are based on an equal distribution of power resources and interactional skills. More usually, the model is a pluralist one where society is seen as constituted by different interest groups each of which exerts pressure and attempts to have its definitions accepted in a process of open, observable conflict. In such a model, the school is an arena where pressure is exerted by teachers, pupils, parents, governors and so forth in a process of conflict-ridden but democratic decision-making. Under this view then, conflict is central and essential to the democratic process in society; its influence is beneficial.

By comparison, all Marxist approaches contain the central assumption that in capitalist societies conflict is not only permanent, but also irresolvable. Problems are conceived not as isolated, unconnected and temporary difficulties but as the expression of an enduring contradiction between the interests of capital and labour. The absence of overt conflict does not necessarily indicate a natural shared consensus for such consensus may be engineered through ideological and political means with only minor residual issues being legitimate subjects for conflict and debate.

For an extended account of the different approaches to 'conflict' see Miliband (1977) especially Chapter 2.

[2] On the degradation of work in contemporary capitalist society see Braverman (1974) and Nichols and Benyon (1977).

[3] For a challenge to the conventional wisdom that improved qualifications lead to better jobs, see, for example Berg (1970) and Bowles and Gintis (1976).

[4] There have been few attempts to provide such forms of inclusive explanation to date, but some recent movements in this area *can* be detected, though the precise nature of the model varies in each case. See especially Sharp and Green (1975) and Willis (1977).

[5] For a more extensive discussion of these schools, and of middle school ideology and practice in general, see Hargreaves (forthcoming).

[6] Pupils' definitions are also, of course, extremely important and will receive some consideration here.

[7] This does not mean that the actual way in which teachers type pupils is necessarily in terms of such categories, as Hargreaves, D. (1977) has pointed out.

[8] This point is made by Hoetker and Ahlbrand (1969).

[9] A. Hargreaves (1979).

[10] The phrase 'irrespective of how they define it' is perhaps a little blunt, though, and overlooks the point that even if 'the situation' proves irresistably oppressive, it still generates defining responses on the teachers' and indeed the pupils' part.

[11] See Woods (1976).

[12] Nichols and Benyon (1977) make this observation in their comments upon 'worker participation' in the chemical factory they studied.

[13] For a discussion of the ideology and practice of 'guided choice' at the routine levels of classroom decision-making see A. Hargreaves (1977).

[14] The block timetable approach entails the inclusion of a large proportion of 'open periods' on the school timetable when assignments (which pupils are given or which they select from a narrow range of alternatives) can be worked upon. The choice which pupils exercise in this system is in the pacing of their work and over the order in which assignments are completed.

[15] This is not of course to suggest that educational reform *ever* took the form of a radical wholesale reconstruction of pre-existing arrangements at any time before large-scale State intervention commenced.

[16] Supportive evidence for this assertion is available in early documents produced by the West Riding when middle schools were first planned. See A Hargreaves (1983).

[17] Matters have improved somewhat since fieldwork was completed. Separate specialist facilities for craft and science are now available and the prospect of a new school opening at Millbeck is now somewhat closer.

[18] These points were also raised by Mr. Butcher in other contexts such as parents' meeting, governors' meetings etc.

[19] At times when teacher unemployment is rising and the opportunities for job mobility decrease, one would expect this effect to increase.

[20] See various *Schools Council Working Papers*, especially numbers 22, 42 and 55 for examples of such ideology. Their ideological content is analysed in A. Hargreaves (1980).

[21] 'Misplaced' refers to a disparity between teachers' orientation and their placement within a particulr kind of school.

[22] The preference for 'indirect' teaching is clearly expressed by Flanders (1970).

[23] The limitations of the Flanderian definitions of 'direct' and 'indirect' teaching have been discussed in Delamont (1976).

[24] A point made and substantiated through analysis of interaction in Hammersley (1974).

[25] Discussion of this point with reference to the United States is made in Bowles and Gintis *op cit.*

[26] Any bias therefore is neither necessarily intentional nor manipulative. That 'bias' is more usually the product of an unquestioned set of value assumptions is most cogently argued by Hall (1973).

[27] Such groups include teachers at Moorhead and, at least for an initial period, students on teaching practice at Riverdale.

[28] A. Hargreaves (1979).

[29] Though this begs the important questions of how far one can have an untheorized observation.

[30] A policy recommended by Blyth and Derricott (1977).

[31] Such statements *are* occasional though, and this is not the usual way in which pupils explicitly talk about school life at Riverdale.

[32] On prisoners see Taylor and Cohen (1972), and on teachers see Woods (1977).

References

Becker, H. (1952) 'Social class variation in the teacher–pupil relationship', *Journal of Educational Sociology*, Vol. 25, No. 4, pp. 451–65.

Berg, I. (1970) *Education and Jobs: the Great Training Robbery*, Penguin, Harmondsworth.

Blyth, W.A.L. and Derricott, R. (1977) *The Social Significance of Middle Schools*, Batiford, London.
Bowles, S and Gintis, H. (1976) *Schooling in Capitalist America* Routledge and Kegan Paul, London.
Braverman, H. (1974) *Labour and Monopoly Capital*, Monthly Review Press, London.
Delamont, S. (1976) *Interaction in the Classroom*, Methuen, London.
Flanders, N. (1970) *Analyzing Teacher Behaviour*, Addison-Wesley, New York.
Gramsci, I. (1971) *Selection from the Prison Notebooks*, Lawrence and Wishart, London.
Hall, S. (1977) 'The determination of news photographs', in Cohen, S. and Young, T. (eds) *The Manufacture of News* Constable, London.
Hammersley, M. (1974) 'The organization of pupil participation', *Sociological Review*, Vol. 22, No. 3.
Hargreaves, A. (1977) 'Progressivism and pupil autonomy', *Sociological Review*, Vol. 25, No. 3.
Hargreaves, A. (1979) 'Strategies, decisions and control', in Eggleston, J. (ed.) *Teacher Decision-Making in the Classroom*, Routledge and Kegan Paul, London.
Hargreaves, A. (1980) 'The ideology of the middle school', in Hargreaves, A. and Tickle, L. (eds) *Middle Schools: Origins, Ideology and Practice*, Harper and Row, London.
Hargreaves, A. (1983) 'The politics of administrative convenience: the case of middle schools', in Ahier, J. and Flude, M. (eds) *Contemporary Education Policy*, Croom Helm, London.
Hargreaves, A. (forthcoming) *The Sociology of Educational Policy and Practice*, Routledge and Kegan Paul, London.
Hargreaves, D. (1977) 'The process of typification in the classroom: models and methods', *British Journal of Educational Psychology*, November.
Hoetker, and Ahlbrand, (1969) 'The persistence of the recitation', *American Educational Research Journal*, Vol. 6.
Keddie, N. (1971) 'Classroom knowledge', in Young, M.F.D. (ed.) *Knowledge and Control*, Collier-Macmillan, London.
Keddie, N. (1973) *Tinker, Tailor... The Myth of Cultural Deprivation*, Penguin, Harmondsworth.
Miliband, R. (1977) *Marxism and Politics*, Oxford University Press.
Nichols, T. and Benyon, H. (1977) *Living with Capitalism*, Routledge and Kegan Paul, London.
Sharp, R. and Green, A. (1973) *Education and Social Control*, Routledge and Kegan Paul, London.
Taylor, L. and Cohen, S. (1972) *Psychological Survival*, Penguin, Harmondsworth.
Westbury, I. (1973) 'Conventional classrooms, open classrooms and the technology of teaching', *Journal of Curriculum Studies*, Vol. 5.
Willis, P. (1977) *Learning to Labour*, Saxon House, Farnborough.
Woods, P. (1976) 'The myth of subject choice', *British Journal of Sociology*, June.
Woods, P. (1977) 'Teaching for survival', in Woods, P. and Hammersley, M. (eds) *School Experience*, Croom Helm, London.

6 Teaching and Learning in English Primary Schools

A.C. BERLAK, H. BERLAK, N.T. BAGENSTOS and E.R. MIKEL

In the following article, Ann Berlak and her colleagues contest the popular view of the 'progressive' English primary school which extols various aspects of their child-centredness. They argue, on the basis of their research among some junior schools in Leicestershire that teachers employ both traditional and progressive methods, and often, apparently inconsistently. The best way to understand this, the authors feel, is by recognizing that teachers are confronted by certain dilemmas in the classroom, which they resolve by making 'trade-off' decisions among various alternatives, depending on such factors as type of pupil, task in hand, and situation.

The English primary school has become the symbol for many school reformers of the 1970s—the standard by which to measure and judge the deficiencies of elementary schooling in America.[1] This paper, based on a six-month participant-observation study of several English informal primary schools, raises questions about the common images of these schools found in much of the popular and professional literature.[2] In particular, the focus will be on three related issues which are central to a discussion of the English informal schools:

1 What role does the child play in making educational decisions?
2 To what extent does the impetus to learn originate in the child and to what extent is it extrinsic?
3 Who sets and maintains educational performance standards?

The analysis of these issues is set within a framework we developed from the observation and interview data we collected and from a systematic effort to use our personal experience in American schools. The framework consists of fifteen basic tensions or dilemmas which we believe confront teachers daily in the classroom. The issues raised are analyzed in terms of three of the dilemmas:

1 teacher making learning decisions for children versus children making learning decisions,
2 intrinsic versus extrinsic motivation,
3 teacher setting and maintaining versus children setting their own standards.
[...]

[...] In order to provide a basis for understanding the framework in this paper, we report the findings using data drawn from interviews with and observations of only two of the twenty-two teachers studied in depth. The two teachers were selected because they manifest patterns common to many of the teachers studied.

We present a general picture of these two teachers and their classrooms before turning to an analysis of the data.

Mrs Lawton
In a primary school in one of the poorer sections of Leicester, Mrs Lawton teaches twenty-five 7-year-olds.. The morning is devoted primarily to work in the 'basics'—reading, maths, and writing—with a brief interruption for assembly. Mrs Lawton sets daily minimum work expectations: everyone will write a story, all but the strongest readers will read individually to the teacher or the head, and each will do a given maths task. Moreover, each child works with a small group at his maths and his story at a specified time. During a work period, Mrs Lawton may tell one child to write a longer story, more often than not ignoring a child's apparent reluctance, but may be satisfied with a shorter story from another child. When a child has finished the required work, or if no work is required at a given time, generally in the afternoons, he may 'choose' from activities such as reading corner, painting, Wendy house, or blocks. At such times, one might see three children in 'dress-ups' wheeling a carriage across the playground unbeknown to the teacher, who might be 'hearing' the last of her students read.

Mr Thomas
On Mondays, Mr Thomas makes explicit the minimum each child should accomplish for the week in a variety of academic areas. Students can choose to go beyond the minimum or to do other activities, including observing pets and discussing football. They can, in general, allocate their own time during the mornings of the entire week. Thus, the observer might, at any given time on any morning, see children working on various academic tasks while others are chatting quietly, painting, or working with a cooking group. On Fridays, Mr Thomas and perhaps the head check to make sure students have completed their assigned tasks to the adult's satisfaction; those few who have not will either confer with the teacher or be sanctioned. In the afternoons the students engage in one of a number of schoolwide 'commitments' or 'minicourses.' At 1:00 p.m. they deploy themselves to various locations in the school to join in dance, music, science, 'topic,' art, or other activity groups.

Patterns of resolutions to the three dilemmas

Teacher making learning decisions for children versus children making learning decisions
Our effort to conceptualize the complexities and apparent inconsistencies in what the teacher and what the child control[3] in the learning situation and under what circumstances differing patterns of control are exercised led us to posit that there was a dilemma facing the teachers we observed. There appeared to coexist a simultaneous pull in two directions—toward the teacher making learning decisions and toward the children making the decisions.

In this section we present a framework which may be used to order the complex ways the dilemma is manifested and resolved. Decisions—not necessarily deliberated—are made about:

1 *whether or not* a child will study in a given area,
2 *what* specifically is to be learned within that area,
3 *when* the task is to begin and when it is to be completed, and
4 *how* the learner is to proceed with the task.

Type of decision	Who decides			
	Teacher decides	Child and teacher decide jointly		Child decides
		Choose from options	Negotiate	
Whether or not to learn				
What should be learned				
When it should be learned				
How it should be learned				

Figure 6.1

In a given learning situation, the child, or the teacher, or both jointly exercise one or more of these decisions. Joint decisions appear to have one of two emphases: either the child chooses from among a set of options or he engages with the teacher in a process that resembles negotiating. The large number of possible patterns of resolution to the dilemma is now evident; a teacher can follow different patterns of resolution for different children, and at different times of the year, or for different subject or learning experiences. Figure 6.1 represents the array of possibilities.

'I think they need freedom but also guidance,' Mrs Lawton claims, indicating that she is drawn to both sides of the dilemma. In fact, she resolves the dilemma by making almost all of the decisions on *whether or not* and most of the decisions about *what, when,* and *how* in the 'basics—reading, writing, and maths—while leaving most decisions in the nonbasics to the children. 'I direct them, but I give them choice as well. Especially with 'activities' and creative work, I allow them to choose more than with written work. I give them suggestions about what to write about, but . . . if they have an idea then they write about what they would like to.'

The class is divided into four groups, and Mrs Lawton sets the time for each group to work on the 'basics.' There are variations; for example, children who want to write first thing in the morning are allowed to do so even if this entails departing from the teacher's schedule. Those few children who do not finish the required work during the specified period will usually be called away from a chosen activity and directed to finish.

Minimal student influence is evident regarding *what* specifically will be learned in academic subjects: children often decide what to write about, and at times they may choose from a very limited number of maths tasks. They have no choice of basal readers, however, as these are selected by the teacher from a sequence of readers prescribed for the entire school. Generally, Mrs Lawton decides *how* a task will be learned; for example, all students will practice 'money' by taking a turn in the 'shop' and by doing a work sheet, though a child may decide when he will 'play' in the shop.

Most decisions beyond the minimum in the academic area and in the creative and nonacademic realm are the child's as long as he had completed the 'basic' work. It is the child who decides whether or not to do the daily art project, read in the reading corner, dabble or work seriously at the workbench (limited only by care of tools and safety considerations), play at the Wendy house, or at learning a game. Choices are, of course, generally limited by the materials placed in the environment. Lego plastic blocks were removed as an option from the room because, as Mrs Lawton said, 'the children were no longer learning anything from their use.'

We observed frequent examples of negotiated decisions, particularly in the nonbasics: the teacher and child discussed a writing topic, what he might construct at the workbench, what he might do in his 'choice' time, or how to best proceed at a given task. Thus, we see that Mrs Lawton many times a day resolves the dilemma of decision making according to a pattern which in her case appears to depend particularly on whether she considers the subject 'basic.'

Mr Thomas explicitly expressed that he feels pulled toward each side of the dilemma:

> I have yet to come to terms with myself about what a child should do in, for instance, mathematics. Certainly I feel that children should as far as possible follow their own interests and not be dictated to all the time, but then again . . . I feel pressure from . . . I don't really know how to explain it, but there's something inside you that you've developed over the years which says the children should do this. . . . I as yet can't accept, for instance, that since I've been here I've been annoyed that some children in the fourth year haven't progressed as much as, say, some less able children in the second year in their maths, because they've obviously been encouraged to get on with their own interests. But I still feel that I've somehow got to press them on with their mathematics.

His resolution to the dilemma is to make most of the decisions about whether or not a child will learn in a given area. In academic areas the child has virtually no control over *whether or not:* 'I insist on what I call the bread and butter.' In fact, Mr Thomas requires work each week in nearly all curriculum areas: art, maths, reading, writing, handwriting, spelling, 'topic' (similar to a research report). This behaviour reflects his expressed desire 'that children take part in practically everything there is to offer.' Students are granted only slightly more control over whether they will work in nonbasic areas. Mr Thomas argued, in opposition to a number of other teachers in the school, that all children be required to participate in Sports Day, and his position on the issue prevailed. Every afternoon all children in the school leave their home teacher to attend 'commitment groups,' courses usually lasting a week in areas such as physical education, dance, science, creative writing, music, or library. Teachers limit students' choice of commitment group by either negotiating with students or requiring them to choose a different group every week or two. Mr Thomas (along with the majority of the teachers) expressed the view that this control over *whether or not* is rightfully in the teacher's domain.

Mr Thomas sets weekly work minimums in each subject area—a specific number of assignment cards or pages to complete. Work minimums are, however, negotiable, and Mr Thomas or the student will not infrequently initiate negotiation in order to adjust minimums to the abilities or interests of the child. In those areas (maths, reading, spelling) where minimums are defined in terms of sets of sequenced cards, children are given almost no choice about *what* or *how* to learn. In handwriting, creative writing, and topic research, Mr Thomas provides sets of non-sequential assignment cards which suggest optional activities from which students may choose if they do not have an idea of their own.[4] In these subjects, although the general area is assigned, the choice of what to work on within an area or how to proceed is up to the children. They choose how they will express what they have learned in the topic area they select, perhaps making a display or giving a play.

The children have almost complete freedom to decide *when* during the week to do their required work, and minimums are set so that perhaps only 60–75 per cent of a child's time each morning is controlled by the teacher. Thus, Mr Thomas argues that it's quite appropriate during a work period for a child 'to tell another what he's done last night or how he got on at football during playtime.'

The foregoing indicates the complexity of decision-making procedures in English informal classrooms (or indeed in any classroom). Barth and Rathbone[5] suggest that the more willing a teacher is to allow children to make independent decisions, the closer that teacher is to the open-education idea and, by implication, the English model. If our data are at all representative of what goes on in English primary schools, then Barth and Rathbone are wrong. In virtually all classrooms, the teachers' resolutions to the dilemma are a combination of opposites—a resolution that takes into account, according to explicit or implicit principles, the claims of both poles of the dilemma. Although we found important variations in the patterns of resolution, the generalization that children in informal classrooms control their schooling—even when qualifications are added—is, we are convinced, gross distortion of the complexity that obtains in the classrooms we observed.

Intrinsic versus extrinsic motivation
The pull of this dilemma is that, on the one hand, teachers are drawn to the idea that the impetus for learning comes—and should come—primarily from within the learner and, on the other hand, to the idea that some kind of action by the teacher or others is required for learning to be initiated and sustained by a child.[6] Action may include urging, threatening, rewarding with praise, candy or tokens, or punishing failure to perform. We present data to demonstrate that both intrinsic and extrinsic motivation are part of the meanings manifest in complex patterns of behavior of the teachers who were studied.

Our analysis suggests three categories of ideas associated with this dilemma. First, teachers have differing ideas about the capacity of a particular subject area or activity to interest, and hence motivate, a child. For example, a teacher will say something to the effect that experimenting with chemicals is 'intrinsically' more interesting to children than learning to diagram a sentence or that children are more likely to be 'intrinsically' motivated to learn measurement than the multiplication tables.

Second, teachers also have different ideas about an individual child's capacity to be motivated. For example, a teacher may say that 'Jane is intrinsically motivated to read, but Joe needs to be pushed.' Thus, teachers have differing views about the capacity of a given child to initiate and sustain involvement in learning without a teacher's push (or other form of action) and differing views about the intrinsic motivating capacity of a subject or activity. The mix of the two we call the 'flash point,' which is the teachers' subjective estimate of how much extrinsic motivation is required to get a child to want to learn in a given area. (Little extrinsic motivation required in a given area for a particular child indicates a low flash point.) Teachers, of course, have differing estimates of the 'flash point' for any group of children in a given area or learning activity. This estimate is only the teacher's best guess as to what is empirically correct, and, as with any empirical judgement, the teacher may be mistaken.

Third, teachers have different valuations of the importance of a child's intrinsic motivation in a given domain of learning. For example, a teacher may feel that it is relatively important for children to be intrinsically motivated to read. This same teacher may believe that the flash point for reading for any given child is high, that is, that the child is not easily motivated to read. Thus, the teacher makes a value judgement (it is important that children be intrinsically motivated to read) and an

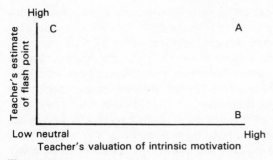

Figure 6.2

empirical judgment about where the flash point is for a given child in a given subject (Jack is not easily motivated to read).

These two sets of judgments—one empirical and the other valuational—may be represented on a two-dimensional space. We are suggesting that those views of a teacher that can be plotted in this space partly account for his pattern of behavior in motivating children. Figure 6.2 is an effort to account for these patterns; the X axis represents the teacher's valuation of intrinsic motivation in a given area, and the Y axis represents the teacher's estimate of the flash point in that area for a given child. Point A in the space would be grounded in a behavioral pattern of richly 'provisioning' the environment, that is, the teacher arranging the environment with stimulating materials and doing a number of other things to spark interest. Point B represents the pattern where there is no use of extrinsic motivation (e.g., candy, threats) and few provisions for stimulating a child's interests, since these are seen as unnecessary. Point C represents the pattern of the popular image of the traditional teacher where there is, as in pattern B, little effort expended by the teacher to spark interest although, in contrast to B, there is much use of extrinsic motivation. Since teachers may see intrinsic motivation as important in one activity but not in another, and estimate that one child is intrinsically motivated but another is not for a given activity, a teacher could be charted with respect to motivation for each child in each subject. However, it seems likely that further analysis will disclose that there are characteristic patterns of teachers in different schooling situations.

Mr Thomas feels pulled toward both intrinsic and extrinsic motivation in the classroom: 'If they are not interested in what they are doing, if I can't interest them in what they are doing then it becomes a case of having to do it.'

On what basis does Mr Thomas decide when to rely on intrinsic motivation? For learning the 'basics' he does not depend on intrinsic motivation: the children are in fact told what they must do, and there are sanctions for those few who fail to do so. He argued: 'If a child doesn't do what I think he should do in a week, then instead of joining his commitment group in the afternoon he'll probably spend time in the library.' This statement suggests what the use of sanctions means to him: that some children are intrinsically motivated in 'commitments' though not in the basics and that the use of extrinsic motivation is not unjustified in such cases.

However, Mr Thomas values 'natural' interest, expects it to appear in some children, and uses it when it appears. 'Richard . . . is a very creative boy . . . he's got to be left alone before he produces his really best work.' Mr Thomas's behavior reflects the value he places on internal motivation: a child who, for example, brought him animals in various conditions of health or who demonstrated interest in pursuing virtually any subject was generally excused from some part of the work minimums.

Mr Thomas frequently spends time evoking student interest. For example, when he requires the children to write a story or read a book, he devotes time to helping them alight upon a book or topic of interest, providing suggestions, pictures, or articles with no manifest pressure to pursue the interest in a particular direction. 'I try to show an interest in their reading. We discuss what they read quite often—we used to do book reviews but this . . . didn't work out very well. I like to call them together, and perhaps it's something somebody's done and I like to get really enthusiastic about it.' At no time did we see Mr Thomas initiate any new activity without attempting to 'motivate' the children; this is consistent with his apparent assumption that the flash point is high in most subjects or activities for at least some children but that intrinsic motivation is valued.

Mrs Lawton does not rely very heavily on intrinsic motivation in the 'basics.' Both observational and interview data suggest that she believes the flash points are high for virtually everyone—'With these children, most of their interests come from what I've put into them'—and that intrinsic motivation is not highly valued in the basics. She forces—gently, but forces nevertheless—children to read, write, and do maths, and forbids them—kindly, but forbids them nevertheless—to 'choose' before they finish assigned tasks. 'I would say, "Finish your maths cards before you build," because Robert is a bit like that. I don't think he finds writing very easy. . . . He does try to dodge written work. If he doesn't do his work in the morning it's there for him to do in the afternoon.' She often 'motivates' with praise, perhaps sending a child to show a particularly good story to the head.

Mrs Lawton seems to value intrinsic motivation more in creative work than in the basics. 'I think in creative work if they do something they want to do, you get better results.' This value, coupled with an assumption of a high flash point in the nonbasics, results in her playing an extremely active role in 'sparking' interest in the nonbasics: 'When I come in at the beginning of the term I don't have ideas on everything I'm going to do, but I've got something to start off with. If I find something that interests them, then I carry on with that.' 'If' suggests that she feels at least uncertain about whether children will display intrinsic motivation. Thus, when she introduced a unit on 'shapes,' she arranged an elaborate display, but she was unwilling to rely on the display alone to spark interest. She conducted frequent short discussions and provided daily optional art projects to encourage interest. She claimed that feeling intrinsic motivation is important in all curriculum areas. 'If I've got a child that's genuinely interested in something I'd never say, "You can't do that,"' but the observational data suggests that she sees intrinsic motivation in some areas as less important than extrinsically motivated work in the basics. Observations indicate that the obligation to write almost always takes precedence over a child's manifest interest in building with blocks, or self-initiated projects in art or at the work-bench.

However, Mrs Lawton resolves the dilemma under consideration differently for different children. For example, at one point the students were working with blocks of different shapes at the maths table. Our notes read: 'One boy says of another, "He's playing with the blocks" (implying he should be working). The teacher allows the boy who is playing to continue. She directs two others to sort the blocks into several groups and to write about what they've done.' Here is an example of simultaneously resolving the dilemma for some in terms of intrinsic motivation and for others in terms of extrinsic motivation.

In summary, our data suggest that English teachers resolve the dilemma of intrinsic versus extrinsic motivation by recognizing the claims of both poles and motivating differently for different tasks and students. Within this range of resolutions, we found many patterns. However, virtually all English teachers, at those times when they did not extrinsically motivate, brought into the classroom stimulating materials and provided options in order to spark interest. We saw few instances of teachers who depended heavily on intrinsic motivation with no provisioning. Classrooms of those few teachers who failed to provision were barren and dull, and these teachers were considered by their heads to be inferior teachers.

Teacher setting and maintaining standards for children's learning and development versus children setting their own standards
What are the patterns of teachers' meanings in the area of setting standards? By now it must be clear that the complexity of this issue is masked by statements such as, open educators believe that 'the preferred source of verification for a child's solution to a problem comes through the materials he is working with'[8] (rather than the imposition of teacher standards).

Analysis of the data suggests that the dilemma as it is manifested in the schooling situation can be better understood if a distinction is made between who sets standards and who decides whether standards have been met by the child. As with the 'decision' dilemma, these responsibilities can be with the teacher (or other school authorities—and the school authorities may be acting only as proxies for standards set by others outside the school), or with the child, or the teacher and child can jointly carry out these tasks in any given activity. The complexity of the issue is increased when one considers that a teacher can follow different patterns with different children and for different tasks or subjects. For example, the teacher may set standards for reading and writing but not for art or 'learning to cooperate,' or he may set standards in art but let the student decide if he has met them. It is also possible for both to agree on the standard of a 'finished painting' or for the child to feel he has finished but for the teacher to disagree.[9]

Figure 6.3 shows the two aspects of the meaning related to this dilemma: who sets the standards and who decides whether a child has met them.

Mrs Lawton's pattern of setting standards is most evident in her response to written work. The absence of data on teacher standard setting in such areas as block building, carpentry, and most art projects suggest that she is concerned primarily with standards in the basics. With respect to daily writing, it is clear that she sets standards such as length of a story or accuracy of spelling, in most cases unilaterally, and decides whether students meet these standards. She called back a boy who put his writing away without finishing and told another boy, 'You've only done one line.' Our field notes report: 'John D. says, "I couldn't do any better on that story." Teacher: "Of course you can."'

Mrs Lawton allows a few children to set standards and to evaluate their work against them while others are made to conform. The data clearly suggest a

| | Sets | |
	Adult	Child
Meets Adult	Aa	Ca
Child	Ac	Cc

Figure 6.3

response to differences among children. She says:

> Usually because Mary works well I let her do what she wants to do... but I know her standards are quite good and she works hard when she is working.... Some children who do bad work I know I could tear the page out and say I'm not accepting that and they would do better. Some children would be absolutely devastated.... It depends on the child. There is no set rule.

Most children measure themselves against Mrs Lawton's standards in maths, but she seems to allow fewer to do so in writing. She is likely to check a child's story before dismissing him from writing, though students rarely check with her before handing in maths work.

Mr Thomas sets clear standards in most areas of work: 'I insist on presentable work. .... I expect [him] ... to do what he's capable of doing and I become annoyed if I feel he hasn't accomplished this.' One child said to the interviewer, 'Mr Thomas told me I could do better, and I do now.'

Many children seem to measure their work against their presumption of what the teacher's standards are. Relatively few regularly asked the teacher whether a story was long enough or neat enough. Relatively few were punished or pushed to go beyond what they were content with; a few received criticism when the record books were checked, on Fridays. The exceptional student was told that he wasn't measuring up: 'You are getting careless' written on a paper. 'I'll chat with them about a story they've done which I've enjoyed, or I'll chat to the children I'm not so pleased with.' Our field notes suggest a number of instances of positive evaluation: 'So far so good.'

In summary, a preliminary analysis of the data again suggests a variety or patterns of resolution to the dilemma of setting standards. Although in general teachers set standards in academic areas, these standards seem to be set for individuals rather than for groups. The data suggest that teachers distinguish between children who can evaluate themselves against the teacher's standards and those who cannot and teachers intervene primarily with the latter group.

Some speculations and implications

[...] What we have attempted to document is that the efforts to describe or to theorize about the English schools have distorted their reality. This distortion, we believe, has occurred because the images of neither the ardent advocates nor the detractors are grounded in a study of the day-by-day occurrences in such schools.[10] The language of freedom, self-motivation, and child-set standards commonly used to characterize these schools does not, even with added qualifications, we argue, capture the complexity of the actual schooling; indeed, such language distorts and, we think, leads others to misunderstand the English experience. It is not an overgeneralization to say that in no school we studied did a child have a choice not to learn to read or do maths, and there are virtually no instances of children being allowed to do nothing. This is no surprise, except perhaps to those who have come to believe that open or informal education is synonymous with permissiveness. Adult standards and sanctions were at all times operative in all the schools and all the classrooms we observed. On the other hand, as we have argued, children did make significant decisions and did follow their interests in the schools we observed.

How can informal education be characterized in terms that more accurately reflect the reality? To answer this, we return to our conception of schooling. We have suggested that a useful way to conceptualize schooling is in terms of a set of persisting dilemmas and that it is the teacher acting as self and agent who makes the de facto resolutions to the dilemmas. We have tentatively identified fourteen basic tensions or conflicts and have dealt with three of them in this essay. We suspect, though we are by no means certain, that informal schooling in England can be described in terms of characteristic patterns of resolving a set of dilemmas, although not in terms of how any one or two dilemmas are resolved. In other words, it is possible to make some generalizations about the grounded rationales of the English teachers we observed and to make comparisons to schooling in other settings.

This view of schooling as personal and complex resolutions to basic dilemmas merely acknowledges that schools, like other institutions, are subject to the complex and diverse influences of the social and political order. As a consequence, it is unlikely that we can have public schools where the immediate desires of children come first in all or even most circumstances (whether this is desirable is a separate question), because window washers, corporation executives, university professors, and teachers who directly or indirectly influence what the schools do want their own children to master and comprehend the intellectual and social traditions they see as instrumental to conventional success. At the same time, these persons, at least to some extent, value personal growth and fulfilment, which, again directly or indirectly, influences what transpires in classrooms. Questions such as whether a teacher is child centered or not are, we believe, better conceptualized in terms of how teachers deal with the conflicting claims implicit in the dilemmas we have identified. In general, we believe that teachers' behavior in the classrooms we observed was responsive to the complex and conflicting claims of the dilemmas. In our view, the English informal teachers' concrete resolutions to these dilemmas may be useful guideposts to American school reformers interested in transplanting English informal methods to American elementary schools.

Notes

[1] There are three types of schools for young children in England, each of which is administered by a separate head or principal: the infant school, for children age $4\frac{1}{2}$ to 7; the junior school, for children age 8 to 11; and the primary school, for infants and juniors. In this paper, unless specified otherwise, the term 'primary school' refers to all three types of schools.

[2] The data for this study were gathered from January to July 1972 by two of the writers, Ann and Harold Berlak, in schools administered by the Leicester and Leicestershire Education Authorities. Three schools were studied in depth during stays of four to six weeks each. Supplementary data from thirteen other schools were collected during visits of from one to four days each. The schools studied in depth were a middle/lower-middle-class primary school located in a suburb characterized by modest tract houses; an infant school in one of the poorer areas of Leicester; and a junior school in an affluent middle-class suburb. The data—consisting of field notes; tape-recorded interviews with all the teachers and heads and at least ten students in each of the three schools studied in depth; interviews and informal discussions with heads and teachers in other schools and with other education officials; documents distributed by school officials, including curriculum guides, memoranda of operational procedures, etc.—represent a combined expenditure of 912 observational hours.

[3] We will here avoid the difficult question of whether the term 'control' is appropriate. There is little question that in English or in American schools, by law and tradition, it is the teacher who has the power to grant decision-making privileges. In the English schools

we observed that the power is real and is used, as evidenced by the many instances in the data where the teacher unilaterally altered the decision-making pattern.

4   Sets of assignment cards from which children may choose are present in almost every classroom. These provide students with options of two sorts: they may provide many alternative forms of the same activity, such as a group of many SRA cards all similar in procedure but differing in the content of the story; or a set of cards may provide many different sorts of activities designed to accomplish a similar goal, such as multiple activities designed to give handwriting practice. The latter sort provides a choice of *how,* the former a very limited choice of *what.*

5   Rathbone, C. (1971) 'The implicit rationale of the open education classroom', in Rathbone, C. (ed.) *Open Education,* Citation Press, New York, pp. 106–7; Barth, R. (1971) 'So you want to change to an open classroom', *Phi Delta Kappan,* October 1971, pp. 97–99.

6   The extent to which teachers believe they can rely on intrinsic motivation has, of course, its counterpart in learning theory, Piaget and Berlyne, e.g. assume natural curiosity, and Skinner and reinforcement theorists assume motivation as the result of a history of reinforcement.

7   A memorable example was a young teacher who was not to be rehired the following year. The head gave precisely this reason: that the teacher failed to provision for the students and spark interest because he believed students would be intrinsically interested and needed no external 'push'.

8   Barth, R. (1971) *op. cit.,* p. 131.

9   While two questions—who sets the standards, and who determines whether for a given area the standards have been met—are logically distinct, in practice the questions are easily confounded. A teacher may intend that a child set his own standards for art; yet, when the child is doing art, the teacher intervenes continually with evaluative statements. From a psychological point of view, the child probably feels that the teacher both sets the standards and determines whether the criteria are being met. It is possible, though unlikely, that the teacher can, as a practical matter, keep these two questions distinct at all times in all areas. The problem of what the standards shall be in a given area, another important source of variation among teachers, will not be examined at this time. Salient concepts here would be whether the standards are qualitative (i.e., is the product 'creative' or 'clear'), quantitative (i.e., how many maths problems should be assigned), temporal (i.e., how long should one work on maths), and absolute vs. relative (i.e., the paper should be neater than the previous paper, or it should approach a given standard of neatness).

10 This includes English writers as well, the Plowden Report no less than the Black Papers: Cox, C.B. and Dyson A.E. (eds) (1971). *The Black Papers on Education,* Davis-Poynter, London.

PART TWO

Teachers as Differentiators

7 Social-class Variations in the Teacher–Pupil Relationship

H. S. BECKER

One of the earliest ethnographic studies of teachers was Howard Becker's celebrated analysis of the careers of Chicago public schoolteachers in the 1950s. In this article, Becker examines how Chicago schoolteachers differentiate their pupils on social class lines according to how far these pupils diverge from the teacher's model of the *ideal pupil*.

The major problems of workers in the service occupations are likely to be a function of their relationship to their clients or customers, those for whom or on whom the occupational service is performed.[1] Members of such occupations typically have some image of the 'ideal' client, and it is in terms of this fiction that they fashion their conceptions of how their work ought to be performed, and their actual work techniques. To the degree that actual clients approximate this ideal the worker will have no 'client problem'.

In a highly differentiated urban society, however, clients will vary greatly, and ordinarily only some fraction of the total of potential clients will be 'good' ones. Workers tend to classify clients in terms of the way in which they vary from this ideal. The fact of client variation from the occupational ideal emphasizes the intimate relation of the institution in which work is carried on to its environing society. If that society does not prepare people to play their client roles in the manner desired by the occupation's members there will be conflicts, and problems for the workers in the performance of their work. One of the major factors affecting the production of suitable clients is the cultural diversity of various social classes in the society. The cultures of particular social-class groups may operate to produce clients who make the worker's position extremely difficult.

We deal here with this problem as it appears in the experience of the functionaries of a large urban educational institution, the Chicago public school system, discussing the way in which teachers in this system observe, classify and react to class-typed differences in the behavior of the children with whom they work. The material to be presented is thus relevant not only to problems of occupational organization but also to the problem of differences in the educational opportunities available to children of various social classes. Warner, Havighurst, and Loeb,[2] and Hollingshead[3] have demonstrated the manner in which the schools tend to favor and select out children of the middle classes. Allison Davis has pointed to those factors in the class cultures involved which make lower-class children less and middle-class children more adaptable to the work and behavioral standards of the school.[4] This paper will contribute to knowledge in this area by analyzing the manner in which the public school teacher reacts to these cultural differences and, in so doing, perpetuates the discrimination of our educational system against the lower-class child.

The analysis is based on sixty interviews with teachers in the Chicago system.[5] The interviews were oriented around the general question of the problems of being a teacher and were not specifically directed toward discovering feelings about social-class differences among students. Since these differences created some of the teachers' most pressing problems they were continually brought up by the interviewees themselves. They typically distinguished three social-class groups with which they, as teachers, came in contact:

1 a bottom stratum, probably equivalent to the lower-lower and parts of the upper-lower class;
2 an upper stratum, probably equivalent to the upper-middle class: and
3 a middle stratum, probably equivalent to the lower-middle and parts of the upper-lower class.

We will adopt the convention of referring to these groups as lower, upper and middle groups, but it should be understood that this terminology refers to the teachers' classification of students and not to the ordinary sociological description.

We will proceed by taking up the three problems that loomed largest in the teachers' discussion of adjustment to their students:

1 the problem of *teaching* itself,
2 the problem of *discipline*, and
3 the problem of the *moral acceptability* of the students.

In each case the variation in the form of and adjustment to the problem by the characteristics of the children of the various class groups distinguished by teachers is discussed. A basic problem in any occupation is that of performing one's given task successfully, and where this involves working with human beings their qualities are a major variable affecting the ease with which the work can be done. The teacher considers that she has done her job adequately when she has brought about an observable change in the children's skills and knowledge which she can attribute to her own efforts:

> Well, I would say that a teacher is successful when she is putting the material across to the children, when she is getting some response from them. I'll tell you something. Teaching is a very rewarding line of work, because you can see those children grow under your hands. You can see the difference in them after you've had them for five months. You can see where they've started and where they've got to. And it's all yours. It really is rewarding in that way, you can see results and know that it's your work that brought those results about.

She feels that she has a better chance of success in this area when her pupils are interested in attending and working hard in school, and are trained at home in such a way that they are bright and quick at school work. Her problems arise in teaching those groups who do not meet these specifications, for in these cases her teaching techniques, tailored to the 'perfect' student, are inadequate to cope with the reality, and she is left with a feeling of having failed in performing her basic task.

Davis has described the orientations towards education in general, and school work in particular, of the lower and middle classes:[6]

> Thus, our educational system, which next to the family is the most effective agency in teaching good work habits to middle class people, is largely ineffective and unrealistic with underprivileged groups. Education fails to motivate such workers because our schools and our society both lack *real rewards* to offer underprivileged groups. Neither lower class children or adults will work hard in school or on the job just to please the teacher or boss. They are not going to learn to be ambitious,

to be conscientious and to study hard, as if school and work were a fine character-building game, which one plays just for the sake of playing. They can see, indeed, that those who work hard at school usually have families that already have the occupations, homes, and social acceptance that the school holds up as the rewards of education. The underprivileged workers can see also that the chances of their getting enough education to make their attainment of these rewards in the future at all probable is very slight. Since they can win the rewards of prestige and social acceptance in their own slum groups without much education, they do not take very seriously the motivation taught by the school.

As these cultural differences produce variations from the image of the 'ideal' student, teachers tend to use class terms in describing the children with whom they work.

Children of the lowest group, from slum areas, are characterized as the most difficult group to teach successfully, lacking in interest in school, learning ability, and outside training:

> They don't have the right kind of study habits. They can't seem to apply themselves as well. Of course, it's not their fault; they aren't brought up right. After all the parents in a neighborhood like that really aren't interested ... But as I say, those children don't learn very quickly. A great many of them don't seem to be really interested in getting an education. I don't think they are. It's hard to get anything done with children like that. They simply don't respond.

In definite contrast are the terms used to describe children of the upper groups:

> In a neighborhood like this there's something about the children, you just feel like you're accomplishing so much more. You throw an idea out and you can see that it takes hold. The children know what you're talking about and they think about it. Then they come in with projects and pictures and additional information, and it just makes you feel good to see it. They go places and see things, and they know what you're talking about. For instance, you might be teaching social studies or geography .... You bring something up and a child says, 'Oh my parents took me to see that in a museum.' You can just do more with material like that.

Ambivalent feelings are aroused by children of the middle group. While motivated to work hard in school they lack the proper out-of-school training:

> Well, they're very nice here, very nice. They're not hard to handle. You see, they're taught respect in the home and they're respectful to the teacher. They want to work and do well .... Of course, they're not too brilliant. You know what I mean. But they are very nice children and very easy to work with.

In short, the differences between groups make it possible for the teacher to feel successful at her job only with the top group; with the other groups she feels in greater or lesser measure, that she has failed.

These differences in ability to do school work, as perceived by teachers, have important consequences. They lead, in the first place, to differences in actual teaching techniques. A young high school teacher contrasted the techniques used in 'slum' schools with those used in 'better' schools:

> At S—, there were a lot of guys who were just waiting till they were sixteen so they could get out of school. L—, everybody—well, a very large percentage, I'll say—was going on to secondary school, to college. That certainly made a difference in their classroom work. You had to teach differently at the different schools. For instance, at S—, if you had demonstrations in chemistry they had to be pretty flashy, lots of noise and smoke, before they'd get interested in it. That wasn't necessary at L—.

Or at S— if you were having electricity or something like that you had to get the static electricity machine out and have them all stand around and hold hands so that they'd all get a little jolt.

Further, the teacher feels that where these differences are recognized by her superiors there will be a corresponding variation in the amount of work she is expected to accomplish. She expects that the amount of work and effort required of her will vary inversely with the social status of her pupils. This teacher compared schools from the extremes of the class range:

So you have to be on your toes and keep up to where you're supposed to be in the course of study. Now, in a school like the D— [slum school] you're just not expected to complete all that work. It's almost impossible. For instance, in the second grade we're supposed to cover nine spelling words a week. Well, I can do that up here at the K— ['better' school], they can take nine new words a week. But the best class I ever had at the D— was only able to achieve six words a week and they had to work pretty hard to get that. So I never finished the year's work in spelling. I couldn't. And I really wasn't expected to.

One resultant of this situation—in which less is expected of those teachers whose students are more difficult to teach—is that the problem becomes more aggravated in each grade, as the gap between what the children should know and what they actually do know becomes wider and wider. A principal of such a school describes the degeneration there of the teaching problem into a struggle to get a few basic skills across, in a situation where this cumulative effect makes following the normal program of study impossible:

The children come into our upper grades with very poor reading ability. That means that all the way through our school everybody is concentrating on reading. It's not like at a school like S— [middle group] where they have science and history and so on. At a school like that they figure that from first to fourth you learn to read and from fifth to eighth you read to learn. You use your reading to learn other material. Well, the children don't reach that second stage when they're with us. We have to plug along getting them to learn to read. Our teachers are pretty well satisfied if the children can read and do simple number work when they leave here. You'll find that they don't think very much of subjects like science, and so on. They haven't got any time for that. They're just trying to get these basic things over ... That's why our school is different from one like S—.

Such consequences of teachers' differential reaction to various class groups obviously operate to further perpetuate those class-cultural characteristics to which they object in the first place.

Discipline is the second of the teacher's major problems with her students. Willard Waller pointed to its basis when he wrote: 'Teacher and pupil confront each other in the school with an original conflict of desires, and however much that conflict may be reduced in amount, or however much it may be hidden, it still remains.'[7] We must recognize that conflict, either actual or potential, is ever present in the teacher–pupil relationship, the teacher attempting to maintain her control against the children's efforts to break it.[8] This conflict is felt even with those children who present least difficulty; a teacher who considered her pupils models of good behavior nevertheless said:

But there's that tension all the time. Between you and the students. It's hard on your nerves. Teaching is fun, if you enjoy your subject, but it's the discipline that keeps your nerves on edge, you know what I mean? There's always that tension.

Sometimes people say, 'Oh, you teach school. That's an easy job, just sitting around all day long.' They don't know what it's really like. It's hard on your nerves.

The teacher is tense because she fears that she will lose control, which she tends to define in terms of some line beyond which she will not allow the children to go. Wherever she may draw this line (and there is considerable variation), the teacher feels that she has a 'discipline' problem when the children attempt to push beyond it. The form and intensity of this problem are felt to vary from one social-class group to another, as might be expected from Davis's description of class emphases on aggression:[9]

> In general, middle-class aggression is taught to adolescents in the form of social and economic skills which will enable them to compete effectively at that level .... In lower-class families, physical aggression is as much a normal, social approved and socially inculcated type of behavior as it is in frontier communities.

The differences in child training are matched by variation in the teachers' reactions.

Children in 'slum' schools are considered most difficult to control, being given to unrestrained behavior and physical violence. The interviews are filled with descriptions of such difficulties. Miriam Wagenschein, in a parallel study of the beginning school teacher, gave this summary of the experiences of these younger teachers in lower-class schools:[10]

> The reports which these teachers give of what *can be* done by a group of children are nothing short of amazing. A young white teacher walked into her new classroom and was greeted with the comment, 'Another damn white one.' Another was 'rushed' at her desk by the entire class when she tried to be extremely strict with them. Teachers report having been bitten, tripped, and pushed on the stairs. Another gave an account of a second grader throwing a milk bottle at the teacher and of a first grader having such a temper tantrum that it took the principal and two policemen to get him out of the room. In another school, following a fight on the playground, the principal took thirty-two razor blades from children in a first grade room. Some teachers indicated fear that they might be attacked by irate persons in the neighborhoods in which they teach. Other teachers report that their pupils carry long pieces of glass and have been known to threaten other pupils with them, while others jab each other with hypodermic needles. One boy got angry with his teacher and knocked in the fender of her car.

In these schools a major part of the teacher's time must be devoted to discipline; as one said: 'It's just a question of keeping them in line.' This emphasis on discipline detracts from the school's primary function of teaching, thus discriminating, in terms of available educational opportunity, against the children of these schools.

Children of the middle group are thought of as docile, and with them the teacher has least difficulty with discipline.

> Those children were much quieter, easier to work with. When we'd play our little games there was never any commotion. That was a very nice school to work in. Everything was quite nice about it. The children were easy to work with ...

Children of the upper group are felt hard to handle in some respects, and are often termed 'spoiled', 'over-indulged' or 'neurotic'; they do not play the role of the child in the submissive manner teachers consider appropriate. One interviewee, speaking of this group, said:

> I think most teachers prefer not to teach in that type of school. The children are more pampered and, as we say, more inclined to run the school for themselves. The parents are very much at fault. The children are not used to taking orders at home and naturally they won't take them at school either.

Teachers develop methods of dealing with these discipline problems, and these tend to vary between social-class groups as do the problems themselves. The basic device used by successful disciplinarians is to establish authority clearly on the first meeting with the class:

> You can't ever let them get the upper hand on you or you're through. So I start out tough. The first day I get a new class in, I let them know who's boss.... You've got to start off tough, then you can ease up as you go along. If you start out easy-going, when you try to get tough they'll just look at you and laugh.

Having once established such a relation, it is considered important that the teacher be consistent in her behavior so that the children will continue to respect and obey her:

> I let them know I mean business. That's one thing you must do. Say nothing that you won't follow through on. Some teachers will say anything to keep kids quiet, they'll threaten anything. Then they can't or won't carry out their threats. Naturally, the children won't pay any attention to them after that. You must never say anything that you won't back up.

In the difficult 'slum' schools, teachers feel the necessity of using stern measures, up to and including physical violence (nominally outlawed):

> Technically you're not supposed to lay a hand on a kid. Well, they don't, technically. But there are a lot of ways of handling a kid so that it doesn't show— and then it's the teacher's word against the kid's, so the kid hasn't got a chance. Like dear Mrs—. She gets mad at a kid, she takes him out in the hall. She gets him stood up against the wall. Then she's got a way of chucking the kid under the chin, only hard, so that it knocks his head back against the wall. It doesn't leave a mark on him. But when he comes back in that room he can hardly see straight, he's so knocked out. It's really rough. There's a lot of little tricks like that that you learn about.

Where such devices are not used, there is recourse to violent punishment, 'tongue lashings'. All teachers, however, are not emotionally equipped for such behavior and must find other means:

> The worst thing I can do is lose my temper and start raving.... You've got to believe in that kind of thing in order for it to work.... If you don't honestly believe it, it shows up and the children know you don't mean it and it doesn't do any good anyway.... I try a different approach myself. Whenever they get too rowdy I go to the piano and ... play something and we have rhythms or something until they sort of settle down.... That's what we call 'softsoaping' them. It seems to work for me. It's about the only thing I can do.

Some teachers may also resort to calling in the parents, a device whose usefulness is limited by the fact that such summonses are most frequently ignored. The teacher's disciplinary power in such a school is also limited by her fear of retaliation by the students: 'Those fellows are pretty big, and I just think it would take a bigger person than me to handle them. I certainly wouldn't like to try.'

In the school with children of the middle group no strong sanctions are required, mild reprimands sufficing:

> Now the children at Z—here are quite nice to teach. They're pliable, yes, that's the word, they're pliable. They will go along with you on things and not fight you. You can take them any place and say to them, 'I'm counting on you not to disgrace your school. Let's see that Z—spirit'. And they'll behave for you .... They can be frightened, they have fear in them. They're pliable, flexible, you can do things with them. They're afraid of their parents and what they'll do to them if they get into trouble at school. And they're afraid of the administration. They're afraid of being sent down to the principal. So that they can be handled.

Children of the upper group often act in a way which may be interpreted as 'misbehavior' but which does not represent a conscious attack on the teacher's authority. Many teachers are able to disregard such activity by interpreting it as a natural concomitant of the 'brightness' and 'intelligence' of such children. Where such an interpretation is not possible the teachers feel hampered by a lack of effective sanctions:

> I try different things like keeping them out of a gym period or a recess period. But that doesn't always work. I have this one little boy who just didn't care when I used those punishments. He said he didn't like gym anyway. I don't know what I'm going to do with him.

The teacher's power in such schools is further limited by the fact that the children are able to mobilize their influential parents so as to exert a large degree of control over the actions of school personnel.

It should be noted, finally, that discipline problems tend to become less important as the length of the teacher's stay in a particular school makes it possible for her to build a reputation which coerces the children into behaving without attempting any test of strength:[11]

> I have no trouble with the children. Once you establish a reputation and they know what to expect, they respect you and you have no trouble. Of course, that's different for a new teacher, but when you're established that's no problem at all.

The third area of problems has been termed that of *moral acceptability* and arises from the fact that some actions of one's potential clients may be offensive in terms of some deeply felt set of moral standards; these clients are thus morally unacceptable. Teachers find that some of their pupils act in such a way as to make themselves unacceptable in terms of the moral values centered on health and cleanliness, sex and aggression, ambition and work, and the relations of age groups.

Children of the middle group present no problem at this level, being universally described as clean, well dressed, moderate in their behavior, and hard working. Children from the 'better' neighborhoods are considered deficient in the important moral traits of politeness and respect for elders:

> Here the children come from wealthy homes. That's not so good either. They're not used to doing work at home. They have maids and servants of all kinds and they're used to having things done for them, instead of doing them themselves. ... They won't do anything. For instance, if they drop a piece of cloth on the floor, they'll just let it lay, they wouldn't think of bending over to pick it up. That's janitor's work to them. As a matter of fact, one of them said to me once: 'If I pick

that up there wouldn't be any work for the janitor to do.' Well it's pretty difficult to deal with children like that.

Further, they are regarded as likely to transgress what the teachers define as moral boundaries in the matter of smoking and drinking; it is particularly shocking that such 'nice' children should have such vices.

It is, however, the 'slum' child who most deeply offends the teacher's moral sensibilities; in almost every area mentioned above these children, by word, action, or appearance, manage to give teachers the feeling that they are immoral and not respectable. In terms of physical appearance and condition they disgust and depress the middle-class teacher. Even this young woman, whose emancipation from conventional morality is symbolized in her habitual use of the argot of the jazz musician, was horrified by the absence of the toothbrush from the lives of her lower-class students:

> It's just horribly depressing, you know. I mean, it just get you down. I'll give you an example. A kid complained of a toothache one day. Well, I thought I could take a look and see if I could help him or something so I told him to open his mouth. I almost wigged when I saw his mouth. His teeth were all rotten, every one of them. Just filthy and rotten. Man, I mean, I was really shocked, you know. I said, 'Don't you have a toothbrush?' He said no, they were only his baby teeth and Ma said he didn't need a toothbrush for that. So I really got upset and looked in all their mouths. Man, I never saw anything like it. They were all like that, practically. I asked how many had toothbrushes, and about a quarter of them had them. Boy, that's terrible. And I don't dig that crap about baby teeth either, because they start getting molars when they're six, I know that. So I gave them a talking to, but what good does it do? The kid's mouth was just rotten. They never heard of a toothbrush or going to a dentist.

These children, too, are more apt than the other groups to be dishonest in some way that will get them into trouble with law enforcement officials. The early (by middle-class standards) sexual maturity of such children is quite upsetting to the teacher:

> One thing about these girls is, well, some of them are not very nice girls. One girl in my class I've had two years now. She makes her money on the side as a prostitute. She's had several children . . . . This was a disturbing influence on the rest of the class.

Many teachers reported great shock on finding that words which were innocent to them had obscene meanings for their lower-class students:[12]

> I decided to read them a story one day. I started reading them 'Puss in Boots' and they just burst out laughing. I couldn't understand what I had said that had made them burst out like that. I went back over the story and tried to find out what it might be. I couldn't see anything that would make them laugh. I couldn't see anything at all in the story. Later one of the other teachers asked me what had happened. She was one of the older teachers. I told her that I didn't know; that I was just reading them a story and they thought it was extremely funny. She asked me what story I read them and I told her 'Puss in Boots.' She said, 'Oh, I should have warned you not to read that one.' It seems that Puss means something else to them. It means something awful—I wouldn't even tell you what. It doesn't mean a thing to us.

Warner, Havighurst, and Loeb note that 'unless the middle-class values change in America, we must expect the influence of the schools to favor the values of material success, individual striving, thrift, and social mobility.'[13] Here again, the 'slum' child violates the teacher's moral sense by failing to display these virtues:

> Many of these children don't realize the worth of an education. They have no
> desire to improve themselves. And they don't care much about school and
> schoolwork as a result. That makes it very difficult to teach them.
>   That kind of problem is particularly bad in a school like —. That's not a very
> privileged school. It's very under-privileged, as a matter of fact. So we have a
> pretty tough element there, a bunch of bums, I might as well say it. That kind you
> can't teach at all. They don't want to be there at all, and so you can't do anything
> with them. And even many of the others—they're simply indifferent to the
> advantages of education. So they're indifferent, they don't care about their
> homework.

This behavior of the lower-class child is all the more repellent to the teacher
because she finds it incomprehensible; she cannot conceive that any normal human
being would act in such a way. This teacher stresses the anxiety aroused in the
inexperienced teacher by her inability to provide herself with a rational explanation
for her pupils' behavior:

> We had one of the girls who just came to the school last year and she used to come
> and talk to me quite a bit. I know that it was just terrible for her. You know, I don't
> think she'd ever had anything to do with Negroes before she got there and she was
> just mystified, didn't know what to do. She was bewildered. She came to me one
> day almost in tears and said, 'But they don't want to learn, they don't even want
> to learn. Why is that?' Well, she had me there.

It is worth noting that the behavior of the 'better' children, even when morally
unacceptable, is less distressing to the teacher, who feels that, in this case, she can
produce a reasonable explanation for the behavior. An example of such an
explanation is the following:

> I mean, they're spoiled, you know. A great many of them are only children.
> Naturally, they're used to having their own way, and they don't like to be told
> what to do. Well, if a child is in a room that I'm teaching he's going to be told what
> to do, that's all there is to it. Or if they're not spoiled that way, they're the second
> child and they never got the affection the first one did, not that their mother didn't
> love them, but they didn't get as much affection, so they're not so easy to handle
> either.

We have shown that school teachers experience problems in working with
their students to the degree that those students fail to exhibit in reality the qualities
of the image of the ideal pupil which teachers hold. In a stratified urban society
there are many groups whose life-style and culture produce children who do not
meet the standards of this image, and who are thus impossible for teachers like
these to work with effectively. Programs of action intended to increase the
educational opportunities of the under-privileged in our society should take
account of the manner in which teachers interpret and react to the cultural traits
of this group, and the institutional consequences of their behavior.[14] Such
programs might profitably aim at producing teachers who can cope effectively with
the problems of teaching this group and not, by their reactions to class differences,
perpetuate the existing inequities.

A more general statement of the findings is now in order. Professionals depend
on their environing society to provide them with clients who meet the standards
of their image of the ideal client. Social class cultures, among other factors, may
operate to produce many clients who, in one way or another, fail to meet these

specifications and therefore aggravate one or another of the basic problems of the worker-client relation (three were considered in this paper).

In attacking this problem we touch on one of the basic elements of the relation between institutions and society, for the differences between ideal and reality place in high relief the implicit assumptions which institutions, through their functionaries, make about the society around them. All institutions, have embedded in them some set of assumptions about the nature of the society and the individuals with whom they deal, and we must get at these assumptions, and their embodiment in actual social interaction, in order fully to understand these organizations. We can, perhaps, best begin our work on this problem by studying those institutions which, like the school, make assumptions which have high visibility because of their variation from reality.

Notes

[1] See Becker, H.S. (1951) 'The professional dance musician and his audience', *American Journal of Sociology* Vol. 57, pp. 136–44, for further discussion of this point.

[2] Warner, W.L., Havighurst, R.J. and Loeb, M.B. (1944) *Who Shall be Educated?* Harper, New York.

[3] Hollingshead, A. de B. (1949) *Elmtown's Youth; The Impact of Social Class on Adolescents* John Wiley, New York.

[4] Davis, A. (1950) *Social-Class Influences upon Learning* Harvard University Press, Cambridge, Mass.

[5] The entire research has been reported in Becker, H.S. (1951) 'Role and career problems of the Chicago public school teacher', doctoral dissertation, University of Chicago.

[6] Davis, A. (1947) 'The motivation of the underprivileged worker', in William F. Whyte (ed.), *Industry and Society* McGraw-Hill, New York, p. 99.

[7] Waller, W. (1965) *Sociology of Teaching* John Wiley, New York, p. 197.

[8] Although all service occupations tend to have such problems of control over their clients, the problem is undoubtedly aggravated in situations like the school where those upon whom the service is being performed are not there of their own volition, but rather because of the wishes of some other group (the parents, in this case).

[9] Davis, A. (1950) *op. cit.*, pp. 34–35.

[10] Wagenschein, M. (1950) 'Reality shock,' master's thesis, University of Chicago, pp. 58–59.

[11] This is part of the process of job adjustment described in detail in Becker, H.S. (1952) 'The career of the Chicago public school teacher', *American Journal of Sociology* Vol. 57.

[12] Interview by Miriam Wagenschein. The lack of common meanings in this situation symbolizes the great cultural and moral distance between teacher and 'slum' child.

[13] Warner, W.L., Havighurst, R.J. and Loeb, M.B (1944) *op. cit.*, p. 172.

[14] One of the important institutional consequences of these class preferences is a constant movement of teachers away from lower-class schools, which prevents these schools from retaining experienced teachers and from maintaining some continuity in teaching and administration.

8   Classroom Knowledge

KEDDIE, N.

The following article is from a study of humanities teaching in a London comprehensive school. The curriculum programme was supposed to meet the needs of pupils of all abilities, but Nell Keddie argues that though teachers espoused these principles outside the classroom, in practice within it they still differentiated their pupils according to their stereotyped conception of them. They then offered these groups different kinds of curricular knowledge. Thus, Keddie argues that, despite the rhetoric of equality, teachers still differentiate their pupils along social class lines even within comprehensive schools.

One consequence of the particular normative orientation of much sociology of education has been its definition of educational failure: explanations of educational failure are most often given in terms of pupils' ethnic and social class antecedents[1] and rely on a concept of social pathology rather than one of cultural diversity. (Baratz and Baratz, 1970) It is only recently that attention has been given to the defining processes occurring within the school itself (Cicourel and Kitsuse, 1963; Dumont and Wax, 1969; Wax and Wax, 1964) and to the social organization of curriculum knowledge. (Bernstein, 1971; Young, 1971) The studies suggest that the processes by which pupils are categorized are not self-evident and point to an overlooked consequence of a differentiated curriculum: that it is part of the process by which educational deviants are created and their deviant identities maintained.[2] Here I hope to raise questions about these processes by considering two aspects of classroom knowledge: what knowledge teachers have of pupils, and what counts as knowledge to be made available and evaluated in the classroom. This involves casting as problematic what are held to be knowledge and ability in schools rather than taking either as given.

The empirical data on which this account is based (Keddie, 1970) were collected by observation, tape recording and questionnaire in a large mixed comprehensive school with a fairly heterogeneous social class intake, although in the school, as in its catchment area, social class III is over-represented. Pupils from social classes I and II tend to be placed in A streams and those from soical classes IV and V in C streams.[3] The study is focused on the humanities department which in 1969/70 introduced an examination course based on history, geography and social science to fourth-year pupils. The course was constructed to be taught as an undifferentiated programme across the ability range, and to be examined by mode 3 at ordinary level and C.S.E. at the end of the fifth year.[4] The course is described as 'enquiry based' and is taught by 'key lessons' to introduce a topic, and a workcard system to allow children to work individually and at their own speed. In the fifth year the work is often organized around topics; in the fourth year it is generally organized in 'blocks' of different subjects. This study is concerned with the first social science block which has socialization as its theme and follows directly after a geographical study of regions of Britain. Both were taught from material prepared by the department's teachers (in this case sociologists, a psychologist, an economist and geographers), so that each class keeps the same teacher for both geographical and social science studies.

The school is probably atypical of secondary schools in this country in its high degree of institutionalized innovation (every subject is now examined by mode 3 at C.S.E.) and therefore if the data has any claim to generality it must be because the school stands as a critical case and illustrates the fate of innovatory ideals in practice. Throughout this account references to teachers and pupils are specifically references to teachers and pupils of this one school.

A central issue for teachers in the school is whether or not the school should unstream. Bourdieu[9] points out that conflict indicates consensus about which issues are deemed worthy of conflict. In this debate consensus that is not articulated is the most interesting because it is not questioned and includes, as I shall show, evaluations of what constitutes knowledge and ability and thus evaluations of what pupils are and ought to be like in critical respects. In the fourth year pupils are divided into three broad bands, A, B and C, and some departments stream rigidly within these bands. The humanities department divides pupils into parallel groups within each band and looks forward to teaching completely mixed ability groups.

In casting as problematic what counts as knowledge and ability, I begin with what teachers themselves find problematic: the teaching of C stream pupils. C stream pupils present teachers with problems both of social control and in the preparation and presentation of teaching material. By their characterization of C stream pupils as 'that type of child' and 'these children', teachers tell that they feel that C stream pupils are unlike themselves. By inference, teachers feel that A stream pupils are more like themselves, at least in ways that count in school. Teaching A stream pupils seems to be relatively unproblematic for teachers: they take the activities in these classrooms for granted, they rarely make explicit the criteria which guide the preparation and presentation of teaching material for these pupils, and what counts as knowledge is left implicit, and, apparently, consensual. [. . .] The assumption underlying my interpretation of data is that C stream pupils disrupt teachers' expectations and violate their norms of appropriate social, moral and intellectual pupil behaviour. In so far as C stream pupils' behaviour is explicitly seen by teachers as inappropriate or inadequate, it makes more visible or available what is held to be appropriate pupil behaviour because it provokes questions about the norms which govern teachers' expectations about appropriate pupil behaviour.

The Ideal Pupil

Becker (1952) developed the concept of the *ideal pupil* to refer to that set of teacher expectations which constitute a taken for granted notion of appropriate pupil behaviour. In examining discrepancies between what I shall call *educationist* and *teacher* contexts I shall argue that it is in the likeness of the images of the ideal pupil from one context to the other that the relation and the disjunction between the views expressed by teachers in these contexts is explained.

The fundamental discrepancy between the views of teachers as they emerge in these contexts can be expressed as that between theory and practice, or what Selznick (1949, p. 70) calls doctrine and commitment:[5]

> Doctrine, being abstract, is judiciously selective and may be qualified at will in discourse, subject only to restrictions of sense and logic. But action is concrete, generating consequences which define a sphere of interest and responsibility together with a corresponding chain of commitments. Fundamentally, the discrepancy between doctrine and commitment arises from the essential distinction between the interrelation of ideas and the interrelation of phenomena.

This is a distinction between 'words' and 'deeds' (Deutscher, 1966) and it is necessary to remember that words like deeds are situated in the ongoing inter-action in which they arise. 'Doctrine' as the ideology and theory of the humanities department is enunciated in the educationist context, which may also be called the context of *discussion* of school politics, in particular discussion which evokes inter-departmental conflicts, especially those about streaming. (The actual context of school politics, for example, heads of departments' meetings, may provoke something else again.) The other aspect of the educationist context is the discus-sion of educational theory, and here talk of the department's policy often evokes statements about its alignment with or opposition to other humanities programmes[6] constructed by other course makers. The educationist context may be called into being by the presence of an outsider to whom explanations of the department's activities must be given or by a forthcoming school meeting which necessitates discussion of policy of how things *ought* to be in school.

By contrast, the teacher context is that in which teachers move most of the time. It is the world of *is* in which teachers anticipate interaction with pupils in planning lessons, in which they act in the classroom and in which when the lesson is over they usually recount or explain what has happened. I shall elaborate on the characteristics of both contexts to suggest their relation to each other and the implications for the possible fate of educational innovation in schools.

The Educationist Context

The educational policy of the course and of the department draws selectively and consciously on education theory and research, and is seen by at least some of the department as an informed and expert view of education, as opposed to the lay and commonsense views advanced by other departments. The 'pure' educational policy of the department seems to contain the following as its components:

1. Intelligence is not primarily determined by heredity. Differential educational performance may be accounted for by differential motivation rather than differential intelligence. Ability is to be accounted for as much by motivation as by intelligence and is largely determined by the child's social class antecedents.
2. Streaming by ability weights the school environment against those whose family background has already lessened their chances of educational achievement, because it 'fixes' the expectations that both teachers and pupil have of a pupil's performance and is thereby likely to lower the motivation of pupils with low achievement-orientation who have been assigned to low streams.
3. The criteria by which pupils are allocated to streams or sets when they enter the school (the mathematics department, for example, are said to use verbal I. Q. scores) have been discredited by both psychologists and sociologists; but their lack of reliability is not understood by those who use them.
4. Streaming perpetuates the distinction between grammar and secondary modern school under one roof, and creates or maintains social divisiveness, since like the grammar school it favours middle-class children.
5. A differentiated curriculum divides pupils. The school should try to unite them.

Those in the school who favour streaming oppose the views given above on the grounds that the individual child is best helped by being placed in a stream with those like himself so that he can receive teaching appropriate to his pace and level.

I have insufficient data about the extent to which teachers in the humanities department hold this educational policy in its 'pure' form. Probably most select out of it aspects of it that are most relevant to them. [...] The main point, however, is that those teachers who will advance the educationist view in the discussion of school and educational policy will speak and act in ways that are discrepant with this view when the context is that of the *teacher*. While, therefore, some educational aims may be formulated by teachers as *educationists*, it will not be surprising if 'doctrine' is contradicted by 'commitments' which arise in the situation in which they must act as *teachers*. [...]

[...] The course is set up with intentions of developing in pupils modes of work and thought which will help them to become more autonomous and rational beings. That is, it is set up in the hope that the conception of enquiry-based work will help to create the ideal pupil. I select three main aspects of the course to show how it also in fact caters for a pupil who already exists: the A stream academic and usually middle-class pupil. Thus the course embodies not only an image of what the ideal pupil ought to be, but also what he already is. These three aspects are:

1. Working at your own speed'—this notion is very firmly embedded in the ideology of the course and it is significant that a teacher I heard 'selling' the course to pupils described it as 'self-regulating work which allows you to get ahead'. The corollary of this is that others fall behind, at least in relation to the pace of the course. Teachers were constantly urging pupils: 'You must finish that this week because next week we're going on to a new topic.' Teachers frequently remarked how much more quickly A pupils work than C pupils, and A pupils generally expressed approval of the notion of 'working at your own speed'—it is *their* speed. It would seem inevitable that the principle of individual speeds should be incompatible with a course that moves in a structured way from topic to topic. The only leeway is for some pupils to work through more workcards than others.

2. All the studies on achievement orientation stress the middle-class child tendency to thrive on an individualistic and competitive approach to learning. It follows that a workcard system which puts a premium on the individual working by himself rather than in a group, is probably set up in advance for the success of some pupils rather than others because they already value that kind of autonomy. [...].

3. Teachers express regret that a problem in motivating C stream pupils is their tendency to see education in vocational terms. It was never made explicit (if realized at all by some teachers) that the educational aims of a course like this one also fulfil the vocational purposes of the more successful pupils. A stream pupils have been told, and they told me, that learning to work independently (of teacher and textbook) will help them 'in the sixth form and at university'. I also heard a teacher telling a B group that 'any worker who can think for himself is worth his weight in gold to his employer'. It is likely that lower stream pupils know this to be a highly questionable statement and do not look forward to this kind of satisfaction from their work. Thus while teachers do not, on the whole, perceive higher education as vocational, C stream pupils do not find the vocational rationale of the course commensurate with their expectations of what work will be like.

Both (1) and (2) suggest that the short-term aims of the course, where it impinges immediately on the pupils' work situation, are weighted in favour of A stream pupils, giving priority to skills and attitudes they are most likely to possess. In its long-term aims the same pattern emerges. It seems likely that an undifferentiated course will be set up with an image of the pupil in mind. Because in the educationist context the perspective is one of how things *ought* to be, it is not so obvious to teachers that they are drawing, albeit selectively, on what already *is*. As I shall show, in the teacher context teachers organize their activities around values which as educationists they may deny. These values arise from the conjunction of social class and ability in the judgements teachers make on pupils. It is by exploring what is judged to be appropriate behaviour that it becomes clear how ability and social class which are held separate in the educationist context are confounded in the teacher context.

The Teacher Context

Normal Pupils

In this context what a teacher 'knows' about pupils derives from the organizational device of banding or streaming, which in turn derives from the dominant organizing category of what counts as ability. The 'normal' characteristics [. . .] of a pupil are those which are imputed to his band or stream as a whole. A pupil who is perceived as atypical is perceived in relation to the norm for the stream: 'She's bright for a B' (teacher H); or in relation to the norm for another group: 'They're as good as Bs' (teacher J of three hardworking pupils in his C stream group). This knowledge of what pupils are like is often at odds with the image of pupils the same teachers may hold as educationists, since it derives from streaming whose validity the educationist denies.

Although teachers in the humanities department might express disagreement with other teachers over teaching methods, evaluations of pupils and so on, there seems, in the teacher context, to be almost complete consensus about what normal pupils are like. It is probable, given the basis of categorization, that members of the department are, in terms of 'what everyone knows' about pupils, much closer to other teachers in the school than they themselves commonly imply. [. . .] It is possible to disagree about an individual pupil and to couch the disagreement in terms of his typical or atypical 'B-ness', but in the teacher context it would be disruptive of interaction and of action-to-be-taken to question that 'B-ness' exists. Like the concept of ability from which it derives it is unexamined in the teacher context since it belongs to the shared understandings that make interaction possible. [. . .]

[. . .] The imputation of normal attributes to pupils by teachers does not tell us objectively about pupils. Rather it is the case that in certain areas of school life teachers and different groups of pupils maintain conflicting definitions of the situation. For the teacher, social control may depend on his being able in the classroom to maintain publicly his definition of the situation. He may do this by attempting to render pupil definitions invalid. Thus he may treat pupils' complaints about the course with scepticism and subsume them under normal categories like: 'he's trying to get out of work', 'it's just a bit of "agro"', 'they'll try anything on'. These explanations may or may not coincide with pupils' explanations of their motives. The general effect of teachers' explanations is to recognize the situation as conflictual, but to render invalid the particular point the pupil is making and thus to delineate the extent of pupils' rights. Equal rights are not granted to all pupils since the 'same' behaviour may have different meanings attributed to it, depending on the normal status of the pupil. In one C stream lesson a pupil asked the teacher:

Pupil: This is geography, isn't it? Why don't we learn about where countries are and that?
Teacher: This is socialization.
Pupil: What's that? I'd rather do geography. . . . Netsilik Eskimo—I don't know where that is.

Teacher   [ironically:] After the lesson we'll go and get the atlas and I'll show you. (Teacher D)

A few days earlier I had asked this teacher whether any pupil had asked in class (as they had in some other classes): 'Why should we do social science?' and had had the reply:

Teacher: No, but if I were asked by Cs I would try to sidestep it because it would be the same question as 'Why do anything? Why work?'
Observer: What if you were asked by an A group?
Teacher: Then I'd probably try to answer.

For me, as observer, learning how to recognize normal pupils was an important aspect of my socialization as observer from the teachers' point of view. Teachers took some care that I should understand what pupils were like, especially C pupils. In my first days in the school they frequently prepared me for what I should expect when I attended their lesson, and they afterwards explained to me why the lesson had gone as it had. These explanations tended to take the form: 'C stream pupils are . . .' or 'low ability pupils are . . .' This aspect of 'learning the ropes' (Geer *et al.*, 1968) is presumably an important element in the socialization of student and probationary teachers.

The 'normalization' of pupils tends to produce a polarity between A and C pupils in which they reflect reversed images of each other. The B stream pupil is left in the middle and tends to shift around in the typology. Generally when special workcards are prepared it is for C groups and it is assumed that Bs will follow the same work as A pupils. On the other hand, teachers often see B pupils as posing the same social control problems as C streams. One teacher saw this as the *result* of their undefined status and characterized B stream pupils as suffering from identity problems. His characterization could as well refer to teachers' problems in being unable to define clearly the normal B pupil, as to the perspective of the pupils themselves, who may have quite clear notions of their own position and status, though they are liable to be defined out by the teachers. Similarly A pupils who present discipline problems to teachers are likely to be described as pupils who 'are really Bs'. This characterization is not necessarily applied to those A pupils who will probably be entered for C.S.E. and not 'O' level in the humanities examinations and might therefore be seen as right for a B stream. This is in keeping with the tendency not only for normative judgements to predominate—teachers speak more about the 'moral' and 'social' qualities of pupils than of their cognitive skills—but for the former qualities to be presented as though they were cognitive skills:

Teacher K: If you want, you can go on to the Depression later in the term. There's also material on America in the twenties.
Teacher B: Isn't it true to say that although it's C material in a sense, the level of response depends on the level of intelligence. For example, some of the moral problems you pose—it would take an A child really to see the implications. Some of the girls would find it interesting.
Teacher K: Yes, it could be used at all levels.   (At a staff meeting)

Ability and Social Class
Most children enter secondary schools with their educational identities partially established in the records, and by the fourth year the question is rather how these identities are maintained than how they were established. Teachers appear to have two principal organizing categories: ability and social class. Social class, however,

tends to be a latent and implicit category for sorting pupil behaviour. On occasion though, some teachers appear to use social class as an explanation of educational performance:

Teacher B of a group of boys he described as 'working class who belong to a B group':

> 'they don't work but they came up high in a test which tested their grasp of concepts'.

On another occasion he spoke of the same boys as

> 'really from a higher stream—able but they don't work'.

Teacher H distinguished between the performance of two 'bright' girls in his A stream class:

> 'one is the daughter of a primary school headmaster; a home with books and lots of encouragement ... [the other one] comes from quite a different kind of home which doesn't encourage homework ...'

He felt that the latter had potential ability she was not using to the full.

Another teacher (L) characterized a girl whom he thought 'works only for grades' as a 'trade unionist'.

Teacher J had a threefold typology of his C stream class (which he told me before I observed his class for the first time) in which he linked certain kinds of psychological disturbance with a working-class culture. It is possible to identify two types of pupil in what follows: the remedial child and the pathologically disturbed child:

> *Teacher:*   The difficulties with the least able child are those of remedial children: children who don't work in normally accepted ways in school—with these children I'm not succeeding, humanities aren't succeeding. The Cs who fail can't meet [the head of department's] criteria [of autonomous work]. They need to be in a group with only a few teachers. .... Many have working-class parents—Jane's got problems. Her father's a not-very-bright milkman and her mother ran away. Lots of difficult children have disturbed backgrounds and this is often more important than innate abilities.
> *Observer:* What do you mean by disturbed?
> *Teacher:*   Fathers who beat mothers, nervous breakdowns in the family, that sort of thing.

He speaks of 'that kind of child' and says they 'fluctuate in behaviour' ... 'Jane has little idea of how to behave generally ... [but Susan] is a big mouthing fishwife who can, on occasion, work solidly and be pleasant.'

The third type of child was identified only after the lesson: the quiet child who works fairly hard through most lessons. In terms of social control this pupil is not a problem and this is why the casual listener-in to teachers' talk might get the impression that all C stream pupils are constant problems for teachers.

After the lesson this teacher, like others, wondered if he were too lenient with the problem pupils; he said of Jane 'Perhaps she gets away with too much ... [but] she can't concentrate and needs the teacher all the time.' The key phrase in his general description is probably the reference to 'children who don't work in normally accepted ways in school'. These pupils' behaviour can be seen as generally inappropriate. Like the concept of the disadvantaged child the reference contains a notion of 'under-socialization' and instability originating in the social disorganization (Cohen, 1959) of the 'background' of the pupil. The dominant notion here seems akin to some social psychological accounts of delinquency (Deutsch, 1963) which specify a multiplicity of factors like a 'bad' home as a cause of deviance without making it clear what a bad home is, how it causes deviance or why other homes, which should on the same criteria be 'bad', do not produce delinquents. Because the social pathology approach allows explanations of pupil behaviour to be made in terms of discrete factors, teachers tend not to perceive the collective social class basis of pupils' experience but to fragment that experience into the problems of individual (and 'disadvantaged') pupils. This makes it likely that the pupils' collective definition of the educational situation will be rendered invisible to teachers,[7] and failure individualized.

This teacher's (J) normal C pupil is probably cast in a more explicit model of psychological disturbance than many, but this does not affect the essential outline of the image, in which instability plays a large part and is frequently linked with aggression. [. . .] This teacher, like most of the teachers in the department, expects his C pupils to behave differently in class from his A pupils: for example, he expects and allows them to make more noise and to achieve a great deal less work than A pupils. [. . .]

[. . .] Another normal characteristic of C pupils is their immaturity.[8] Thus after showing a film called *The First Fifteen Minutes of Life* to groups of pupils, the noise made by B and C groups was described as 'covering up embarrassment' and as 'the back row of the cinema', indicating the pupils' response had been characterized as contextually inappropriate. A pupils who were much more silent (but were also hushed quite systematically) were characterized as more 'mature' in their response, although the comments of a girl to her friends: 'they shouldn't show films like that to fifteen year olds', suggested that some of these pupils, at least, found the film difficult to accept. It may have been relevant to the C pupils' response that they were quite unable to see a rationale for the showing of the film since the label 'socialization' had no explanatory significance for them. Many defined the film as 'biology' and said 'we've done it before'.

Clearly, A stream pupils' definition of appropriate behaviour in the situation was taken over from or coincided with that of the teachers. It is already clear that teachers are most concerned with what they perceive as the negative characteristics of C pupils' behaviour and that this is to some extent linked with expectations of appropriate behaviour that have a social class basis and differentiation. C stream pupils are often seen to lack those qualities which are deemed by teachers desirable in themselves and appropriate to school,[9] whereas A stream pupils appear to posses these qualities. The negative aspects of the normal C pupil emerge whenever a teacher compares C and A pupils:

'It's amazing how much quicker As are than Cs. The As have almost caught Cs now.' (Teacher D)

'I did it slightly differently with the As because they're rushed for time. With the As I used the pink card more, but I still put diagrams on the board. But it was still quicker.' (Teacher J)

'I meant to find out [what "ulu" an Eskimo word, meant] but I knew the Cs wouldn't ask. It's remarkable how they can read through and not notice words they don't understand.' (Teacher D)

'I didn't know any more than was on the workcard—this was all right with Cs, but it wouldn't be with As.' (Teacher G)

These comments indicate that teachers have notions about the organization of time and material (and the degree of preparation necessary) in the classroom which depend on the normal characteristics of the ability group they are teaching. Thus what teachers 'know' about pupils as social, moral, and psychological persons is extended to what they know about them as intellectual persons, which as I shall show leads to the differentiation of an undifferentiated curriculum.

Ability and Knowledge

One of the remarkable features of the tendency to attribute to pupils the normal characteristics of their ability band is that what is held to constitute ability is rarely made explicit. When teachers discuss whether material is suitable for teaching to A, B or C streams, the criteria on which they make judgements remain largely implicit and consensual. Throughout it is difficult to separate out references to cognitive skills from imputed social and moral characteristics on the one hand and from characterization of teaching material on the other. This comment on teaching material about the Depression is typical:

> 'Some of the economic implications are difficult—it's O level type of material . . . but some of the human elements may be C material.' (Teacher at staff meeting)

Material is categorized in terms of its suitability for a given ability band and, by implication, ability is categorized in terms of whether or not these pupils can manage that material. Like the pupils who are categorized in terms of levels of ability, knowledge in school is categorized in terms of its supposed hierarchical nature with reference to criteria of age and ability. I shall be concerned with how teachers organize knowledge in relation to the normal attributes of the pupils they are teaching, according to criteria used to establish the hierarchies of ability and knowledge. This approach involves starting from the assumption that not only is ability not a given factor but also that we do not know what the knowledge to be got or the subject to be mastered properly is. We can only learn what they are by learning what teachers and pupils who are involved in defining that knowledge claim to be doing: subjects are what practitioners do with them.

Within the course itself, the enquiry-based mode is intended to change the emphasis from mastery of given contents of a subject to mastery of the method of enquiry itself. The workcards are to some extent structured around the 'concepts' it is desirable for pupils to acquire through working through the material. [. . .] Yet although the course was deliberately set up by teachers as educationists to counteract what they saw as an inappropriate exercise of authority by the teacher in the traditional talk-and-chalk presentation of material, in the teacher context enquiry for the pupil is still heavily teacher directed.

In the following extract from a C stream lesson, the teacher (E)—who is not a sociologist and has to rely on prepared material on a pink card[10] which includes a description of the joint family, but not of the extended family as it is defined in Britain today—rejects alternative definitions to the nuclear family suggested by pupils because his reading of the material leads him to see common residence as a critical criterion:

> Teacher: Now who'd like to tell me what we mean by the family? [Pause] It's not as obvious as you might think. What is a family? Derek?
> Derek: A mother, a daddy.
> Teacher: Yeah.
> Derek: A couple of kids if they got them.
> Teacher: Yes.

Derek: A granddaddy, a grandmummy.
Teacher: Yes.
Derek: An aunt, an uncle.
Teacher: You'd include that in the family.
Boy: Yes, you would.
Girl: [untranscribable]
Teacher: Anybody disagree with that—that in a family you'd include grandparents?
Derek: Well they are 'cos they're your mother's and father's mothers and fathers.
Teacher: And it's all part of one family?
Boy: Yeah.
Teacher: Anybody disagree or like to add to it at all? What we mean by the family?
Girl [she has probably been reading the pink card]: It's also a group of people living under one roof.
Girl: No, it's not. [Other pupils agree and disagree].
Teacher: Ah, a group of people living under one roof—aah—that differs from what Derek said, isn't it? Because the group—ssh, Derek . . .
Derek [his voice emerges above the teacher's voice]: . . . would still be the same as your mum, wouldn't it? It'd still be your family.
Teacher: Yeah, the group that Derek mentioned doesn't live under one roof. Now we can limit the family to say its a group of people related by blood, er, who live under one roof; or we can extend its meaning to include what Derek said: grandparents, aunts and uncles and so on, who may in individual cases live under the same roof, but it's not normal. The British family, I say the British family because the idea of families differs, as we shall see, over the world. Peter and Derek, you're not listening.
Peter: I am.
Teacher: . . . British family is parents and children, that is what you might call the, er, nuclear family; in other words, the core of the family. They tend to live together until the children have developed, matured, if you like, into adults. . . .

The way the exchange goes is not entirely a matter of 'how much' sociology this teacher knows; it is also a question of the relation between the categories he is using to structure this knowledge in the classroom and those used by the boy which derive from his everyday knowledge of 'what everyone knows' about families. The teacher moves outside this everyday knowledge since there must be occasions when he refers to his own relations as 'family' even if his ties with them are less close than those of Derek with his extended kin. The teacher cues the class that he wants them to move into another reality[11] with the words: 'It's not as obvious as you might think.' The C girls who said to me 'why should we learn about families? I mean we know about families, we live in them,' have not made this shift to seeing that the family might be viewed as problematic. It appears at this point [. . .], that the ability to 'grasp a concept' in the context of the course [. . .], refers to a pupil's willingness or ability to take over or accept the teacher's categories. This may mean, as it would have done for Derek, having to make a choice between apparently contradictory sets of statements unless he can see a reason for shifting his perspective to another set of categories. I shall suggest that Derek's stance is common among C pupils and differs from that of A stream pupils, who assume that the knowledge the teacher will purvey to them has a structure in which what they are asked to do has some place. This does not mean that the A pupil expects that knowledge to be relevant to his everyday experience. The argument is that A and C pupils tend to approach classroom knowledge from different positions and with different expectations.

The Teaching Material: 'Subjects' and Pupils
When teachers talk about how they have taught or will teach material they speak

nearly always about the problems of teaching C stream pupils. Teaching the material to the A stream pupils for whom it is primarily prepared and who stand in some sense as ideal pupils appears relatively unproblematic [...]. I have already quoted comments from staff meetings which showed the difficulty of 'economic implications' as opposed to 'human elements'. Similarly the comments showed a link between the level of response to 'moral problems' and the 'level of intelligence'. The following extracts from teachers' comments bring out these points more clearly:

> 'Yes, worth bringing out with the more able group.' (Teacher B)

> 'I envisage problems with 4Cs in understanding unusual relationships. The meaning of relationships, it's going to be very difficult to get this over to them.' (Teacher J)

> 'Yes, um, when we did it with the 4Cs before they, er, didn't seem particularly interested that, er, other people had family groups of their own. Because it wasn't real to them, it was so far removed, it didn't seem of complete ... of any relevance to them.' (Teacher L)

> 'I think if you're dealing with it purely in terms of kinship diagrams and white sheets [see Ref. 10], again you're actually reducing the interest again, if you make it too intellectual. What illustrative material is there on this? ... I think I've said this before ... that sociology has its validity in its abstractions and in its intellectual [untranscribable] ... to what extent the 4Cs will take that or to what extent it will remain a series of stories about families ...' (Teacher J—not himself a sociologist)

The picture that emerges from these comments which are highly representative, is one of oppositions that describe material and pupils: 'intellectual' is opposed to 'real', and 'abstractions' to 'stories'. One teacher implies that so long as the material is accessible only in terms of kinship diagrams and buff cards it will be too 'intellectual'. To make it 'real', illustrative material is needed. The points they make are not ones simply of method, but are about methods relating to C stream pupils, and so questions arise not only about why C pupils are believed to need non-intellectual material, but also why A pupils are believed not to need illustrative material and not to have problems in understanding 'the meaning of relationships'. The suggestion in these comments is that there is something in the material which 'it might be possible to bring out with the As'. The phrases 'bring it out', 'make explicit', the 'implications of moral problems', 'economic implications', seem to point to a range of understanding that is not available to C pupils who can engage only marginally with the material. Teacher J provides a further gloss (Garfinkel and Sacks 1970, pp. 342–5, 362–6) on this when he says after a lesson with a C group:

> 'This stuff [on language] is much too difficult for them. .... On the other hand they could cope with the family stuff. They could say something in their own words about different kinds of family, because they already knew something about them even if they did not know the corect term.'

'The correct term' implies something about how status may be attributed to knowledge. The pupils' ignorance of the 'correct term' suggests their deficiency. In the following discussion it is futher suggested that the range of understanding that is available to C stream pupils must be rooted in their 'experience', and that this is linked with another phrase teachers often use about adapting teaching material for C pupils: 'putting it in language they can understand':

> *Teacher J*:   How about the family for the Cs? It may have more in it for them because it's nearer home.

Teacher B: There'll be a lot of visual stimulus for discussion. . . . The Cs should be able to get somewhere with discussion. . . we won't do the history of the family with them, it's too difficult, probably too difficult for anyone.

What seems to emerge overall from the way teachers discuss teaching material in relation to pupils' abilities is an assumption that C pupils cannot master subjects: both the 'abstractions of sociology' and the 'economic implications' are inaccessible to them. The problem then in teaching C pupils is that you cannot teach them subjects. When A pupils do subjects it can be assumed by teachers that they do what, in terms of the *subject*, is held to be appropriate, and material is prepared with regard to what is seen as the demands of the *subject*. In teaching C pupils modifications must be made with regard to the *pupil* and it is as though the subject is scanned for or reduced to residual 'human elements' or a 'series of stories'.

The clearest statement of the differential emphasis on subject and pupils is that made by Teacher K. He is describing how he is able to 'gear' his study of the British economy for a C pupil at 'quite a different level' from the level at which he teaches it to his A group. He says:

'I can streamline it so it's got various grades of content and I can, I hope, do things which are very useful and valuable to the C child which I don't feel are as necessary for the A child. But they're all doing economics, they're all doing certain vital basic studies in how the economy works. . . .'

He describes how the study is dealing with 'land, labour and capital . . . in answer to what we call the "for whom" question in economics':

'Well, that leads on to a special study of labour for the Cs. Rewards for labour—wages. Wages can then be considered for girls in terms of why they're paid often lower than men's pay and what sorts of factors determine the different wages rates for different sorts of employment—something that's very immediate for these children.'

Later he says:

'Looking at a mixed economy he can angle that study much more towards taxation and the practical elements of how to fill in tax forms and what you get relief for, whereas . . . I'd be much more concerned with how the different types of taxation work, with the higher ability child: the difference between direct and indirect taxation and S.E.T. and so on. And also the effects that different forms of taxation have on the rates of economic growth—the more sophisticated elements which the lower ability child, it may not be possible for him to grasp the ideas that are part of that type of study but he's still able to study taxation and at a simpler level; but he's not being discriminated against.'

Here it is clear that one consequence of a differential treatment of the economy is the way in which categories of analysis are made available to or withheld from pupils. This teacher held the educationist view in almost its pure form, and the political implications of his teaching of economics should probably be seen as an unintentional and unrecognized manifestation of consensus politics arising from an image of society as consensus. The teaching cannot be said to be intentionally prescriptive: it is presented as an objective account of the economic system rather than one of a number of possible accounts. He is not deliberately restricting the categories that are available to A pupils, since his teaching reflects his own thinking. When he further restricts C stream pupils to a study of labour and that in terms of differential wages, he sees this as 'valuable' for the C pupils in terms of their ascribed status as workers. He does not intentionally withhold the framework which would allow the pupil to raise questions about the taxation policy as a whole, but he does effectively prevent, by a process of fragmentation, the question of how such knowledge becomes available.[12] [...]

Conclusions

In the presentation and discussion of data an attempt has been made to examine what teachers 'know' about their pupils and how that knowledge is related to the organization of curriculum knowledge in the classroom. Ability is an organizing and unexamined concept for teachers whose categorization of pupils on the grounds of ability derives largely from social class judgements of pupils' social, moral and intellectual behaviour. These judgements are frequently confounded with what are held to be rational values of a general nature. There is between teacher and A pupils a reciprocity of perspective which allows teachers to define, unchallenged by A pupils, as they may be challenged by C pupils, the nature and boundaries of what is to count as knowledge. It would seem to be the failure of high-ability pupils to question what they are taught in schools that contributes in large measure to their educational achievement.

It seems that one use to which the school puts knowledge is to establish that subjects represent the way about which the world is normally known in an 'expert' as opposed to a 'commonsense' mode of knowing. This establishes and maintains normative order (Blum, 1970) in and within subjects, and accredits as successful to the world outside school those who can master subjects. The school may be seen as maintaining the social order through the taken for granted categories of its superordinates who process pupils and knowledge in mutually confirming ways. The ability to maintain these categories as consensual, when there are among the clients in school conflicting definitions of the situation, resides in the unequal distribution of power. There is a need to see how this enters into and shapes the interactional situation in the classroom. Clearly there is also a need to examine the linkages between schools and other institutions, and attempt to understand the nature of the relationship between what counts as knowledge in schools and what counts as knowledge in other relevant societal areas. In particular, there is a need to understand the relationship between the social distribution of power and the distribution of knowledge, in order to understand the generation of categorizations of pupil, and categories of organization of curriculum knowledge in the school situation. (Because these linkages are unspecified here, the comments I have made about teachers may at times appear to be critical of the 'failures' of individuals.)

In the wider context of educational discussion, two panaceas currently put forward to reform the educational system are unstreaming and an undifferentiated curriculum. It seems likely that these prescriptions overlook the fact that streaming is itself a response to an organizing notion of differential ability. It seems likely that the hierarchical categories of ability and knowledge may well persist[13] in unstreamed classrooms and lead to the differentiation of undifferentiated curricula, because teachers differentiate in selection of content and in pedagogy between pupils perceived as of high and low ability. The origins of these categories are likely to lie outside the school and within the structure of the society itself in its wider distribution of power. It seems likely, therefore, that innovation in schools will not be of a very radical kind unless the categories teachers use to organize what they know about pupils and to determine what counts as knowledge undergo a fundamental change.

Acknowledgements

My thanks are first and foremost to the teachers and pupils of the school of the study. The teachers in the humanities department were, throughout the time I was at the school, unfailingly helpful in giving me their time and allowing me into their lessons with a tape recorder. I am indebted to Gillian Frost, who was also carrying out research at the school, both for the discussions we had, and for the data she made available to me.

The London Borough of Bromley made it possible for me to study for the Master's Degree of the University of London, by seconding me for a year, giving me the time to carry out the study on which this paper is based. I should like to thank Professor Basil Bernstein for his encouragement and for his assistance in getting the tape recordings transcribed. My thanks are also due to John Hayes and Michael Young with whom I discussed the material at various stages and to whom I owe very many insights that helped me to organize the data. I owe similar thanks to my fellow graduate students, in particular to John Bartholomew, and also to John Beck. My thanks are also to Michael Young for reading this paper in an earlier draft and making many detailed and constructive comments which helped me to clarify confusions and inconsistencies.

Notes

1. The direction of mainstream sociology of education in this respect can be seen in the very comprehensive account of available studies in Chapters 3, 4 and 5 of Banks (1968).
2. Cicourel and Kitsuse (1963) shown the importance in this context of the processes by which students are allocated to college or non-college courses. The Schools Council's acceptance of a differentiated curriculum, like the Newsom Report, maintains a distinction between the 'academic' and the 'non-academic' child.
3. I have to thank Gillian Frost for making this information available to me.
4. This mode of examination allows teachers to construct and examine their own courses with moderation from an external examiner.
5. Selznick (1949), p. 70. I have to thank John Bartholomew for bringing this to my notice.
6. For example, the Humanities Curriculum Project of the Schools Council directed by Lawrence Stenhouse.
7. Dumont and Wax (1969) make a similar point about the culture of the Cherokee Indian. There is clearly a relationship between individualization of failure and the psychologistic notion of a curriculum based on pupils' 'needs'. See also Friedman (1967).
8. This relationship is also apparent in the data of Hargreaves (1967, p. 95): 'On one occasion a teacher left the room to investigate some noise in the corridor. "Who are you lot?" he cried. "3B, sir", came the reply. "You sound more like 1E than 3B", was the master's crushing retort.'
9. Wax and Wax (1964) find the same situation in what they call a 'vacuum ideology' which is attributed to the Cherokee Indian by white teachers.
10. Workcards for pupils are of three kinds: pink cards written by a member of staff which give an overview of the topic to be studied ('concepts' are generally printed in capital letters to point the organization of material to the pupils); buff cards which are also referred to as 'documents' because they often reproduce original sources and deal with areas of the topic in more detail; yellow workcards which have questions intended to guide pupils in the use of the other workcards. Many pupils treated these straightforwardly as question sheets.
11. The concept here is that of 'multiple realities' developed by Schutz (1967). In organizing the data I have also been greatly influenced by the distinction between 'common-sense' and 'expert' knowledge made by Horton (1967). I have also used this article in attempting to conceptualize A and C pupils' approaches to knowledge as the outcome of alternative thought systems, as opposed to seeing the differences in terms of a hierarchical relationship.
12. There is a need for studies of the models of society inherent in subjects as they are taught in schools and in textbooks. T.S. Kuhn (1970) suggests how an authoritarian model of science is built into science subjects as they are taught and the textbooks as they are used. Other studies might cast light on how a normative order is transmitted through the

contents of subjects in schools and, in relation to this, what counts as 'objectivity' in that subject and how it operates to maintain that normative order.

[13] Barker Lunn (1970) suggests that teachers often carry attitudes appropriate to streaming into unstreamed classes and that this is particularly damaging for the 'low-ability' working-class child.

References

Banks, O. (1968). *The Sociology of Education*, Batsford, London.

Baratz, S. and Baratz, J. (1970) 'Early childhood intervention: the social science basis of institutionalized racism', *Harvard Educational Review*, Vol. 40, February.

Barker Lunn, J.C. (1970) *Streaming in the Primary School*, National Foundation for Educatinal Research, Slough.

Becker, H.S. (1952) 'Social class variations in the teacher-pupil relationship' *Journal of Educational Sociology*, Vol. 25, April.

Bernstein, B.B. (1971) 'On the classification and framing of educational knowledge' in Young, M.F.D. (ed.) (1971) *Knowledge and Control*, Collier-Macmillan, London.

Blum, A. (1970) 'The corpus of knowledge as a normative order'. Reprinted in Young, M.F.D. (ed.) (1971) *Knowledge and Control*, Collier-Macmillan, London.

Bourdieu, P. (1967) 'Systems of education and system of thought' *International Social Science Journal* Vol. XIX, No. 3.

Cicourel, A.V. and Kitsuse, J. I. (1963) *The Educational Decision Makers*, Bobbs-Merill, Indianapolis.

Cohen, A.K. (1959) 'The study of social disorganization and deviant behaviour' in Merton, R.K., Broom, L. and Cottrell, L.S. (eds.) *Sociology Today: Problems and Prospects*, Basic Books, New York.

Deutsch, M. (1963). 'The disadvantaged child and the learning process', in Passow, H. (ed.) *Education in Depressed Areas*, Teachers College Press, New York.

Deutscher, I. (1966) 'Words and deeds: social science and social policy', *Social Problems*, Vol 13 (Winter).

Dumont, R.V. and Wax, M.L. (1969). 'Cherokee school society and the inter-cultural classroom' *Human Organization*, Vol. 28, No. 3.

Friedman, N.L. (1967) 'Cultural deprivation: a commentary in the sociology of knowledge', *Journal of Educational Thought*, Vol. I, August 1967.

Garfinkel, H. and Sacks, H. (1970) 'On formal structures of practical actions' in McKinney, J. and Tiryakian, E. *Theoretical Sociology: Perspectives and Development*, Appleton-Century-Crofts, New York.

Geer, B., Haas, J., Vivona, C., Miller, S.J., Miller, C. and Becker, H.S. (1968) 'Learning the ropes: situational learning in four occupational training programmes' in Deutscher, I. and Thompson, E. J. (eds) *Among the People: Encounters with the Poor*, Basic Books, New York.

Hargreaves, D. (1967) *Social Relations in a Secondary School*, Routledge & Kegan Paul, London.

Horton, R. (1967) 'African traditional thought and western science', *Africa*, vol. 67.

Keddie, N.G. (1970) 'The social basis of classroom knowledge: a case study', M.A. thesis, University of London.

Kuhn, T.S. (1970) *The Structure of Scientific Revolutions*, University of Chicago Press, Chicago.

Schutz, A. (1967). *Collected Papers. Volume I: The Problem of Social Reality*, Martinus Nijhoff, The Hague.

Selznick, P. (1949) *T.V.A. and the Grass Roots: a Study in the Sociology of Formal Organizations*, University of California Press, Berkeley and Los Angeles.

Wax, M. L. and Wax, R. H. (1964) 'Formal education in an American Indian community', *Social Problems Monograph*, II, Spring.

Werthman, C. (1963) 'Delinquency in schools. A test for the legitimacy of authority' *Berkeley Journal of Sociology*, Vol VII.

Young, M.F.D. (1971) 'An approach to the study of curricula as socially organized knowledge', in Young, M.F.D. (ed.) (1971) *Knowledge and Control* Collier-Macmillan, London.

9 Social Stratification in the Classroom

SHARP, R. and GREEN, A.

One of the places one might least expect pupils to be differentiated on social class lines is in the infant school. Yet, Sharp and Green argue, in this excerpt from their study of three classes in Mapledene Infant School, that this is precisely what happens. For in reconciling the individualistic requirement of child-centred education with the constraint of high teacher–pupil ratio and the like, teachers, they claim, adopt a strategy of encouraging ordinary and less able children to 'be busy', while devoting disproportionate amounts of their time to giving individual attention to the able few. The authors conclude that general social class differences are thus confirmed, but are masked at school behind a rhetoric of progressivism.

[. . .] In this chapter, our intention will be to try to show how elements of their situation and the teachers' perspectives together produce what could be regarded as essentially similar formal properties of the stratification system in three infants school classroom settings. The analysis will suggest that certain key elements are present in each. This will be explained in terms of common features in the material and social environment of the teachers which cannot merely be intended away in consciousness, and which structure the activities of each and produce similar patterns in the social structuring of pupil identities. [. . .] We are not claiming that the careers of individual pupils would be identical regardless of which classroom they happen to enter, but instead wish to concentrate upon the overall similarities, reducible we argue, to constant parameters contingent on each of their social contexts. [. . .] These parameters are not metaphysical absolutes, but are themselves historical products of social structural formations [. . .] The analysis will proceed ideal typically. That is to say an attempt has been made to isolate the essential and key features of the stratification system in all three classrooms. A useful entry into the analysis is to note two significant paradoxes. The first paradox is that all three teachers claim that their approach is child centred and oriented to the needs and requirements of individual pupils. All claim to want to get to know their pupils in their idiosyncracy and uniqueness and are aware of the dangers of premature labelling, preferring to retain open minds regarding the potentialities and capabilities of their pupils. Nevertheless, in their substantive practice the quality of intersubjectivity between teacher and pupil varied considerably. Some pupils seemed to have acquired reified identities and were thought of as really 'thick', 'peculiar' or had other stable and hard categorizations applied to them. Thus whereas in the teachers' ideology as educationalists, open mindedness towards all pupils should prevail, in their substantive practice it only seemed to apply to some of them.

The second paradox is related to the first. Whereas all three teachers would claim to be supporters of the egalitarian principle that all pupils are of equal worth, having an equal right to receive an education appropriate to their needs, in practice there was a marked degree of differentiation among the pupils in terms of the amounts and kinds of interaction they had with their teachers. Now the principle of equality does not necessarily commit one to identity of treatment. Nevertheless, it is significant that those pupils whom their teachers regarded as more successful tended to be given far greater attention than the others. The teachers interacted with them more frequently, played closer attention to their activities, subtly structuring and directing their efforts in ways which were noticeably different from the relationship with other pupils less favourably categorized.

Such paradoxes could be seen to be related to certain inner tensions and ambiguities in the teachers' perspectives but they should not be interpreted solely as the products of such processes at the ideological level in the teachers' consciousnesses. Indeed we shall argue that these very ambiguities are in themselves reflections of the structuring of material and social constraints, external to the classroom which impinge upon the teacher and structure her activities. The understanding of stratification in the classroom, whilst it may be related to and affected by the teachers' consciousness, cannot be solely explained by it. In our analysis we shall suggest that the teachers are encapsulated within a context which produced the necessity for some hierarchical differentiation of the pupils in order that the teacher may solve the problems she is confronted with and provide some legitimation for the allocation of her time and energies.

The teacher is faced with an immediate problem of 'what do do' in the classroom which itself is embedded in a wider structure of material and social relationships. In this situation the following are of importance for the teacher's practice: expectations are placed upon her from professional colleagues and superiors, from parents and others regarding the levels of achievements she is to maintain. Similarly she will be required to live up to certain standards of 'good pedagogical practice' set within the wider community of professional colleagues and more crucially by those who are in a position of power over her within the school itself. In addition parents and colleagues will look to her to maintain social order in the classroom. Moreover, her pupils are not merely passive 'objects' but will exert some influence on the teacher. Such constraints on her practice could be regarded as social and are traditionally analysed within a discussion of role theory and the teacher. Role expectations on the teacher may well be incompatible thus creating the potentiality for role conflict. Other constraints are of a more material or physical nature. Of particular importance are such factors as the teacher–pupil ratio. An obvious physical constraint on the teacher relates to the sheer number of pupils with whom she has to deal. Teachers frequently cite overcrowded classrooms as causes of their difficulties but it is significant that the pedagogical implications for the teacher of having large classes have not yet been systematically explored. Other physical constraints relate to such factors as the architecture and layout of the classrooms, the 'materials' therein, and other human and non-human resources at the teachers' disposal.

Within this situation are generated a series of concepts and categories with which she orders the situation and objects in the world of her practice. The categories 'work' for her. They have a pragmatic basis for their existence [. . .], they have an affinity with her situation and projects. This is not to suggest that they are completely unstructured nor that she has complete freedom to select her categories. She operates within systems of available and legitimized categories within the community of her colleagues [. . .] The acceptability of these categories will relate also to the teacher's prior experiences, her history and socialization in other contexts of relevance. Clearly the teacher will operate with a stock of knowledge influenced by each of these factors. Given these social and physical constraints, there will be an ongoing attempt to accommodate her stock of knowledge and her projects to the situation and the physical and social opportunities it offers. The outcome of this dialectic will form her behaviour and her consciousness; the one cannot be understood without the other.

Some of the categories with which the teacher orders her experience will be stable, others unstable or transitory or developing dynamically over time. For the observer it is most easy to chart the contours of the social structure of the classroom *vis-à-vis* the teacher's practice where routine can be identified. Such routines refer to the key [...] categories related to activities of relatively high importance to her. In the teacher's perspective there are at this point notions like 'busyness', 'good pupil', 'bright pupil', a 'good day', 'maladjusted child', and so on. We can divide these types of category used by the teacher into categories of situation, categories of activities and categories of persons. The distinctions are analytic and only arise from our interest in the generation of and consequences for categories of pupils as the main focus of attention, whilst retaining an interest in the context of social action as important for explanation. Such key and stable categories tend to relate also to the unproblematical nature of aspects of the classroom as seen by the teacher.

[...] The changes in the teachers' perspective and practice are more elusive to chart and understand. In addition, the precise technical relationship between the teachers' categories and the elements of the situation or types of pupil they purport to describe is problematic. With both stable and unstable categories there is a level of ambiguity *vis-à-vis* practice [...]

We have referred to the paradox that some pupils take on a reified identity and are categorized as abnormal, 'really' peculiar, despite the ideology prescribing open-mindedness. In contrast most are thought of as not 'really' anything other than complex, slightly baffling but normal children within the parameters of the teachers' background expectancies. The key feature associated with the abnormal children was that the teacher's approach manifestly did not work for them. These were children who were 'difficult to get through to', who did not get there by 'leaving out a stage' or 'going round the back way' who 'dribbed and drabbed' or 'wouldn't show an interest' in anything. These children did not get there at all, or when they did it was at the expense of great effort on their and the teacher's part. With these children the teacher had, in consequence, become less openminded, had developed a clearer typification of each child, in Schutz's terms, as more contemporaneous than consocial and a prognosis was in the making both in the teacher's perspective on such a child and in the social structure of the classroom and the school. By this, we mean that the child was becoming clearly distinguishable as a 'problem' to the teacher. In addition and, for the child, more importantly it became increasingly likely that the teacher's colleagues and outside agencies would become involved in the categorization of the child as a 'problem'. Thus for such a child, a career is potentially being generated beyond the classroom context by the involvement of increasingly anonymous agencies as structural features of his fate. As this occurs the teacher may receive feedbacks from the agencies which feed into her present definition of the child and in so doing tend to further reify the categorization she has of him.

On the other hand, there was a majority of pupils in the class to whom the teacher when trying to understand their intellectual accomplishments would give the benefit of the doubt when a failure occurred. Thus when a child was unable apparently to understand a particular point or had slowed down or come to a halt in its progress at reading this was interpreted as a temporary lapse and that if carefully handled the child would soon recover. It was not interpreted as an indication that, within the parameters of her overall conception of normality-for-these-children, this particular child was 'slow', 'dim', 'thick', 'peculiar', etc. So in effect, no adverse prognosis or prophecy of deviance other than a conception that the child is pretty normal, at least 'for these children' is made. Thus to all intents and purposes the current failure of the child is no great problem and is not dealt with in any particular way. The important aspect of the teacher's prognosis in this case is that it is relatively loose and open-ended, just as her behaviour towards the child, when having initially failed to elicit the required response is noncommittal and to a large extent nondirective. At this point the teacher is realizing the child centred vocabulary in her classroom practice from within her own perspective. It is important to note that this approach 'works' for her, and is linked closely or has a logical affinity with the teacher's understanding of how children learn. In this connection, it is interesting that none of the teachers seemed to have very clear understandings of how children acquire or develop knowledge. This could be an example of what P.W. Jackson (1968) refers to as the 'mystery' among teachers of what the learning process might be in young children. Yet for the teachers, this does not appear to be a problem because in their perspective most children achieve normally or normally 'for this sort of child' most of the time and their classroom practice reflects this.

The children who are normal in the teacher's perspective are such because they can be comprehended easily within the structure of the teacher's common sense, especially the ideal 'good pupil' where teacher–pupil intersubjectivity is high. In commonsense understanding the actions of these children are obvious and can be satisfactorily comprehended with minimal reflection [...]

We will, at this point, expand one discussion by Schutz (1964) of common sense. Schutz notes that in commonsense knowledge other human objects, present in the phenomenal world of the actor, may be placed on a continuum from consociates to contemporaries. Consociates are people whom the actor knows in their unique individuality, while contemporaries are more remote and appropriated in consciousness via typifications. In the we-relationship shared with consociates typicality of the other does not exist, while in the actor's perception of contemporaries it does. A type is generated by taking a set of characteristics formed by 'anonymization', by which is meant that the subjective meaning of immediately experienced individuals is omitted.

Schutz's construction is useful but needs to be expanded and fitted into the material context of the teacher's project to provide a more complete explanatory model for understanding the structure of the self-fulfilling prophecy. For Schutz, anonymization appears to arise because of the *ad hoc* invocation of physical remoteness in time and space of the object. In the infant classroom this manifestly is not the case on the scale Schutz would imply is appropriate for his constructs. The teacher and the pupils are contemporaneous and yet a structure similar to Schutz's anonymization arises. Certain children appear in the teacher's perspective of them as closer to the contemporaneous than consociate end of the continuum. These latter arise as phenomena in the teacher's perspective not because they are remote in time and space but because the teacher's commonsense knowledge is no use to her in handling them, given her classroom management problem. Whilst consociates fit easily into the actor's common sense, other children arise as contemporaries because of the ignorance which is part of the structure of the teacher's knowledge *vis-à-vis* her practice with these children. While the consociate is known in a relatively complex and personal but generally unreflective way, certain children emerge as contemporaries because it is impossible to communicate with them. This is not to suggest that the impossibility of communication between the teacher and her pupil would occur, whatever the circumstances. The teacher involved in a one to one relationship with such a child over a long period of time would undoubtedly develop a relationship of high inter-subjectivity and consociality. Nevertheless, given the material and social constraints on the teacher in this context the contents of the teacher's consciousness which lead to anonymization between the teacher and certain pupils reflect these constraints. Her consciousness is not the prime independent causal variable. Thus such pupils present themselves as strangers to the teacher's cognitive paradigms and routine practices in this context and this generates problems for the teacher which in her theoretical practice entails the need for non-common sense, reflective theoretical knowledge where the categories are drawn from 'esoteric' or abstract knowledge. This is an initial process in the reification of the child's identity as a social structural process and phenomenon in the classroom. The category tends to be hardened, the fit being more convincing to its user (the teacher) the more the child continues to feed back the appropriate behavioural cues. We may widen the context of this phenomenon and in so doing indicate that the process of hardening in the child's identity is related to the degree to which extra-classroom audiences come to accept this reified definition of the child. Parents, other teachers, social workers, etc., may be brought in and so increase the likelihood of the implementation of structures such as psychiatric testing, special schooling and the wide range of administrative techniques for the processing of 'social problems'. In so doing, pressure is taken off the teacher and her management problem is reduced.

The child who has acquired the identity of 'really peculiar', 'dim', 'difficult' is unlikely to become less problematic to the teacher and so to change in identity the less time he spends interacting with the teacher. The central aspect of the contemporary-consocial continuum lies in the level of communication links or intersubjectivity. The more remote the child is from the teacher's common sense the less will intersubjectivity be a feature of their relationship and the less individuality a feature of the teacher's perception of the child. It was noticed that in each classroom in the deployment of time-space resources the teacher tended to spend less time interacting with the 'peculiar' children than with the 'normal' ones and, particularly much less time than with those (abnormal for this context) who were good pupils or approaching the conception of the teacher's personal conception of the ideal client. This was as much a product of the pupil's own choice or style of being in the classroom as a function of the teacher operating within the structure of an informal child centred classroom regime (Jackson, 1968; Jackson and Lahaderne, 1967).

It is interesting to note that many of the key categories in the teacher's perspective on her work relate to control rather than learning, teaching or instruction. To explain this it is important to reiterate that each teacher is faced with the practical problem of how to implement in the classroom a child centred philosophy given the nature of the school ethos and the expectation that each teacher will operationalize the key features of that ethos. [. . .] The 'integrated day' and 'freedom of choice' are of crucial significance in the school philosophy. In attempting to put these into practice the teacher is confronted with a major problem of 'what-to-do-with-freely-choosing-children'. It is suggested that the notion of 'child directed learning' is related to the categorization of the pupils via the control problems presented to the teacher in this open fluid context. The bright ones are the 'biddable' easily controllable ones who are on the teacher's wavelength. The dull ones are those who are not motivated to be 'indirectly directed' to the activities the teacher defines as important. Given this very complex problem in the practical implementation of a 'progressive' approach to pedagogy the teacher's practical solution is 'busyness', where children do something they have chosen and are thus engaged in activity without requiring the constant attention which the teacher is unable to give them. To the teacher there is a logical relationship between her notion of busyness, her educational philosophy and her actions. However, there is also a contingent relation in that the situation is objectively given in the sense of the limitation of her time-space resources. Thus the notion of 'busyness' is not merely a second order construct based upon a rather limited aspect of her work as the teacher would see it but indicative of a social structural phenomenon characteristic of control in this type of fluid situation, and as such is a construct which has ramifications latent to the teacher's perspective. Thus the teacher's major working concept, or central technique in her operational philosophy, is her emphasis upon 'be busy' or 'get on, on your own' or 'find yourself something to do'. Such exhortations to the pupils are a frequent occurence. As this becomes acted out by the teacher and by the child, certain types of pupils as social structural position in the classroom are generated as the teacher in her practice solves the problem of 'what to do' in the classroom. The key feature of 'being busy' for the teacher is that in a situation perceived by her of fluidity and constant change in the children's interest and activities, the more they take seriously this command, the greater the area of freedom it allows her and thus the more manageable her task becomes.

'Normal pupils' in this context account for the identity of the majority of the children in the class in this way. They form a 'bedrock of busyness', that is, for the most part, they settle down to follow the routine of self-directed activity within the range offered. They are normal in the sense that they can be accounted for generally within the framework of the teacher's commonsense perceptual structures and rationales. As manageable problems in terms of behaviour and intellectual attainment they fit mundane common sense and require little by way of esoteric understanding. In this way children occupying this social position are invisible to the teacher and can be handled with little reflection.

By contrast, the problem child, the one labelled 'disturbed', 'very maladjusted' or 'peculiar', illustrates a key form of deviance. While the normal child is no threat to the teacher's competence or the underlying social order of the classroom, and can be readily dealt with on a commonsense basis and fits into the classroom routines, this type does not.

The low level of intersubjectivity between the teacher and this type of child makes him extremely problematic to her commonsense perspectives and at a wider level presents a serious threat to the school's accountability to the parents and other interested parties. The teacher is assisted with dealing with such pupils, however, by those elements of the school ethos which support the view that these sorts of children benefit most from this unthreatening atmosphere, as well as through the tendency to employ esoteric or 'scientific knowledge' from psychology of psychiatry which 'explain' the child's deviance in terms of some inner pathology. The teacher is thus enabled to integrate the child into her practice for he can now legitimately be left alone to 'work through his problems' to pursue 'what interests him according to his needs'. This, then reduces the management problem of having to devote too much time to these difficult children and in so doing integrate him and his activities into the 'bedrock of busyness' discussed above. [...]

The third type of pupil is the teacher's ideal client in the sense which the other categories discussed are not. This sort of pupil fits the teacher's ideal for children 'from a good area' or a 'middle class district'. This type is bright and articulate, interested and interesting and would 'get on' in other schools. This type of child most approximates to the teacher's own ideal of what school children should be like.

It is crucial now to understand the operational philosophy of 'busyness' as it relates to the social stratification of pupils in this social structure. One of the central functions of busyness is to free the teacher to handle the ever changing situation in the classroom. The latent function, however, is to free the teacher to be engaged by the articulate, bright, 'pushing' or teacher directed children who tend to take up disproportionate amounts of her time and energies. The level of inter-subjectivity between this type of pupil and the teacher is extremely high, and given the egalitarian ideal central to child centredness it is with these children that an egalitarian relationship most clearly develops. While the 'problem' child is a contemporary and anonymous stranger requiring esoteric rationales, this type of child is a relatively consocial companion with whom a joking relationship may develop and who can be expected to carry out tasks successfully and responds to the wide range of subtle cues the teacher emits.

The social stratification that is thus generated operates in the following way. The 'problem' child is in a position of low status which is relatively rigid and binding. His life chances in the classroom, to the extent that he has relatively little contact with the teacher and so is unlikely to alter his identity from that of peculiarity, are severely limited. Being really 'odd' in the teacher's account he has a reified identity to her which is socially structured and reinforced at the classroom level as he has less opportunity to develop contradictory cues and at a wider level, as his identity is accepted by other teachers, parents and social workers. The normal child for this school is in a relatively more fluid position with the chance of moving upward or down the hierarchy of social status to the extent that he or she moves from the low profile position of the normality of adjustment to the routines of busyness.

The élite of the social structure are the few 'bright' children who are able to take most advantage of the 'free day' and 'leading from behind', in that they readily know what it is the teacher wants and can reward the teacher for the time spent with her thus confirming her in her identity as a competent teacher. While the maladjusted or problem child can be used by the teacher as an illustration of the difficulty of her task and the need for this type of approach to pedagogy, so the bright ones can be cited as the operational indicators of the teacher's success, i.e. confident readers, articulate interactors, the child who produces 'interesting', creative work. Thus the structure of pupil stratification illustrates a central paradox of the child centred approach. In practice, though attempting to generate the lowest possible degree of boundary and hierarchy in pupil identities, social stratification does occur. The pressures on the teacher require her to produce certain goods such as competent standards of reading and number work. The generally low level can be accounted for by citing the maladjusted children as examples of the operational problems. The bright ones can be cited as evidence of the successful working of the whole approach. Within this pupil differentiation is generated and justified. The teachers recognize differentiation among their pupils but within the child centred philosophy differentiation does not entail hierarchy. What we are suggesting is that hierarchization, and the differentiation of the material life chances of the children, is being produced within the social structure of the classroom. Neither from the child centred ethos of the school, nor the immediate personal common sense of the teacher embodied in her operational philosophy is it recognized that these phenomena are a part of the social structure of teacher-pupil relations in the classroom. Where it is recognized that some children 'get on' better than others the individualistic and psychological vocabulary is invoked to illustrate the personal problems of the non-achieving child, or the social pathology of their deprived home environment.

The major irony in the situation, however, is that the position of the *élite* in the classroom depends upon the other pupil's nonconformity to the teacher's personal ideal. Were all her pupils 'interested', keen and teacher directed, the management problem thus presented to the teacher would be insuperable in a context where the school ethos requires informality and pupil choice. It appears that the latent function of allowing pupils choice is that the onus of responsibility for the child's success or failure in the classroom lies with the child. The child determines his own mode of being in the classroom and in so doing the teacher is liberated to perform those activities she defines as important. [. . .]

[. . .] To sum up: we have considered the extent to which teachers are encapsulated within a context where the problems of management and control require some implicit hierarchical differentiation of pupils in order to solve the problem of order and provide some legitimation for the allocation of scarce resources, i.e. the teacher's time and energies. In addition we have suggested that in the process of the construction of pupil's identities through the differential management of pupils' careers in the commonsense world of the teacher, the pupil plays a highly significant part in his own identity construction. The kind of style-of-being adopted by the child in the classroom is crucially related to his being integrated in varying ways into the teacher's common sense and practice as she tries to solve various management dilemmas. Thus rather than seeing the labelling process as one where the social controller, in this case the teacher, applies some hard label to her pupils, we should instead see it as a far more subtle process where the rigidity or variability of the labels are as much related to the state of social control within the organization, and to the social control implications of varying ways of acting therein as to the rigidity of the social controller's thought processes. Therefore in our analysis we have tried to show how the meaning of the child as an object of the teacher's attention is influenced by the social structure in which she works which partly she creates and which partly creates her. The social structure throws up problems and allows her, given her projects and the field of constraints, only certain solutions or structures of opportunity to solve them.

References

Jackson, P.W. (1968) *Life in Classrooms*, Holt, Rinehart & Winston, London.

Jackson, P.W. & Ladahere, H.M. (1967) "Inequalities of Teacher-Pupil Contacts", *Psychology in the School*, vol. 4.

10

One Spell of Ten Minutes or Five Spells of Two...? Teacher–Pupil Encounters in Art and Design Education

L. TICKLE

In the previous article it was argued that, even in what was claimed to be progressive, child-centred teaching, more teacher time and attention was given to privileged, more able pupils. In this article, Les Tickle takes issue with the argument, on the basis of his research with art and design teachers in three middle schools. These teachers, Tickle found, spent *more* time with the *less* able. However, it is not the allocation of time per se that seems to matter. For it was in *how* that time was spent that teachers appeared to discriminate against their pupils.

The charge of Pink Floyd that pupils are regarded as no more than bricks in a wall and that teachers are engaged in a process of mind control over their pupils may be written off as extreme adolescent-like protest. Yet the charge echoes much earlier ones which are illustrated by the work of many distinguished educationists. One, Krishnamurti (1953), claimed that the system of education, whilst perhaps doing something to awaken the intellect, also makes people subservient, mechanical and deeply thoughtless, and leaves the individual incomplete, stultified and uncreative. Furthermore, Torrance (1962) argued that teachers are actually punitive towards pupils who show creative potential. And from a Marxist perspective Bowles and Gintis (1976) have asserted that by serving the needs of capitalism for a stratified, compliant workforce, schools inhibit and distort personal development and prevent the achievement of that very social equality which they purport to serve. Thus, while the relationship between schooling and personal development has usually been associated with an optimistic public view that education is concerned with maximizing that development in intellectual, physical and social/emotional terms, the arguments of critical educationists and some sociologists have run counter to that view: for them contemporary schooling is essentially anti-creative and inegalitarian in nature.

Despite the strength of these claims and counter-claims, however, little evidence about the nature of schooling has been produced which would allow us to arbitrate between them. The production of such evidence is an important priority for in their different ways the two perspectives—one of teaching as a controlling mechanism which tends to stunt growth through punitive action; the other of education which by its very nature develops the creative potential of individuals—highlight a major conflict for teachers. That conflict is especially acute at the very centre of the classroom enterprise where teachers and pupils are involved in interactional and curricular processes; particularly so in those parts of the curriculum—art, design, English, etc.—which are explicitly concerned with creativity and personal growth. This chapter focuses on one such area of the curriculum—art and design—and is derived from my analysis of classroom processes in that subject in two middle schools. In art and design the relationship between 'greater control and rigour' by teachers and 'freedom for children to do things their own way' is a contentious one which has been widely voiced and recorded (Schools Council, 1974). In addition to offering insights into art and design teaching *per se*, therefore, this study also provides an important testing ground for the examination of wider pedagogical and curricular issues concerning the effect of curriculum practice on personal development.

The view that schooling essentially inhibits development and stunts personal growth might be expected to induce particularly grave concern among teachers of art and design. For some, these subjects provide the key to the whole span of education, being the means by which individual potential can be fulfilled (Read, 1934), even if in practice they have more often been simply interludes in the school curriculum during which pupils can indulge the luxury of pursuing 'creative expression'. In either case, though, artistic work in schools has come to be seen as intrinsically, essentially and necessarily 'creative', providing a vehicle for the fostering of personal growth in children. Most teachers of art and design intend that pupils should engage in some form of creative activity, and recent curriculum development projects (Schools Council, 1974 and 1975), as well as other publications in this area (Field, 1970; Shaw and Reeve, 1978), explicitly demand that children should be involved in problem-solving processes and creative experience.

\ssertions about schooling's restricting effects on creativity and personal development offer a devastating blow to teachers who subscribe to a more optimistic view of education, where children are seen as exploratory, creative, problem-solving beings who engage actively in learning. While existing evidence suggests that teachers of this kind may be thin on the ground (Bennett, 1976; Galton *et al.*, 1981; Boydell, 1981), they are probably more concentrated in art and design teaching than almost anywhere else. Also, arguments that schooling is inimical to personal development and creativity either because of the institutional character of schooling (Illich, 1971) or through its relation to the needs of capitalism (Bowles and Gintis, 1976; Sharp and Green, 1975) run counter to the assumptions of art and design educators about creativity and personal growth. Those optimistic assumptions (particularly at points in the school system far removed from formal selection and examinations) and their more critical counter-arguments pinpoint the need for a study of art and design education as a test case for these claims. In this study I will examine some of the effects of schooling on personal development, creativity and the equality of pupil treatment in an area of the curriculum and at a point in the school system where one might reasonably expect to find individual potential being fulfilled. This will be achieved by studying how teachers allocate their time among pupils, and by examining the kinds of educational content and experience that are offered to different pupils within this time.

The research on which the chapter is based (Tickle, 1979) examined aspects of classroom practice in art and design, involving four teachers[1] with third- and fourth-year pupils in two 9–13 middle schools. The study focused on teaching strategies; the teachers' perspectives relating to classroom practices; and the outcome of these perspectives and strategies for the pupils' experience in art and design subjects. Data were collected by observing how teachers interacted with their pupils (recorded in field notes and on tape) and by formal and informal interviews with the teachers. The data used here relate to practical sessions which took place after lesson introductions with whole classes.

The 'main dilemma' of art and design teachers identified by the Schools Council (1974)—between imposing 'skills' on pupils yet granting feedom for children to do things their own way—is one which reflects conflicting pressures in creative activities not only in schools but in the social production of art generally (Wolff, 1981). In classrooms the conflicts and dilemmas impinge everywhere, not only on the content of learning but also on the form of its transmission and on the criteria by which learning products are judged; on curriculum, pedagogy and evaluation, that is. In the case study each of the teachers was concerned with the didactic teaching of 'basic skills' while also fostering (in varying degrees) creativity, problem-solving and individuality in the pupils' expression of personal ideas. They identified basic skills as manipulative craft skills; knowledge of tools, equipment and craft processes; kinaesthetic experience in the use and control of a variety of materials; and aesthetic skills and modes of visual representation. At the same time, expectations for creativity, problem-solving and use of personal ideas played an important part too. These involved the use of 'design ideas' which incorporated individual decision-making; problem-solving in open choice situations; kinaesthetic exploration of materials; and the expression of personal ideas and image-making.

The conflicting demands of imposing 'basic skills' in which all pupils are expected to succeed on the one hand while valuing personal growth and fulfilment for individual children on the other has been discussed by Berlak and Berlak (1981) in the context of the primary school curriculum. These demands, they point out, are part of a wide variety of influences acting on teachers, who respond to the dilemmas these influences present in different ways. In this case study, the conflicting demands of imposing basic skills in art and design on the one hand and fostering creativity and individuality on the other were reconciled through similar strategies by each teacher. These strategies ensured that pupils received instruction in manipulative and technical skills while incorporating some, albeit limited, elements of freedom for children to express ideas and make choices.

The balance between the opposing principles did not occur equally for all pupils, however. Some were granted greater opportunity to pursue individual ideas and engage in problem-solving while others' learning experiences were more closely controlled and restricted. Those deemed to be 'more able' were engaged increasingly in the 'creative' elements while others continued to work under pressure to perform in 'basic skills'. Moreover, these different categories of pupil received different allocations of teacher time, not only in quantity but in quality too.

I shall now examine in detail the classroom practices of the three teachers — Mr Penketh, Mr Tansley and Mr Sankey — to show how the dilemmas were experienced and resolved in each case.

Mr Penketh

Mr Penketh can be typified as being a 'discipline-based' teacher (Hammersley, 1977). The traditional craft teacher element was dominant within his professional identity yet he had also been influenced by a number of different orientations to teaching since working within the middle school. These included the organizational demands of mixed ability teaching; the headteacher's perspectives on individualized teaching and the integration of subjects; and the views of two LEA advisers who shared a 'progressive' view of education (Hammersley, 1977) and who had close contact with the school and with the art and design department in particular.

Mr Penketh's strategies centred on notions of *limited choice* and *choice of jobs*. At the beginning of their course every pupil did the same job—a model railway engine or similar toy. Later, different jobs were available, in the form of models made by the teacher, the patterns of which could be copied. As pupils progressed through the course more open choice was offered, without models to be copied. During the first year of the course pupils who were perceived by the teacher as 'less able', 'average', or 'more able' respectively in terms of performance in basic skills were then 'turned' towards 'appropriate' tasks, with increased 'choice' over time. As Mr Penketh himself put it: 'I think in the fourth year you've to give them some choice of jobs. By the fourth year I think you've got to, I think they need it. It's not complete choice, they've got limitations.' It is the ways in which 'choice' and 'limitations' were applied by Mr Penketh in relation to pupils' perceived abilities in basic skills which will be considered.

Choice of jobs was implemented by producing models on a simple-to-difficult scale, whereas 'limited choice' allowed pupils only to make simple modifications to the job set for the whole class. Mr Penketh explained the choice of jobs: 'I've done three carts, one's a tip cart, one's called a Devon Wain which is a haycart, and one is . . . just a cart. That one is quite a difficult one, it's the most difficult of them all, the tip cart is a bit easier, the Devon Wain is much easier . . .' The range of jobs from which pupils could 'choose' was extended further into allowing the pupils to design their own jobs, as illustrated in the case of a class doing metal/forge work:

> I'm going to explain to you what jobs you are going to do next week when you come to Design. I'm going to show you various processes in metal and you're going to design certain jobs . . . So between now and next week you can think of the type of work you would like to do. You can bend it round, you can twist it, you can shape it, you can make sculptures . . .

Within both frameworks—a range of set jobs or the opportunity to design jobs — Mr Penketh incorporated the option of *changing the job* which a pupil chose. For instance, when we discussed a group of 'less able' boys in the fourth year who were making the less difficult of two types of marionette, and I asked what would happen if they chose the more difficult one, Mr Penketh replied: 'They wanted to make the puppet so I suggested that they try the simpler one, otherwise they'd get frustrated . . . . Well if they chose that [the difficult one] I'd have to change he job.' An example of how this operated when pupils designed their own jobs occurred when the class doing metal/forge work presented ideas for the type of work they 'would like to do'. Each pupil in turn showed the design to Mr Penketh for approval. Some were given the 'OK' with little more than a nod of approval; some received brief comment regarding dimensions or similar detail; others were scrutinized more closely:

Mr Penketh to Janice:	I don't like your 3. Do you? [Mr P. hands a book of lettering to the pupil.] Take that away, see if you can find a large 3 in there, OK. You might, have a look. Can you improve your 3 and then we can get to work.
Mr Penketh to Melanie:	How many of those [supports on a plant stand] are you going to make?
Pupil: [Pause]	Two
Mr Penketh:	Are you only having two? Are you sure? Are you positive you only want two? Are you sure? (This was said in a pleasant joking manner, reciprocated by the pupil.)

Mr Penketh:	Watch
	Mr Penketh turned to another pupil in the class, standing nearby, to illustrate the point he wanted to make:
	Open your legs, stand with your feet wide apart, right.

He then turned to the girl again.

Now look. He's difficult to push over there isn't he? [pushes boy gently] He's difficult to push over there [pushes other side of boy gently] but he's easy to push that way isn't he? [pushes boy from front and he begins to fall backwards] It's the basic principle of Judo that is [joking again] How many are you having?

| Pupil: | Four. |

Like Janice who was now redesigning her figure 3, Melanie left to redesign the supports. The next pupil in line was Russell. Russell had been pointed out to me as a boy with learning difficulties. He was also new to the school. He offered his design for approval:

Mr Penketh:	You want to do that, do you? Can you wait a moment and I'll see you last Russell. Don't go away.
	[Later, at a time when the queue had disappeared and more time could be devoted to Russell.]
	I think I'll find you a slightly different job Russell. Unless you specially want to do that one, do you?
Russell:	Yes
Mr Penketh:	OK, Russell, I'll let you have a go at it but don't be disappointed if you have trouble will you? [undistinguishable ... _] to give me trouble if you have trouble with your job. Good, but we'll see what we can work out for you, OK?

Russell was seen the following week doing a different job, one which Mr Penketh had given him to do.

I asked if it was necessary to sort out which children would want to do a particular kind of job. Mr Penketh replied:

Yes. At the moment I'm giving them limited choice, so it sorts itself out, and guiding certain children where I can. But of course within this guidance you're going to have a certain amount of ... [pause] ... what you might call slack. You know, one or two children that's ... it's like the 11+, isn't it, you have fifteen per cent that you're sort of going to lose if you're not careful ... .

The notion of limited choice and a choice of jobs amounted to no choice at all for pupils like Russell and the boys working on the less difficult marionette. But changing the job as a mechanism for fitting pupils to appropriate tasks could also apply upwards in the hierarchy of difficulty where differentiated models were involved. If 'more able' pupils chose a simple job they could be guided to more difficult ones. Where jobs were not of the set kind and pupils were asked to design their own jobs, the possibility of using design ideas incorporating individual decision-making was available to some pupils, while others were prevented from pursuing their own ideas and were given jobs set by Mr Penketh.

From classroom observation it became clear that limited choice within a set job, some choice of different jobs, and in the case of some pupils freedom to design jobs, all operated within the same classes. Some pupils were granted greater freedom to make major design decisions, and were expected to do so, while others, like Russell, were given jobs which they could attempt to copy as a means of developing (or *not* developing!) basic skills. With pupils like Russell, proof of their incompetence in and lack of opportunity to develop basic skills was confirmed in teacher-pupil interaction, where the teacher often took over the pupil's work, effectively doing the job for him or her.

With 'more able' pupils who exercised a wider range of choice, teacher intervention of a quite different kind was provided. This difference is well illustrated in the case of two boys (as recorded in field notes):

Boy 1
trying to make wire 'eyes' for the joints of the limbs of a marionette; having obvious difficulties. Mr Penketh arrived at the workbench.

Mr Penketh: How many do you need?

Boy: Lots.

Mr Penketh proceeded to make 'lots' with the boy looking on. Some minutes passed.

Mr Penketh: Hey, it's like going into production, this. There you are then, you can get on with those, you should be alright now.

The boy had not been shown explicitly how to make the loops, the teacher making them as quickly as possible while other pupils waited for attention.

Boy 2
making a stool, asked Mr Penketh for some plywood and was given a large sheet of it. He proceeded to clamp the plywood to a sawing bench, measured and marked a required price, using rule, tri-square and T-square as needed, selected a saw and began to cut it, though apparently not accurately. I held the wood for him and commented, 'are you supposed to cut to the line?' He replied that he did not want to make the piece too small. He completed cutting, thanked me, and took the tools and remaining plywood away. Taking his own piece to the bench it was checked, planed, sanded, and checked for 'fit' on the stool.

I later established that Boy 1 was regarded as 'less able' and Boy 2 as 'more able' by Mr Penketh. While both boys were offered guidance from time to time, the exact nature and amount of contact over time differed between the two, even though the classroom circumstances were similar. In the case of Boy 1 intervention by Mr Penketh was characterized by frequent, short periods of contact during which the teacher gave specific instructions, solved problems for the pupil, or actually did the work. With Boy 2 the pupil worked for long periods without contact with Mr Penketh. When it did occur contact was of a 'servicing' kind when the boy asked for and was granted the use of tools and materials, or it involved discussion of design ideas being incorporated into the job.

Sharp and Green (1975) have argued that one reason for the existence of inequalities in achievement among pupils is that they receive different amounts of teacher time, the more able being more favourably treated. They claimed, in other words, that teachers in the progressive infant school they studied interacted more frequently with those pupils they construed as being more successful. In addition, the attention these pupils received, along with the way their learning was structured and directed, was different from that of pupils who were viewed less favourably (Sharp and Green, 1975, p. 115). However, evidence to support these assertions is rather thin (Hargreaves, 1978; Boydell, 1981). The data from the present case study, interestingly, cast further doubt on the details of Sharp and

Green's claims, for Mr Penketh seemed much more concerned with and aware of the dealings with the less able than Sharp's and Green's teachers were alleged to be. Moreover, although Mr Penketh did give pupils unequal slices of his time, more of these interactions were with the less able.

Mr Penketh recognized clearly the problem of the unequal allocation of his time to different pupils—a problem which he had to overcome in order to achieve success in learning for *all* his pupils. It was the greater allocation of time to the 'less able' which he saw as the major problem area.

> theoretically, educationally, that [different approaches to match different rates of progress] shouldn't happen, but it doesn't work like that in practice. I've got two choices. I could give them [the less able] all my attention and ignore the others, but then the others would miss out .... One answer would be to make the work so they could cope, but then you'd have the problem at the other end [the more able] with the others getting frustrated.

Solving the less able's problems for them went some way towards a solution:

> There's a new lad, Russell, who's got very low ability, cannot concentrate, cannot hold on to anything for any length of time, so I gave him a little job. He chose a giraffe, and he made a sketch and it was a mess, so I sent him away. Remember I had a whole class with me He came back and it was not much better but we improved it together.

But an alternative solution also emerged in the shape of offering a 'choice' of jobs, or 'changing the job'. The solution in these cases was to provide a limited choice of projects which allowed the more able to progress (within limits) while the less able could be controlled and 'helped' more closely.

> This is the crux of the whole matter, in that, do I develop them up in skills slowly to a point where I can say the whole class can handle that job, or do I go along as I am, trying to keep my eye on those who are lagging a bit, or those who are struggling, or even those who are a bit lazy, don't want to make that extra effort. It's difficult to assess on that one.

Crucial to Mr Penketh's problem was the difficulty of reconciling the didactic teaching of craft skills with the encouragement of individuality, the expression of personal ideas, and problem-solving. These two aspects of curriculum content related closely to the difficulty of reconciling intentions for equal treatment and success for all pupils in a given curriculum, with the provision of opportunities for the personal development of individual pupils through creative activities. The strategies of offering pupils limited choice in modifying the end product, of offering a choice of jobs and of providing the opportunity to design their own jobs were seen as different ways of reconciling the problem of *what* was done. Changing the job was an attempt to control *when* pupils should be exposed to basic skills or allowed to engage in design/problem-solving experiences. The nature and amount of teacher attention allocated to particular pupils demonstrates one of the mechanisms of *how* these strategies were used between different groups.

In this latter sense the strategies adopted by Mr Penketh varied depending on the pupil. With some—the less able—acts of imposition and close structuring of jobs along with much 'helping' and 'improving it together' were invoked in attempts to develop competence in manipulative skills. The 'more able' pupils, on the other hand, experienced less imposition over time, and were presented with work which involved decision-making, problem-solving and the use of design ideas. These differences became acute in mixed ability classes where, because of the large numbers, Mr Penketh had yet further difficulties in providing for individual pupils' personal development, particularly in the management, allocation and use of his time. When a class worked on the same job, the management of time was relatively easy. But when work was differentiated, Mr Penketh's concern for those 'lagging a bit' or 'struggling' led to further acts of imposition on his part, with continued stress upon skills and a consequent restriction of personal development. Thus, while, in contrast to Sharp's and Green's teachers, Mr Penketh allocated the greater part of his time to less able pupils, the way he *used* that time confirmed the two curricula for less able and more able pupils respectively: a curriculum of imposition for 'the less able' and one of opportunities to engage in creative work for 'the more able'.

Mr Tansley

Unlike Mr Penketh, Mr Tansley did not identify himself with traditional craft teachers. He had made a number of changes in his teaching since working in a middle school, and his current ideas reflected an amalgam of traditional and progressive views. Despite these differences, however, the pattern of events in Mr Tansley's classroom closely paralleled that in Mr Penketh's. When pupils started the course in 'technical studies'—at the beginning of their third year—they were all presented with exactly the same tasks: to make a pencil box using the same materials, tools and skills, and at approximately the same pace. From this kind of activity Mr Tansley claimed to be able to identify which pupils were the more or less creative ones. This indicated who could be guided towards different kinds of learning, who could be given greater degrees of freedom, choice, decision-making and problem-solving, and who needed more careful guidance in manipulative craft skills. Controlling who did what and guiding individual pupils was achieved by similar means to Mr Penketh's, as illustrated in Mr Tansley's explanation of his strategies and tactics. He felt that the kind of work provided in the early stages formed a base upon which later learning was built, but that elements of both 'skills' and 'creativity' were important in all work:

> In both [skills/creativity] you build on what's gone before and you deviate from it in some particular direction. The creative aspect in the very first instance with the eleven year olds is as simple as giving them the opportunity to govern the basic shape and then a few trimmings added on ... from that you go to things where the choice is greater.

> I do set out to allow for both. A good many teachers don't, but I think it's much more worthwhile to put them side by side. If you separate them then you've got to start with skills and then follow up with perhaps the design aspect, but to take away all creativity and to lay it straight down the line for a child exactly what he's got to do defeats a lot of the aims of my teaching ... you've got to pre-determine to some extent what skills are involved, and teach the necessary ones ... and at the same time allow the child some freedom as to what the final result is.

When I discussed with Mr Tansley those pupils who had been granted more choice he pointed out that choice and freedom for these pupils operated 'within your direction': 'to give them complete choice of ideas for half of them is a formula for disaster in the size of group I get. If you'd got, say, nine children of varying ability a choice of ideas might be on.' The curriculum was 'set for them, but, of course, the choice comes in exactly what they produce within that framework.' The framework itself and the degree of choice within it varied from pupils being given no choice at all, as in the pencil box job which they all did, to subtle expectations for 'design considerations' to be included in closely restricted jobs, to a choice of different jobs or to granting approval for some pupils to deviate from an 'expected course'.

As pupils gained experience in the manipulative skills, knowledge of tools and materials and understanding of processes, Mr Tansley viewed increased freedom in decision-making and the development of personal ideas in pupils as both necessary and desirable:

> Initially the amount of freedom has got to be very constrained, but gradually the brakes can come off and with each child it's a matter of releasing the brakes at a slightly different rate, and certainly by the time the child leaves the middle school, the more advanced children at least, the brakes can be ... not removed entirely, you've still got to direct their operations but, emmm ... you don't need to stamp on every little deviation from the expected course. You can allow them not to go almost exactly as they want, but within your direction. ...

This led to a strategy of *directing pupils towards appropriate tasks* and of *pointing them in the direction you want them to go in*. Such guidance and direction was closely related to Mr Tansley's perception of pupils as 'bright' or 'backward'. These two types of pupils were consequently offered quite different curricular experiences, not only in what was done, but in the allocation of teacher time and in the nature of the teacher–pupil interaction which filled that time.

> Occasionally the bright child gets a poorer deal, and as he's not coming to see me every five minutes there are occasions when he gets left out altogether. He feels that he can get on on his own .... The backward child falls into a pattern of rushing to me more frequently than even they need, and perhaps I tend to get too involved with them, and perhaps tend to solve too many problems for them. I'm not saying that they get a very good deal, but, emm ... I find myself involving myself a little too much with them at the expense of the brighter ones.

The brighter ones had certain compensations. They were not totally 'ditched' by the teacher but gained their 'independence':

> ... You've got to give them that independence, but even with them there has got to be limits, because if you don't impose some limits on them at some stage even they are capable of hanging themselves. And there's got to be a success factor with them just as much as the others, probably equally important. In fact I don't always set the same work for the whole class.

The relationship between the different degrees of freedom intended by Mr Tansley and the ways in which the 'real guidance' occurred was critical to the experiences of the pupils. Central to that relationship was the frequency and nature of contact with the teacher.

> What I like to feel happens is that the less able need me at very regular intervals, usually very short intervals, but their problems can often be solved very quickly because there's no great depth to them. The brighter child doesn't need me anywhere near as often but when they do need me I like to think that I go into things in some depth, I should have one spell of say ten minutes with a bright child or several bright children who are doing similar things. And then with the less able probably five spells of two minutes. The rest will fall between these two extremes, they need me less frequently than the less able child and probably for a little longer.

Mr Tansley recognized the difficulty of achieving such an accurate share-out of time, and he recognized that he became 'too involved' with the pupils deemed less able: '[that's] ... what I like to feel happens, although I know it doesn't always.'

To sum up, Mr Tansley's notion of giving 'more able' pupils greater independence to pursue design ideas and engage in individual problem-solving activities was realized through less frequent but longer encounters during which problems were considered in depth. When Mr Tansley attempted to achieve a balance in the management of classroom time, he was conscious that the demands of the 'less able' predominated. But this did not mean that the 'more able' were neglected. Rather, in the extended periods when they were left to their own devices, and in their less frequent but more sustained interactions with the teacher, they enjoyed greater opportunity for the development of their own personal ideas. In Mr Tansley's classes, therefore, while the less able get more of his time the fact that the time is used up in frequent short bursts of routine managerial activity actually seems to reinforce the differentiation between pupils in their experience of design activities. In effect, it confirms restrictions upon and opportunities for personal development for 'less able' and 'more able' pupils respectively.

Mr Sankey

Mr Sankey regarded himself as a 'progressive' teacher adopting a child-centred approach to teaching and learning (Hammersley, 1977). The development of the creative process was central to his aims, as was his desire to extend to the child as much autonomy as was consistent with the development of 'personal ideas' in a 'free' environment. On the face of it both the perspectives and the classroom activities of Mr Sankey offered a dramatic contrast to those of his colleague, Mr Penketh. Mr Sankey's views of teaching and learning were radically progressive. His actual practice, however, shares many similarities with Mr Penketh's, indicating major discrepancies between intention and action. Stimulating children to develop and express ideas of their own, through exploration of their environment, was central to his teaching perspective. His ideal was for each individual to have personal ideas which they wanted to express and for the teacher to facilitate such expression. This ideal was not matched in practice because of various influences, not least the activities of the pupils themselves: 'If I give them too many alternatives I find they can't cope and in the end they come back and ask me to tell them what to do ... !' These influences resulted in his adopting a strategy of using a *common starting-point* for all pupils, in the form of visual stimuli to generate ideas.

Following the common starting-point with the whole class, individual pupils were then expected to *develop an idea*—an individual, personal idea. In practice, this use of ideas, along with the promotion of personal expression in pupils' work, was followed by teacher sanctions upon the art products and the ideas that pupils represented in them, particularly with regard to aesthetic composition and modes of visual representation.

> One girl's produced a super piece of work. She put this hand in up here, so I had to explain to her that it was a still life and you don't have living things in it. She made the whole thing up though, it's come from us doing pencil shading and she did it all on her own at lunchtime.

Such inconsistencies between Mr Sankey's stated intentions and his classroom practice were particularly noticeable in his concerns for developing skills in the control and knowledge of materials. In this respect he adopted a strategy of *'experimenting with skills'* at the beginning of each session. This, in sharp contrast to his stated aims, led to identical class exercises in pencil shading and colour mixing, using the same sized paper, the same tones and colours, organized in exactly the same way on the paper. In this way all pupils were expected to learn the same skills, at the same time, under close direction from the teacher. Mr Sankey also wanted children to understand the creative process, and to engage in qualitative problem-solving. The responsibility for generating problems was vested in the pupils. It was Mr Sankey's hope that over time the visual forms used—paintings, colleges, ceramics, etc.—would develop through different aesthetic 'styles' or modes of representation as the pupils became accustomed to and ready for their use. Thus, for example, he would not 'teach perspective', but would encourage its use in drawing and painting if an individual pupil 'needed it' or was 'ready for it'. He did not want to set the same work for all pupils, though he hoped that they would all encounter the same range of experiences over the duration of the course. For example, Mr Sankey hoped that pupils would choose to work in a range of media. If they did not, he would implement a strategy of *'guiding them in that direction'*: 'If that happened [pupils chose a range of media] it would be ideal, but I don't think it will happen, it would be nice if it did. If it didn't then I'll suggest it, guide them in that direction.' What varied for different pupils was the form of guidance. Pupils who 'tuned in', who 'understand what I want' and who gave Mr Sankey the feeling that he had 'projected myself very well in the first place', were permitted to proceed 'independently'.

> If I can get them to understand then in any new piece of work there shouldn't be any reason why they can't come up with a statement that's fair for that individual child. I'm taking individuals you know ... and then from that understanding they can develop their own work, if they've got the inclination.

Some pupils, however, did not 'tune in'. They did not achieve the prescribed learning which underlay much of the work Mr Sankey set (as distinct from his ideals). As I have already indicated, allowing pupils to express individual ideas was difficult enough in itself. Discussing individual pupils' ideas with them proved even more problematic.

> Well, I'm trying to. I can do it more simply if I tune all the kids in to the same piece of work ... I know there are kids who need attention and the ones who can't quite tune in are demanding more attention. I think this is the mixed ability thing coming into the class, there's such a diverse ability range.

Some pupils, on the other hand, 'work so well you hardly need to bother them at all.'

The difference between those pupils demanding more attention and those hardly needing any at all is paralleled by differences in the amount and kind of attention Mr Sankey gave to different pupils. There were those 'like that girl last week, the still life ... I want to let her get on with that', and those like 'that lad who did that bizarre landscape. I've made him go back and back to that ... I'm going to make sure he sticks with it.' Pupils of the first kind who were left to 'get on with it' were usually identified as 'more able', 'tuned in' and of 'innate ability'. The second group, identified as 'less able' (or even 'remedial' or 'dyslexic'), received or demanded more frequent 'help' or intervention from the teacher. Such attention was also qualitatively different from that devoted to the 'more able', and usually involved closer control and explicit, specific directives about the requirements of work. Pupils' freedom to make decisions was contained within limits of particular aesthetic values, as illustrated in the following incident (as recorded in field notes):

> A girl was working on a large painting of a landscape which was mainly tones of blue, green and yellow. In the lower right hand corner she had put a large crimson shape.
>
> Mr S: You'll have to be careful there ... that colour's very strong.
>
> He took the painting and stood a short distance from her, holding it for her to see.
>
> Mr S: Look [he covered the red shape, then uncovered it]. Your eye goes through it. Before your eye went up here, now it goes straight to that shape because it's so strong. You'll have to be careful with the colours.
>
> At the end of the lesson Mr Sankey spoke to the class: OK, next lesson we'll look at some of the problems some of you are having and talk about them. One girl was putting ...' [He described the problem of the red shape.]

Mr Sankey was unhappy about pupils 'like that girl there, she'll ask me if it's the right blue!' In his ideal teacher perspective Mr Sankey related success to individual pupils' own ideas, and measured achievement against criteria which were related to each pupil's development. In practice, however, the achievement of success also required pupils to satisfy certain implicit criteria which Mr Sankey applied. These criteria differed sharply between 'problem' and 'ideal' pupils. Such differences were reflected in the nature and amount of teacher interaction each received:

> *Group work*
> A group who had 'performed disastrously' when asked to present ideas without directives were addressed by Mr Sankey: 'Look at this one of Sandra's. Now try to do one like that.' After the pupils began work, individuals approached Mr Sankey to ask if their work was 'alright'. This pattern was common in several groups observed. One boy had made a painting of a section of rose tree. He approached Mr Sankey for 'approval' and was told that the spikes were not pointed enough—the wrong shapes had been used. Most noticeable was the number of children who came to Mr Sankey for approval. He discussed the work and gave explicit directions about what they could or should do. A girl had made pencil sketches of a cluster of Scots Pine needles. She was told to choose the centre detail of one drawing and to enlarge it, using pastel, on a sheet of paper approximately 30×50 cm. She did an enlarged drawing of the centre point or bud and approached the teacher. He said she had not done the needles and demonstrated how this should be done. She followed instructions for *one* needle and returned. Mr Sankey said: 'But now you've got to darken them down on one side, haven't you?' She went to a table and did so, and soon returned. Mr Sankey told her to include the other needles in the drawing in the same way, and similar interaction continued for most of the lesson with the girl doing one part and returning for further instructions at each stage. (Field notes)

In instances of this kind Mr Sankey repeatedly issued directives on technique in the application of media and on composition. Type and size of paper, media to be used, colours allowed, ideas to be incorporated and length of time to be devoted were all included in the decisions that Mr Sankey took for such pupils. At times it seemed that he even tried to enjoy the work for them:

> Joanne, looking unhappy, approached, handed over a drawing of a teasel and stood silently. Mr Sankey enquired what she wanted. She shrugged. Others approached and he attended to them, then turned to Joanne and asked what she wanted. She didn't answer. He was distracted by further demands and whilst attending to another pupil, Joanne was approached by a friend:
>
> Friend: [showing Joanne her work] I did this in one lesson.

Joanne: Yeh, but did you like doing it?

Friend: No.

Joanne: I hate it, I'm bored.

Mr Sankey returned. Joanne told him she was bored. He took her to the display boards and showed her some examples of work she could do if she wished. He suggested she use an object: 'to take out simple shapes, limited colours, and so on', and tried to stimulate her ideas. Fully aware of Joanne's lack of involvement, he was trying, he said, to get her to involve herself with her own ideas but was finding it very difficult. (Field notes)

Mr Sankey was aware of some of the differences that occurred in the kind and amount of his interactions with different pupils. This presented him with a major dilemma which was most acute in his imposition of aesthetic standards with 'problem' pupils. As Mr Sankey put it when asked how he conveyed appropriate standards: 'On a personal ... yeh ... I think ... I put it across ... [long pause] ... it might be a personal thing of my own ... yeh ... ... it could be indoctrination.'

'Indoctrination'—the imposition of particular aesthetic standards and modes of image-making—was not a problem with those pupils who 'tuned in'. These pupils, ones who were seen as having 'innate ability' in the subject, were Mr Sankey's ideal. Such was the case of a boy I observed painting a landscape, meticulously mixing tones of colour in small quantities, quite dry, applying it by a stipple technique. The boy had worked quietly at this on one side of the room, with no intervention, for most of the lesson. I saw Mr Sankey watching the boy but not intervening; then he came to speak to me: 'Have you seen his tree over there, it's beautiful.' This kind of interaction was emphasized further in the case of a girl making design decisions:

Melanie
After an introductory session when pupils had been asked to 'develop ideas' from stimuli, Melanie approached Mr Sankey with her idea. She had drawn a small triangle on a piece of paper and tried to explain her intentions. The explanation was incomprehensible. Mr Sankey suggested she should sketch her ideas more fully: 'Can you put them down on paper, whatever ideas you want to use?' He was distracted by other pupils. Melanie started to section off the paper in triangular shapes, and showed that each was to be enlarged on to a triangle of cardboard, with folded edges which would cause the triangle to stand in relief (a double fold) to give a deep section and allow for fixing onto a base. The sections would be mounted with small spaces between each, so that each contained an independent section of a larger whole picture. The idea was communicated to me without interjection. It was very carefully thought out and had not come from the teacher, with whom I discussed the incident later. It was 'far better' that the idea had come from the girl. He was very aware that in 'telling them what to do' he was not fulfilling his intentions with some pupils. (Field notes)

The success of such pupils was measured by implicit criteria linked to displayed achievement in 'adult' modes of image-making. Because they satisfied such criteria these pupils were presented with opportunities to engage in qualitative problem-solving and to express personal ideas through the use of a particular sequence of experiences with media.

Imposition of aesthetic standards and tight control over pupil time ran counter to Mr Sankey's idea of encouraging pupils' personal development. Yet 'problem' pupils were expected to 'stick with it' and experienced more frequent contact during which standards in aesthetic qualities and the requirements of particular modes of image-making were consistently and explicitly imposed. On the other hand, pupils who 'tuned in' satisfied Mr Sankey's criteria and were able to pursue his ideal of using personal ideas, exploring media and engaging in problem-solving. The differentiation among pupils in the amounts of time allocated, and their different experiences within that distribution of time, confirmed the restrictions upon and opportunities for personal development for 'problem' and 'ideal' pupils respectively. In both cases the teacher imposed standards which were derived from models of 'adult' aesthetic competence. This occurred through interactions which were qualitatively different for each 'type' of pupil, giving some support to the assertions of Sharp and Green in their study of infant classrooms. But, in contrast to Sharp and Green's findings, it was those pupils seen in favourable terms by the teacher who received *less* interaction, and engaged in more exploratory learning, while those seen in less favourable terms experienced frequent, brief and closely directed interactions with Mr Sankey.

Conclusion

What, then, do the perspectives and practices of these three idealistically inclined art and design teachers reveal about the effects of teaching on creativity and personal development? And do these effects vary for different kinds of pupils? Each of the teachers held different pedagogical perspectives. Yet the patterns of inter-action and the distribution and nature of teacher–pupil contact time were similar in each classroom. Although there were differences in perspectives about how learning should occur, each teacher intended that creativity should play an important part in pupils' development, and that it should be encouraged and fostered through clearly established expectations about the kinds of creative experiences which pupils should engage in—including the establishment of their own expressive, aesthetic or design problems. Yet in the classroom these intentions were continually frustrated, acutely so in relation to the 'less able' pupils. I have shown that from the two main strands of curricular intention—basic skills and creativity—there evolved two curricula, one which involved the imposition of basic skills for pupils seen as 'less able', the other involving opportunities to engage in creative work for those seen as 'more able'. I have also shown how these different curricular experiences became predominant for each group, and how this occurred through the unequal distribution of teacher-pupil contact and differential treatment of pupils during interaction with the teachers. Pupils seen unfavourably in terms of a perceived lack of success in basic skills received greater amounts of attention and closer structuring of their experiences than those seen more favourably by the teachers. What is more, each of the teachers was conscious of these differences in treatment even though it was their intention to treat pupils equally. Thus with these teachers of art and design in these two middle schools creativity and personal development of many pupils were persistently inhibited, despite intentions to the contrary.

Ironically, it was the closer structuring of skills teaching with the 'less able', arising out of teacher concern for those pupils' success, which enhanced opportunities for others to engage in creative dimensions of experience. Restricted chances for some ran side by side with afforded opportunities for others to fulfil creative potential. Within that divisive curriculum the teachers' management of classroom time mirrors a major dilemma of art and design education and opposing views about the nature of schooling in general. Conflicting views about whether art and design curricula are concerned with imposing control through the rigorous teaching of predetermined practical skills, or with fostering personal growth through problem-solving processes and creative experience met head-on in these classrooms. Furthermore, more general images of education concerned with maximizing personal development and creative potential came face to face with ones in which schooling is anti-creative, inegalitarian and stultifying to the individual.

Given the variable experiences of these pupils in art and design within the same classroom—indeed, within the same curricular intentions—to assume that art and design education necessarily or even usually offers the chance for individual potential to be fulfilled would be to dismiss the perspectives and practices of these teachers and the experiences of their 'less able' pupils in particular. But if the optimistic assumptions about education are clearly problematic, so too are the charges that education is essentially controlling in nature. These are not equally applicable to all pupils—pupils' experiences of art and design are, in this sense clearly variable, but systematically so.

What assumptions are highlighted in these experiences of art and design? That skills of a specific kind precede and are a prerequisite to creative, problem-solving learning experiences was a predominant feature. That success in the former signals ability and likely success in the latter was a view which had a strong influence on the way classroom time was managed. Further, that more 'help' with skills would enhance individual, creative development was assumed. If change in classroom practice is to be effected these assumptions deserve and require reappraisal.

What are the implications for art and design education policy? If policy is not to be unrealistic and unrealizable, further and more extensive scrutiny of the classroom experiences of teachers and pupils is obviously needed. In this way informed understanding rather than trendy slogans about creative development might lead the way for teachers and pupils. In particular, the demands of curriculum projects (Schools Council, 1974 and 1975) as well as art and design educators (Read, 1943; Field, 1970; Shaw and Reeve, 1980) need to take full account of classroom experiences and the perspectives of teachers and pupils, such that any statements about the importance of creative activities in school experience are made with pupils like Russell in view. And what of schooling in general? This case study suggests that even where optimistic public and professional assumptions about the nature of education are strong—as with these middle school teachers of art and design—their picture of aesthetic experience at the point of classroom interaction is often out of focus with those assumptions. For some pupils at least the messages of increasing failure and increasing control, in the face of assertive attempts to raise success, are painted both clearly and early on the walls.

Note

[1] For reasons of brevity, data relating to only three of them will be used here.

References

Bennett, N. (1976) *Teaching Styles and Pupil Progress*, Open Books, London.

Berlak, A. and Berlak, H. (1981) *The Dilemmas of Schooling*, Methuen, London.

Bowles, S. and Gintis, H. (1975) *Schooling in Capitalist America*, Routledge and Kegan Paul, London.

Boydell, D. (1981) 'Classroom organization 1970–7', in Simon, B. and Willcocks, J. (eds) *Research and Practice in the Primary Classroom*, Routledge and Kegan Paul, London.

Field, D. (1970) *Change in Art Education*, Routledge and Kegan Paul, London.

Galton, M., Simon, B. and Croll, P. (1980) *Inside the Primary Classroom*, Routledge and Kegan Paul, London.

Hammersley, M. (1977) *Teacher Perspectives*, Course E202, Units 9 and 10, The Open University Press, Milton Keynes.

Hargreaves, D. (1978) 'Whatever happened to symbolic interactionism', in Barton, L. and Meighan, R. (eds) *op. cit.*

Illich, I. (1971) *Deschooling Society*, Penguin, Harmondsworth.

Krishnamurti (1953) *Education and the Significance of Life*, Harper and Row, New York.

Read, H. (1943) *Education through Art*, Faber and Faber, London.

Shaw, D.M. and Reeve, J.M. (1978) *Design Education for the Middle Years*, Hodder and Stoughton, London.

Schools Council (1974) *Children's Growth through Creative Experience, Art and Craft Education 8–13*, Van Nostrand Reinhold, London.

Schools Council (1975) *Education through Design and Craft*, Edward Arnold, London.

Sharp, R. and Green, A. (1975) *Education and Social Control*, Routledge and Kegan Paul, London.

Tickle, L. (1979) 'A sociological analysis and case study of the organization and evaluation of Art and Design subjects for third and fourth year pupils in a 9–13 middle school, unpublished MA thesis, University of Keele.

Torrance, P. (1962) *Guiding Creative Talent*, Prentice Hall, New York.

Wolff, J. (1981) *The Social Production of Art*, Macmillan, Basingstoke.

11 Girls on the Margins: A Study of Gender Divisions in the Classroom

M. STANWORTH

In this extract from her study *Gender and Schooling*, Michelle Stanworth argues that teachers view and treat boys and girls unequally and thus contribute towards a hierarchical system of gender divisions in the classroom. Her evidence is drawn from detailed individual interviews with teachers and pupils in seven 'A' level classes in the Humanities department of a college of further education. The extract concludes with a consideration of how the kinds of differentiation illustrated might be reduced.

The significance of gender in teachers' views of their pupils

Teacher: As I told his father, he's not really got any friends in our group. Because, he's not like Norman, who's the acting one, and he's not like Sebastian who's the public school type. He is just a nice quiet ordinary sort of lad. In the back row, I'm afraid, the boys have got their own groups of friends. One of them is a rugger player, and the other two stick pretty closely together. He doesn't seem to fit. And the rest are girls.

How important a factor is gender in teachers' perceptions of their pupils? The obstacles confronting systematic research into teachers' orientations towards male and female pupils are formidable. Differential perceptions of boys and girls may be so taken for granted by teachers that they will rarely, and only with great difficulty, be explicitly articulated. Furthermore, differential attitudes towards *particular* groups of girls and boys may co-exist with egalitarian principles which inhibit their expression anywhere but in the classroom itself; as Nell Keddie demonstrated in her study 'Classroom Knowledge', there may be a gulf between the ideals teachers profess in the abstract, and the prejudices they enact in the classroom. With these difficulties in mind, teachers were not asked direct questions about their attitudes to gender. Instead, the interviews concentrated on their attitudes towards, and perceptions of, the particular pupils whom they regularly teach; and did so in such a way that attitudes to male and female pupils can be systematically analysed, and can be compared with the comments of the pupils themselves.

Segregation in co-educational classes?
Teachers carry in their heads an impressive range of information about individual pupils for whom they are responsible; this is true at least of the teachers I know, and certainly of the teachers interviewed in this study. But is it the case that the male/female distinction acts as a fundamental anchor point for the way teachers categorise their pupils?

A special procedure was used to investigate the possiblity that teachers would be more sensitive to similarities between pupils of the same sex, than to characteristics which girls and boys may have in common. Each teacher was presented with a number of co-ed triads (a set of cards bearing the names of two boys and one girl, or two girls and one boy) and invited to pair the two pupils who were, in some educationally relevant way, most alike. A calculation was made of the number of occasions on which teachers paired the two pupils of the same sex. Overall, there was only a moderate tendency for teachers to confine their comparisons to pupils of the same sex. There were, however, marked differences between the choices made by female teachers and those made by men. Of the co-ed triads considered by female teachers, only 39 per cent were sorted into same-sex pairs. Male teachers, by contrast, selected same-sex pairs in 80 per cent of the cases.

There might be several ways of explaining this finding. First, it might be suggested that male teachers consider gender itself to be evidence of, or explanation for, different educational skills. Such attitudes are not unknown among the teachers interviewed, as the following comment suggests; the remark is, however, atypical of teachers' statements, and was made by a woman rather than a man.

> *Female teacher*: On the other hand, Nick, being a boy, he's rather slapdash. The girls write more diligent essays.

Another explanation for same-sex pairings might be that, perhaps because of different upbringings, girls are more likely to resemble their female classmates than their male ones, in ways that are significant within an educational context; and that, therefore, the pairing of girls with girls, and boys with boys, merely reflects teachers' perceptions of the 'actual' characteristics of their pupils. This suggestion must be rejected, because it cannot account for the different patterns of choice between male and female teachers. If girls are radically different from boys in the classroom, how is it that male teachers paired pupils of the same sex twice as frequently as female teachers?

The most adequate explanation of the findings is that male teachers tend, far more than their female colleagues, to view the sexes whom they teach in mixed classes as relatively discrete groups. If male teachers are particularly attuned to dissimilarity between the sexes, this orientation may, in turn, be translated into actions which have the effect of further polarising girls and boys in classes which they teach. (As we shall see later on, this possibility is borne out by pupils' comments.) In sum, the pairings made by male teachers may reflect both their own way of looking at the world (through a framework which emphasises male/female dissimilarity), and behavioural differences between girls and boys which the men's own attitudes may help to create.

Attachment, concern and rejection

Teachers were asked a series of questions to elicit the names of pupils to whom they were most attached, for whom they were most concerned, and those whom they would most readily reject. In analysing the responses, an effort was made to control for pupils' academic standing: whether, that is, pupils are classified by teachers as likely to pass, on the borderline, or likely to fail. Even when academic standing is taken into account, it is clear that gender plays a large part in the character of teachers' involvements with their pupils.

Teachers are most often attached to, and concerned for, pupils who are expected to pass. Within this group, however, boys are twice as likely as girls to receive 'concern' from their teachers, and three times as likely to receive 'attachment' choices. In addition, the only pupils among those classified as borderline or fail for whom teachers showed concern, were boys.

'Rejection' was most often directed at pupils who were in danger of failing their examinations. But a girl in this category is twice as likely to be rejected as a boy of the same standing. Furthermore, the only pupils from the pass category to be rejected were girls.

The evidence that teachers are more attached to and concerned for boys, and more often reject girls, applies to teachers of both sexes. However, the trend is more pronounced among the male teachers; the chance, for example, that a boy will be the recipient of his teacher's concern is twice that of a girl if the teacher is a woman, but ten times greater if the teacher is a man.

Initial impressions of pupils: 'Just three quiet girls'
In the early weeks of the academic year, teachers are faced with the arduous task of getting to know not just one, but several, groups of pupils; it is not surprising that it takes a while for the name and face of every pupil to be clearly linked in teachers' minds. What is remarkable is that the pupils who were mentioned by teachers as being difficult to place were, without exception, girls.

Interviewer:	What were your first impressions of Emma?
Male teacher:	Nothing really. I can only remember first impressions of a few who stood out right away; Adrian of course; and Philip; and David Levick; and Marion, too, because among the girls she was the earliest to say something in class. In fact, it was quite a time before I could tell some of the girls apart.
Interviewer:	Who was that?
Teacher:	Well, Angie, and her friends Leonore and Helen. They seemed rather silent at first, and they were friends, I think, and there was no way— that's how it seemed at the time—of telling one from the other. In fact, they are very different in appearance, I can see that now. One's fair and one's dark, for a start. But at the beginning they were just three quiet girls.
Interviewer:	What were your first impressions of Lucy?
Female teacher:	I didn't start teaching that class until a bit later, by which time my mind was dulled. Although I had seen them once a week, she hadn't made any impression on me at all. I didn't know which one she was. She was one of the people who it took me longest to cotton on to her name. She was one I got mixed up, actually, with Sharon, who was equally quiet and somewhat the same build. Now they're quite different, I realise, but at the time I was never quite sure which one it was.
Interviewer:	So Lucy was very slow to make any impression at all then?
Teacher:	Well, a positive impression, yes. I won't say she made a negative impression, but . . . well, you see the trouble is that that group had got more girls in it, which makes a difference. The other group had a lot of foreigners, and within a day or two I knew Belinda, who was the only foreign girl. And Dennis had curly hair and Tony had straight hair, so they were well fixed in. In fact, in that group there were only Lyn and Judith who took me a few days to get straightened out, and the rest I knew straight away. Whereas in this group, there were only seven boys and about ten girls, I suppose.
Interviewer:	So you found it easiest to learn the names of the boys, did you?
Teacher:	Yes, that's it.

As these quotations suggest, the anonymity of girls is due in part to their reticence. The girl who is mentioned as speaking out early is instantly 'fixed' by her teacher; she has, among the girls, a sort of rarity value. However, this cannot entirely explain the greater readiness with which teachers identify boys, for the few male pupils who were reported by their teachers to be exceptionally quiet in class were, nevertheless, clearly remembered. Teachers' slowness at identifying girls has strong implications for the comfort and involvement of female pupils for, as we shall see later on, pupils take it as a sign of approval if teachers know their names right away.

Advice and expectation

Teachers were asked what advice they would give to particular pupils if they were considering abandoning 'A' levels either in order to get married, or to take a job. Many of the teachers refused to accept that marriage might imply an interruption of studies; as one woman exclaimed (perhaps drawing on her own experience in combining marriage and academic work), 'I don't know why you think marriage is such a disruptive activity!' For the rest of the teachers, the advice offered was often cautionary, and female pupils were warned against giving up 'A' levels as often as males—although, as the first passage below indicates, some men were worried that to advise a girl against early marriage might be taken as a slur on her character.

> *Male teacher*: Don't do it. I would say, 'Don't do it.' Don't get me wrong, she could certainly cope with marriage, she wouldn't be an inept house-keeper or a child-beater or anything like that. But if she could get her qualifications before she took all that on, I'd say stay.
>
> *Male teacher*: If Sheila's getting married meant giving up her chance of getting 'A' levels, I'd say it would be disastrous.
>
> *Male teacher*: I'd probably tell Howard the story of my life, how easy it was to get married and how difficult it was to get back. I would remind him of the disadvantages.
>
> *Female teacher*: I think I'd say that nowadays, in her age group, half the marriages will end in divorce by the time they're thirty. And although she may have got a boyfriend whom she feels she's going to love for life, you don't know what's going to happen. I've told some of them in the past, that your husband may die (because accidents do happen!) and you'll have to support the family, and if you don't have two 'A' levels it is much harder to start again.

Largely because of the steadier academic record of their female pupils, teachers were less likely to dissuade boys than girls from giving up 'A' levels to take a job; only one teacher made the point that it might be more risky for girls in general to abandon their studies than for boys:

> *Female teacher*: I think I would say no... The type of jobs girls get offered are rather different from the ones boys get offered. It's likely to be a job lacking in prospects; and it's also quite a lot harder for girls to come back to academic study than it is for men.

The most important point to emerge from this section of the interviews is that teachers tended to find the questions much less credible for their male pupils than for their female ones. When asked about their male pupils, teachers commented that it was very unlikely the boy would contemplate leaving college for employment (in one-third of the cases) or for marriage (in one-half).

> *Male teacher*: To take a job? Now? I don't think that's even conceivable. It's like having Alastair McMaster (a teacher noted for being very untrendy) announce he was off to join a rock group.

Female teacher:	I'd be amazed. I can't imagine Ted thinking of marriage. He's definitely still got the schoolboy atmosphere. I don't think he'd have the kind of maturity to cope with a girl at this stage.
Male teacher:	Well, it wouldn't arise, would it? Boys don't usually give up their studies when they get married, that's what girls are more inclined to do.

No equivalent comments were passed about girls. It appears that while teachers are equally concerned that girls and boys should avoid a disruption of study due to marriage, and more concerned to prevent the girls abandoning their studies for employment, teachers expect such disruptions more often from girls than from boys. In other words, teachers feel at least as strongly that girls should complete their 'A' levels compared with boys; but they combine this with a lower expectation that girls will actually do so.

Looking to the future

Teachers were asked to predict what each of their pupils might be doing two years, and five years, from the time of the interview. Boys—even those in danger of failing their examinations—were seen in jobs involving considerable responsibility and authority, the most frequent predictions being for civil service or management careers. One boy, for example, of whom his teacher had earlier said—'His essays are bald, childlike and undeveloped; his statements are simple and naive'—was expected to rise to head office:

> *Female teacher*: I suspect he might be quite good at summing things up. I don't know quite whether local government or civil service, but I can't just see him pushing paper around. I can see him writing reports on things. Perhaps an information officer, or sales planning, or something like that; something in head office.

Marriage cropped up in teachers' predictions of boys' future only once, in the case of a pupil who was academically very weak, but in whom his teachers recognised exceptional personal qualities; they described him as having 'a warm streak, almost Mediterranean', and 'the gift of communication' (a reference to his sympathetic manner in face-to-face encounters, for he was reported not to speak in class). He alone among the boys is defined more in terms of his personality than his ability, and it may be no accident that he is the *only* boy for whom the future anticipated by his teachers includes marriage and parenthood.

Male teacher:	I wonder if he's the kind of boy who will marry fairly young, once he's sure of his sexual self as it were.
Female teacher:	I see him having a frightfully happy girlfriend who's terribly fond of him. So long as she's not ambitious, I think they'll be very happy. He would be a super father. I think children would adore having him for a father, though I'm not immediately sure what he'd be doing to support his family.

By contrast, the occupations suggested for girls seldom ranged beyond the stereotype of secretary, nurse or teacher. These predictions do not match either the girls' academic standing or their own aspirations. For instance, the girl who is envisaged as a secretary in the following quotation is thought to be fully capable of getting a university degree, and is herself considering a career in law.

> *Female teacher*: I can imagine her being a very competent, if somewhat detached, secretary. She looks neat and tidy, her work's neat and tidy, she's

	perfectly prompt at arriving. And she moves around with an air of knowing what she's doing. She doesn't drift.
Interviewer:	Why would she be a *detached* secretary?
Teacher:	I can't imagine her falling for her boss at all! or getting in a flap.
Interviewer:	What about in five years' time?
Teacher:	Well, I can see her having a family, and having them jolly well organised. They'll get up at the right time and go to school at the right time, wearing the right clothes. Meals will be ready when her husband gets home. She'll handle it jolly well.

Another girl, who intends to qualify as a professional psychologist, is predicted, in five years' time, to be at home with the children:

Female teacher:	I don't know what she's got in mind, but I can imagine her being a nurse. She's got a very responsible attitude to life. I don't know if nursing would be the best thing for her, but something like that, something which is demanding.
Interviewer:	What about being a doctor, say?
Teacher:	I don't think she has quite enough academic capacity for that, but she might go into teaching. A caring kind of vocation, that's what I see her in.
Interviewer:	What about in five years' time?
Teacher:	Obviously married. She's the sort of girl who could very easily be married in five years' time.
Interviewer:	Would she be working then do you think?
Teacher:	She might. But she's the sort of girl, I think, to stay at home with the children. She's a caring person, as I said.

Remarks such as this indicate an implicit assumption that girls' capacities for efficiency and initiative will be channelled into nurturant or subordinate occupations (and, of course, into childcare and housework) rather than into other, less traditional, spheres.

Marriage and parenthood figure prominently in teacher's visions of the futures of their *female* pupils: teachers volunteered that two-thirds of the girls would be married in the near future. The prediction of marriage was applied not only to girls whose academic record was unremarkable, as here:

Male teacher:	She is the sort of girl who might up and get married all of a sudden, and kick over the traces.
Interviewer:	You mean she might abandon her 'A' levels?
Teacher:	I'm not saying she would, but I wouldn't be surprised.
Interviewer:	What do you imagine her doing in five years' time?
Teacher:	Definitely married.

but also to girls who were considered to have outstanding academic capacity.

Male teacher:	Well, I'd be surprised if she wasn't married.
Interviewer:	Is she the sort of person you would expect to marry young?
Teacher:	Well, not necessarily marry young, but let's see ... 16, 17, 18, 19 years old ... somewhere along the line, certainly. I can't see what she'd be doing apart from that.

In only one instance when teachers anticipated the future was the possibility of early marriage viewed regretfully, as a potential interruption to a girl's development:

Male teacher:	I should like to see her doing some kind of higher education, and I wonder whether something in the HND line might be more suitable than a degree course.

Interviewer:	Because it's slightly more practical?
Teacher:	Yes. This is pure supposition, but it does seem to me that there is a practical vein in her. She successfully holds down a job in one of the chain stores. I can see her making a very great success of management, retail management, because I would have thought she would be very skilled at dealing with people. And though she's a little unsure of herself still, there is a vein of sureness in her. She wouldn't be taken aback by awkward situations, for instance.
Interviewer:	What about in five years' time?
Teacher:	Quite possibly early marriage, which I think would be a pity. Not because I'm against the institution of marriage, but because I think that an early marriage would prevent her from fully realising her potential.

Apart from the reaction to marriage, the preceding quotation is a-typical of teachers' comments about their female pupils in other respects. First, it is the only prediction in which a management post was suggested for a girl. Second, the fact that a possible career was specified by a male teacher is itself unusual; in two-thirds of male teachers' discussions of female pupils, the girl could not be envisaged in any occupation once her education was complete. In some cases, it is almost as if the working lives of women are a mystery to men:

Male teacher:	She would be competent enough to do a course at a university or polytechnic, though not necessarily the most academic course.
Interviewer:	What sort of a course might suit her then?
Teacher:	I can't say. I don't really know about jobs for girls.
Male teacher:	She will probably go on to further or higher education. You'd know better than I what a young girl with an independent sort of mind might be doing in five years' time!

The type of futures teachers anticipate for girls seem to be related to classroom interaction in two important ways. First, teachers' views of 'women's work', and their emphasis upon the centrality of family in women's lives, are likely to make high achievement at 'A' level seem less urgent for girls than for boys. To the extent that teachers underestimate the ambitions of their female pupils, they will be reluctant to make girls prime candidates for attention in the classroom. Second—and more pertinent to this study—it seems likely that the current dynamic of classroom interactions does nothing to undermine stereo-typical views of appropriate spheres for women and men. The reports gathered here from both teachers and pupils indicate that (whatever girls may be like outside) they are in the classroom quieter more diffident and less openly competitive than their male classmates. No matter how conscientious and capable female pupils are, they are perceived by their teachers to lack the authoritative manner and the assertiveness which many teachers seem to believe to be pre-requisites of 'masculine' occupations.

This interpretation seems to be the best way of accounting for a curious anomaly in the teachers' predictions. One girl who is ranked as the top performer in both her main subjects, and who wants a career in the diplomatic service, is envisaged by her teacher as the 'personal assistant to somebody rather important'. In contrast, the girl with the poorest academic record is one of only two girls to be suggested for a job that is not in traditional feminine mould. The comments made about these two pupils are reproduced below; they indicate that teachers attach a great significance to assertiveness in classroom situations.

Interviewer:	And can you think ahead to five years' time, what Clare might be doing in five years?

Female teacher: I could possibly see her as a kind of committee type person. She's not a forceful public speaker, you see. She says something rather quietly, and it's absolutely right. The people next to her take it in, but it doesn't have any impact if you see what I mean. I can imagine her as the personal assistant to somebody rather important, dealing with things very competently, and arranging things very competently, and giving ideas backwards and forwards, and dealing with individual callers face to face. She's good at face to face things, or in small groups, rather than in large groups.

Interviewer: What about Alison in five years' time?

Female teacher: She could have a professional job of some sort, I think. I can imagine her in publicity or almost anything. She's got a strong presence, and she definitely makes an impression. She's pretty downright and forthright and forthcoming in her opinions. In fact, she is a very good stimulus in the group, though she does make some of the pupils feel a bit antagonistic.

It is, apparently, only when a girl's behaviour in class sharply contradicts the retiring feminine stereotype (a contradiction that may produce antagonism from classmates), that teachers are likely to imagine her in a career at odds with highly traditional expectations. [...]

Intervention in the Classroom

How may the devaluation of female pupils in mixed classes be minimised? Whatever initial tendencies girls may have towards passivity (and boys, towards dominance) in classroom encounters, these are likely to be reinforced by the attitudes of their classmates. Girls are caught in a double-bind. Those who are most quiet in class are likely to be despised by their male classmates; while those who speak out most confidently may win the grudging respect of boys, but sacrifice the approval of members of their own sex. In deciding whether to participate, and how often or how forcefully to put their point of view, girls, it seems, are required to strike a particularly delicate balance.

Greater emphasis deserves to be placed, however, on those attitudes and actions of teachers which keep girls on the periphery of classroom activity. Teachers are (on their own accounts, and those of their pupils) concerned for boys, and attached to boys, more often than girls. They identify boys more readily than girls, and are reported to direct more questions and comments to their male pupils. Teachers of both sexes appear to permit the girls—even when they form the majority in the class—to be up-staged by the boys. In short, instead of drawing girls out, teachers in this study tend to go along with, and to reinforce the dominance of boys. A vicious circle is established: the less frequently girls are addressed, and encouraged to engage in classroom activity, the more that traditional beliefs about gender will appear to be vindicated—and the more girls are likely to be regarded as having nothing of value to communicate in the first place.

Male teachers have, on the evidence offered here, a heightened responsibility with regard to sexual divisions in the classroom. On their own accounts, men tend to differentiate more sharply between girls and boys in their attitudes and expectations than do women. Furthermore, pupils report that certain male teachers are noticeably more warm and sympathetic in their dealings with boys. In discussing what they experience as the favouritism of some male teachers towards boys, pupils often ventured to comment that male teachers experienced embarrassment or uneasiness in their relationships with girls. It is indeed possible that the age structure of teaching situations (older men dealing with younger girls, older women with younger boys) intersects with expectations about sexuality in such a way that it encourages male teachers to keep their distance from girls, in other words, if teachers wish to protect themselves from the appearance of sexual involvement with their pupils, then at present the male teacher–female pupil relationship is the one which is most likely to arouse suspicion. This may partially explain why female teachers seem to find less difficulty in expressing warmth towards pupils of the other sex than do men. But whatever the reasons for their attitudes and actions, male teachers must be encouraged to recognise (and to rectify) the damaging effects which their apparent leaning towards boys has on the class as a whole.

Discussion of the particular case of male teachers should not, however, be allowed to obscure a more central problem: why is it that teachers of both sexes are more likely to 'reject' girls, while showing a greater readiness to express attachment and concern for boys? Teachers involved in this study were, on the whole, conscientious and strongly committed to the welfare of their pupils. Some of the apparent insensitivity towards girls is, it seems to me, an *unintended* consequence of the guidelines teachers adopt when deciding how they will distribute, amongst their many pupils, their limited time and attention. Three major criteria for distinguishing 'deserving' pupils were mentioned by teachers in this study. Teachers felt that pupils who are trying hard, those who display outstanding ability, or pupils who are obviously experiencing difficulties with their work, should have first claim on their energies. On the surface, these criteria of commitment, talent and need may seem to be reasonable; but all three intersect with the initial reticence of girls in class so as to favour the choice of boys, rather than girls, as objects of the teacher's attention and concern.

The process by which teachers identify pupils with commitment, talent or need is problematic, involving evaluations of oral as well as written contributions. For example (as the teacher quoted below points out), it is easy to underestimate the commitment of a pupil who completes assignments adequately but who says little about the amount of effort expended:

Interviewer: So, to sum up what you just said, the attitude you take towards pupils who are finding the course a bit a difficult varies according to how deeply the pupil is committed to the subject?

Female teacher: Yes. But I think commitment is very hard to judge. Because, to a degree, your perception of commitment depends on the noise a pupil makes. A quiet, hard-working pupil may not appear to be very committed, because all the effort goes on behind the scenes.

If girls speak less in class, they have fewer opportunities than boys for displaying either 'need' or 'talent' to their teachers. On the one hand, as long as a girl's written work is adequate, teachers are likely to assume that she understands the topic; confusions and misunderstandings which may be glossed over in her written work will go undetected and unresolved, while a boy with a similar level of comprehension is more likely to have his problems noted—and worked on in the course of class discussions. On the other hand, the impression teachers gain of a 'merely competent' female pupil from looking at written work is less likely to be offset by judgments of 'perceptive and original' commentary in class. There is less chance that girls will impress their teachers with the gap between written and oral expression—and more chance that a girl who writes passable essays will be assumed to be working 'up to capacity'.

In short, the criteria according to which teachers divide their energies among their many pupils would seem to have the *unintended* consequence of disadvantaging the girls. These criteria may constitute a form of indirect discrimination. Where teachers err in their judgments about female pupils, it is likely to be in the direction of underestimating girls' talent, their commitment and their needs. This tendency is illustrated in a view of female pupils that was expressed by teachers on several occasions: that of the 'schoolgirl', able to follow instructions, but not capable of, or interested in, breaking new ground.

> *Interviewer:*   Which two of those three pupils are most alike?
> *Male teacher:*   Penny and Anna. They're standard school-leaver young ladies, of no great difference in social background. Well, some difference in social background, but schoolgirls in their attitude ... adequate, but no outstanding ability.

There are two important consequences of the priorities of teachers which have been discussed here. First, though it need not be the case that teachers grade girls more harshly than their present performance warrants, female pupils are less likely to be challenged and stretched academically, with serious implications for their *future* performance. Second, girls are less likely than boys to be singled out as worthy recipients of the teacher's attention; this (quite apart from its academic consequences) makes girls feel less valued in the classroom, and reinforces other pressures urging them to take a back seat in classroom activity.

The attitudes and orientations of teachers which may inform their classroom behaviour represent only one half of the equation; the other relevant consideration is pupils' initiatives, and the ways in which teachers may respond. Some writers have argued that male pupils place greater demands on teachers—demands in the form of questions, comments, gestures which invite attention or disruptive activity—and that teachers' greater attention to boys may be partially a straight-forward response to these immediate 'pupil presses'. If it is the case that teachers are faced with such demands from boys more than from girls (and the pupils in this study seemed to think it to be so), they have two options other than outright acquiescence.

In the first place, teachers should make a conscious effort to channel more of their attention and energies to quieter pupils—to those who, like 'Edith' in the following quote, do not put themselves forward in class:

> *Interviewer:*   Who, all in all, does Mrs. Symonds pay most attention to in this group?
> *Male pupil:*   She pays a lot of attention to Bob and me. Steve gets a lot of attention. And Tristan.
> *Interviewer:*   Who gets paid least attention, do you think, in this class?
> *Pupil:*   Edith, I think. She gets least attention in Mr. Morgan's class as well. Then there's those other two girls, Judy and Eve. Those three, they are very quiet, they don't say very much. They are just bumbling along so they get left alone. Well, perhaps that's not quite right. Edith, she's touch and go, but the other two are more intelligent, they are just quiet ...
> *Interviewer:*   Who does Mrs Symonds seem most concerned about in this group?
> *Pupil:*   I think Mrs. Symonds is a bit worried about me, and about Steve and Tristan, because we miss classes a lot. She mentions it in a roundabout way, and seems concerned. I don't think she worries much about the others, about Edith and Judy and Eve, say.
> *Interviewer:*   Even though they are very quiet?
> *Pupil:*   Judy and Eve are quite competent. But Edith, I don't think she can handle it, I don't think she understands what's going on.
> *Interviewer:*   It's strange, though, that if Edith doesn't know what she's doing, that the teacher doesn't worry about her.
> *Pupil:*   Yeah, but you just completely don't notice Edith. You just forget her existence. Whereas if me or Steve or Bob or Tristan are away, Mrs. Symonds notices that, because we usually make a lot of noise in class.

Though there are some quiet boys in secondary classrooms, the neglect of quiet pupils works, on the whole, to the disadvantage of girls.

Secondly (and more fundamentally), if girls do make fewer demands than boys, teachers could give a higher priority to re-shaping the sexual distribution of interaction in the classroom. We have seen that pupils place a considerable significance on what might otherwise be trivial aspects of social relations in the classroom—on being singled out of the group, having one's name known, being addressed individually: such actions could be taken account of by teachers in an effort to create an atmosphere in which girls (and other reticent pupils) can more readily participate. As has been demonstrated in linguistic experiments, fluency is very much dependent on social context: children who confine themselves to monosyllabic answers in situations they see as threatening may become extremely talkative and articulate when placed in more congenial surroundings, with an obviously sympathetic adult. It is, arguably, only when teachers create an atmosphere in which girls and boys are (and know themselves to be) equally valued and equally welcome, that girls will be positively encouraged to voice their opinions and ideas.

A reluctance on the part of teachers to bring girls more to the forefront in classroom activity may be based on at least two grounds: a concern not to embarrass or cause distress to timid pupils by putting them on the spot; and a commitment to non-interference with 'normal' patterns of classroom interaction. Both these grounds are open to question.

In the first instance, the potential embarrassment to timid pupils which may in some cases result from being 'put on the spot' may be outweighed by the constant undermining of confidence that stems from being (apparently) ignored. Moreover, the notion that reticent pupils will shrink under the direct gaze of the teacher may sometimes contain an element of myth which, if untested, will simply force those pupils to remain in the shadows—as one teacher discovered in a telling example:

Interviewer: Would you describe Martin as outspoken or reticent in class?
Female teacher: Well, I would have described him as exceptionally reticent, for a boy. He hardly ever said a word; and I was worried that if I leaned on him too hard, he might be embarrassed and withdraw. But you see, all that's changed since the conversation with his father.
Interviewer: How's that?
Teacher: Well since his father said he wasn't shy, since that time, I've made a point of trying to make Martin speak. And in fact, in the several times I've seen him since then, he has made a contribution.
Interviewer: How did the change occur?
Teacher: Well, it was very simple really. I've looked at him directly when I posed a problem, or just outright asked his opinion. Somewhat to my surprise, he responded right away. When I just direct a comment at the group, though, he won't offer any comment.

The attempt to engage less forthcoming pupils requires both ingenuity and effort on the part of teachers; there are no ready-made solutions. But just as teachers seek ways of encouraging students to improve their capacity for written expression—and as many manage to do so without causing undue embarrassment—so too it should be possible for concerned teachers to create for girls a more central place in classroom life.

As for the commitment to 'non-interference', I would argue that intervention in the learning process, aimed at encouraging the development of pupils in valued directions, is (almost by definition) a fundamental part of teachers' responsibilities.

Participation in classroom activities is valued; it enters into pupils' assessments of the relative capacities of themselves and their male and female classmates, and may influence teachers' judgements of the needs and abilities of girls and boys. It would seem both illogical and unjust if, on the one hand, teachers regarded the encouragement of participation as an illegitimate sphere for intervention. Toleration by teachers of practices which reinforce the devaluation of girls in their own eyes and those of their classmates, contributes directly to maintenance of the status quo: non-intervention (as much as intervention) consititutes a significant political act.

A parallel may be drawn with Bernstein's observations about the discontinuities between past and present faced by working class children entering primary school; such children are in a difficult position, he argues, because they have not only to learn new things, but also, more importantly, to unlearn patterns of interaction that have been established in earlier contexts.[1] Similarly, the teachers interviewed in this study were very anxious that pupils should realise that Advanced level study is different in quality from anything that preceded it—requiring analysis rather than description, originality of style rather than rote recitation of facts, and so on. It may be that the quiet conformism to which many girls are so effectively groomed in earlier years is suddenly in the view of 'A' level teachers, deemed inappropriate; if this is the case, and girls are having to unlearn patterns of behaviour they learned earlier, then it is reasonable to expect that teachers will give them firm and explicit guidance in the process of re-socialisation.

Note

[1] Bernstein, B. (1971) *Class, Codes and Control*, Vol. 1, Routledge & Kegan Paul, London.

PART III:

Teacher Cultures and Careers

12 What Teaching does to Teachers: Determinants of the Occupational Type

W. WALLER

Occupations tend to have a powerful effect on the identities of those who perform them. Teaching is no exception. In this extract from his classic book *The Sociology of Teaching*, Willard Waller considers what personal characteristics and qualities are induced by the circumstances of teaching. Though Waller wrote this over fifty years ago, on the basis of what he had 'seen and thought and done' in American schools, many of his insights continue to be relevant today.

[...] Before we can understand the occupational type to which the members of any profession belong, we must take account of the operation of four sorts of factors:

1 selective influences affecting the composition of the profession,
2 the set of rôles and attitudes which the member of the profession must play consistently,
3 the effect upon individuals of the opinion which the community has of the profession, and
4 traumatic learning within the occupation.

1 Following out the operation of the first of these factors, we find that one reason for the similarity of doctors to each other is that there is a type of personality which is especially attracted to medicine. Likewise a certain type is attracted more than others to law, another type to engineering, another to the ministry, etc. There is in no case complete consistency, but there is a sufficiently heavy aggregation of one sort of personality type in a given profession to justify the assumption of a selectivity affecting the composition of the professional population.
2 Those who follow certain occupations are continually thrown into certain kinds of social situations. These social situations call for, or are best met by, a certain kind of reaction on the part of the professional. The individual thus plays certain rôles and shows certain attitudes habitually, and there is a tendency for him to distort other social situations until they conform to a pattern which can be met by his habitual rôles and attitudes. [...] Training an individual for the practice of such a profession often consists in teaching him what he is expected to do or say upon certain occasions, as when the minister offers the consolations of religion to a bereaved family, a teacher assigns a lesson, a doctor enters a sick room, or a lawyer threatens suit. Long practice in the social techniques enjoined upon one in a profession makes those the deepest grooves, and at length they grow so deep that there is no getting out of them.
3 From community experience of persons playing certain kinds of rôles in the

practice of certain callings, worked over and somewhat distorted by the conscious and unconscious attitudes of the community toward that profession, arise certain subjective patterns, or stereotypes, which embody the community idea of the individual belonging to a certain occupational group. The stereotype helps to determine the true occupational type, for it affects the selectivity of the occupation, and it limits and canalizes the social experience of the member of the occupation. The attempt of the individual to escape from the stereotype may itself become as in teaching and the ministry one of the important determinants of the occupational type proper.

4   The social situation surrounding the practice of any occupation is set to inflict upon the individual whose occupational behaviour is eccentric certain shocks, or trauma. From the viewpoint of social organization, these shocks or penalties are means of enforcing conformity to social codes. Upon persons they produce special effects due to psychological shock. Though not easily differentiable from situational moulding, these effects seem to deserve special discussion [. . .]

[. . .] The economic standing of a vocation is one of the most important factors determining its selective pattern. In this are included the matter of financial return, immediate and future, the opportunity for advancement (more or less graded into steps to consititute a career), and economic security. Economic considerations do not solely determine the power of an occupation to attract desirable individuals, but they are an important part of the general configuration in which the occupation makes its appearance in the minds of individuals, for some callings have a 'personality wage,' and others have not. The social standing of the occupation is also important. Under this, it needs to be considered what social circles those in the occupation move in, and what stereotyped ideas the community has concerning the profession; for women, the question of marriage opportunities is not a slight one. The nature of the work is another condition of its attractiveness or unattractiveness to particular individuals. Some persons take naturally to routine; others are satisfied only with an occupation which presents a series of crises to be met and conquered. For some, obscurity is no hardship, but for others it is necessary always to be in range of the spotlight. There are yet other persons in whose minds the opportunities which an occupation yields for self-expression outweigh all other factors. The amount and kind of special training required for entry into the ranks of a given occupation are futher considerations which select out some few of the many called. [. . .]

But choice is rarely rational. When these considerations appear in the human mind, they are distorted by wishful thinking, altered to conform to the prevalent stereotype, colored by fancy. It is the logic of the impulses that finally determines choice. The choice of a vocation is more likely to be dictated by the family pattern and the supposed conformity of an occupation to class tradition than by a rational consideration of pay, opportunity, and the nature of the work. The social experience of the individual, too, often gives him a preference for a certain occupation on a basis that is scarcely conscious. Not all personal considerations, of course, are irrational in their nature; the possession of special aptitudes or marked disabilities often affects choice. [. . .]

The selective pattern which teaching presents to prospective teachers has never been adequately described, and the present writer does not presume to be able to deal with it any better than have his predecessors. It is a known fact that the financial rewards of teaching are not great; the pay low, and opportunity for advancement, for most teachers, slight; and economic security little. Most writers have concluded that this is in itself an explanation of the known failure of the profession to attract as large a number of capables as it should. Yet one may wonder whether merely raising salaries all around would cause the mediocre to be crowded out by the influx of the talented. The social standing of the profession is unfortunately low, and this excludes more capable than incapable persons. Particularly damaging, probably, is the belief that is abroad in the community that only persons incapable of sucess in other lines become teachers, that teaching is a failure belt, the refuge of 'unsalable men and unmarriageable women.' This belief is the more damaging for the truth that is in it. The nature of the work of teaching, with its overwhelming mass of routine and its few opportunities for free self-expression, may both deter and attract to the ultimate damage of the profession. On the one hand, the drudgery of teaching, combined with the many restrictions which the community places upon the personal conduct of teachers, may eliminate from teaching many of those virile and inspiring persons of whom the profession has such need, for it is a known fact that such pronouncedly individual persons often have little respect for purely negative morality, and react vehemently against living within the community stereotype of the teacher. On the other hand, teaching, along with the ministry, is known as one of the sheltered occupations, as an occupation where those persons who shrink from the daily battle of life, often very esteemable persons, by the way, may find refuge. This quality of not wishing to do battle in the front rank, which would perhaps show a high correlation with introversion, by no means detracts from the teaching ability of every person who has it, but on the whole it probably operates to the detriment of the profession. [. . .]

[. . .] Perhaps it is an inherent need of the personality for being in some sort of managerial position which prompts one to take up teaching as an occupational goal. Perhaps it is a training which has interested one in the things of the mind so that the attractiveness of other occupations has been dulled and that only teaching is left as a compromise (creative art being left out of consideration for lack of talent). Perhaps it is a training which has made one almost able to enter some other profession, such as law or medicine, but has left him at the door. (Students of one midwestern institution refer to the customary fifteen hours of education as an 'insurance policy.') [. . .]

[. . .] Unfriendly commentators upon the manners of teachers are able to compile a long list of unpleasant qualities which, they say, are engendered in the teacher's personality by teaching experience. There is first that certain inflexibility or unbendingness of personality which is thought to mark the person who has taught. That stiff and formal manner into which the young teacher compresses himself every morning when he puts on his collar becomes, they say, a plaster cast which at length he cannot loosen. One has noticed, too, that in his personal relationships the teacher is marked by reserve, an incomplete personal participation in the dynamic social situation and the lack of spontaneity, in psychological terms, by an inhibition of his total responses in favor of a restricted segment of them. As if this reserve was not in itself enough to discourage ill-considered advances, it is supplemented, when one has become very much the teacher, by certain outward barriers which prevent all and sundry from coming into contact with the man behind the mask and discovering those inhibited and hidden possibilities of reaction. Along with this goes dignity, the dignity of the teacher which is not natural dignity like that of the American Indian, but another kind of dignity that consists of an abnormal concern over a restricted rôle and the restricted but well-defined status that goes with it. One who has taught long enough may wax unenthusiastic on any subject under the sun; this, too, is part of the picture painted by unfriendly critics. The didactic manner, the authoritative manner, the flat, assured tones of voice that go with them, are bred in the teacher by his dealings in the school room, where he rules over the petty concerns of children as a Jehovah none too sure of himself, and it is said that these traits are carried over by the teacher into his personal relations. It is said, and it would be difficult to deny it, that the teacher mind is not creative. Even the teacher's dress is affected by his occupational attitudes; the rule is that the teacher must be conservative, if not prim, in manner, speech, and dress. There are other traits which some observers have mentioned: a set of the lips, a look of strain, a certain kind of smile, a studied mediocrity, a glib mastery of platitude. Some observations have remarked that a certain way of standing about, the way of a person who has had to spend much of his time waiting for something to happen and has had to be very dignified about it, is characteristic of the teacher. Sometimes only small and uncertain indications betray the profession. Sometimes, as a cynical novelist has remarked of one of his characters, one cannot see the man for the school master. If these traits, or those essential ones which make up the major outlines of the picture, are found among the generality of teachers, it is because these traits have survival value in the schools of today. If one does not have them when he joins the faculty, he must develop them or die the academic death. Opinions might differ as to how widely these characteristic traits are found among the members of the profession and as to how deeply they are ingrained, as to whether the ordinary man might see them, or only one with the curse of satire. But Henry Adams has said that no man can be a school master for ten years and remain fit for anything else, and his statement has given many a teacher something to worry about.

There is enough plausibility in the above description to make us teachers ponder about the future, if not the present, of ourselves and our friends. But there is another side, and we may well pause to look at it before going on with our analysis. Teaching brings out pleasant qualities in some persons, and for them it is the most gratifying vocation in the world. The teacher enjoys the most pleasant associations in his work; he lives surrounded by the respect of the community and the homage of his students. Teaching affords a splendid opportunity for a self-sacrificing person (how many of these are there?) to realize his destiny vicariously; in any case the teacher is less soiled by life than those who follow more vigorous professions. It may well be questioned, too, whether there is any occupational conscience more strict than that of the teacher. Teaching breeds patience in some teachers, patience and fairness and a reserve that is only gentlemanly and never frosty. There are some persons whom teaching liberates, and these sense during their first few months of teaching a rapid growth and expansion of personality. While we are stating this side of the case, we must record the pointed observation of one person on the constructive side of the argument that those very teachers who are bitterest in the denunciation of teaching would not for a moment consider doing anything else, and that even the most discontented teachers can rarely bring themselves to leave the profession. These considerations should be enough to convince us that there are two sides to everything that can be said about the teacher, perhaps that teaching produces radically different effects upon different types of persons. But whatever the classification of the qualities which are produced in the teacher by teaching, they all mark the occupational type. Our theoretical problem should now be clear; it is to account for the genesis of the character traits belonging to the teacher by showing how they flow out of the action of his life situation upon his personality, if possible, to show how different effects are produced upon different basic personality types.

The weightiest social relationship of the teacher is his relationship to his students; it is this relationship which is teaching. It is around this relationship that the teacher's personality tends to be organized, and it is in adaptation to the needs of this relationship that the qualities of character which mark the teacher are produced. The teacher-pupil relationship is a special form of dominance and subordination, a very unstable relationship and in quivering equilibrium, not much supported by sanction and the strong arm of authority, but depending largely upon purely personal ascendency. Every teacher is a taskmaster and every taskmaster is a hard man; if he is naturally kindly, he is hard from duty, but if he is naturally unkind, he is hard because he loves it. It is an unfortunate rôle, that of Simon Legree, and has corrupted the best of men. Conflict is in the rôle, for the wishes of the teacher and the student are necessarily divergent, and more conflict because the teacher must protect himself from the possible destruction of his authority that might arise from this divergence of motives. Subordination is possible only because the subordinated one is a subordinate with a mere fragment of his personality, while the dominant one participates completely. The subject is a subject only part of the time and with a part of himself, but the king is all king. In schools, too, subordinated ones attempt to protect themselves by withdrawing from the relationship, to suck the juice from the orange of conformity before rendering it to the teacher. But the teacher is doomed to strive against the mechanization of his rule and of obedience to it. It is the part of the teacher to enforce a real obedience. The teacher must be aggressive in his domination, and this is very unfortunate, because domination is tolerable only when it stays within set bounds. From this necessary and indispensable aggressiveness of the teacher arises an answering hostility on the part of the student which imperils the very existence of any intercourse between them. The teacher takes upon himself most of the burden of the far-reaching psychic adjustments which make the continuance of the relationship possible.

That inflexibility or unbendingness of personality which we have mentioned as characterizing the school teacher flows naturally out of his relations with his students. The teacher must maintain a consistent pose in the presence of students. He must not adapt to the demands of the childish group in which he lives, but must force the group to adapt to him, wherefore the teacher often feels that he must take leave of graciousness and charm and the art of being a good fellow at the classroom door. The teacher must not accept the definitions of situations which students work out, but must impose his own definition upon students. His position as an agent of social control, as the paid representative of the adult group among the group of children, requires that when he has found a pose he must hold it; to compromise upon matters where adult morality runs would be thought treason to the group that pays his salary. There is added a necessity of his professional career which, since men and careers are always mingled and never appear separately, is also of the greatest personal importance: he must maintain discipline, and it is easier to maintain discipline by making continual demands of the same sort and by keeping one's social rôle constant in conformity with those constant demands than by changing rôles frequently and making demands consistent with those changing rôles but inconsistent with each other. It is, furthermore, very wearing to change rôles when one is responsible for a group, for one must make the fact of the change and all its implications clear to the entire group; it usually requires a certain effort to constellate all the members of the group in the new set of attitudes which take their key from the teacher's changed rôle; there are laggards who never quite catch the point, and some lacking in social comprehension who cannot know that the teacher is joking or do not observe that he has stopped; there are risks to the teacher-dominated order in the straggling march to a new mental alignment. Therefore the teacher cannot change his rôle as often as the fulfillment of his personal impulses might dictate. When he does change it, he must label the transition in such a manner as to destroy its point, erect sign-posts, take the salt from his humour by broad hints that he is joking now. But the ability of a person to hold our interest as a person depends in large part upon a shifting of social rôles so rapid that the eye must look closely to see it and so subtle that no ready-made lables can fit it.

If there are few rôles which classroom life permits the teacher to play, he must put on each of them many times a day. The teacher must alternate his rôles because he is trying to do inconsistent things with his students, and he can bring them about only by rapid changes from one established pose to another. He is trying to maintain a definite dominance over young persons whose lives he presumes to regulate very completely. This requires of the teacher aggressiveness, unyield-ingness, and determination. If persisted in, this attitude would exterminate in students all interest in subject matter and would crush out every faint inclination ·to participate in the social life of the classroom, which presents no very alluring vistas at the best. And the teacher who went very long upon this tack would be known for a knave and a fool, and justly hated for a martinet. Sometimes an unimaginative teacher runs into just this situation. The solution is found in alter-nating this authority rôle with some other which is not altogether inconsistent with it but which veils the authority so that hostility is no longer aroused. But the authority impression must be continually renewed, and there ensues a long series of rapid but not subtle changes of rôle. As a result, the limitations and implications of the teacher-pupil relationship are made clear to the pupil group.

A clever friend has perhaps summed up the matter by saying, 'The successful teacher is one who knows how to get on and off his high-horse rapidly.' (As it happened, the author of this remark did not himself possess this skill, and failed in teaching, as so many other clever men have done, for want of dignity.) Thus one says, 'I am your teacher,' in a certain unemotional tone of voice. This begets discipline, perhaps some sullenness, certainly emotional and personal frustration on the part of both student and teacher. Before this reaction has been carried through to completion, one says 'But I am a human being and I try to be a good fellow. And you are all fine people and we have some good times together, don't we?' This is rôle number two, and if taken at its face value it begets a desirable cheerfulness and a dangerous friendliness. If he tarries too long upon this grace note, the teacher loses his authority by becoming a member of the group. He must revert to rôle number one, and say, with just a hint of warning and an implication of adult dignity in his voice, 'But I am the teacher.' All this occurs a hundred times a day in every school room, and it marks the rhythm of the teacher's movements of advancement and retreat with reference to his students, the alternate expansion and contraction of his personality. It does not occur, of course, in so obvious a form as this; it is perhaps only the very unskillful teacher who needs to put such things into words. This pulsation of the teacher's personality, with its answering change of posture on the part of students, is usually reduced to a mere conversation of gestures. This conversation, for all that habit has stripped it so bare of identifying characteristics and drained it so dry of emotion, is the most significant social process of the classroom. It is also a very important determinant of the teacher's personality, and one of the points on which transfer is said to be made most easily. After all, it need cause us no amazement if one who has learned to get his way in the school by alternate applications of hot and cold water should fall into that technique of control in his more intimate relationships. In the life of every teacher there is a significant long-term change in the psychic weight of these rôles, a not unusual result being that rôle number one, the authority rôle, eats up the friendly rôle, or absorbs so much of the personality that nothing is left for friendliness to fatten upon.

The authority rôle becomes very much formalized, both because of the psychological law that performances lose their meaningfulness by frequent repetition and because there is an advantage in having it so. Army men speak of a voice of command, a flat, impersonal, unquestionable, non-controversial tone of voice in which commands are best given. It is a tone of voice without overtones, representing only a segment of the officer's personality and demanding obedience from only a segment of the subordinate. School teachers learn by trial and error, by imitation and practice, to formalize their commands. They develop, too, the voice of exposition, which is a voice perfectly dry and as mechanical as a dictaphone, a voice adapted to the expounding of matter that has long since lost what interest it may have had for the expounder. Lack of enthusiasm has survival value. Hence the paradox that sometimes the best teachers are those least interested in their work, and that others do their best work when least concerned. But all these things contribute to the final flatness and dullness of the teacher who falls a prey to them.

It has often been remarked that a certain kind of dignity is characteristic of teachers. It seems that teachers develop a certain way of carrying themselves which sets them out from the rest of the world. This we may call school-teacher dignity. There seems to be two major roots of school teacher-dignity. One is in the community and in the attitude which the community takes toward the teacher; the other is in the nature of the teacher's work. (These are not unconnected, for the community attitude is determined by the school experience of the adult members of the community.) What happens when a new and unformed teacher first goes about in the community in which he is to teach? Let us say that a person who has never before known deference takes up teaching. Suddenly he finds himself the object of flattering attention from students, catered to by them and addressed respectfully and ceremoniously by fellow teachers. In the community he is called 'Professor.' Tradesmen approach him obsequiously; plain citizens kow-tow. People profess to show him special consideration on the grounds that he is a teacher. He is supposed to be more trustworthy than other mortals, more moral, more learned. A place of honor is prepared for him. It is a dignity that is unearned, and it is empty because it is unearned. In any other occupation, with the same training and experience, he would still be a menial of low degree, but if he ever fought through the ranks in another profession and attained to his top hat at last, he would merit the distinction, and it would fit him well. Not so teacher dignity, for it is too cheap; only the finest man can give it a high value, and then it is not the profession, but the man, that counts. Some young teachers, knowing that they merit no deference, endeavor to fend it off as gracefully as they can. Others realize vaguely that this external respect of the community is a part of the school-teacher stereotype, that it is the obverse side of a latent hostility and is more than balanced by an inclination to ridicule; sometimes they know that this respect is part of the iron framework that shuts the teacher, as a sacred object,[1] out of society and keeps him from acting as a human being—these rebel against teacher dignity. Perhaps their rebellion brings them personal disaster, and they are forced to compromise at last with dignity. Perhaps they merely suffer a myriad of tiny hurts from the satire of the dignity, and that gives them dignity by a process of scar-tissue. But dignity they must get, rebels or no—somehow. Others accept teacher dignity, and make the most of it. It is a flattering rôle. They live it. They live it the more determinedly if they ever become aware of the irony that comes with it to the lips of the average man.

The second root of teacher dignity is in the nature of the teacher's work in the classroom. The teacher lives much by the authority rôle; his livelihood depends upon it. Those who live much by one rôle must learn to defend its ultimate implications. Dignity is a means of defending the authority rôle. The necessity of maintaining dignity is increased by the fact that the rôle which gives rise to it is peculiarly liable to attack. On the objective side this dignity which arises in the classroom is an exaggerated concern over all the ramifications of respect and all the formal amenities due to one who occupies a narrow but well-defined social status. On the subjective side, dignity is first an inhibition of all action tendencies inconsistent with the major rôle of the school teacher. What is inhibited is usually the teacher's responsiveness to the more minute and subtler stimuli; what the teacher must crush out in himself is his alertness for human participation in unimportant by-play. But since it is this little responsiveness that makes us human, or makes us seem to be human, we say that the teacher, when his dignity has become habitual, has lost the human touch. Since, furthermore, the teacher must demand and obtain respect in all the ramifications of his authoritative rôle, he must develop certain mechanisms in himself which will defeat any attacks made by others upon that rôle. Among these mechanisms, perhaps chief among them, is the hair-trigger temper so often observed in the man with the pointer. The person learning to teach must recondition his anger response. The teacher must learn when to get angry and how to get angry quickly. He must learn every by-path of the social interaction of the classroom so that he may know what does and does not constitute an attack upon his dignity. To keep little misdeeds from growing into great ones, he must learn to magnify them to the larger size originally; this is easy because the more his habits are concerned with the established order the more heinous breaches of it will appear. What is even more important, he must learn that breaches of order committed in his presence or when he is responsible constitute direct attacks upon his authority. Teachers are cranky because crankiness helps them to hold their jobs.

If by virtue of unusual personal force or some psychological sleight of hand the teacher is able to dispense with dignity, or if there is in him no need for playing an authoritative rôle, but rather a revulsion against it, so that he pays the price and goes all undignified, he still stands to have dignity forced upon him by others. Though he avoids the open disrespect which most teachers without dignity encounter, or thinks *camaraderie* a compensation for it, he may still be wounded when he learns that his students compare him unfavourably with their other teachers on account of his lack of dignity or his lack of concern for the respect due him. Or he may find that he loses the friendship of the few students who matter to him because of his tolerance for the affronts of those who do not matter. But most of all is dignity enforced by one's fellow teachers. The significant people for a school teacher are other teachers, and by comparison with good standing in that fraternity the good opinion of students is a small thing and of little price. A landmark in one's assimilation to the profession is that moment when he decides that only teachers are important. According to the teacher code there is no worse offence than failure to deport one's self with dignity, and the penalties exacted for the infraction of the code are severe. A more subtle influence of the teacher group arises from the fact that it passes on its tradition to the new member of the profession and furnishes him with his models of imitation.

One has become a school teacher when he has learned to fear the loss of his dignity. Not that a greenhorn can resolve to be very dignified on the morrow, and become a full-fledged teacher by virtue of his resolution. He must learn to be dignified without the slightest effort, and without being conscious of the fact that he is being dignified; it must be so natural for him to ride upon the high horse that he fears alighting as he would fear falling from a balloon. Usually the psychological process by which one comes to fear the loss of dignity and to be bound by iron habit to the dignified pattern is not at all understood by the person who is going through it. He rarely knows that he is acquiring dignity, and when he has acquired it he does not know that he has it. The process by which dignity is built up in the teacher is apparently about as follows. A few unpleasant experiences build up a feeling of insecurity or a fear of what will happen if one lets the situation get out of hand. This fear produces a limitation of intercourse with students to the starkest essentials and an inhibition of other tendencies to respond to the persons about him. One does not love children when they are likely to become dangerous; one does not even trust them. This paralysis of part of the personality and limitation of action is school-teacher poise and school-teacher dignity; it enables one to cut through all extraneous matter to that core of behavior which involves discipline. The teacher who has it is 'all business.' When it has become habitual and one has built up a new conception of his rôle around his delimited activities, one has acquired dignity and one has become a school teacher. Though confidence returns, as it usually does, and though that confidence grows to great proportions, as it sometimes does, the limitation of behaviour remains. It should also be noted that the necessity of treating all students alike contributes to the school teacher's dignity, in so far as that is a matter of the social distance between student and teacher.

This wonted seeking-avoiding balance of the teacher, connected with dignity, is not maintained without some inner conflict. Teachers tend to withdraw from non-institutional contacts the while they yearn for the opportunity and the strength to live a life of dust and danger. Their customary routine of duties, their well-known ceremonial of personal relations, come to be their world, a world which they think of as in some sense a shelter. Thus in one mood the teacher reflects that the school year draws to a close and he shudders slightly at the thought of the new contacts which the summer may bring him. Some budding orators have found their powers deserting them as they developed into school teachers; their growing shell made the self-revelation and expression of emotion which are the soul of successful speech-making increasingly difficult; perhaps they even came to take pride in the fact that 'gush' was no longer in their line and to look back with shame to their spectacular behaviour in the days when their habits of social expression were less restricted. 'Don't be an ass,' is a rule of conduct which has a special appeal to teachers and to all others who live much in a dominant rôle. Yet it is a principle that paralyzes, too, and one that cuts the person off from communion with his naïve fellows, and the teacher often feels the isolation which his personality traits impose upon him.

Enthusiasm does not comport well with dignity. Enthusiasm, therefore, is bad form. 'I rather resent your inference that anyone who believes in the Dalton plan is a "progressive" teacher, an enthusiast,' said a headmaster at a regional meeting of private-school teachers. Maugham has furnished a classic bit:

> It was Winks who summed up the general impression and put it into a form they all felt conclusively damning. Winks was the master of the upper third, a weak-kneed man with drooping eyelids. He was too tall for his strength, and his movements were slow and languid. He gave an impression of lassitude, and his nickname was eminently appropriate.
>
> 'He's very enthusiastic,' said Winks.
>
> Enthusiasm was ill-bred. Enthusiasm was ungentlemanly. They thought of the Salvation Army with its braying trumpets and its drums. Enthusiasm meant

change. They had goose-flesh when they thought of all the pleasant old habits which stood in imminent danger. They hardly dared to look forward to the future.[2]

One is puzzled to explain that peculiar blight which affects the teacher mind, which creeps over it gradually, and, possessing it bit by bit, devours its creative resources. Some there are who escape this disease endemic in the profession, but the wonder is they are so few. That the plague is real, and that it strikes many teachers, the kindest critic cannot deny. Those who have known young teachers well, and have observed the course of their personal development as they became set in the teaching pattern, have often been grieved by the progressive deterioration in their general adaptability. [. . .]

[. . .] Some of the gradual deadening of the intellect which the observer remarks in the teacher as he grows into his profession may no doubt be explained as an effect of age. Perhaps age does dull some persons, and certainly experience disciplines the creative impulse out of many. But if all the deterioration in the teacher is due to age, there must be a special type of short-blooming mind that is attracted to teaching; if this is so, we are thrown back upon the unanswered question of occupational selection. Another type of explanation could be based upon the tendency inculcated upon one practising any profession to respond to recurring social situations in stereotyped ways. The deepening of some grooves of social expression is apparently inevitable in any occupation, and, this emphasis of the part must involve deterioration of the whole. The mental structure of the unspecialized person is necessarily plastic; by specializing and developing particular proficiency along some one line, one nearly always loses some of his general adaptability. Perhaps that was why the elder James regarded so many of the established pursuits as 'narrowing.' The extent to which a profession stereotypes and narrows the social expression of the individual depends upon the range of variation in the social situations which the practice of the profession presents. The situations which the teacher faces are somewhat more stereotyped than those which the lawyer and the doctor must confront. Perhaps teaching is only a little more rigid in the social patterning which it imposes upon its devotees, but it is a very important little. The over-attention of teachers to tool subjects must certainly be called in to help explain the smallness and unimportance of the contributions which teachers have made to the arts and sciences. The teacher, from the very nature of his work, must spend most of his time in the classroom in drilling his students upon those subjects which may later open to them the doors that lead to wisdom. Other men, when they have reached maturity, may themselves use those tools to unlock the doors of the place and enter within. But the teacher, unfortunately, must always sit upon the front steps and talk about the means of opening the door; he must instruct others in the technique of door-opening, and usually he finds when he has finished his task that he has no energy left for explorations of his own. All this is incidental to the fact that the teacher must deal with persons living in a world of childish attitudes and values, and comes himself to live in it part way. This is what one teacher called 'the drag of the immature mind.'

The routine situations which the teacher confronts give rise to routine habits of social expression adapted to meet them. This we have mentioned. What we have not dealt with is the influence of these routinized reactions upon the selective pattern of experience which the teacher builds up within himself. Actually the teacher faces a narrow but complex and dynamic social situation, one from which he might well receive a liberal education in adaptability, but from this complex network of human attitudes and activities he is forced to select mainly those which affect his discipline. He may peer into the book of human life, a various volume which has many obscure and devious passages, but he is privileged to read in it only the insults to himself. As to subject matter, the teacher's possibilities of reaction are equally limited. Not confutation, nor understanding, nor yet the notation of the heart must be his aim as he reads, but merely the answering of the most obvious questions and the prevention of the most stupid errors. The selectivity which the teacher builds up must be one which will give him a maximum of discipline and a minimum of subject matter. We have noted the partial paralysis of the teacher's personality through a fear of possible consequences if he allows himself freedom in his social life; this is a sort of self-frustration produced by the elaborate system of defence reactions which the teacher builds about himself. We have mentioned, too, a certain tenseness as characterizing the teacher, a tenseness which arises out of the conflict implicit in the inhibition of the major part of his potentialities of response in favor of a few necessary but personally unsatisfactory responses. This tenseness prevents the wholesome fulfillment of creative process. Creation requires motivation with control; the teacher has an excess of motivation with an even greater excess of inhibition.

There is something in the attitude of grading, too, which makes against change, and renders mental growth difficult. One who presumes to rate the performance of another must have a very definite idea of the perfect performance, and he judges other performances, not by their inner, groping onwardness, but simply by their resemblance to the perfect performance. This perfect performance is a thing finished, for nothing can ever be super-perfect except for advertising writers, and so the teacher need not think about it any more. Yet the teacher must have in mind a perfect performance, or he is no very accurate marker. The grading, marking habit assumes increasing importance as one becomes a teacher. The new teacher rarely has definite standards of grading. Often he does not consider that part of his task important. But sceptical though one be concerning the numerical evaluation of so subjective a thing as learning, he must at length conform. From habit, from the importance which others (especially the persons graded) attach to grades, and from the involvement of the teacher's status feelings with the development of rigorous standards, there arises a change in the teacher's attitude. His status feelings become involved when he realizes that students believe that he is 'easy,' and preen themselves upon their ability to deceive him. (Sometimes there arises a circular interaction as a result of the alternate stiffening and relaxation of academic standards. These changes in the standards produce changes in the attitudes of students, and these in turn work upon the teacher to effect the relaxation or stiffening of standards, according to the place in the cycle where the group happens to be.) The teacher must establish standards of grading; he must identify himself with them and make them a part of himself.

The creative powers of teachers disappear because the teacher tends to lose the learner's attitude. As Burnham has put it, 'Again, one's own opinion based upon personal experience and strengthened by daily repetition[3] is apt to develop a didactic attitude that makes learning impossible. With this mental set, teachers cannot learn because so eager to teach; and nothing perhaps wearies them so much as to hear again what they think they already know. This inhibition of learning by the attitude of the teacher as such, combined with the common critical attitude, made it impossible for a large part of the teachers to profit greatly by the teachings of genetic pedagogy and genetic psychology.'[4][. . .]

[. . .] It is likely that the general adaptability of the teacher suffers also from the over-stable adjustment which the teacher makes to a number of simple, changeless rhythms. Teaching, perhaps, exceeds other professions only in the unvarying quality of these rhythms and the tightness with which they are bound together. There is the rhythm of the class period, which becomes so exact and unvarying that the experienced teacher often has a feeling for the end of the hour which no delayed bell can delude. One teacher has reported that when he had taught for some years in a school where the daily regimen was adhered to strictly he developed a time mechanism which always told him when two minutes only were left of the hour; at this time, contrary to the rules of pedagogy, he assigned the lesson for the next day. He said that if he forced himself to assign the lesson at the beginning of the hour, as he occasionally did, he might fail to note the nearness of the end, but if the bell were delayed by so much as two or three minutes, he always noticed it. This is no doubt rather an unusual case, but similar mechanisms operate in other teachers with less perfection. Then there is the daily rhythm, with its high points and low, its crises relieving monotony, its automatic transition from one class to another, and its alternation of school duties. There is a weekly rhythm, marked by Monday and Friday, and by special days devoted to special tasks. Where the daily routine differs much from one day to the next, the teacher tends to live by the week; this seems to be true of the college teacher. There is a monthly rhythm; payday, quizzes, grades, and the completion of certain tasks mark off the month. In certain communities, the life of the teacher is from one spring to the next, for at that time it is decided what teachers shall be retained and what ones dismissed, and it is never altogether a foregone conclusion in what class one is going to be. In any case, one reckons time from his years of teaching for the first few years. The myriad smaller habits which cluster about teaching (usually interpretable as the manifestations of central, determining rôles) are organized into the pattern of life by being made a part of one of these basic rhythms, and this in part accounts for the meaning which these habits have; a violation of the rhythm in even its smallest detail throws the whole scheme of things out of joint. This extreme routinization amounts almost to stereotypy. Thus a certain man reports that he used to pass a very bad day if he did not have time in the morning to read his paper carefully and smoke his pipe. This external scheme of things, bound together by basic simple rhythms, has a deeper basis in the fundamental motives of the individual, or acquires it by the internal reworking of externals by which time gives values to any life arrangement. Habit, bound together by rhythm, reworked by and in terms of fundamental motives, twisted about until it expresses those motives, accounts for most of the rightness and oughtness of the existent social order. The moss of meaning upon the stone long ago given us for bread can make it bread.

We have touched upon fear in its relation to the non-inventiveness of the teacher mind, and we have elsewhere identified the wish for security with certain mental mechanisms called into action by definite fears. It seems worthwhile to analyze a little further the results of the dominance of this security motive, based upon fear, in the life of the teacher. That security does receive preferential treatment as contrasted with the other possible values of the teacher's life is obvious enough to one who has known a number of teachers intimately. This preference for security, whether it is a constitutional quality which causes one to choose teaching rather than one of the more risky callings, or whether it is produced by the conditions of teaching, makes for the development of an early and rigid conservatism. When teachers meet and talk freely, one hears talk of positions and the hold that one has upon them; one hears as well of the things that threaten seisin. When it is a group of college teachers, one hears of academic freedom, and though the talk is often bold, one senses the fear it covers up. The established teacher has been playing safe so long that he has lost that necessary minimum of recklessness without which life becomes painful. A realization of the strength of this security motive enables one to understand some of the suspicion with which teachers regard each other; certainly one does not exceed the truth when he asserts that a very large percentage of the numerous quarrels between teachers arise from a belief of one teacher that another is sawing at the strings with which his job is held.

There is basis enough in the conditions of the teacher's life for the existence of many fears and the consequent dominance of security. The teacher's hold upon his students is constantly threatened by the students themselves, and there are many reasons other than inefficiency for a teacher's losing his position. The occupational risks of teaching are high, and there is no Compensation Act which covers them. The insecurity of the teacher's tenure of office profoundly affects the inwardness of the teacher's life. This prevalent insecurity has apparently given rise to a social type which is very common among teachers, that of the 'warner.' One informant relates his experiences with persons of this species as follows:

> One thing I soon noticed about teaching was that wherever I went I had to fight off a whole coterie of 'warners.' These people, seeing that I was new in the system, would come to me with an offer to set me right about the people there. They would say, 'Look out for Smith,' 'Don't trust Jones,' 'The less you have to do with Robinson the better,' 'Johnson's a snake in the grass,' 'Keep your eye on this chap Brown,' 'I wouldn't trust Thompson any further than I could throw a bull by the tail,' etc. With the utmost show of secrecy, they would announce the generous intention of giving me a tip.' Usually I did not want a tip, but I nearly always got it, and when I did get it it was perfectly meaningless. Sometimes they would hint at dire disclosures they could make about the principle, but when the disclosures were made they were rarely important. Sometimes they would tell one baldly that So-and-So was 'making a fight on you,' or was 'after your job.' Details were rarely forthcoming. All this was done in the name of friendliness, but its egotic character was perfectly apparent. These warners got a great deal of ego-gratification from their activities, and demanded a corresponding abasement of self from the warned one. The warners themselves were rarely important in the school system, perhaps because their oversuspicious disposition kept them in trouble; apparently, too, the warning was a compensation for lacks within themselves. Sometimes these warnings covered an opposition of the warner to the administration and at other times they were an attempt to get the newcomer enrolled on the right side in the war of faculty cliques and factions. I found that I did much better to disregard warners altogether. When I did follow their advice it nearly always got me into trouble. (Life history document.)

Undoubtedly these talebearers and self-appointed tipsters contribute much to making the life of the teacher a hard one. [...]

[...] Some observers have spoken of a certain habit of impersonality which grows upon teachers and finally shuts them off from all the subtler kinds of personal interchange with their fellows. In addition to certain things which we have already considered, the fact that the teacher must produce results in human materials conduces strongly to this habit of impersonality. This is an essential of the peculiar distance between teacher and student, that the student is at best material in which the teacher works, at worst, a means for the attainment of the teacher's personal ends. A similar but separate split of the teacher's personality arises because the teacher is forced to say over and over things so elementary that they have no interested for him and so many times repeated that they have lost what meaning they once had. Part of him must serve as an animated phonograph while another part stands aside and jeers. He must inhibit the normal mental processes of the adult in order to think as a child and speak as a child; it follows inevitably that he is shut out from both worlds. If Thornton Wilder had never been a school master he could not have known that it is a luxury to speak out of one's whole mind. Extreme introverts, because of their tendency to speak from the whole mind or not at all, make poor teachers. An additional cause of impersonality, and of unpleasantly toned impersonality, inheres in the fact that the teacher is rarely on good terms with all his students at the same time. As his eye runs over the class he sees two or three particularly interested students and a much larger number of persons who are at best apathetic. Always there are sore spots in the class, and although the teacher averts his gaze from these they still produce an effect upon his attitude. There is Laura Baker; she has always looked a bit disdainfully at him. There is Stanley Brown, who still resents his failing grade in the last examination. There is George Adams, whom only yesterday it was necessary to send from class. Rosie Allen is going to flunk the course; she sits and glares and does not understand. All failing students are potential enemies. And Johnny Jukes, deficient in gray matter and short of food, is a constant worry in the classroom. It will be well to be wary, to watch, watch, watch. One must guard one's behavior in this group.

Notes

1 C.f. Durkeim, Emile, *Elementary Forms of Religious Life*.
2 From *Of Human Bondage* by Somerset Maugham, copyright 1917 by Doubleday, Doran & Company, Inc., pp. 58–59.
3 Strengthened by repetition, we should say, under circumstances which do not admit of challenge. The preacher and the teacher are infallible because it is not permitted to argue with them.
4 Burnham, Wm. H. *Great Teachers and Mental Health*, p. 211, New York, 1926. (By permission of D. Appleton & Company.)

13   Teacher Career and Work Rewards

D.C. LORTIE

In the following extract from Dan Lortie's classic work, *Schoolteacher*, based on interviews with teachers in five American towns, the argument is advanced that the characteristic features of teaching as an occupation and a career are derived not only from the *constraints* of the occupation, but from the *rewards* that teachers find in it too—most especially the rewards of close personal contact with children in the classroom.

Unstaged Careers and Disjunctive Rewards

[...] The burgeoning schools of the nineteenth century faced the problem of recruiting thousands of teachers each year—they developed a system of remuneration that would attract new members and paid little attention to those who already taught. I suspect they did not have to worry about losing women who did not marry—they had few alternatives. A pattern was established: teachers with long service earned relatively little more than beginners. Subsequent efforts by teachers to raise salaries relied on a standardization strategy; the resulting salary schedules incorporated limited increases through time, usually at a ratio of two (for highly experienced teachers) to one (for beginners). High turnover within teaching continued well into the twentieth century, and teacher organizations consequently had many members with limited experience. The strategies of teacher organizations have reflected this influence; they have pressed for higher beginning salaries rather than for more income for experienced teachers.

The cellular pattern of organization developed during the nineteenth century also affected payment arrangements. Although teachers might teach in different grades and specialize in different subjects, they were largely generalists; each had many tasks in common with other teachers. The logic of the organization favored teachers when they pressed for single salary schedules which equalized payments across grades; how could one argue that particular grades were 'more important' than others? Standard schedules also spared school boards the embarassment of having to assign some students to highly paid teachers and others to low-paid teachers; in a system of common schools, such inequities would have aroused objections.

The result is that income profiles of teachers today are predictable, comparatively unstaged, and 'front-loaded.' A beginning teacher knows what he will earn and can see that long service brings limited reward. Those who persist in teaching experience the drop-off in percentage gains associated with fixed dollar increments: each pay increase is a smaller percentage of the salary base than the previous one. Earnings are 'front-loaded' in the sense that one begins at a high level relative to one's ultimate earnings potential.[1]

Compared with most other kinds of middle-class work, teaching is relatively 'career-less'. There is less opportunity for the movement upward which is the essence of career.[2] People who work in highly established bureaucracies, for example, can move up a hierarchy of statuses, each movement involving a significant gain in income, and they can frequently do so without endangering their occupational identities. (A soldier is still a soldier when he is promoted.) White-collar work is often highly stratified; secretaries' career lines may be attached to the fates of their bosses. Even ostensibly nonorganizational professionals who work for fees have powerful interpersonal networks which produce career stages involving income, prestige, and control over one's tasks and clientele (Hall, 1948).

The potential upward steps in teaching are fewer and hold less significance than one normally finds in middle-class work. Becoming an administrator or specialist (e.g., a counsellor) blurs one's identity as a teacher and means abrupt discontinuity in tasks. High-school teachers may assume part-time administrative duties as department chairmen; such promotion normally entails modest financial and prestige gains (Maguire, 1970). A teacher may make a lateral move to another school within the same system, which may offer advantages of clientele and so forth (Becker, 1951). Some teachers increase their earnings by moving to more prosperous school systems (Pedersen, 1973). Seniority may bring certain informal benefits (e.g., more options in students and facilities). But in contrast to the larger packages of money, prestige, and power usually found in other careers, the typical career line of the classroom teacher is a gentle incline rather than a steep ascent. The status of the young tenured teacher is not appreciably different from that of the highly experienced old-timer.

Does the lack of staging in teaching careers make any appreciable difference in the work of teachers? That is obviously a difficult question, but there is a way to attack it. We can identify the functions performed by stages in other kinds of careers and inquire into the state of such functions within teaching. We can, for example, state that one function of staging in careers is to institutionalize the delay of gratification; stages force younger people to expend effort in the hope of ultimate gain. Beginners in staged fields may have to accept considerable deprivation in the early years—the professions offer good examples. A brilliant law student may go from the high estate of law review editor to service alongside a judge of the Supreme Court; but his next position may be as a lowly clerk in a large law factory (Lortie, 1958). The beginning physician finds himself, after twenty years of continuous schooling, putting in months and perhaps years as a low-paid, low-ranked, and sleep-deprived intern and junior resident (Doctor X, 1965). Young professors may wait years before they can teach courses which reflect their specialized interests. Career lines of this nature orient people to the future; personal ambition is successively whetted and satisfied as the individual moves from one stage to the next. The law student strives for good grades so he can get a good position in a law firm; if he succeeds, he finds himself confronted with new challenges and strivings—this time, to get a partnership. Staged careers produce cycles of effort, attainment, and renewed ambition. In tying the individual to the occupation they give him a stake in its future. Staging gives reality and force to the idea of the future; it generates effort, ambition, and identification with the occupation.

Career staging may also serve another function; it may balance the relationships among effort, capacity, and reward. Not all who begin staged careers go the full route, but where the reward system is seen as legitimate, people believe that the largest rewards go to those who earn them through effort and talent. Supporting beliefs emerge to buttress the contention that reapers deserve the harvest; it is interesting how rarely Sumner's 'aleatory element' (sheer luck) is mentioned in journalistic accounts of outstanding success (Sumner, 1906, p. 6)

There are mechanisms which give credibility to the beliefs; people who fail to get the scarcer rewards (e.g., promotion) may 'confirm' the negative judgment made about them by reducing their effort. In short, there seems to be a strain toward consistency in reward systems which justifies their outcomes.

If stages perform the functions I have attributed to them, we should find that their absence has consequences for teaching. We would expect that teachers would be less future-oriented than people in staged career systems and that disjunctions would appear between effort and reward. Since a high proportion of the available rewards are quickly received—and subsequent rewards are less impressive—it makes little sense to sacrifice present earnings for future prospects. The delay of gratification becomes irrelevant. Since benefits are not highly differentiated within the teaching group, and since extra effort brings scant reward, those who do exert extra effort are likely to feel underrewarded. People who work long hours and commit more of their life energies to work will realize that others who give less get similar rewards. I will hypothesize, then, that the lack of stages in the teaching career results in:

1   the dominance of present versus future orientation among teachers and
2   a sense of relative deprivation among those who persist in teaching and work at above-average levels of effort.

The balance between effort and reward in teaching is complicated by the presence of members of both sexes in similar roles and the divergent life contingencies experienced by man and women. We will have to take account of these complications as we examine data on time perspective among teachers and the issue of disjunction between effort and reward.

The Tentativeness of Future Commitments

Although teachers tend to serve for more years now than they did in the past, available data indicate that a minority of beginners expect to teach continuously until retirement. In his survey of beginning teachers, Mason (1961, chap. 10) found that only 29 percent of the men and 16 percent of the women projected uninterrupted futures in the classroom. Men and women have different prospects and emphasize divergent contingencies in thinking about the future. Although most women expect their careers to be interrupted, the vast majority think of teaching as a terminal status. Most men reject teaching as an ultimate goal; they see teaching as a means toward another end—as an interim engagement. We will discuss women and men separately since the patterns differ by sex.

Beginning women teachers do not hide their intention to put family matters first; 65 percent of Mason's respondents planned to leave the classroom within five years and 84 percent expected to leave it before they reached retirement age. When asked what circumstances would induce them to leave, 80 percent of the young women mentioned family-related events. The teaching futures they project are contingent on relationships outside work. Seventy-eight percent of the single teachers said that marriage would cause them to leave; 60 percent of the married women cited childbirth as the key contingency. Married teachers also mentioned occurrences in their husband's lives, such as completion of schooling (24 percent), changes in employment (27 percent), and increases in income (31 percent). Fifty-eight percent of the beginning women teachers thought they would return to the classroom after they had raised their children. In sum, more than half looked ahead to teaching as an 'in-and-out' engagement hinging on marital and maternal commitments. Few women expected to work outside classrooms; only 9 percent expressed interest in administrative or specialized positions. Mason's respondents were ready to commit themselves to teaching as long as they worked, but work itself was a secondary commitment.

Marital status influences the amount women invest in preparing for their careers. Single women begin to teach with more schooling than married teachers; 73 percent of the single women versus 68 percent of the married fell into the highest preparation category in Mason's sample (1961, chap. 4). The contingent schooling pattern I mentioned in chapter 1 widens the gap with time. Single women continue to teach while married women may drop out, and so unmarried women accumulate more course credits. An NEA survey conducted in 1966 disclosed that 22 percent of the single teachers had master's degrees, compared with 14 percent of the married ones (NEA, 1967, p. 71). Single women invest more in their education; we shall see that this is not the only respect in which their investments exceed those of married women teachers.

The majority of beginning male teachers have no intention of ending their work careers as classroom teachers; that is a major finding in Mason's study. Seventy-one percent said they intended to leave the classroom; 51 percent hoped for higher-ranked positions within education, and the rest (20 percent) anticipated working outside education altogether. Asked what would influence them to leave, they answered 'pay, salary, and standard of living.' Sixty-three percent said they were concerned about 'being able to support a family on a teacher's salary.' Married men were more likely to express economic apprehensions; 71 percent of them, versus 51 percent of the single men, mentioned financial worries. The major projection of male beginners is temporary engagement in teaching but continued involvement in education; they hoped for positions which would yield greater income than classroom work. But one out of five showed no persisting interest in education as a field of work. [...]

[...] Several characteristics of teaching join to reduce future orientation among members of the occupation. Since access is not particulary difficult, people with low commitment can enter, and many begin teaching without plans to persist. Women may enter expecting to work for a short period before marriage or childbearing; they may or may not plan to return later. Twenty percent of beginning men expect to leave education altogether; most of the ot'ers are hoping for jobs other than teaching. The career line has little appeal for most entrants.

Men and women react differently to the nature of the career line. The steps upward within teaching are too small to satisfy the ambitions of most male entrants; they want the greater rewards associated with administrative positions. But the gentle incline of teaching fits the aspirations most women bring with them; it facilitates their 'in-and-out' plans. Absence would be costlier if teaching careers were staged; the reentering teacher would have lost more in comparison with those who stayed on and moved into higher statuses. Under the present system, the major cost is the loss of incremental earnings, and for married women this is probably not perceived as serious. (Married women might be expected, therefore, to resist moves to stratify teaching careers.) We also note that 'in-and-out' rests on the assumption that no major technical changes are likely to take place while one is absent; so married women may also (consciously or not) have a stake in slow rather than rapid change in teaching technique.[3]

Most young teachers do not consider a lifetime of classroom teaching 'enough.' Men want to move through teaching to other work; women see it as supplementary to marriage and motherhood. But not all who make plans on these grounds will be able to attain them. Many male teachers will not be promoted into administrative work; some women who plan to marry will not do so. We expect, therefore, that men who are not promoted and women who do not marry will have to adjust to these realities. To persist in teaching is, in a sense, to be 'passed over' for higher position or marriage. Do such experiences affect the person's satisfaction with teaching? Do other obligations influence commitment to the occupation? It is to questions of this kind that we turn next. [. . .]

The Disjunction between Engagement and Work Satisfaction
[. . .] It was possible to develop overall measures of involvement and satisfaction using the questions asked in the Five Towns interview. Effort-involvement was based on three questions:

1 total hours put in during an average work week;
2 number of professional associations to which the teacher belonged and the level of activity within them; and
3 proportion of 'life space' the teacher allocated to teaching work (questions 27, 80, 82, App. B-1).

Three items were used to indicate the level of satisfaction:

1 a direct question asking respondents to select their level of satisfaction with teaching;
2 readiness to repeat the choice of teaching as one's occupation; and
3 citing (or not citing) specific costs when asked about losses attendant upon being a member of the teaching occupation (questions 44, 47, 83, App. B-1).

A simple score of satisfaction was developed, with the higher score indicating greater satisfaction.[4]
Because of the sample size, it would not be wise to attach great weight to these distributions, but it is interesting that the pattern found is similar to a national sample (NEA, 1967); cross-tabulation of levels of satisfaction and involvement disclosed no positive association. The patterns involving men and women and single and married women, however, were similar to those in the national sample study. We turn to these now, discussing first the women and then the men.
Single women in Five Towns report somewhat higher involvement in work than their married colleagues. They put in slightly more time (one-half hour per week on the average) and join slightly more associations (.6 more). They are more active in the associations they join; 53 percent report active levels compared with 22 percent of the married teachers. Thirty-seven percent of the single teachers, compared with 6 percent of the married, engage in the highest levels of activity. It seems that differences in the involvement of time between single and married teachers occur primarily *outside* regular school activities. It is highly probable that married women allocate outside time to their families rather than to their work.
There is also an interesting difference in responses to the life space question; married women report a mean of 3.9, and single women a mean of 5.4. Married women group their responses around the midpoint of 4, probably circumventing the pan of underinvolvement and the fire of overinvolvement. Their remarks suggest that according teaching too small a place in their lives would imply inconveniencing husbands and children frivolously; some teachers said they would not feel justified in being away from home for work which was not truly important. But to accord teaching more than half of their life space is also problematic—it subordinates husband and children to work. These responses, in short, are a paradigm for the situation of the married woman who works; occupancy of two sets of demanding roles requires careful and diplomatic

balancing of their claims. The responses of single women, on the other hand, show great variation, reflecting their comparative freedom to allocate their resources as they see fit. Where single women are so inclined, they can express all-encompassing commitments to work without normative restraint.

The age of women teachers in Five Towns is also related to their level of involvement; in general, women over forty are more involved than those under forty. The main difference lies in the number of weekly hours they report (four hours more) and the proportion of life space they allocate to teaching; older women typically assign five-eighths, young women four-eighths. Inspection of the distributions reveals that few women, single or married, become deeply involved during their twenties; they seem to be hedging their bets if single and if married awaiting the arrival of a child or a change in their husband's status (e.g., completion of training). Married women who have returned to work are those who typically choose the carefully split (four-eighths) response; the truly high allocations of life space to teaching occur among the older single women. It seems that commitment to work expands when women conclude that they will remain single (Peterson, 1956).

Reading an entire interview at one time provides an overall impression of the quality of a respondent's involvement. The cumulative impression gained is that women vary their definition of teaching work according to their life stage and what is happening at the time; Hughes's observations about phases and facets are germane.[5] In some interviews (especially when the interviewer was a sympathetic woman), respondents talked of adjusting work plans to marriage prospects; some single women, for example, moved in order to keep a promising relationship going. Young married women placed their work futures in the context of their husband's careers. Older married teachers tended to be serious about their work and frequently mentioned the difficulties they encountered in convincing their husbands that household rearrangements were worth it. The strongest commitments came from some older single teachers; it was in this group that one heard statements like 'teaching is my life.' Such teachers connected travel and other activities to their classroom work; teaching was definitely the master role which organized other aspects of their life. (But of course there were exceptions.)[6]

Charters (1970), a serious student of 'teacher survival,' concludes that women's participation in teaching is a function of the life cycle; such considerations outweigh specific working conditions in school districts. The Five Towns data support this view; age and marital status, rather than grade level or socioeconomic conditions, show the larger associations. The energies and interests of women teachers flow back and forth between family and work claims in discernible, regular rhythms. Those who marry follow different courses than those who do not. Further research could profitably focus on these processes, for the evidence suggests that they are more important than the incentives provided by school systems. My findings underscore the relative weakness of organizational resources in mobilizing the involvement of women; the capacity of school officials to influence the engagements of female subordinates is sharply constrained.

As in the case of the national data, men in Five Towns (without disentangling differences due to level) are slightly more involved than women teachers. They work a little longer each week (one and one-half hours), belong to slightly more associations (.8 on the average), and are somewhat more active in their associational life—55 percent report active levels compared with 42 percent of the women. When we control for level, their edge in involvement becomes too thin to warrant attention. The position of men falls between single women and married women.

The small number of cases makes internal comparison statistically risky, but differences observed in Five Towns are suggestive for further research. Involvement apparently varies with age for men as it does for women, but the bases for variation are probably different. Younger men (under forty) put in longer hours (three and one-half hours more), but older men accord teaching a higher proportion of their life space (5.2 to 4.5). There is more variation in the life-space scores of the younger men: two groups, elementary teachers and those planning to leave education altogether, report low scores. But men high school teachers under forty who hope for promotion have the highest scores among the younger teachers; their involvement probably reflects the wish to create the impression needed for promotion. The older men, on the other hand, cluster around a similar life-space allotment, roughly five-eighths. Their involvement patterns suggests stabilization. Teaching occupies a definite niche within their life, but they normally have strong outside interests.

Impressions drawn from reading the total interviews support inferences we can draw from the involvement data. The model young male teacher is a man 'on the way up,' eager for promotion and ready to show his capacity through hard work; Griffiths et al. (1965, p. 137) has described this orientation among New York City teachers. But two subgroups differ. The first consists of the few male elementary teachers in the sample who from all appearances are relatively passive, with low commitment. They so described themselves, saying their interest in work was low. Ironically, each hoped for promotion to principal within five years. The second subgroup consisted of young men using teaching as a temporary haven while preparing for work elsewhere. The presence of these two subgroups reflects one of the consequences of the eased entry syndrome: people with limited commitment can get into and stay in teaching. The Five Towns pattern is similar to that described by Mason; only a small proportion of the men intend to stay in teaching for a lifetime. Most hope for promotion into administrative work or for other positions outside the classroom.

One feature in the life involvement of male teachers over forty is especially interesting; almost every such man in Five Towns had either a strong avocational interest outside teaching or an additional source of employment income. One of the high schools had a very complicated administrative structure in which many teachers occupied minor positions. Teachers in that school emphasized such semiadministrative duties. Most talked about engagements outside education, however, such as ancillary careers in business and athletics or hobbies which consumed much of their interest. Sometimes the other positions they held seemed more important to them than their teaching. I could not tell whether these outside interests had always been important or had become more so after chances for promotion waned; the respondents did not seem eager to talk about earlier aspirations that had not been realized. But it is interesting that low salaries favour lower involvement for men; they may take on outside work primarily for the income and gradually become more involved in it. Although these respondents did not say they had hoped for promotion, several went out of their way to allege that promotions in their school system were based on political connections, not on merit. To the extent that patterns in Five Towns reflect those within the occupation, men may temper their involvement in teaching by developing strong outside interests. It may be that one of the major mechanisms men use to adjust to lack of promotion is partial disengagement from their roles as teachers.

The relationship between reported satisfactions and involvement among Five Towns teachers matches that found in the national survey discussed earlier. We find a similar pattern of imbalance between effort and satisfaction.

Married women report higher satisfaction levels than their more heavily involved single colleagues; the mean score of the married teachers is 7.5 and that for single teachers is 6.2. Despite the fact that they put more of themselves into their work, single women are less satisfied with teaching. The difference between married and single teachers apparently increases with age, with a 1.0 edge in satisfaction among marrieds under forty but a difference of 2.2 points in the older group. We recall that although married women over forty reported steady, balanced involvements, the highest scores were obtained by single women in that age category. The spinster teachers who have historically symbolized high commitment to teaching (e.g., the Miss Dove ideal) describe themselves as less satisfied with their work than married teachers who dedicate less of themselves to it.

Men in Five Towns, taken together, are somewhat more involved than women in toto; the mean satisfaction score of the men, however, is lower by 1.1 points (5.8 versus 6.9). Younger men—most of whom are striving for promotion—report lower scores than older men: 5.5 compared with 6.3. The lowest satisfaction scores in all subgroups occurred among young men who did not yet know whether they would be promoted. One is reminded of Stouffer's soldiers awaiting word on their disposition. Those with the lowest morale—even lower than those who knew they were getting undesirable assignments—were men uncertain of their fates. It seems that a process of reconciliation occurs as older men realize they will not be promoted.[7] But this does not occur rapidly enough to prevent considerable anxiety among male teachers under forty.

Two subgroups, therefore, show a negative balance between involvement and satisfaction—young men and older single women. Married women are most likely to show a positive balance. We can get further insight into the reasons for these differences by examining data on the 'costs' associated with being a member of the teaching occupation. Responses to a question about what it cost to be a teacher correlated with the categories we have been examining (question 47, App. B-1).

More than a quarter of the teachers (28 percent) denied the premise of the question, saying that teaching had *not* entailed costs for them; this response, however, was given by twice as many women as men—36 percent, versus 16 percent. More than half the married women, however, gave such an affirmative assessment of teaching; 53 percent of them, compared with 26 percent of the single women, denied that they had lost anything by choosing to teach. When men and women cited costs, they differed in their selections; 59 percent of the men said 'inadequate money income', but only 4 percent of the women referred to low salaries. Women who cited costs were much likelier to say 'teaching is isolated work'; they said that in 42 percent of the cases while men did so in 22 percent. Since the teaching roles of men and women are largely similar, the differences point to divergent perspectives and concerns.

Three times as many single as married women mentioned the isolation involved in teaching (59 percent versus 18 percent). *Every* single woman under forty citing costs mentioned isolation; the modal response of married women, on the other hand, was 'no costs.' The specific meanings attached to isolation were not always made explicit, but some variations could be identified. The young single women stressed that teaching is a poor base from which to meet people (including eligible males) and that the social life of the teacher is normatively constrained.

> One of the things you lose is personal contact with other people. You're not meeting new people all the time ... I think if you were outside the school, if you were in an office or some other kind of job, you would be meeting more people, adults. [#67 F-24-3d]

That Waller's descriptions of special moral controls over teachers are not completely outmoded is also evident (Waller, 1961, p. 45):

> Teaching is confining, emotionally and socially. I mean a teacher has to be a Caesar's wife, beyond reproach, particularly in the eyes of the community. You think twice about doing things. [#7 F-34-5th]

> Teaching is too confining ... You find that you're always watching who is around who might know you from school, and how you have to behave and who shouldn't I be seen with here and all this and that. [#9 F-32-2d]

Schools are 'guarded' sites; adults in the community do not casually move in and out of them. Many schools (particularly elementary) have few males on the staff. The young woman who teaches encounters obstacles in her movements outside school; some said that they were not free to frequent places where singles meet one another (e.g., bars) since 'everyone is watching.' (Such moral controls may produce different results in different eras; in earlier times, they permitted young girls to work away from home and meet people they would not otherwise get to know. Today the reverse is true.)[8]

Other meanings were attached to the term 'isolation,' and these were alluded to by both married women and men. Teaching controls one's daily interactions so that most take place with children; some teachers expressed concern about the effects of protracted contact with children.

> I think in other occupations you may meet more people with different interests. I think you are limited as to the interests of the people you meet. It gets to be 'Well, Johnny ...' or 'In my school, they do so and so.' That's about all you can talk about. [#73 F-57-3d]

> I think you lose an opportunity to meet a certain group of interesting people. Many teachers are not too broad-minded about things; they lead a somewhat narrow existence. [#34 F-45-4th]

Some teachers worried aloud about how constant interaction with children might reduce their degree of adulthood and injure their intellectual functioning (Haller, 1966).

> If you stay with the students too long, you get to talk like them sometimes. You don't come in contact with too many adults, and your students, you are supposed to talk down to their level so that they can get it. [#25 F-28-Business]

> I just think you sort of stagnate in a way. You could stagnate more if you wanted to let it happen, if you did not read, etc., but I would just like to give and take with adults once in a while. Just to be able to be in [a large office building complex] once in a while and be talking to someone in my same age bracket. [#42 F-31-1st]

Isolation can be perceived as a cost by both men and women and by both single and married teachers. Yet we can see why it is mentioned most often by single women; isolation makes it harder for them to meet potential mates. (Some unmarried teachers blame the occupation for their difficulties.) But older single women are also affected; modern family life makes the position of the single person socially marginal; single teachers are thrown back upon each other's company to a considerable degree. Relying upon other teachers to prevent loneliness intensifies the role of teaching in one's life; cultural isolation follows personal isolation. Waller (1961, p. 420) was much concerned with the narrow social range of teachers, arguing that it restricted their outlook. It is difficult to see how it could be otherwise given the life circumstances of unmarried women in modern society.

We can understand the preoccupation young men (particularly in their thirties) show with promotion and additional income. [. . .] This is typically a period of life in which their obligations expand rapidly and their income increases slowly. There is, moreover, the discomfort involved in feeling that one is not succeeding; when others are being offered administrative positions, the sense of being 'passed over' can become painful. It seems likely that many men who leave teaching do so at this point; unfortunately, the studies of teacher dropouts do not pay close attention to these issues. Yet we must also observe that people who persist in teaching often come to terms with their situation. Wives may work outside the home to ease the economic load, and male teachers may redistribute their involvements so that teaching plays a smaller part in their lives. A small promotion in school may help, as may the informal benefits associated with seniority. Data gathered in Dade County suggest that by the time they reach their fifties, most men in teaching have made peace with their status; in fact, many no longer find the possibility of administrative rank attractive.

Summary and Implications
Teaching presents a relatively unstaged career. The main opportunity for making major status gains rests in leaving classroom work for full-time administration. The primary benefits earned by persistence in teaching (annual increases in pay) are the outcome of seniority and course-taking; the incentive system is not organized to respond to variations in effort and talent among classroom teachers.

My data support the expectations with which we began this chapter. Few beginning teachers project long futures in the classroom; men expect, in the main, to leave, and women see their participation as contingent. Entrants project a somewhat hazy picture of the future; the system does not require them to sacrifice current gratifications for long-range goals once tenure has been gained.

We expected that the lack of stages would be associated with lower rewards for those who invest much of themselves in teaching. This seems to be true; persisters are relatively disadvantaged. Men who are not promoted and women who do not marry are not defined as having made voluntary commitments. Most men work for promotion; if they fail and continue to teach, they must resign themselves to classroom teaching as a terminal status. Young single women hold off their work commitments, increasing them when they conclude that they will not marry; those who throw themselves into their work do not, it seems, earn extra benefits of satisfaction. Married women are comparatively satisfied; a flat career line permits them to come and go without serious loss of status. The system of career rewards, in sum, works most satisfactorily for those who give teaching less than full commitment; 'gainers' are teachers who plan on short-term or less than full-time engagement. We are witnessing consequences of a historical pattern; the career system in teaching continues to favor recruitment rather than retention and low rather than high involvement.

There are other implications associated with this kind of reward system. It subtly depreciates the status of classroom teaching; it is not enough to be 'merely' a teacher, for one must also be on the way to higher rank or, if a woman, married. This pattern of depreciation probably gives a certain fragility to relationships between younger and older teachers. Young men do not see older male teachers as models for emulation—their models are likely to be administrators. Young women probably show respect for older married teachers and qualify their admiration for those who have not married. Such discontinuities weaken the solidarity of the occupation and should receive independent research and analysis;

they may be major obstacles to more effective collegial relationships among teachers. Tensions between older and younger teachers may complicate the problem of collegial leadership: a 'natural' elite of highly experienced practitioners is missing. Patterns of deference and tension among members of different generations and marriage groups could provide a useful perspective for the study of organizational affairs. We might speculate that age and marital cleavages within teaching reduce the collective power of the teacher group and thereby contribute to its subordination within the system.

There is another side to this system of weak career incentives, however, which enhances teacher autonomy: it works to reduce the capacity of officials to exert influence over *individual* teachers. Although young male teachers must be sensitive to the evaluations of superordinates (they play a large part in the distribution of promotions), most other teachers have less stake in superordinate assessments. Experienced teachers, moreover, are protected by tenure and automatic pay increases; the sanctions superordinates possess have limited impact. This leverage allows married women to vary their involvement (to some extent) depending on family demands and allows men to engage themselves in activities outside teaching. Older single women can quietly define themselves as the teachers who 'really care' and probably acquire moral authority as a consequence; such moral authority may provide them with considerable freedom from superordinate intervention. The system of rewards, therefore, contributes to teacher individualism by permitting variations in involvement.

Career arrangements seem to be integrated with other aspects of the occupation. Like recruitment and socialization, they foster private rather than shared orientations. Career rewards complicate vigorous collegiality among teachers. Their joint status is depreciated, few consider it 'enough' for a lifetime, and those who persist occupy ambiguous positions. The peer group has no effective control over the distribution of rewards, and its most experienced members may encounter resistance when they attempt to assume leadership. On the other hand, most teachers are not greatly constrained by the set of career incentives, since money rewards do not depend on the individual decisions of superordinate officials.[9] The system permits teachers a significant degree of personal autonomy.

The Primacy of Psychic Rewards

The organization of career rewards in teaching fosters a present-oriented rather than future-oriented point of view; those who intend to stay in the classroom have limited need to delay gratification in the hope of future gain. Few beginning teachers intend to stay very long, and the majority of teachers are women who have little interest in leaving the classroom for other work. Most teachers will therefore emphasize rewards they can earn in the present; this propensity affects the *kinds* of rewards which will matter to them.

The thesis of this section is that cultural and structural aspects of the occupation influence teachers to emphasize psychic rewards in their work. The cultural influences stem from a long tradition of teaching as service; that tradition [. . .] affects recruitment into the occupation and the outlook of those who are drawn in. Structural considerations affect the differential responsiveness of various rewards to teacher effort; teachers consequently tend to concentrate their energies at points where effort may make a difference (Lortie, 1969).

We can classify rewards into three types: extrinsic rewards, ancillary rewards, and psychic or intrinsic rewards. The first includes what we usually think of as the 'earnings' attached to a role and involves money income, a level of prestige, and power over others. These earnings are 'extrinsic' in the sense that they exist independently of the individual who occupies the role; since they are experienced by all incumbents, they have an 'objective' quality. Ancillary rewards are simultaneously objective and subjective; they refer to objective characteristics of the work which may be perceived as rewards by some (e.g., married women might consider the work schedules of teaching to be rewarding while men might not). Ancillary rewards tend to be stable through time, and to be 'taken for granted' rather than specified in contracts; for example, people expect teaching to be cleaner than factory work. Psychic rewards consist entirely of subjective valuations made in the course of work engagement; their subjectivity means that they can vary from person to person. But they are also constrained by the nature of the occupation and its tasks; we would not expect lighthouse keepers to list sociability as a work reward or street cleaners to rejoice in opportunities for creative expression. It is an empirical task to find recurrent patterns in such subjective, psychic rewards; the goal is to uncover rewards which cut across the preferences of individuals.

The culture and surrounding structure of an occupation are likely to influence the emphasis on some kinds of rewards rather than others. We get the types of variations I mentioned at the beginning of the chapter; in one occupation, achievement will be defined essentially in money terms; in another it will be measured by rank attained or power acquired. The values of the occupation work together with the core tasks to produce a characteristic reward structure among the membership. For example, deference and approval flow to the wealthiest financiers, the most powerful politicians, and the highest-ranked bureaucrats.

The culture of teachers and the structure of rewards do not emphasize the acquisition of extrinsic rewards. The traditions of teaching make people who seek money, prestige, or power somewhat suspect; the characteristic style in public education is to mute personal ambition. The service ideal has extolled the virtue of giving more than one receives; the model teacher has been 'dedicated.' (I suspect these values are linked to the sacred connotations of teaching in early American history.) Some will assert that teachers abandon this tradition when they organize and strike; this is probably so in some respects. But we cannot conclude that collective aggressiveness legitimates *individual* ambition; group activity to raise salaries is not the same as individualistic attempts to raise one's standing. Nor can we infer that it will produce a normative change in which teachers channel deference and approval to those who make idiosyncratic gains. There may be instances, in fact, where the opposite is true and group mobility reduces support for individualistic ambitions; if the group is successful in getting more money and other rewards, the individual's claims may be weakened. Teachers continue to oppose internal differentiation in rewards on grounds other than seniority or education; their behavior has been consistently egalitarian.

The way extrinsic rewards are distributed makes it difficult for individual teachers to influence their flow in the short run. Salary payments are fixed annually; one's income goes up primarily as one acquires seniority and takes courses. The formal standing of teachers within a given system tends toward equality; the major distinction is between beginners (probationary teachers without tenure) and others. (Some teachers, of course, develop informal reputations as outstanding or ineffective, but these are not reflected in formal status.) Important research could be done on the issue of power and teachers; officially, however, teacher power is limited to specified authority over students; teachers are not supposed to *enjoy* exercising power per se. Extrinsic rewards tend to be comparatively undifferentiated.

Opportunities to increase extrinsic rewards are also limited in the long run. Some teachers improve their lot by moving to more prosperous school systems; we recall, however, that many teachers are place-bound, particularly women with family responsibilities. Teachers who accept intermediate positions of responsibility (e.g., department chairmen) are likely to complain that the obligations exceed their authority and that money rewards are inadequate for the effort required. Fame and fortune are rarely the lot of the classroom teacher.

Ancillary rewards affect entry to a given line of work more than the effort of those in it; organizational theorists make the distinction between incentives which affect membership and incentives which affect participation (March and Simon, 1958). People may be attracted to teaching partly because it offers economic security or has a schedule perforated by frequent holidays and vacations; but once they are in teaching, they probably take such advantages for granted (for one thing, they are also enjoyed by everyone else around). Ancillary rewards are present whether one makes high or limited effort on the job. The significance of ancillary rewards, in sum, lies in the contrast with other kinds of employment; they may restrain a person from leaving the occupation, but they are unlikely to affect the effort he exerts on a day-to-day basis.

Unlike extrinsic and ancillary rewards, the psychic rewards of teachers fluctuate; the teacher's enjoyment of his work can vary. Effort will not make much difference in the flow of extrinsic and ancillary rewards, at least in the short run. Effort, on the other hand, might increase task-related satisfactions. Nor are teachers so constrained that they feel their decisions make little difference in their work; they are not assembly line workers whose every move is paced by externally controlled systems of production. (Jackson, 1968, reports that teachers make well over two hundred decisions hourly.) One would expect teachers, then, to concentrate on psychic rewards; energy directed toward their realization can affect total rewards. The structure of teaching rewards, in short, favors emphasis on psychic rewards. When we recall that the culture emphasizes service, we should not be surprised if the data underscore the significance of psychic rewards in the work life of classroom teachers. We turn next to such data.

The marked tendency for teachers to connect their major rewards with classroom events was first noticed in the Five Towns interviews. Respondents fused the idea of work gratification and the idea of work goals; they made little distinction between deriving satisfaction from their work and reaching classroom objectives. In answering questions which asked specifically about the satisfactions they received from teaching, they overwhelmingly cited task-related outcomes. On one question, for example, 125 mentions were coded as psychic reward references, while 11 dealt with ancillary rewards and 9 with extrinsic; on a follow-up question, all but 4 of the responses were connected with work outcomes (question 40, App. B-1). The major emphasis in answers to both questions was that satisfaction accompanied desirable results with students; respondents experienced gratification when they felt they had influenced students.

Similar data are found in a national survey conducted by the National Education Association (NEA, 1963, p. 69). Twenty percent of respondents were asked on open-ended question in which they were requested to identify 'sources of professional satisfaction and encouragement.' 'Students' was selected by 78.9 percent of the respondents, and 18.3 percent said 'teaching in general.' All other sources mentioned received fewer mentions; they included administrators,

Table 13.1 Types of rewards, Dade County teachers

Extrinsic Rewards	(N)	(%)	Psychic Rewards	(N)	(%)	Ancillary Rewards	(N)	(%)	All Combined	(N)	(%)
Salary	835	14.4	Chance to study, read, and plan for classes	200	3.4	Security of income and position	1,302	22.4	Extrinsic	693	11.9
Respect from others	2,127	36.6	Discipline and classroom management	69	1.2	Time (esp. summers) for travel, etc.	1,348	23.2	Psychic	4,463	76.5
Chance to use influence	2,083	35.8	Knowing that I have 'reached' students and they have learned	5,067	86.1	Freedom from competition, rivalry	288	5.0	Ancillary	681	11.7
No satisfaction from these	773	13.3	Chance to associate with children or young people	470	8.0	Appropriateness for people like me	1,977	34.1			
			Chance to associate with other teachers	63	1.1	No satisfaction from these	890	15.3			
			No satisfaction from these	17	0.3						
Total	5,818	100.1	Total	5,886	100.1	Total	5,805	100.0	Total	5,837	100.1

working conditions, teachers, parents, facilities, and the community. The typical quotations presented in the text reveal that concern with classroom results dominates the modal replies, teaching is satisfying and encouraging when positive things happen in the classroom.

The most detailed and relevant data were those I gathered in Dade County, Florida, Respondents were asked a series of four questions; the first listed alternative extrinsic rewards and asked respondents to select the one which provided them the greatest satisfaction. A similar procedure was used in two additional questions which asked about psychic and ancillary rewards. The fourth question asked respondents to select from the three clusters of extrinsic, ancillary, and psychic rewards (questions T8, T9, T10, T11, App. B-2). The data are presented in Table 13.1.

The answers to the last question indicate that these teachers consider psychic rewards their major source of work satisfaction; 76.5 percent chose psychic rewards compared with 11.9 percent selecting extrinsic rewards and 11.7 percent ancillary rewards. The modal response is *six times* as frequent as the closest contender. It is also noteworthy that the psychic income responses 'piled up' under one of the alternatives listed; the modal answer got 86.1 percent of the choices. That alternative was 'the times I know I have "reached" a student or group of students and they have learned.' The next most frequent response also dealt with students, but the emphasis was on association with them rather than discernible results. Fewer than 1 percent said none of the psychic rewards was important; 13.3 percent selected that response for extrinsic rewards, and 15.3 percent did the same for ancillary rewards. Since the vast majority of responses to this question dealt directly with classroom and student events, it is clear that these teachers consider the classroom the major arena for the receipt of psychic rewards. Thousands of teachers in Dade County report the same 'joys of teaching' which Jackson and Belford (1965) found among teachers who were rated as especially competent.

It is of great importance to teachers to feel they have 'reached' their students—their core rewards are tied to that perception. Other sources of satisfaction (e.g., private scholarly activities, relationships with adults) pale in comparison with teachers' exchanges with students and the feeling that students have learned. We would therefore expect that much of a teacher's work motivation will rotate around the conduct of daily tasks—the actual instruction of students. In that regard, the exertion of effort and the earning of important rewards are congruent; they are not in the position of those who must trade away psychic rewards in order to make a living (Becker, 1951). Teachers face different problems [. . .]

Notes

[1] It is true, of course, that older teachers working today earn more than twice their initial salary in real income terms. It is unlikely that their earlier decisions, however, were based on the expectation of a general rise in income. Nor is there cause to believe that teachers beginning today expect an equivalent rise in the future, although it would be an interesting point for research.

[2] The root of the word career is the same as that of *car* (*Shorter Oxford English Dictionary*)

[3] This is conjectural and should be the object of inquiry. Married women who return after a protracted absence could, of course, be trained into newer techniques; this necessity, however, would increase the overall cost of employing older married teachers compared with younger single or married teachers.

[4] Level of satisfaction was divided into four possibilities (1–4), repeat readiness into four, and presence/absence of costs into two; scores could range, therefore, from 3 to 10.

5 E.C. Hughes developed the ideas of facets and phases in a memorandum written in the 1950s. Work can be seen as one facet of a person's life which, like other facets, takes on different meanings in various life phases. I do not believe that the memo was published.

6 Some of the older women teachers varied markedly from this depiction. Their interviews were characterized by repeated complaints about fatigue—they mentioned time and again how tired they were. Some, for example, said they went to bed as soon as they got home from school. One got the distinct impression that they were looking forward to retirement.

7 Dade County respondents were asked whether they thought it likely that they would be asked to take a position one step up within the next five years (question 44, App. B-2). Of men in their thirties, 43 percent thought it likely, 34 percent unlikely. Men in their fifties, on the other hand, had quite different expectations; 21.7 percent thought it likely, 61.1 percent unlikely. Asked how they would react to such an invitation, 9.5 percent of men in their thirties would refuse while 29 percent of men in their fifties signaled unwillingness to be promoted (question 43, App. B-2)

8 That such controls continue to exist—even in urban areas—is indicated by responses to the Dade County questionnaire. Asked whether they felt they had to be careful about doing things publicly which they considered acceptable but others might not, 45.2 percent of Dade County teachers replied either 'I feel I must be very careful' or 'I feel some pressure to be careful' (question 38, App. B-2).

9 One could understate the influence administrators have in salary matters. They have some discretion, I understand, in a teacher's initial placement on the salary schedule; they can also influence a teacher's mobility potential through the power of recommendation.

References

Becker, H. (1951) Role and career problems of the Chicago public school teacher. Ph.D. thesis, University of Chicago.

Charters, W.W., Jr (1970) 'Some factors affecting teacher survival in school districts', *American Educational Research Journal*, Vol. 7, pp. 1–27.

Griffiths, D.E., Goldman, S. and McFarland, W.J. (1965) 'Teacher mobility in New York City', *Educational Administration Quarterly*, Vol. 1, pp. 15–31.

Hall, O. (1948) 'The stages of a medical career', *American Journal of Sociology*, Vol. 53, pp. 327–336.

Haller, E.J. (1966) Teacher socialization. Pupil influences on teachers' speech. Ph.D. thesis, University of Chicago.

Jackson, P. (1968) *Life in Classrooms*, Holt, Rinehart and Winston, New York.

Jackson, P. and Belford, E. (1965) 'Educational objectives and the joys of teaching', *School Review*, Vol. 73, pp. 267–291.

Lortie D.C. (1958) 'The striving young lawyer: A study of early career differentiation in the Chicago bar', Ph.D. dissertation, University of Chicago.

Lortie, D.C. (1969) 'The balance of control and autonomy in elementary school teaching', in Etzioni, A. (ed.) *The Semi-professions and Their Organization*, Free Press, New York, pp. 1–53.

Maguire, T.F. (1970) Exchange and interaction in academic departments. Ph.D. thesis, University of Chicago.

March, J.G. and Simon, H.A. (1958). *Organizations*, Wiley, New York.

Mason, W.S. (1961) *The Beginning Teacher*, U.S. Department of Health, Education, and Welfare, Office of Education, circular no. 644, Washington D.C.

National Education Association (1963) *The American Public-school Teacher, 1960–61*, Research Division, research monograph 1963-M2, Wshington D.C.

National Education Association (1967) *The American Public-school Teacher, 1965–66*, Research Division, research report 1967-R4, Washington D.C.

Pedersen, K.G. (1973) *The Itinerant Schoolmaster: A Socio-economic Analysis of Teacher Turnover*, Midwest Administration Center, University of Chicago.

Peterson, W. (1956) Career phases and inter-age relationships: The female high school teacher in Kansas City. Ph.D. thesis, University of Chicago.

Sumner, W.G. (1906) *Folkways*, Ginn, Boston.

Waller, W. (1961) *The Sociology of Teaching*, Russell and Russell, New York.

14   The Meaning of Staffroom Humour

P. WOODS

In the following article, Peter Woods outlines one of the most prominent features of the staffroom at a secondary school: its laughter. Woods describes the nature and analyses the functions of staffroom laughter, arguing that it is a major means by which teachers come to terms with their job and reconcile their selves with the demands of the teacher role.

Sociological analyses of schools invariably leave an impression of grim institutionalization, and analyses of teachers, one of either sinister conspirators in the service of the dominant groups in society or of judgmental dopes, innocently but naively unaware of what they are doing. Neither of these is the view I have formed of teachers, at least in as simple a form as that; and that particular image of the school [. . .] is one-sided.[1] [. . .] A large amount of rhetoric pervades the teaching game. Many ingenious explanations are devised to provide accounts that square with the professional ethic and naturally enough, when interviewed on this plane by researchers, teachers answer in those terms with entire conviction. However, it is a curious fact in a society characterized by sharply differentiated functionary roles that we can 'split' ourselves into components, each one self-sufficient and insulated from the others. So that we can, if we wish, stand outside ourselves and comment on the actions of another 'self'.[2] I take the line that much personal investment in the advanced industrial society is made in the private, as opposed to the public, sphere. [. . .] For the moment it is clear that [. . .] certain elements of the 'private' self are not to be found in the teaching process at Lowfied. But they are there in school, and performing an important function.

At Lowfield, I found them in the staffroom. There I discovered a great deal of awareness of the restrictions, ruses, shortcomings and subterfuges that make up teacher activity. This awareness posed a problem, namely how to resolve the great conflict and discrepancy between the appearance on the one hand, and the reality on the other. [. . .] Rhetoric solves a problem of dysfunction on the plane of professionalism. But where the dysfunction arises as a result of the invasion of the professional by the personal plane, rhetoric is clearly highly inappropriate. The panacea in this instance is laughter. Thus we have, by my analysis, the greatest paradox of all, namely that what appears to be the most trivial and peripheral activity of the school could be interpreted as the most serious and central. For it is through laughter that teachers neutralize the alienating effects of institutionalization; that they synchronize the public and private spheres.

In this chapter I examine the phenomenon of staffroom humour. First I look at the significance of its location—the staffroom—and its incidence. Then, to give some perspective to the examples that follow, I give a summary of sociological accounts of laughter and humour. The examples are arranged according to the main contexts that have been developed in these accounts. It will be seen that these are insufficient within the framework of my analysis to do justice to the essential properties of staffroom laughter. My alternative explanation sees staffroom humour against a broader backcloth. The key role played by laughter is further supported by the conflicts that arise when its emergence is obstructed. I conclude the chapter, therefore, with a consideration of laughter-inhibitors.

The staffroom—the laughter arena

It is important to grasp the physical and temporal properties of staff laughter. Here I refer to several staffrooms of my acquaintance, which all seem of a type, though I make no other claims to wider generalizations. In these schools, the main arena is the staffroom, the teachers' collective private area. Its privacy is well respected by headteachers and pupils alike. Pupils are often debarred from knocking on the door, or even approaching its vicinity, by 'out-of-bounds' corridors. Headteachers usually knock before entering, limit their visits to urgent matters of business, and conduct themselves discreetly while there. Its boundaries are usually clearly demarcated. One I know, regarded as ideal by its inmates, was a cellar in an outbuilding, protected from the rest of the school by ancient stone walls and two car-parks. It was the 'men's' staffroom, and the strength of its boundaries was well indicated by the women's confessed trepidation at entering it. 'Solidarity' was here expressed in distance, construction, site, and reinforced by others' recognition of it. The 'properties' of the staffroom often lend it a distinctive character—perhaps old battered armchairs which the teachers who 'belong' to them defend with great vigour, resisting charitable urges from the headteacher to buy 'brand new ones'; or stained tea mugs, which carry the evidence of many a happy break—both symbols of individuality; and frequently too, signs of vast disorder—masses of papers, books, journals strewn around flat areas—which contrasts strongly with the system and order outside. Above all the staffroom is characterized by a euphoric atmosphere, given off by the reactions of the people in it, whether they be smoking, doing crosswords, playing bridge, conversing or just relaxing.

This is indeed a haven in stormy seas, and recourse must be had to it at regular intervals. The 'collective' periods are again well indicated. The initial gathering at the beginning of the day is a leisurely and tension-free gathering, after which teachers register their forms, then go to assembly. This is followed by a short, transient but often highly significant episode in the staffroom, before lessons begin in earnest. There is then a mid-morning break of some twenty minutes, a lengthy dinner-hour and a mid-afternoon break. Some often stay behind after school for an 'unwinding session'. In between these times the staffroom is populated by one or two teachers enjoying 'free periods', but as these are used in preparatory work, or in marking, they are not our concern—the staffroom is being used on these occasions as a 'quiet area' in the service of the official work of the institution. [. . .]

Staffroom laughter

[. . .]. My impression was that some of the staff were as much on the lookout for laughs as the kids. 'You have to make a laugh of it', Harry Timpson told me after one uproarious session. Often it might have its origins in conflict, control, order or some frustration, but equally as often it would seem to lose that initial referent to which it was a reaction, and become a growth experience in itself. The main social referent then would be the immediate company, the function, the delight and pleasure of sociation.[3]

Conflict-initiated humour frequently involves the attacking through laughter

of attempted subversions of status by senior personnel combining excessive bureaucratic features, which themselves call for neutralization. It is not surprising, therefore, that much staffroom humour takes the form of mocking, embarrassment, or compromise of senior personnel, often by 'subversive ironies'. [...]
[...] But there is a more general principle involved than the expression of aggression through humour, and the undermining of the moral position of the enemy in the context of the school and their relative positions and statuses within it. That is the celebration of a common principle among people in general which calls for equalizing and levelling.[4]

> The humor in such situations is seen in the attempt to be something one is not or in trying to assume characteristics which one cannot have by virtue of his previous experience. These jokes thus function to express the value of being one's self, average, and 'just like anybody else'

[...] Thus the headmaster's fire drills were passed off and acted out as Nürnberg rallies, complete with the caretaker's wife being sent to the gas chamber for not clearing up the school yard properly. (Of course, when somebody told Barney that he could take his gas-mask off, he replied he hadn't got one on!) And his hymn practice assemblies were similarly acted out as if at the palace of varieties, or a Frankie Vaughan attempting, vainly, to conduct the Wembley multitude. Here is an extract from my notes of one such assembly:

> 'Lester introduces the hymns, and talks about how the chaps on the football trains used to sing in four-part harmony. Then he announces the first hymn, "Alleluia, sing to Jesus". Both Barney and Lester open their mouths wide and sing very loud indeed. The band also play very loud, but there is not much coming from the body of the hall. Barney comes round from behind the table to the front of the stage to inspire. Lester, who had been conducting the band, turned to face the assembly, emphasizing once more the last lines of the verse.

> > Hark! the songs of peaceful Sion
> > Thunder like a mighty flood;
> > Jesus out of ev'ry nation,
> > Hath redeemed us by his blood.

> Barney stops the band with a wave of the arm. 'The band is playing! Me and Mr Lester are singing, with about twenty others in the hall, now come on, heads up, books up, fill your lungs with air and sing!" After another verse, with no perceivable increase in volume, Barney suddenly shouts, "Girls only!" ("Oh Christ!" says the girl next to me.) There is a pathetic noise, like a behind-the-hand mumble, for Barney and Lester, of course, are no longer singing. "Now come on!" urges Barney. "This is a damn good tune, some good words..." and he intones roundly the words of the next verse:

> > Alleluia, Alleluia
> > Glory be to God on high;
> > To the Father, and the Saviour,
> > Who has gained the victory...

> "... now come on, sing up, sing up!" After this first hymn, Barney says, "It's coming. It takes a lot out of you, doesn't it? It takes more out of you than a game of rugby, but if you want enjoyment you've got to pay for it. The more you put into it, the more you get out of it. Thank you, Mr Lester." Lester introduces the next hymn. He runs on about background, capabilities, etc., philosophical stuff. The hymn is softer, more dulcet, "Take May Life". the band plays the introduction, then Barney interrupts. "Now come on, heads up, books up, let's hear it!" After one verse, it was, "Girls! 'Take my voice'." But they were still unable to find theirs.

After that verse it was "Without the band, this time!", which yielded the most miserable noise of the morning, like one or two creaky doors opening and shutting. One girl later told me she actually started to sing, but they all stared at her so she stopped. "Boys! 'Take My Silver, take my gold!'" Oh, what a groaning!'

The headmaster and music master achieved little in terms of their intentions during this hymn practice, despite formidable exertions. Teachers on the stage said they could see whole wedges of silent faces. [. . .] But it was an extremely important component of the teachers' day, a brilliant start, in fact. I could see faces twitching as they sat at the back on the stage. And as soon as they reached the staffroom, Harry Timpson went into his master of ceremonies routine.

'For this verse, I give you your own, your very own, Flossie Sparkes!'
'This time we'll have the boys, the girls, the band, but chiefly—yourselves!'
'Is there any truth in the rumour that he's practising for Wembley next year?'
'It's sing-a-long with Cheetah time, folks.'
'He gets just about as much response.'
'When the band stops you can hear a pin drop, can't you?'

The staff went off happy to their lessons, and when they returned at break they immediately recaptured, some of the early morning mirth, '. . . but chiefly yourselves!' [. . .]

[. . .] These incidents [. . .] quite clearly promote solidarity. With a large school staff there is always some regular turnover, and the input of new personnel unacquainted with [. . .] backroom legends and traditions offers an excuse for their regular recall. The spontaneous laughter of the initiates is shared by those familiar with the tales, even if they have rehearsed it a hundred times. The humour in the material is constant. The laughter is sparked off, and then spread, contagiously, and then frequently compounded by other tales.

'Do you remember the time the head announced in assembly about the kids coming over from the hills? "When you get to the gym, you must go straight on, you must not fork off to the dining-room."'

The mental image of those kids 'forking off' to the dining-room was another 'banker' among the staff's humour sessions. There would be input from others' experiences elsewhere, contributions heightening the individual's identification with the group. Laughter is an enormous aid to solidarity, and in the harshness of the conditions in which teachers work it is important that they have this support. Group solidarity is often aided by demarcation from other groups, hence the persistence of such themes as 'senior personnel' or 'the women's or 'men's staffroom' (if indeed they are separate), or 'the kids', or other departments (such as 'the PE department'). The more ludicrous or ridiculous these can be made to appear the better—hence the added spice in the examples above that were public announcements to very large audiences. But it would be quite wrong to present this as entirely a kind of vindictive delight in the failures and embarrassments of superiors. There might be some of that, more especially when less amusing consequences of incompetence are actually being experienced. Then there might be an overriding tone of ridicule.

But on occasions, especially in recollection, and in legends, the ridicule and ill-feeling has evaporated, and the overriding tone is one of fondness. These howlers, errors and misjudgments are accepted as a contribution to sociation, and the endearing qualities of human failure, and that is how they are celebrated. The ecstasy of the humour lies not so much in the content by itself, as in the extreme incongruity, in relation to it, of the people perpetrating it. These are senior personnel—headteachers, their deputies—who, as previously noted, are more committed to the institutionalized structure and have perfomed more accommodations. In their responsibility for, and dedication to, the overall running of the school, they have a preoccupation with administration and policy, with rules and timetables, with 'appearances' (e.g. the public image of the school) and the 'forms' (i.e. the way in which things are done) of a completely different degree and order from the rest of the staff. That such institutionalized people can, on occasions, act in such outrageously 'foolish' fashion is an implicitly shared delight, where all concerned are allies, and the common foe, the institutional framework of the school. 'There's nowt so queer as folk', one member of staff was always declaiming. The comedian or fool who sets off a chain of humour is a person of special worth, since he promotes 'a bit of the transcendence designed to make sport of those situations, events and taboos that lie heaviest upon us if seen only from an earnest and serious perspective'.[5]

There is a lot of this in the sniping at rituals, as in assemblies, hymn practices, fire-drills, as discussed above. There might be elements of personal animosity and restoration of professional status, but there is also ridicule of the ritual as an enterprise in itself, as some kind of uncomfortable transmutation of life. It needs this humorous treatment to expose its pretentiousness. Laughter can be a great leveller. One example of this was the school's Sports Day, one of the great annual rituals of the school year. This called for considerable organization on the part of the games staff and complete co-operation from the rest, who were required to act as starters, stewards, convenors, recorders, announcers, calligraphers, policemen and cheer-leaders. It was not to everybody's taste. Indeed, to many it was an added burden, completely incidental to their main function as teachers. There were problems of motivation and order—since for many pupils it was simply a bit of a giggle—of a change of role and arena and of interdepartmental rivarly. This latter was particularly acute among some members of staff who resented the PE department's assumption of plenipotentiary powers on these occasions especially as they were using those powers to subject them to unpleasant experiences.

The gloom that had settled over the staffroom during the dinner-hour break in anticipation of the sports afternoon was suddenly dispelled when it was noticed that it had begun to rain, very, very slightly. The 'wits' went quickly to work:

'Can I have a runner—I mean a swimmer—please?' (Using pretend binoculars, through the window.) 'Are you ready? On your marks!'
Calling Mr Lewis, glug, glug, glug . . .'
'Can we have all runners at the deep end?'
'That boy with the outboard engine is disqualified!'
'The shot is sinking!'
'With a boy underneath!'
'Ten to one on the one in the diver's helmet.'
'Don't forget to go straight to the decompression chamber when you've finished the race.'
'I've just seen Julie Marne. She said it was only a little shower. "We're certainly going to get a little wet this afternoon, but I don't think it'll be too bad," she said.'
'So saying, she dived into the playground and struck out manfully for the gym.'
'Ted, can you get your band to strike up "A Life on the Ocean Wave", and a few sea shanties, just to drop her a hint? Or "Fierce Raged the Tempest o'er the Deep"?
'We'll all change into bathing costumes, goggles and flippers and come and join in.'
'I hear they're going to issue us with shooting-sticks and polythene bags this year.'
'Cor, look at it, it's making dents in Sandra's car roof!'
'Where's Fuller, for heaven's sake!'

'He was last seen tacking up the causeway . . .'
' . . . dropping anchor over the girls' changing room.'

The joking intensified with the rain, and eventually Julie Marne came in and announced to universal applause and merriment that the sports had been cancelled. The feelings that lay behind this humour were articulated to me by Ted Lester. He was quite happy to miss 'sports afternoon'. He was envious of the PE department—it was one of the 'sacred cows'.

> 'The kids don't want to watch, they don't want to run, you're forever chasing them up for being in school, writing in the toilets, smoking and so on. It's a hell of a job to get them to compete, or to watch, worse than trying to teach them—at least you know where you are with your own room and your own subject. Then they have their hierarchy of jobs. If you're a starter for the 400 metres that's a cushy number. But if you're race co-ordinator, that's a hell of a job. You've got to get them all together. They're in these four pens, and they're always going missing. Jack Fuller allocates jobs all off his own bat, without the courtesy of asking.'

In short, sports afternoon challenged the day-to-day survival mechanisms which were the ordinary teacher's safeguard, and disturbed the status equilibrium of the staff by elevating the PE department to a position of high authority. These two factors deprived the great amount of organizational detail that was necessary of its credibility, thus laying it open for ridicule. In the example above, certain features of it are seized on with alacrity and lampooned in the overall expression of opposition to the activity. It is a good example of the use of humour to disguise enmity, anger and frustration, but again, with evidence of the 'growth' element, which appears, is indulged in and enjoyed on its own account. [. . .]
[. . .] Humour can often be seen running along the edges of the institutional framework. The line of quivering lips on the stage during hymn practice assemblies, the asides during fire-drills, the ruses to alleviate the boredom of doing reports (such as trying to fill a whole line with 'satisfactory', or drawing pictures and running a book on what it is, with such comments as 'Fair' and 'Good') all indicate the fine balance between role and person, paradigm and practice, programme and survival. One hilarious lunch-hour was spent in filling in forms (than which there is no more bureaucratic feature) for a colleague doing a project for a diploma:

> 'What have you put for "occupation"?
> 'Teaboy to a steeplejack, What have you put?'
> 'Deep sea diver, unreturned.'
> 'Irish peat-cutter's mate.' . .

[. . .] At times, someone will, deliberately I suspect, aim to create a mirthful atmosphere, again through the well-known technique of incongruities, offering him or herself as the butt of the joke. Thus one whole mid-day break was once taken up with Frank Boundley's defence of queueing as a restful experience.

> 'You're in the queue, you can't do nothing about it, so you might as well relax and shut off. Everybody else is hustling and bustling about. There's too much dashing about in this world, not enough pausing to think . . . queues stop you dashing around, make you stop and think. You know you won't do it unless you're forced to do it, and queues are the only thing I known about that make you do it . . . Oh yes, if I go to the bank, or Sainsbury's, and see a number of queues, I'll always join the largest one, or if I'm on the road and get in a jam or come up behind one of them MIT lorries, I'll think, "Good, we're in for a nice, relaxed drive now." I'll never try to overtake; why should I deprive myself of what I enjoy most?'

Frank sustained this line of talk for the whole of the lunch-hour, while the staffroom 'wits' spun variations on it:

> 'Oh dear, I've punctured my basket, I'll have to sit down till the floor manager repairs it.'
> 'What do you do, Frank, if when you come to go out, there aren't any queues? Keep going round till there are some?'
> 'Sometimes I will actually go looking for queues, if I'm feeling in need of relaxation. If I see a big one I'll get in it, whatever they're queueing up for.'
> 'Now, sir, when is your baby due?'
> 'When did you have your last period?'
> 'Is this the tooth that's hurting?'
> 'This is the last job we're offering you; you've refused six already.'
> 'Men's toilets are round the other side, sir.'

Thus a pleasant dinner-hour was passed and people went off smiling to their lessons. The humour was developed out of nothing in particular; in other words it could not be represented as a reaction or response to threatening people or situations, or as dissipating conflict or as tension release. It was a creative act in itself. This gives it a broader setting. 'Humour as an example of the creative act in its full range of potential, or humour as play, is a sensitive means of coping, an adaptive vehicle for making life's compromises, and is, therefore, a *growth experience*.[6] This fondness and affection which marks the human bond is often forgotten amid the overriding conflict that prevails in many schools. [...]

[...] Fondness for the pupils as individuals is evident in the following teacher's remarks on some of her pupils:

> 'John Hurley, he's charmer; he always says "Cheers, Miss!" if I ask him to do something. I think he fancies his chances with me, always telling me risqué jokes, and I'll laugh, others are quite embarrassed. Paul Hopkins is very expansive. If I'm trying to find something out, he comes in saying, "You'll never find out, Miss, you'll never find out!" I say, "Do you mind, I'm conducting this!" "Oh, sorry I spoke, sorry I spoke!"'

The sense of individuality coming over from these comments contrasts strongly with [...] laughter arising from conflict, or from professional failure. This is certainly very common. As with the writing of reports, laughter helps sustain a view of self as expert, and infallible. Shared experiences of failure are accounted for in terms of the object, and often ridiculed. Thus one teacher read out to the class a 'hoot' of an essay somebody had written during an examination. Killing himself with laughter as he read it (it was a preposterous tale about the Last Supper), he left the class in no doubts about the idiocy of the author. A similar motive might be held to lay behind the recounting of howlers.

> 'Queen Elizabeth was known as the virgin queen. She had a unique way of getting what she wanted.'
> 'The ancient Britions had rough mating on the floor.'
> 'The French executed people in a pubic place.'

Again these have an earthy ring and the laughter raised is serving a variety of functions. The professional motive appears uppermost, though glee at the enormous incongruity revealed by the slightest human error is a universal phenomenon. Teachers, too, can make 'howlers', such as the one who wrote on a girl's report, 'I do not like to see her bottom.' There is nothing as tedious, or professional, as writing reports. Such slips provide personal relief for all concerned, including the perpetrator. [...]

Laughter inhibitors

Occasionally, however, certain combinations of factors produce incidents for which laughter is no antidote. These are the real disturbers of the peace and it is important to identify them. I have noticed the following factors obstructing laughter:

1 *The psychological and physiological state of the teacher.* There seems to be a higher incidence of staffroom 'explosions' towards the end of a term, during or just after examinations, or at other times of high tension. With some, all social poise is lost and customary civilities, such as passing the time of day, forgone. Others might invert the process and actually invade the staffroom with their distress. The staffroom has been swamped by the tide of their misery and offers no relief; and, like drowning men, they threaten to pull the others down with them. At such times staffrooms are 'unhappy' places, and staff sectionalize, some going to the local pub, or to department rooms, store-cupboards, the games field, or even home.

2 *Injustice.* Some things just are not funny and cannot be made so. Bureaucracies operate on the assumption of equal work and responsibilities according to status, and equal distribution of resources. If you get less work and more resources than average, that might be cause for self-congratulation—but if you get more work and less resources, that is without doubt the very worst thing that can happen to you in state secondary schools. Hence the trauma of the 'free period' ritual every morning. The teacher who can smile at the loss of a 'free' is very rare indeed. He is more likely to have others smiling at him, in relief that it is not them.

3 *The undermining of status, or threats to professional equilibrium or personal insults.* Of course, some pupils threaten teacher status continually but not, usually, irretrievably. Sometimes, however, they go too far. Also it is up to [. . .] teachers to negotiate their own position not only *vis-à-vis* the pupils, but also [their] colleagues and the headmaster. Laughter presupposes this kind of equilibrium. It assumes that though there may be frustrations, difficulties and altercations, on balance the flow of activities is on the credit side, and that, to some extent, one is achieving one's personal aim, however negotiated that might be. Otherwise, sour feeling is likely to predominate, unrelievable by humour.

All these factors are evident in the following examples which all promoted 'heavy' conflict (as opposed to 'negotiable' conflict):

Example A
One particular instance that occurred during my stay concerned Jerry Horne and Harry Timpson, major laughter-makers as a rule. They discovered one day, from pupils as I gathered, that there would be no spectators at the swimming gala. Disappointment at not gaining some extra 'frees' was compounded by the empathetic feeling of injustice they felt on behalf of the kids and their resentment at the high-handedness of the PE department in making decisions they felt should be more appropriately made by the headmaster. Significantly this lunchtime debate was totally lacking in humour, and highly charged with inter-staff animosity. It came to light that, because of problems of discipline, Jack Fuller had decided that the staff-school hockey match was better played in the lunch-hour. Again the autocracy of the decision, the loss of valuable free time and the denial of the gain of free time doing a pleasurable activity—a great aid to survival—led to disappointment, frustration and anger, and totally precluded laughter. The very

next day, Jerry Horne learnt, again from the kids, that some House cricket matches were to be played during two periods when there was to be a staff meeting. Five teachers had been 'excused' the staff meeting to supervise the rest of the school, but these cricket matches would consume three of them, leaving two—Jerry, since he knew nothing about cricket, and a student—to 'control' the five hundred other pupils, who would in all probability be rather boisterous at the break in routine. Jerry felt particularly aggrieved, since the other form teachers concerned had volunteered their absence from the staff meeting, cutting the ground from under his feet. When the headmaster asked him, he felt he had little option but to agree. Now there was this further injustice.

> 'Jack Fuller says he's been to higher authority, but I know the old man—Jack would mumble something to him and Barney would mumble "Yes, all right" back without realizing what was going on. It's Fuller's direct responsibility . . . It's all right for him . . . "I'm all right, Jack" . . . He'll get his cricket in, get his umpires, and be nice and comfortable in the staff meeting. What about us poor sods trying to cope with that mob out there?'

As noted, laughter is frequently both a symptom and a reinforcer of solidarity. Threats to, and rifts in, solidarity promote the obverse, conflict and anger.

Example B

Another outstanding example was the shattering of David Sylvester's 'inner peace'. Here was a man of great conviction who lived the message that he put about, that peace lay within the individual, not in all these frenzied activities that took place outside. This extract from my notes of an assembly talk given by him one morning gives some idea of the history of arriving at that conviction. It is much condensed.

> 'The story of his life was basically one of anti-establishmentarianism throughout school and college. He had all the feelings and trappings, supported the right groups. He championed the "Rolling Stones" against the establishment's "Beatles", grew his hair long, wore zany clothes. He went crazy when Pete Townsend smashed his guitar on the microphones, ecstatic when Jimi Hendrix performed. As he went up the school he changed, from supporting the "Stones" to Hendrix for example. None of them quite suited exactly. Later, at college, he met many people who claimed to have found the ultimate solution, but none of them suited him. Then he went to America and he came across a group who made a lot of sense to him, called the "drop-ins". One guy there particularly drew his attention. He stood apart from the others, a gentle, quiet, guy. He plucked up courage one day and went up to him and said, "This is it, man, this is where it's all at!" He said gently, "That may be so, but it's what goes on in here (i.e. in the mind) that matters, this has to be at peace with itself." And that guy really put him in his place. He realized that all his previous attatchments had been based on hate. What he sought was peace . . . The talk was illustrated by appropriate tracks. Yes, he had always aligned himself to movements that promised revolution in some form or another—until he found peace with the "drop-ins". And he hoped he still carried a bit of it around with him. It was not too late for them—yet. After the talk, Clem Marne sang a song to his own guitar accompaniment of a dream he had had about no more war . . .'

This is interesting in several respects, but here let us note the firmness of the conviction and the length and highly-charged nature of the journey getting to it. David's 'peace' withstood all manner of buffetings, but Barney, the headmaster, managed to undermine it, and in a comparatively short space of time. They had had several altercations along the lines of Barney's traditionalism versus David's libertarianism, all successfully resisted by David, until the day Barney visited one of David's lessons. Again I quote from my field notes the story as told me shortly afterwards by a far from peaceful David.

> 'David was showing a film to a 5th form on housing. All had gone pretty well in the project they were doing. Barney came in and stood at the opposite end of the room, hesitated then came in far enough, so a number stood up, whereupon he waved them down. David wished he'd make up his mind what he wanted. "Anyway I went over to him and thought I'd better say something, so I started to tell him what the film was about, putting it in context. Half-way through—he clearly hadn't been listening—he suddenly bellowed to Mervyn Waters to get his feet down—and strode across the room to him, thus obscuring the film and concentrating all attention on him and Mervyn Waters. There was some altercation with Mervyn, remonstrating as is his wont, then Barney finally stormed back across the room, his image all over the screen, and out, having taken over and ruined the entire lesson. I'd resisted getting steamed up over him till then—but it went then—I seethed! (He gestures.) The ignorance of it!"'

In fact Barney's intervention in this way might not have been all that ignorant—on the contrary. Up to that point, David had resisted all Barney's attempts to 'cut him down to size'. Humour had been a useful weapon in his defence, joining in the general lampooning of the headmaster. But it was of no avail to him now. We might interpret what happened like this: Barney, continuously on the look-out for 'constitutional' ways of putting down David, found one in this film lesson in the form of Mervyn Waters's lounging posture, which epitomized for him the dangers in David's radical style of teaching. Using this symbol, Barney conveyed a loud and clear message to David, nicely dramatized by the circumstances:

(a) that this form of teaching was unwelcome, and
(b) that he was headmaster, and would, if necessary, use his superior authority.

David's distress was an indication that he had got the message. He now had to decide whether to allow himself to be socialized into the Lowfield way of doing things, or whether to continue to go his own way and develop unbearable conflict. In fact, the commitment to his ideals allowed for no compromise, and it was the latter course that he took, ultimately to resign his post after a stay of little over a year. The point, for our present discussion, is that this conflict, bared of all its camouflaging gloss, allowed for no mediation by humour, or by any other device. It was too open, too revealed, too frank, too oppositional, and the opposing parties' commitments to their respective positions too complete, to allow any room for reconstruction or manoeuvre. From this point on David saw nothing funny whatever in Barney no matter what high pitches of merriment on that account were struck in the staffroom. For him, the issue was much too real, much too earnest to allow for its transcendence.

Example C
A typical laughter-resistent item occurred in the last week of the Christmas term. During a 'reading competition' two 4th-year boys—Clanton and Willcock—hid under the stage and refused to come out. They made noises through the grill, such as 'Yoo-hoo, Miss Travis!', thus effectively spoiling proceedings without actually stopping them. However, the headmaster was on the stage behind the curtains (unbeknown to the boys, in the staff's opinion) but was unable to detect their presence conclusively. One teacher thought this was what irked him—they were getting the better of him. He had the piano moved over the trapdoor to block their

escape. Then, coming down the steps from the stage he forgot the organ and banged his head, much to the glee of the children in the hall. There was a welter of suppressed giggles hurriedly stopped as he glowered at them. He then 'had a go' at Miss Travis and Mr Whitlock, who were supervising the reading competition, in front of the assembled children.

Paternalism will become inverted if its own armaments are turned against it, and will reply with vindictive assault. In this case the headmaster had been well and truly 'shown up' and Clanton and Willcock had scored a great triumph. Barney had contributed to his own discomfiture by banging his head, which compounded the irresolution and failure to detect. The balance of respect had to be restored. For Clanton and Willcock it was the worst punishment he could administer—suspension. But he had been shown up before the senior school, so they too must be made to pay. They were assembled in the hall and given a general dressing-down. Things were going to be different from then on. They were 'denigrated as human beings', according to one account. School uniform was going to be rigorously inspected and boys were to have hair cut above collars. David Sylvester, now continually smarting from his losing battle with the head, and whose own hair was shoulder length, came into the staffroom afterwards and declared, 'That's it, I'm leaving, I'm off, can't stay in this school any longer.' Even Jack Fuller, with what he called his 'armchair traditional views', disliked it intensely. The staff said it was his 'tone' and 'irrationality', especially the fact that 'the huge majority of kids in there were completely innocent of any wrong-doing'. Moreover, he associated his staff with this 'new totalitarian, oppressive policy'. Sylvester resented this. He wasn't 'going to bloody do it'. [. . .]

[. . .] It would appear that the only beneficiaries of this incident, and the only ones entitled to 'laugh', were Clanton and Willcock. Everyone else—headmaster, staff and pupils—were outraged. Thus a situation which might have been interpreted as a bit of innocent mucking about was transformed into a criminal and rebellious assault on the headmaster's status, the restoration of which had to be made up by sacrifices from the rest of the school. No 'fun' could be made out of this incident by anybody—except perhaps the two perpetrators. It was too wilful, irrational, vicious, unjust, arbitrary. It overstepped the limits of accommodation. [. . .] 'The most original thing Clanton's ever done,' commented Sylvester. 'And he gets suspended for it!' There were, of course, no mass hair-cuts, nor uniform reformations—the display of rage and power had been sufficient.

This incident combines all three of the conflict-producing contingencies mentioned above—exhaustion at the end of a term, a felt injustice and a disturbance of the finely balanced equilibrium in the school, which takes weeks and weeks of subtle and complex negotiation to attain. Both staff and pupils were deprived of the right of appeal to secondary adjustments. Laughter was no antidote. It is not difficult to see that it would not take many such incidents to reduce the whole school to strain and misery, making survival for all intensely difficult.

Example D
Another instructive incident arose during the school examinations. Because of different 'sets' in maths, and because each set had different teachers for different aspects of the subject, the circumstances arose where nine different examination papers were needed within the same rooms. Some did not appear. Allan Groves, for example, had only seven, though he searched diligently for the other two, even asked some of the maths staff for them. There was general chaos. Many had finished their 'bits' of papers by break, others had not even started. The maths

department were outraged that their examination had been 'sabotaged'. The staff who had been supervising were equally outraged at the incompetence of the maths department's arrangements. Insults were hurled about, and physical assault threatened:

'He was bloody rude to me ...' 'If he says that to me I'll stick him one on ...!' 'Ridiculous! Forty minutes for a 1¼-hour paper! ...' 'I'm not marking 2Ws, I'm *not* marking them, and that's that! ...' 'It's the kids I think about, done all that revision, one little lad came to me this morning, crying he was ...

Allan Groves astutely observed that because so many people were involved in the difficulty, the maths department should have known it was not the supervisory teachers' fault as individuals but the system's. By causing so much disturbance they were covering their own tracks, or trying to. Disguising professional failure is one of the functions of staff laughter, but sometimes it is inappropriate; for example, when the failure is peculiar to one group on the staff and not others, when it adversely affects the others, and when its consequences are going to be evident and incriminating. Bigger guns are then brought to bear, and heavier smokescreens laid.

Interdepartmental rivalry frequently hovers on the borders separating humour from malice, in ridicule for example. But it is a thin divide, and the scales are often tipped by minor, even trivial, factors. If there is humour, it disguises the real grievance within, and helps one to conduct one's business.

Some other examples

Some relationships are unamenable to rescue by laughter. While some might joke about 5L, Jim Martell was unable to see anything funny in them at all.

'They're terrible, particularly the girls, they're revolting, they really are—filthy, vile, despicable. (*I asked him in what way.*) In their minds ... I don't catch what they say, thank God, I just hear the guffaws—you wonder how much is directed at you. There's Carol Landers and Sandra Turner—great big lump—really coarse, horrible she is, disgusting. The boys aren't so bad, just won't work—idle and lazy. Yet on their own they're different. Sharman, for example, that very tall boy, an idle waster in class, yet as an individual ... I had a talk with him the other day—his background, family, what he's going to do—and for the first time I felt I was getting through to him. They're all OK as individuals, I suppose, but in a group! If there were a 5th-form dinner this year, I wouldn't go. It will be the first one I've missed for over twenty years, but I shan't go. Yet there was no group we did more for, as a staff, by way of preparation, countless hours spent, hundreds of meetings among staff making sure we didn't overlap on subject-matter.'

Even here one sees redemption in the individual, but as a group, for Jim, 5L were beyond the pale. The feeling, it must be said, was mutual. They staggered on, from lesson to lesson, under clouds of bad feeling and perpetually on the brink of breakdown. Some individual relationships were of this kind; for instance, those between Ted Lester and Phil Harman. Quite regularly, each would tell me how much he hated the other. Senior and long-serving teachers both, they had not spoken to each other for eight years. 'Loathsome, pompous individual!' said Harman. 'I'll never understand', said Lester, 'why someone who hates kids so much could stand teaching so long. He's a funny feller, you know!' Therein lies the irony. There was no fun. Their gorges rose at the mere thought of each other, so much so that Harman had removed himself from the staffroom and lived a hermit's life in his formroom, in a separate building.

Thus the psychological and physiological state of the teacher, perceived injustices, the undermining of status, threats to professional equilibrium, inter-departmental and interpersonal rivalry or hatred, and the obstruction of routes to secondary adjustments, all work as blockages to laughter, either dispelling its efficacy or pre-empting its use. But these all imply breakdown or non-survival. They represent cracks in the system. Invariably they are repaired by humour, or at least humour is a sign of its repair. Laughter is the coping mechanism *par excellence*. Lack of it might suggest non-survival. Its presence is a sure indication of managing. [...]

Notes

[1] See Walker, R. and Adelman, C. (1976) 'Strawberries', in Stubbs, M. and Delamont, S. (eds) *Exploration in Classroom Observation*, Wiley, London, and Walker, R. and Goodson, I. 'Humour in the classroom', in Woods, P.E. and Hammersley, M. (eds) *School Experience*, Croom Helm, London.

[2] Goffman, E. (1971) *The Presentation of Self in Everyday Life*, Penguin, Harmondsworth.

[3] On the influence of different compositions of groups see Furlong, V. 'Interaction sets in the classroom', in Stubbs, M. and Delamont, S (1976) *op. cit.*

[4] Stephenson, R.M. (1951) 'Conflict and control functions of humour', *American Journal of Sociology*, Vol. 56, pp. 569–574.

[5] Pollio, H.R. and Edgerley, J.W. (1976) 'Comedians and comic style', in Chapman, T. and Foot, H. (eds) *Humour and Laughter*, Wiley, London, p. 240.

[6] Fry, W.E. and Allen, M. (1900) 'Humour as a creative experience: the development of a Hollywood humourist', in Chapman and Foot, op. cit., p. 252.

15   Staffroom News

M. HAMMERSLEY

In the following article Martyn Hammersley looks at certain features of the occupational culture of teaching as revealed in staffroom talk. He takes what, on the face of things, appears to be the harsh and condemnatory staffroom talk of secondary school teachers about their pupils and the community, and explains it in terms of the functions that talk serves for the teachers as a group.

In the last twenty years a considerable body of ethnographic research has been carried out in schools. The bulk of this has focused on classrooms. Such a focus is not unreasonable, of course, since the classroom is the place where one might expect the most important work of the school to take place. But there is much to be learned from looking at other parts of schools; and indeed at other aspects of schooling than teacher–pupil interaction.

One important but neglected area is the structure of social relationships to be found among teachers.[1] This is a key issue in itself from the point of view of the sociology of occupations, but, of course, staff relations are also likely to be a significant factor shaping what occurs in the classroom. This article looks at one aspect of relations among the teaching staff of a small, inner-city, boys' secondary modern school (to which I have given the pseudonym 'Downtown'). It focuses on the exchange of 'news' about pupils in the staffroom and seeks to identify its functions.[2]

In the morning, before school starts, the teachers at Downtown sit or stand around in the staffroom reading papers, chatting and smoking. At dinnertime they eat in the hall with the pupils and then come to the staffroom; or eat sandwiches in the staffroom and stay there until afternoon lessons begin, talking, playing cards, etc. During free periods they read newspapers, chat with whoever else happens to be there, or mark books.

While there was some variation in who sat where, there were informal groups centred on each of the three coffee tables in the staffroom. For much of the time the three tables formed self-contained interaction groups, although the staffroom as a whole was occasionally the audience. At other times, smaller standing or sitting groups straddling the usual groups were formed.

The typical distribution of the teachers across the three tables partly reflected friendship networks, but the tables were also sites for different activities. Table III was invariably occupied with bridge at lunchtime and sometimes at break. Table I was often a solo whist game at lunchtime. A regular member of Table II mentioned that at one time they had done crosswords, though during the period of fieldwork they merely talked, ate sandwiches and read newspapers.

Talk was undoubtedly the major staffroom activity, ranging in focus from football to classical music. However, most staffroom conversation was shop talk, and usually about Downtown and its pupils.

Types of Staffroom News

A consequence of the structure of the teachers' work situation at Downtown is that while the information acquired by one in the course of his work is likely to be different from that acquired by others, it is nevertheless of potential relevance to the whole staff. This arises in particular from the fact that, because classes move around between them, the teachers all face the same pupils at one time or another. A premium is thereby placed on the gathering and trading of 'news' about pupils.

Some of this 'news' is about specific events and derives from direct experience:

1   [Greaves enters the staffroom and speaks to the whole room:]

Greaves: Don't anybody hit Storey for a bit, lay off Storey for a week or so everyone.

T: Why?

Greaves: His mother's just been in.

T: What happened?

Greaves: She came up to me an' said 'I'll push yer glasses through yer face'.

T: What did you say?

Greaves: I raised myself up to my full height and said: 'Madam, if you have a complaint you must see the headmaster' and I walked down to the office with her muttering behind me. Anyway, the head saw her off. He told me to hit him on the shoulder in the future, where it doesn't mark. I haven't heard of that before.

Webster: That's what Freddy Carpenter used to do, lay about the shoulder [laughter].

T: Aye, after he'd kicked them in the crutch.

(Greaves mentioned that the mother had said that someone else had hit him on Monday)

Baldwin: I think I hit him yesterday.

Denison: I kicked him out.

T: I don't think he went up to games.

Baldwin: Oh well I can't have hit him then, my conscience is clear.

Denison: Well, I kicked him out [laughter]. Oh no, not literally, I think he did go up to games.

Baldwin: Oh don't say that.

(At lunchtime Greaves tells the story again, this time mentioning that Storey's mother was accompanied by another woman)

T: For support I suppose.

T: What did you do to him?

Greaves: Oh I hit him across the face three times, he reckons he counted five as his head hit the desk.

T: What had he done?

Greaves: Oh you know what Storey's like, he's one of those lads who acts just at the wrong moment, he goes just too far, just tips the balance.

On other occasions there is a pooling of news about the same event from multiple sources, including information gleaned from the pupils themselves:

2 [Staffroom]   There is talk about a fight that had taken place in the hall, a prefect had hit three fourth year pupils and one of the latter had tried to hit the prefect in the face with a piece of slate [there are builders in the school]. The prefect put his hand up to prevent this and his hand was cut. There was much talk abut why the prefect had hit the pupils. I think the teachers were in a quandary. On the one hand, he was apparently provoked, on the other prefects are not supposed to inflict physical punishment. One teacher says 'The head is very concerned and came into the classroom and gave the fifth form a rollicking without mentioning the prefect by name'. Another points out that they had had trouble with that form [the fifth form] when it had been a third form. Holton asks: 'Who got the best of it?' There's a discussion between Webster and Denison [the latter very concerned about likely repercussions on the prefect]. Webster reports that 'There's a rumour among the boys that a fourth year gang are going to get the prefect, forty of them, it's no joke, they could disable a teacher'. Some comments were also made to the effect that the prefects represented the teachers.

Staffroom news is selected and presented in terms of its relevance to common problems and issues. The two extracts just quoted are clear examples of this. Thus in extract 1 the account of the irate mother is prefaced by a summary of its implications for colleagues: 'Lay off Storey for a while'. Furthermore, this account relates to some major teacher worries: possible interference by parents, and being prosecuted for hitting pupils. The former concern is well-documented in other schools (Becker, 1951; Sharp and Green, 1975; Lortie, 1975) and emerges clearly in this example; the latter came out quite explicitly at other times in the staffroom:

3 [Staffroom: Larson to Walker in MH's presence]
Larson: You ought to be official NUT convenor.
Walker: I'm only in the NUT for one reason.
[Larson looks significantly towards MH]
Larson: In case you get prosecuted for hitting someone.
Walker: That's right.

While the news about the fight in extract 2 doesn't include any specific guidance for future action, it too is relevant to a prevailing staff concern: the danger of pupil violence towards teachers. If the pupils can hit a prefect, a representative of the teachers, might they not start attacking the teachers themselves? While as far as I could tell this had never happened, the possibility was mentioned several times in the staffroom and seemed to underly much talk about the pupils:

4 *Webster*: I don't know what'll happen this term, it'll be a matter of containment, it's the last two days I'm worried about.
  Dixon: We'll be issued with guns for the last two days, Thompson sub-machine guns mounted on our desks.

5 [Talk about Wilson [a pupil] between Baldwin and MH after a lesson]
  Baldwin: When you face him his chin's up here [about nose level] and I'm fairly tall, it's quite alarming in a physical sense. I wouldn't like to control him for another two years.

This concern about the danger of pupil violence perhaps explains the staffs' somewhat ambivalent attitude towards the prefect and his actions in extract 2. On the one hand, as their representative he should be respected by the pupils, and to ensure this he must be supported in his dealings with them; just as a teacher must be supported by his colleagues, and in particular by the head (Becker, 1951). On the other hand, the teachers were clearly concerned that this prefect's possibly illegitimate action might itself actually spark off physical attacks on teachers.

Much staffroom news though is not about specific events at all. Some, for example, concerns pupil moods:

6 [Staffroom]
  Webster: 4T are playing up today.

7 [Staffroom]
  Greaves: I don't know what's happened but 3T are working this morning.

8 [Staffroom: Webster to Marsden]
  Webster: What mood's [name] in today?

Who's here and who's absent is also reported; though it is only the presence and absence of 'problem' pupils which seems to be newsworthy:

9 *T*: All the clowns in that form are away at the moment, [name] was being very stupid.

10   T: Donald Channing has been put into detention centre.
    Greaves: Good. Has Hughes been excluded because of window breaking?
    T: No, because of the nurse.
    Greaves: Oh pity, that means he'll come back. Still I suppose we should be thankful
         for small mercies.

11   [Denison and Webster] Denison recounts who in a particular class is away to
    indicate that it won't be too bad taking 3T. Webster tells how he tried to persuade
    a pupil to bunk off [i.e. to truant]

12   Greaves: O'Brien's been suspended.
    T: Where from?
    T: By the neck I hope.

13   Webster: [Aldwych] is back, horrible child.

Once again this news is closely tied to classroom concerns and is made relevant
by the fact that the pupils pass round from one teacher to another for different
lessons. Given the assumption that there are certain 'prime-movers', getting such
information may enable a teacher to anticipate how a lesson will go and what
problems are likely to arise.

    The primary concern underlying all this news is with sources of trouble and
the most common kind of staffroom news retains this interest while being even
further removed from specific events. Here teachers' current characterizations of
problem pupils are exchanged:

14   [Philipson and Baldwin talking about 2T]
    Baldwin: There's seven good lads but there's some little buggers: Short, Cook,
         Mills, Dunn's top of the list. Arnold's vicious, aggressive, resentful . . .
    Philipson: [laughing] Is that all?
    Baldwin: Richardson, I can get along with him, he's just a bit loud that's all.
    Philipson: Gary's not so bad.
    Baldwin: He's easily led that's his trouble. I get no pleasure out of taking 2T, no
         pleasure at all, I get more pleasure out of teaching third year classes.

15   [Staffroom]:
    Webster: [name], he's an oaf.
    Walker: Well y'know why, he's stupid, can't even read or write.
    Webster: O'Brien's going off his head.
    MH: [Laughs]
    Webster: It's not just an expression, I mean it, he's going off his head, but nobody
         does anything about it of course.

What we have here is the trading of summary typifications of pupils.[3] Teachers
employ typifications of pupils to guide their actions (Rist, 1973; Hargreaves, Hester
and Mellor, 1975). 'Knowing what to expect' from different quarters minimizes the
cues required to come to some conclusion about what's going on, what's about to
happen, who is involved, in what role, and what can be done about it. Knowing
what 'type' a pupil is is important, otherwise one might be caught unawares.
Teachers' reliance on typifications is heightened by the immediacy of the classroom
(Jackson, 1968; Doyle, 1977) and their responsibility for what goes on there. Yet,
at the same time, these features of classroom interaction also minimize the
evidence available for the construction of typifications. Given this, it is perhaps not
surprising that the teachers at Downtown seem to supplement their own
observations with information from colleagues.

Teachers' Typifications of Pupils

There is now a considerable literature on teacher typifications (Hargreaves, 1977). The impetus for this derived initially from the concept of the self-fulfilling prophecy (Merton, 1957), dramatically and controversially demonstrated in the classroom by Rosenthal and Jacobson (1968).[4] Their experimental approach has been followed up by more ethnographic work, notably that of Rist (1970, 1973), Nash (1973) and Sharp and Green (1975). More recently, however, attention has shifted somewhat, away from the consequentiality of teacher typifications for pupil careers, and towards an examination of their structure and process. Thus, for example, Leiter (1974) investigated the processes by which kindergarten children are assigned to different ability groups within the class and to different classes in the first grade. In doing this he focuses on the structure of social interaction in assessment interviews and assignment meetings, and the typifications and criteria involved in the decisions. Similarly, but this time in the field of secondary education, Hargreaves *et al.* (1975) have developed a complex model of the process by which pupils are typed as deviant and how these types underpin teachers' responses to classroom events.

Most research in this area to date has sought to identify the typifications used by teachers in the classroom or other assessment settings. While the importance of the staffroom as a place where teachers 'compare notes' about pupils has been recognized (Hargreaves, 1972, chapter 12; Hargreaves *et al.*, 1975, pp. 62–5), the nature of such discussions has not been investigated. But the analysis of staffroom typifications has methodological as well as substantive significance. Existing research on typifications has relied almost entirely on interview data, and questions inevitably arise about the relationship between the typifications elicited in that context and those which are actually operative in the classroom. After all if, as is generally accepted, action is always tailored to the situation in which it occurs, this is no less true of interview talk than of action in any other setting. How much, then, do the typifications elicited owe to the interview context itself? There is no basis for claiming that staffroom talk about pupils is any closer to classroom operative typifications than that elicited in interviews; but it does provide us with another source of evidence.

Crucial to the nature of both staffroom typifications and those elicited in interviews is that they are two-stage productions. In the classroom the teachers are constantly monitoring and making sense of pupil behaviour, and the products of this process are sedimented as typificatory knowledge. We can expect that this material is then reworked to one degree or another to produce staffroom typifications. Unfortunately, there is no direct way of identifying the nature of this production process and how it differs from that involved in interviews. One indirect line of attack, however, is to compare the typifications produced in the two types of context. Thus, for example, one can compare the staffroom typifications reported here with those elicited in interviews by Hargreaves *et al.* (1975).

At a superficial level, at least, the *content* of the typifications produced in the two contexts does not seem all that different. They are both structured around what are generally regarded as the two basic classroom concerns of teachers: order and learning (Stebbins, 1975, p. 45). Even though in both sets of data general descriptors are used much of the time (e.g. in example 14 'good', 'little bugger', 'vicious', 'aggressive' etc.) it is quite clear that the typifications are formulated in terms of how much trouble the pupil is for the teachers: 'I can get along with him', 'I get no pleasure from taking 2T ...'. There may, of course, be more subtle differences in the way in which these themes are handled in the two kinds of data; and indeed my subsequent analysis of staffroom talk will suggest that this is likely to be the case.

In one respect typifications in the two contexts are strikingly different. Those reported by Hargreaves *et al.* (1975) are extensive and elaborated, those exchanged in the Downtown staffroom highly abbreviated. An explanation for this immediately suggests itself on the basis of the nature of the two contexts. Where interaction between the same participants is recurrent, processes of routinization and institutionalization occur and interaction becomes more economic; much is taken for granted as no longer needing to be spelt out (Berger and Luckmann, 1967). On the other hand, in interactions with relative strangers, and especially strangers who occupy a strange and ill-defined role such as that of researcher, much will be spelt out at length, especially when the researcher encourages long, open-ended responses.[5]

Underlying some staffroom news is a standard set of pupil types. Sometimes the pupils are described as unpredictable and dangerous:

16 *Webster*: Wilson, he's going to kill someone one day, he's got the killer instinct. How he's changed, you can see the mentality breaking up, he's unstable.
    Denison: You should have seen him loping across the road at four o'clock yesterday, like a prehistoric animal

On other occasions they are simpley 'buggers', 'bastards', 'yobos' or 'louts', showing little respect for authority and often setting out to cause trouble.

17 [Staffroom]
    Greaves: His balls haven't dropped yet and he's the worst bastard I've had to deal with in eighteen years teaching.

Perhaps the key feature of the 'unstable' and the 'lout'[6] is that there is little a teacher can do to change them; he must simply recognize how they are and deal with them accordingly, for example by avoiding confrontations:

18 [Staffroom]
    Denison: You've got to try and avoid confrontations, although they sometimes force confrontations on you. [He later explained how he had spent twenty minutes telling a class off today.] You could spend all your time trying to persuade or force the reluctant to work, if there are some who are willing to work it's better to concentrate on them.

However, there are some pupils who appear to be louts but are actually more manageable: they are simply 'easily led':

19 [Staffroom]
    Philipson: Gary's not so bad.
    Baldwin: He's easily led that's his trouble.

These three types of pupil relate primarily to the concern with classroom order and possible pupil violence towards teachers. They each pose a threat, though the third is the weak link, the one where pressure may work. Other problem pupils pose more of a nuisance than a threat, they are 'immature':

20 [Classroom talk between Denison and MH after a lesson]
    Denison: [Name's] an immature lad, cards stuffed in his pockets

The 'immature' do not challenge teacher authority in any serious or effective way, nor are they physically dangerous. Their deviance is simply an irritation, and results primarily from intrinsic interest in 'childish' actvities that are proscribed by school rules.

However, despite these standard types the nature of the pupils is not treated as static, and much news concerns changes in the pupils, almost always for the worse:

21 *Holton:* Has Mills been suspended then?
   Roach: Well he's here this morning.
   Holton: Oh so he's not been suspended, after all the head's great threats. It's funny that lad should have gone that way in the last few months. Nobody had ever heard of him before, I mean he's been here four years someone must have heard of him, y'know as an odd fellow, but not for creating violence.

22 [Marsden about a pupil to other teachers in the staffroom]
   Marsden: He's getting worse he needs taking to the head, that'd do him good.

23 (Staffroom discussion)
   Bolton: I'll tell you who's becoming a very silly lad. X [pupil's name]
   Scott: I pointed that out a few weeks ago, he should be put in front of the head, it's a phase.
   Holton: Everything Jerry Roach [student teacher] told him to do he did in the most silly, stupid way
   Scott: [And yet] he's potentially one of the best lads, potentially way beyond the rest.
   Holton: The intelligence is there but he will constantly do the wrong thing.

24 [Staffroom discussion]
   Webster: I'll tell you who's turning nasty: Gary.
   Walker: Johns you mean, well that's because he's stupid he can't read or write. He reminds me of something in an African jungle.

There is considerable agreement on a list of the infamous, but the list changes over time, stars rise and fall.[7]

An important feature of staffroom news at Downtown is the predominant concern with the 'behaviour' of pupils; in other words with those features of them relevant to the problem of maintaining 'order' in the classroom. Only a few staffroom comments included in the data relate to the 'ability' of pupils and their 'response' to teaching:

25 *Philipson:* O'Brien is in the top set in Maths.
   Baldwin: [to Philipson] Has O'Brien got anything upstairs?
   Philipson: No, neither has [Name], he got an E in the test, oh n'then a B I think.
   T: He doesn't even know his three times table.
   T: Most of them don't.
   Denison: Some of them don't even know how many inches in a foot.

26 *Webster:* [name], he's so lazy it takes him twenty minutes to pick up the pencil and twenty minutes to put it down. [Name] looks prehistoric, I wonder if he's on drugs.

27 *Webster:* Gibbs is dead to the world.

In summary, then, while some staffroom news is concerned with specific events or the moods, presences and absences of particular pupils, most of it reports how the teachers are finding particular pupils troublesome in the classroom and what conclusions they have come to about what can be expected from them. What is involved here is a process of collective sense-making and stock-taking.

The Rhetorical Functions of Staffroom News

It must not be assumed, however, that typifications necessarily have a purely referential function. In the Downtown staffroom, typifications of pupils are frequently used in a more rhetorical fashion than the idea of 'comparing notes' or 'stocktaking' suggests, being dismissive as much as descriptive:

28 *Webster:*   They're all louts.

29 [Staffroom]
    Baldwin: X [Pupil's name] is bright.
    Denison: Potentially, but he's got a quirk.
    Baldwin: They've all got their quirks I suppose.
    Denison: But his quirks are between wider extremes, he's got a nice side and a nasty side. Most of them have just got quirks within the nasty.
    Marsden: The rest of them come to school to be nasty.
    Baldwin: They are nasty.
    [Also, see examples 14, 15, 16, 17, 20, 25, 26 and 27.

Both the form and content of the accounts given in the staffroom seem to be shaped to this rhetorical function. For example, a striking feature of staffroom news about pupils is that it generally concencetrates the nature of particular pupils rather than describing their actions in detail; and even where their actions are reported these are described without reference to the features of the particular interactional context in which they occurred:

30 *Vaughan:*   Mills went beserk this morning, he's a bit unstable that lad.

31 *Vaughan:*   Mills really blew his top today. He'll be inside soon I know it, he's going that way.

32 *Vaughan:*   Mills is going to end up on a manslaughter charge.

33 *Vaughan:*   The slightest thing can set him [Mills] off, someone's only got to stand on his toe and he's off.

34 [Vaughan talks about Mills now and last year]
    Vaughan: If he can't conform reasonably to society then society'll have to kick him out and treat him as an exceptional case.
    Philipson: He's got a tremendous persecution complex.

According to these descriptions this pupil is liable to explode at any time for no reason at all, 'the slightest thing can set him off'! This is reminiscent of some of Smith's (1978) data, in particular:

Nearly every morning K would cry in the car, being upset about little things, and the girls would comfort her'.

In this instance, the reasons for K's crying are taken to be those immediate occasions which were directly observable to 'the girls' and which were 'little things', not sufficient to warrant her weeping. Angela does not raise the possibility that there might have been features of K's biography unknown to her and the others which would provide adequate reasons for K's disposition to cry so readily.

Accordingly also it is not a problem or ought not to be a problem for the reader/hearer who properly follows the instructions for how the account is to be read, that no explanation, information, etc., from K is introduced at any point in the account. And it is not or ought not to be strange that at no point is there any mention of K being asked to explain, inform, etc.

In sum then, the rules, norms, information, observations, etc. presented by the teller of the tale are to be treated by the reader/hearer as the only warranted set. (Smith, 1978, p. 35)

This 'cutting out' of context occurs in staffroom talk at Downtown even where the events concerned have had important consequences and where a teacher is specifically asked 'what happened' by a colleague (see example 1 above). In all the examples of staffroom talk I collected,[8] the setting, including the actions of the teacher, is taken for granted as natural and normal and as warranting certain behaviour. For the teachers the occurrence of that behaviour does not require explanation, and indeed it does not normally constitute staffroom news. What is a recurrent topic for comment and discussion in the staffroom is the 'failure' of pupils to conform to those expectations.

The rhetorical function of staffroom news can also be detected in the kinds of explanation implied in the typifications. For the most part these appeal to psychological characteristics of pupils: moods, characters and mental disorder. Thus, in the case of Mills quoted above (in examples 30–34), there is apparently something about him, or in him, which makes him 'unstable' and results in him beng unable to 'conform reasonably'. Moreover, it seems (see example 21 above) that this aspect of his nature has 'emerged' relatively recently and if it continues he will 'end up on a manslaughter charge' and go 'inside'. In the teachers' account Mills' 'condition' has its own dynamic. All of the psychological characteristics attributed to pupils in these teacher typifications, then, are presented as underlying generative features which produce typical behaviour in diverse contexts; indeed irrespective of the context. Nor is there any attempt to trace the causation of these features, to ask why the pupils have these moods for example. Even the notion of behavioural contagion, a more sociological theory (Sutherland, 1956), is psychologized: some pupils are simply 'easily led'.

There has been some discussion in the literature of the 'ideological' role of psychological explanations, notably in individualizing failure, explaining it in terms of the characteristics of the individual rather than in terms of the structure of society[9] (Ingleby, 1976; Bowles and Gintis, 1976). But, even if the form of explanation employed by the teachers at Downtown does indeed fulfil some larger social function, we must still ask why they adopt it. We cannot assume it is simply because they have the interests of the system at heart. While remote causes may well be involved, these would operate through more proximal phenomena and it is these which are my concern here.

In discussing teachers' reactions to badly behaved and below average pupils, Stebbins (1975, p. 64) suggests the following explanation for the common tendency to blame the pupil:

There is something disquieting about these students to their teachers; despite their often exceptional efforts to instill respect for classroom rules and raise levels of achievement, the latter still fail. Teachers can blame only two sources for their lack of success: themselves or others. As in other conventional occupations, they choose the latter alternative and thus contend that there is an important aspect of the students' lives or personalities affecting their behavior at school which is beyond their [the teachers'] ability to manipulate.

This seems a plausible explanation for the nature of the typifications of pupils that Downtown teachers exchange in the staffroom. But we must ask why it is that these teachers are faced with the choice of blaming either themselves or their pupils. After all, they might equally appeal to the conditions in which they are forced to work or to the nature of the society in which they live as the source of their, and their pupils', problems. To understand why they do not do this I think we have to look at the conception of teaching to which Downtown teachers are committed. Theirs is a very traditional aproach to pedagogy, according to which teaching is a skill which one either has or does not have:

> 35   [Staffroom: Walker and Baldwin talking about resources]
> *Baldwin:*   Sarge and I calculated we needed £700.
> *Walker:*   I couldn't spend £200. Whatever the school it's the teacher that's important, it doesn't matter what books and equipment there are if the teacher's no good.
> *Webster:*   A good teacher can teach in a henhouse.
> *Walker:*   Whatever the school you must teach basically the same material: the basic skills.

In these terms any failure on the part of pupils to 'behave' and 'learn' is the product either of teacher incompetence or of the ignorance, stupidity and/or loutishness of pupils. From this point of view the characteristics of the pupils referred to in staffroom news represent obstacles to be recognized, not problems that can be solved by the adoption of appropriate methods. In fact the explanations for pupil behaviour implied in Downtown teachers' typifications of their pupils are not strictly speaking explanations at all, they have the form of predictions and function as excuses (Lyman and Scott, 1970). They specify dangers and limits involved in teaching Downtown pupils, rather than being concerned with identifying problems and finding strategies for solving them.

The construction of descriptions of pupils which cut out the context of their behaviour, and the kinds of explanation for pupils' behaviour employed, both operate to explain away poor pupil performances as the product of ineducability. Through trading news in the staffroom about their pupils Downtown teachers defend their collective sense of competence in the face of potentially discrediting evidence.

Conclusion

I have argued that one important function of staffroom news at Downtown is a kind of collective stocktaking in which teachers compare notes and bring themselves up to date about the pupils whom they all face in the classroom. However, this does not provide an entirely satisfactory explanation for the nature of this staffroom news. The form and content of the accounts of pupils which the teachers exchange suggests that they also serve a rhetorical function. They seem to be designed to protect the teachers' professional identities in the face of the threat to their sense of their own competence posed by the behaviour of the pupils. However, it is important to remember that this threat derives in part from the teachers' commitment to 'traditional' teaching. Moreover, the process of collective self-protection which underpins the exchange of staffroom news at Downtown serves at the same time to preserve this commitment from pressure for change.

Notes

[1] There has been some empirical research in this area. See Lortie (1975), Woods (1979) and Hitchcock (1983). For valuable, though speculative, discussions see Waller (1967) and Hargreaves (1972) and Hargreaves (1980).

2 Other aspects of staff relations at Downtown are discussed in Hammersley (1980).

3 For the most part these fall into Becker's (1952) categories of relevance to 'teaching' and 'discipline'. Only one example seems to relate simply to what Becker calls 'moral acceptability':

> *Webster*: You can smell him two classrooms off.

4 Rosenthal and Jacobson's results have been challenged. See Good and Brophy (1978) for a discussion.

5 On this interpretation my evidence is compatible with that of Hargreaves *et al.* (1975). However, this does not necessarily suggest that their findings actually reflect teachers' classroom typifications. It may reflect instead some correspondence at another level between staffroom and interview talk. In fact, elsewhere Hargreaves (1977) actually suggests such a correspondence, dubbing it 'third party talk'. Woods (1979) also questions the relationship between the kind of typifications documented by Hargreaves *et al.* (1975) and teachers' classroom practices. In addition, he provides some data which do not fit the superficial contrast I have drawn between staffroom and interview data. He presents an interview transcript in which the typifications are highly abbreviated. However, there is a possible, and plausible, explanation for this which leaves my argument substantially intact. This is that the distinction between staffroom and interview contexts is analytically unsatisfactory. What is crucial is not the way settings are conventionally defined but how actors *actually* define them. I suggest that perhaps in Woods' interview the informant treated him as a colleague as much as a researcher, and that this shaped the nature of his response. This fits Woods' account of his research strategy, in Woods (1977) and (1979). Regarding the more fundamental issue of the relationship between any of this data and the typifications used by teachers in the classroom, at the moment we are simply in the dark.

6 It is of some interest that these two categories of pupil closely parallel some accounts of pupil and youth typifications. Thus 'the mentally unstable' seems to match the 'nutter' among football fans (Marsh, Rosser and Harré, 1978), the 'louts' are perhaps similar to Willis's 'lads' (Willis 1977).

7 See Hargreaves' (1967) account of the rise and fall of reputations among pupils. I am not suggesting that teachers' perceptions of the rise and fall of pupils as 'louts' will be an accurate representation of reputations among the pupils, though there may be some relation. Note, however, that the two reputations interact (there may of course be more than two). While a pupil's reputation among teachers will be related to his actions, teachers' actions affect pupil reputations and pupil choices of courses of action. While Hargreaves does not mention this, and it goes against his argument in that he seems to see the pupil subculture as autonomous once established, evidence for this interaction can be found in his account of the beginning of Clint's rise to become 'Cock of the School'.

8 For a discussion of the problems involved in assessing the representativeness of this data see Hammersley (1983).

9 However, frequently the falsity of psychological explanations is taken for granted. While I think it can be quite satisfactorily demonstrated that there are social structural conditions for 'success', psychological attributes no doubt also play a role in determining who 'succeeds' and who 'fails'. One should not simply reject a form of explanation on the grounds of unpalatable political implications.

References

Becker, H.S. (1951) Role and career problems of the Chicago public school teacher. PhD dissertation, University of Chicago.

Becker, H.S. (1952) 'Social class variations in the teacher–pupil relationship', *Journal of Educational Sociology*, Vol. 25, No. 4. Reading 7 in this volume.

Berger, P. and Luckmann, T. (1967) *The Social Construction of Reality*, Allen Lane, London.

Bowles, S. and Gintis, H. (1976) *Schooling in Capitalist America*, Routledge and Kegan Paul, London.

Doyle, W. (1977) 'Learning the classroom environment', *Journal of Teacher Education*, Vol. 28, No. 6, pp. 51–55.

Good, T.L. and Brophy, J.E. (1978) *Looking in Classrooms*, Harper and Row, New York.

Hammersley, M. (1977) Units 9–10 Teacher Perspectives, *E202 Schooling and Society*, The Open University Press, Milton Keynes.

Hammersley, M. (1980) A peculiar world? Teaching and learning in an inner city school. Unpublished PhD thesis, University of Manchester.

Hammersley, M. (1983) 'The researcher exposed: a natural history', in Burgess, R.G. (ed.) *Qualitative Research in Educational Settings*, Falmer Press, Brighton.

Hargreaves, D.H. (1967) *Social Relations in a Secondary School*, Routledge and Kegan Paul, London.

Hargreaves, D.H. (1972) *Interpersonal Relations and Education*, Routledge and Kegan Paul, London.

Hargreaves, D.H. (1977) 'The process of typification in the classroom', *British Journal of Educational Psychology*, Vol. 47, pp. 274–84.

Hargreaves, D.H. (1980) 'The occupational culture of teachers' in Woods, P. (ed.) *Teacher Strategies*, Croom Helm, London.

Hargreaves, D.H., Hester, S. and Mellor, F. (1975) *Deviance in Classrooms*, Routledge and Kegan Paul, London.

Hitchcock, G. (1983) 'Fieldwork as practical activity: Reflections on fieldwork and the social organization of an urban open-plan primary school', in Hammersley, M. (ed.) *The Ethnography of Schooling: Methodological Issues*, Nafferton Books, London.

Ingleby, D. (1976) 'The psychology of child psychology', in Dale, R. *et al.* (eds) *Schooling and Capitalism*, Routledge and Kegan Paul, London.

Jackson, P. (1968) *Life in Classrooms*, Holt, Rinehart and Winston, New York.

Leiter, K. (1974) 'Ad hocing in the schools' in Cicourel, A.V. *et al.* (eds) *Langauge Use and School Performance*, Academic Press, New York.

Lortie, D. (1975) *Schoolteacher*, University of Chicago Press.

Lyman, S.M. and Scott, M.B. (1970) *A Sociology of the Absurd*, Appleton Crofts, New York.

Marsh, P., Rosser, E. and Harré, R. (1978) *The Rules of Disorder*, Routledge and Kegan Paul, London.

Merton, R.K. (1957) *Social Theory and Social Structure*, Free Press, New York.

Nash, R. (1973) *Classrooms Observed*, Routledge and Kegan Paul, London.

Rist, R. (1970) 'Student social class and teacher expectations', *Harvard Educational Review* Vol. 40, No. 3.

Rist, R. (1973) *The Urban School*, MIT Press, Cambridge, Mass.

Rosenthal, R. and Jacobson, L. (1968) *Pygmalion in the Classroom*, Holt, Rinehart and Winston, London.

Sharp, R. and Green, A. (1975) *Education and Social Control*, Routledge and Kegan Paul, London.

Smith, D. (1978) '"K is mentally ill": The anatomy of a factual account', *Sociology*, Vol. 12, No. 1.

Stebbins, R. (1975) *Teachers and Meaning*, Brill, New York.

Sutherland, E. (1956) *The Sutherland Papers* (eds Cohen, A., Lindesmith, A. and Schuessler, K.) Indiana University Press.

Waller, W. (1967) *The Sociology of Teaching*, Wiley, New York (first published in 1932).

Willis, P. (1977) *Learning to Labour*, Saxon House, New York.

Woods, P. (1977) 'Stages in interpretive research', *Research Intelligence*, Vol. 3, No. 1.

Woods, P. (1979) *The Divided School*, Routledge and Kegan Paul, London.

16 Contrastive Rhetoric and Extremist Talk

A. HARGREAVES

Here, Andy Hargreaves examines one particular set of strategies and cultural assumptions which underlie staff decision-making in a middle school. He points to the use of *contrastive rhetoric* by members of senior management—the introduction into discussion of outrageous and stereotyped examples of alternative practice which, by implication, quickly serves to mark the boundaries of reasonable and acceptable decision-making. The use of such a strategy to create and maintain staff consensus on educational issues, Hargreaves argues, can be compared with forms of *extremist talk*, which are deployed by certain junior members of staff to push the boundaries of discussion outwards.

Introduction

In one of the first British ethnographic studies of a school, Nell Keddie (1971, see Reading 8) made a crucial distinction between two contexts in which teachers' knowledge is displayed and applied: the teacher context and the educationist context. *The teacher context* concerned the teacher's routine daily contact with pupils in the classroom, and all the practical activities such as lesson planning and marking that surrounded it. This was a highly pragmatic world; the world of *is* rather than *ought*; deeds not words; practice not theory. It was therefore a world that was fundamentally organized around the principles of habitual and pragmatically based commonsense thought and action. *The educationist context* was very different. This was a 'context of discussion of school politics' which 'draws selectively and consciously on educational theory and research' (p. 135). This context was realized in situations like school meetings or in teachers' encounters with influential and/or inquisitive outsiders, such as HMIs and educational researchers, which entailed their explaining and justifying school policy. It was a context where fine ideals were espoused even if, as Keddie argued, they would later be shattered on the rocks of classroom reality.[1]

This distinction between teacher and educationist contexts is an important one, but the very emphases which Keddie made in the details of her analysis marked out the lines on which the research preoccupations of people in the discipline were to develop over the next decade.[2] The major focus of Keddie's argument, as the title of her article 'Classroom Knowledge' indicates, was on the classroom: the teacher context. Seventeen pages were devoted to this while there were less than four on the educationist context, and these contained very little data indeed. It is unfortunate that as Keddie shifted from her scant discussion of the educationist context to her more detailed analysis of the teacher context in the classroom, most sociologists of education sympathetic to ethnographic study seem to have followed suit.

Apart from a few studies of school staffrooms (e.g. Hammersley, 1980a, 1981; Woods, 1979, and see Readings 14 and 15) we have learnt very little about the ways in which teachers interact with one another and with senior members of the school hierarchy—in particular the head and deputy headteacher.[3] This neglect of the sociology of educationist contexts is not just one small gap among many others waiting to be plugged in a vast programme of sociological inquiry, but a vital absence, the remedy of which is of the utmost urgency for two reasons. First, there are signs that recent changes in patterns of curriculum innovation are bringing the educationist context into greater prominence in the life of teachers. In particular the emergence of school-based curriculum development as a response to the expense and failure of large-scale and nationally-based programmes of curriculum change and to problems of teacher morale and curriculum innovation within a contracting educational system where the opportunities for career mobility have been severely curtailed, has thrust many teachers into a relatively unfamiliar arena of decision-making, debate and reflection about educational activity. The educationist context in this sense appears to be moving inwards from the periphery of the teacher's world.

Second, the study of educationist contexts provides a critical testing ground for the thesis that teachers' everyday thinking is hegemonically determined. There is not the space here to provide a comprehensive account of the nature of hegemony. All that can be done is to give a brief glimpse of some of its constituent features which are pertinent to the nature and determinants of teachers' thinking.

Those who advance the view that the thinking of teachers is hegemonically determined do not suggest, like Althusser (1971) that teachers subscribe to or are the victims of any particular monolithic ideology, be it conservative, social democratic, or whatever. Nor even do they argue, like Dale (1977) that teachers share what he calls a basic 'cognitive style' of liberal individualism which 'sees educational problems as deriving from individuals and the solutions to them as lying in individual treatments' (p. 20). Rather, they stress the existence of considerable variation among teachers' perspectives. For them, the central issue is that while teachers hold a range of views about education and exhibit a diversity of patterns of thought in this area, *they do so within very definite and unquestioned limits*. Beyond these limits lie a set of educational and social practices which would be viewed by most people as potentially threatening to the existing order of capitalism and the broad social and political assumptions which help sustain it. Existing practices (what passes for normal teaching and education under capitalism that is), therefore become not one version of reality among many, but the only conceivable ones; standing at the deepest levels of teachers' consciousness as the only normal, natural and reasonable ways of proceeding (Williams 1973, 1977). Through this process, dominant versions of reality (of which there are several) become deeply sedimented into people's consciousness and mark the boundaries of their commonsense, for the most part remaining beyond analysis and question. In the case of schooling, alternative educational practices are therefore not only regarded by teachers and other educators as extreme or utopian, but frequently as being simply unworthy of serious discussion. They just don't get talked about (Apple, 1979).

As insightful as this analysis is it must be said that, to date, it has been founded more upon theoretical speculation and an almost religious conviction that the essential principles of the present social order have been grasped, than upon any kind of empirical demonstration. What is therefore required is some adequate empirical justification for claims about the limits of teachers' commonsense. These limits are confirmed not only by the absence of oppositional views in teachers' thinking but also, and perhaps more crucially for the purposes of empirical demonstration, by the way in which oppositional views are treated on those rare occasions when they are actually introduced into discussion in staff meetings and so on. The following case study of the ways in which educational alternatives are introduced into discussion and the kinds of response those introductions elicit provides one (although by no means the only) empirical test of the hegemony thesis as it applies to teachers.

The empirical research is drawn from a study of curriculum decision-making in an open-plan, suburban middle school in the mid 1970s. My overall study of middle schools as such is a large project embracing investigations of their history, ideology and practice.[4] The data here are drawn from one small part of that study; a series of weekly curriculum decision-making meetings held mainly on Wednesdays after school in the Summer term and involving the participation of the Head, his Deputy and the full staff of thirteen. These meetings were tape-recorded, transcribed and analyzed. Their purpose was to decide upon a curriculum for the following year. The programme of meetings was instigated by the Head and his Deputy who was nearing the end of secondment on a one-year in-service course at a nearby university where curriculum studies was one of the major areas of enquiry. The first meeting commenced with the Deputy Head using the overhead projector (to appropriate theatrically orchestrated gasps of astonishment from the rest of the staff) to outline a model of curriculum planning. The remaining weeks were then taken up with discussion of educational questions in decreasing order of generality; covering in sequence such things as the purposes of education, choice and responsibility, moral education, areas of knowledge; then, following a division into working groups according to the identified areas of knowledge, a programme of aims and objectives in each case. The data discussed in this paper come from the earlier meetings.

The transcripts provide fascinating documentation of the complexities of the curriculum decision-making process. My specific task, in this paper, is to focus on the ways in which educational alternatives were introduced and discussed and thereby to clarify the nature of teachers' thinking and its boundaries as displayed in what Keddie would call the educationist context. [. . .] There are few acid tests for the thesis of hegemony. But if any empirical test of an ethnographic kind can turn the theorist's litmus paper red (or blue), this is probably it.

I make no claims that the case I discuss is a typical one—that it is characteristic of most educationist contexts, that it typifies the usual ways in which teachers' thinking is hegemonically determined or that it is representative of the ways in which educational alternatives are normally introduced into discussion. Rather, it is my contention that the case is a *critical* one, an *exceptional* instance which highlights the theoretical problems and social processes under review.[5] In other words, Riverdale School is a place where one might most expect educational alternatives to be introduced seriously and discussed rigorously, where studied reflection and the discussion of school politics and educational theory would be in abundance. At Riverdale, that is, one might *most* expect the characteristics of the educationist context as outlined by Keddie to be present, and *least* expect hegemonic influences on teachers' consciousness to prevail.

What are the factors which enable Riverdale to be credited with the status of a critical case? First, its teachers were, at least initially, strongly involved in and committed to the process of discussion and debate. There were several reasons for this. The school was a new one; little more than a year old in fact. Moreover, it was not part of an immediate programme of comprehensivization and as such was not staffed by compulsorily 'reorganized' teachers who held long-standing commitments to grammar, secondary modern or primary schools and who, consequently, felt any marked antipathy towards middle schools. Being a new school, it had attracted a young staff as yet untarnished by the cynicism that often comes with a long teaching career. Because of all these things, an unquestionable vitality permeated the discussions and many of those who participated considerably enjoyed much of the decision-making experience. The comment of Miss Rogers at the end of the first meeting that 'I haven't done anything as exciting as this since college' (*not* spoken tongue-in-cheek) epitomized the general tenor of early staff responses.

Furthermore, in terms of topics selected and issues raised, the discussions were far from superficial. Particularly in the early meetings, the teachers often touched on some of the deepest and most complex social issues with which schooling is concerned—for instance, whether it fosters the development of individuals or secures social integration, whether it is a potent agent of social change or whether its influence in this respect is minimal, and so on. The meetings therefore occasioned not only critical and vigorous staff involvement, but also consideration of serious, indeed fundamental social and educational questions. These features would certainly accord with many of the characteristics of the educationist context to which Keddie alluded in her seminal article. But what was the character of discussion in that context? What kinds of alternative practices and social forms were discussed? How were they introduced? Who introduced them? And what do the identified decision-making practices reveal about teachers' and headteachers' knowledge and about the exercise of power and control in the decision-making process? I want to propose that within the educationist context— the ways in which educational alternatives are introduced and discussed [. . .], can be elucidated by the use of two concepts: *contrastive rhetoric* and *extremist talk*. I shall discuss the two processes denoted by these concepts in turn.

Contrastive Rhetoric

[. . .] *Contrastive rhetoric refers to that interactional strategy whereby the boundaries of normal and acceptable practice are defined by institutionally and/or interactionally dominant individuals or groups through the introduction into discussion of alternative practices and social forms in stylized, trivialized and generally pejorative terms which connote their unacceptability.* The concept is in part derived from research on interactional practices among professional groups and from the sociology of mass media and deviance; but in the main it is a *grounded concept* (Glaser and Strauss, 1968) formulated [. . .] as the most satisfactory method I could evolve of explaining the data to hand.[6] Some indication of the detailed elements and effects of contrastive rhetoric can best be gauged by considering specific examples.

One of the clearest and most lengthy instances of the use of contrastive rhetoric took the form of a discussion about Countesthorpe College, a well-known comprehensive school lying very much outside the mainstream of educational practice. The discussion was initiated by the deputy head, Mr. Pool.

> Mr. Pool: Perhaps I could quote an example where they took it [pupil choice] not only on an individual, intuitive basis of what's right and wrong, but at Countesthorpe...I don't know if you've heard of this school in Leicestershire?
> [Laughter]
> You have. Yeah. Well, you know what happened there.
> They gave the kids an awful lot of choice.
> Mr. Stones: I've been there.
> Mr. Pool: You went, Alan?

Mr. Stones: Well, my friend lives in Countesthorpe and she's ... um ...

Mr. Pool: Well, can you tell us more about it? You'll know more than I do.

Mr. Stones: Well, she's one of ... she's a twenty-five year old who goes in with the kids to do her O-levels. She's doing O-level biology and they just sort ... well, I've not actually been round while it's working. I've been to have a look at it. But from what she says, you know, they're given free choice that the pupils ... on what they want to do ... you know ... they can walk out half way through a lesson if they're bored and all this sort of thing. There are grown ups and children in together on O-levels and A-levels and it's all sort of first name terms with staff. She only knows the two that are taking her for biology as Jim and Bill. It's that sort of set up.

Mr. Pool: Mmm ... And did she approve of it, or ... or what? What kind of benefits or ... or ...

Mr. Stones: She doesn't ... doesn't like it. She doesn't like it. But then she's been brought up in a formal atmosphere.

Mr. Pool: On what grounds? Just because it's ... it's different, you know, or has she got some sort of thing that she's got against it?

Mr. Stones: Well, she doesn't like the way they can sort of just walk in and walk out and come in at any time and all this sort of thing.

Mr. Pool: Yeah, yeah.

Mr. Stones: She doesn't think that should happen. I don't know, she's got a bit of ...

Mr. Pool: The bits ... the bits that I read the reports about it was that the kids were appointed to a ... a home basis and then there were a variety of choices which they could make, whether they went and did ... uh ... O-level science courses or whether they went and did CSE science courses, or just a general thing anyway, or whether they didn't do science in fact. This went through a whole load of things. These specialist things were provided for them and whether they chose these was a matter of counselling on the part of the staff for the kids, and the parents' pressure and their own wishes of course. But apart from that, there was no ... no compulsion to go. In fact, stay in home base all day and read ... just read comics until they got so bored with it, in theory, that they wanted to do something else. And if you walked around the school, you could see kids eating crisps and sitting around, you know. But that's, that's right at the far end of what we're talking about.

Mr. Stones: A long way [muttered].
[Concurring laughter]

Mrs. Home: A very long way.
[More laughter]
Cos I can see the kids that once they get bored sitting around and eating crisps and reading comics, will just go out of the school and find something more ... more exciting.

Mr. Stones: Oh, they had the ... the trouble with the smokers' room, didn't they, which ... there was a great big kick up about under fourteen ... over fourteens select smokers' room. The headmaster there was the headmaster at my school. Mr. X in Southshire. He was the headmaster for the first term that I was there and he tried to get something off the ground like that, but it ... he couldn't. It's a bit of a stronghold.

Mr. Pool: Really, I think it's ... it's worth looking at these things when ... you know ... you do hand things right over to the kids and see what happens.

As some of the better known and more unconventional features of Countesthorpe were introduced into discussion, laughter broke out. That laughter was elicited by virtue of the fact that potentially serious (and conceivably threatening) educational questions and practices were reduced to trivial, peculiar and highly visible features of Countesthorpe culture—smoking, reading comics, eating crisps, calling staff by first names etc. There is much in common here with what Cohen (1973) observes to be the usual way in which instances of deviance and dissent are portrayed in the mass media. In such coverage, Cohen argues,

> Symbolization and the presentation of 'the facts' in the most simplified and melodramatic manner possible leave little room for interpretation, the presentation of competing perspectives on the same event or information which would allow the audience to see the event in context.
> (Cohen, 1973, p. 76)

What Cohen means by symbolization is a process whereby,

> Communication . . . of stereotypes, depends on the symbolic power of words and images. Neutral words such as place names can be made to symbolize complex ideas and emotions: for example, Pearl Harbour, Hiroshima, Dallas and Aberfan.
> (ibid., p. 44)

Even though it cannot be shown that it was anyone's particular intention to introduce 'Countesthorpe' into debate for just these reasons, the effect of the mere mention of the name—the evoking of a heightened emotional response (in this case through the medium of laughter)—is undeniable. In the world of teachers, certain schools like 'Countesthorpe' or 'Tyndale' become eponymous. Their very mention triggers off a vast array of educational fears and uncertainties and symbolizes the threatened extension and incursion of extreme, unreasonable or simply meaningless educational practices. In the terse though graphic descriptions of such schools, particular words and phrases are selected out to conjure up generalized images of apparently anarchic and bizarre educational practices. These images become so strongly embedded in teacher folklore, that they need no detailed elaboration, only the merest allusion to exert their emotive effect. Thus, after noting that his friend knows only the first names of her biology teachers, Mr. Stones adds without further explanation, 'It's that sort of set up'. As with some of his other statements, the rest of the staff are simply left to 'fill in' most of the additional and presumably obvious details of 'this sort of thing' and 'that sort of set up' themselves. The statements are taken to be and treated as if they were self-explanatory. The interchangeability of teachers' standpoints is assumed[7].

The elements of exaggeration and stylization that permeate the discussion of Countesthorpe College add to the humour of the account and to the laughter it evokes. Like much routine staffroom humour, this serves to neutralize the threats presented by alternative practices and thus implicitly reaffirms the teachers' broadly shared existing conceptions of good versus bad teaching. Indeed, there is a sense in which Countesthorpe is depicted as being *devoid* of teaching rather than simply representative of an alternative tradition (see Hammersley, 1980a). An important feature of contrastive rhetoric, therefore, is the sometimes humorous but always dramatic definition of normality by reference to its opposite, deviance; and thus the demarcation (albeit a hazy one) of the outer limits of existing practice (Durkheim, 1964, chapter 3; Taylor, Walton and Young 1973, chapter 3)

One possible response to that observation is 'So what?'—for even if this portrayal of the way in which Countesthorpe is discussed is accurate, it does not necessarily follow that these features result from the pervasive influence of a dominant hegemony, social-democratic or otherwise, on teachers' thinking. Indeed, they may provide no clarification whatsoever about the special character of schooling or of teachers' thinking under the ideological influences of capitalism.

There are several respectable lines of sociological argument which suggest that the business of making contrasts is a widespread, if not universal, feature of social, interactional and conversational practice and therefore, by implication, not specific to discussion and decision-making practices in capitalistic social democracies.

First for instance, is it not the case, following Durkheim, that definitions of the normal are conventionally and universally construced by reference to the pathological—is it not this fact indeed which gives deviance its socially necessary role in society as a marker of the boundaries of morality? (Durkheim 1964, chapter 3; Hargreaves, D.H., 1979). As Erikson (1964) puts it:

> People who gather together into communities need to be able to describe and anticipate those areas of experience which lie outside the immediate compass of the group—the unseen dangers which in any culture and in any age seem to threaten its security. Traditional folklore depicting demons, devils, witches and evil spirits, may be one way to give form to these otherwise formless dangers, but the visible deviant is another kind of reminder. As a trespasser against the group norms, he represents those forces which lie outside the group's boundaries: he informs us, as it were, what evil looks like, what shapes the devil can assume. And in doing so, he shows us the difference between the inside of the group and the outside. It may well be that without this ongoing drama at the outer edges of group space, the community would have no inner sense of identity and cohesion, no sense of the contrasts which set it off as a special place in the larger world.
> (Erikson, 1964, p. 15)

Secondly, isn't the business of rhetorically making contrasts one important means by which occupational identities are protected and consolidated against counter conceptions of the tasks in question? Anselm Strauss and his colleagues, for instance, observed, in their study of *Psychiatric Ideologies* (1964), that psychiatric workers subscribing to different conceptions of 'treatment', developed rhetoric which 'blazed back and forth between the treatment and chronic wards' and which opposed custody and therapy in particularly stylized and exaggerated ways, such that each groups of workers was equipped with a 'ready vocabulary for explaining difficulties and conducting battles' (p. 364). Dingwall (1977) in his research on health visitors argued that atrocity stories they told about social workers with whom they had to deal and from whom they wished to distinguish themselves, performed similar functions.

Thirdly, following the findings of ethnomethodology and conversational analysis, are not contrasts either explicitly or implicitly involved in all descriptions, since all our conceptions of what things *are* are also constructed according to corollaries of what they are *not*? (Gazdar, 1977; Schegloff, 1971; Sacks, 1972).

I would not seriously contest any of these claims. Contrastive rhetoric *does* draw on the universal and indispensable ability of individuals to build descriptions by implicit or explicit reference to comparative cases; it *does* reinforce collective occupational identifications of pertinent tasks against those of other occupations or occupational segments, and it also functions to define and redefine the boundaries of normal practice against deviant and therefore unacceptable alternatives. The interesting thing about contrastive rhetoric, though, is that it does not consist of any one of these features, but all of them—and more besides. In this respect, there are at least two additional and important points to note about the concept.

The first concerns the power dimension: *who* is it who introduces the stylized alternatives, who opposes deviance and normality, and consolidates a particular conception of occupation identity? When the transcripts were analyzed, one of the most startling facts to emerge was that in all cases the contrasts were introduced by either the headteacher or his deputy; the instigators of the programme of curriculum change.[8] In the Countesthorpe case, for instance, it is Mr. Pool who initiates discussion and later reminds the staff of the extreme character of the cited example ('That's right at the far end of what we're talking about'). The contrasts, that is, are introduced by the more senior members of the school hierarchy, the holders of formally designated institutional power.

The second point is that over time, the users of contrastive rhetoric demarcate the boundaries of existing practice at *both* ends of the educational spectrum. In other words, by excluding extreme and unacceptable alternatives of both progressive and traditional kinds, contrastive rhetoric specifies the *range* of acceptable practice. It is by no means the case that contrasts are made solely with reference to extreme progressivism. Archaic traditionalism is just as much a *bête noire* for the head and his deputy. Thus, in the case of traditional schools, Mr. Kitchen argues that

> If we took conformity, a way to make them conform would be to blow a whistle and they'd stand still. Blow another whistle and they'd move into a line and the teacher would move them in. And I know a school that was like that. They conformed! But, my God, I wouldn't like it here!

And Mr. Pool spins out a favourite haberdashery metaphor of his:

> Many tight schools tell the kids what they have to do from thread to needle. They don't have to do any of that kind of (independent) thinking at all.

Very occasionally, the extremes at each end of the spectrum can be highlighted by their juxtaposition in a single dramatic paradox which shows them to be only different sides of the same rather grubby coin. A well known example outside education was Shirley Williams' vitriolic comment during the 1980 Labour Party leadership debate that 'there can be a Fascism of the Left as well as of the Right'. In the case of Riverdale School, this essential and awesome unity of apparent opposites was skilfully displayed by the headteacher on one occasion when he combined the worst of two twilight worlds, mixing together dark visions of pupil anarchy with salutary images of headteacher despotism.

> I mean, one of my lines has always been I want people to have as much choice as possible—that is, staff to be able to use their expertise, to feel that, 'Yes, I would like to try this out. I've got reasons for doing this.'
> [Mmm]
> Because in many, many places ... I've been in so many places where ... where they go on this choice business. Uh ... one in particular I can think of in Halford where choice is the thing running across everything in that the children choose the colours the loo doors will be painted—and, you know, there's rainbow colours of them. They choose a lot of pencils they'll have in school. They go to the County Supplies Link and choose the type of books they'll have. It goes to these lengths. And yet the head has got a most rigid grip on the staff, really and truly. They have no choice at all! He's got this choice firmly fixed in his mind and he jolly well makes sure they carry it out to give children choice. And this is my big criticism of the place, you know, the staff have no choice at all. And he ... he boasts that he always takes probationers. Now I know, he always ... *always* takes probationers.
> [Laughter]
> That's right. That's why he does it!

In this expertly constructed paradox signalled by the grammatical force of what Smith (1978) calls a contrast structure ('And yet ...'), many of the same elements are presented as in the Countesthorpe case mentioned earlier—the laughter (the meaning of which is taken to be obvious—'That's right') the indications that the case being discussed is an extreme one ('It goes to these lengths'), the introduction of graphic images of the trivial and outrageous (loo doors, choice of pencils, etc.). Progressivism and traditionalism are, therefore, simultaneously united and distilled into a single fearful phenomenon; extremism, which is to be avoided at all costs.[9]

This is an appropriate point to recap on the major features of contrastive rhetoric as outlined so far. I have argued that it presents stylized and trivialized images of alternative practices, characterizing them as unacceptable extremes and thereby implicitly drawing the boundaries around the permissible range of present practice. Moreover, this definition of a professional and pedagogical consensus is occasioned by the strategic intervention of those holding institutional power—the head and deputy. Contrastive rhetoric is therefore a major part of their strategic repertoire; a crucial means by which they translate institutional power into interactional power and thus exercise control over the decision-making process. But the effective use of contrastive rhetoric is not simply a matter of head and deputy head-teacher strategy, however, for just as teachers trade on their pupils' ability to interpret the messages contained in their classroom strategies (Edwards and Furlong, 1978; Hargreaves, A., 1979), so the users of contrastive rhetoric rely on the capacity of other teachers to recognize the message connoted by the particular images and symbols they present and the trivialized and stylized mode of description in which those symbols are enshrouded. The success of contrastive rhetoric in screening out undesirable alternatives is therefore contingent on the kind of knowledge, assumptions and interpretive schemes that teachers bring to the interaction, and on the capacity of its users—the head and deputy—to trade on these components of teachers' culture.

The presence of laughter is one testimony to the existence of shared understandings of the symbols and descriptions in contrastive rhetoric; although, like silence, laughter is also a possible indicator of the existence of many other things too—the presence of tension for example. (see Reading 14).

Perhaps the most telling illustration though, of the kinds of response generated by constrastive rhetoric is to be found in the extended contribution of Mr. Stones to the Countesthorpe debate. This is an exceptional piece of data, for at no other time did anyone respond to the use of contrastive rhetoric as he did. Furthermore, he not only reacted to contrastive rhetoric, thus indicating his ability to interpret its symbols and mode of description, but formulated a considerable part of it himself. Much of the description of Countesthorpe College, as you may already have realized, was his. If we examine this case closely, we might be able to determine what it is that makes the case an exceptional one; why, that is, Mr. Stones was able to contribute to the extent that he did. Accordingly, this might also tell us something about the normal pattern; about why other teachers made no such contribution. In short, why were most teachers receivers and not producers of contrastive rhetoric?

The reason, I want to propose, is to be found in the way that teachers draw on their own experience in educational discussion. Experience, especially professional experience, lay at the heart of virtually all the contributions that teachers made to discussion. It supplied most of the justifications for the accounts they presented. [. . .] But since most teachers' experience excluded even the most fleeting of encounters with educational alternatives, it is hardly surprising that they made little or no contribution of their own when the question of such alternatives was raised. Like Mrs. Home, who speculated that 'the kids . . . will just go out of the school and find something more exciting' after they have got bored with eating crisps and reading comics', the teachers could only take the sketchy images with which they were presented at face value and react accordingly within the conceptual limits of their shared interpretative scheme. Since, in their experience, they had no previous acquaintance with the particular reality to which the image referred, they could not substantially elaborate on the image or dispute its accuracy.

Mr. Stones was no exception to the rule of experience. What distinguished him from the rest of the staff was not that he used criteria other than experiential ones to present and justify his accounts but that one fragment of the *content* of his experience—the Countesthorpe connection—was different. It was this that enabled him to talk about that particular alternative at unusual length; to produce his own formulation, that is. The *fact* that he produced a formulation was a mark of the atypical nature of his experience; but the fact that his formulation was consistent in form with the other instances of constrastive rhetoric used by the head and deputy was indicative of the sort of cultural resources on which he drew. In effect, Mr. Stones constructed his unflattering description of Countesthorpe College by drawing on a standard repertoire of symbols of outrageous progressivism that carried the appropriate pejorative connotations: 'they can walk out if they're bored', 'all sort of first name terms with the staff', 'they can sort of just walk in and walk out and come in at any time'. To these symbols of first naming of staff, walking in and out and so on are added important descriptive and indeed implicitly contrastive qualifiers. Thus, the fact that 'first name terms' are, in effect, *'all sort of* first name terms' established that the first naming of staff is but the visible tip of an enormous and dangerous iceberg of unacceptable pedagogical relationships. And the fact that pupils do not simply 'walk in and walk out' but *'just* walk in and walk out ... *at any time'* reflects on the shared assumption that in *normal* pedagogical relationships there are appropriate and inappropriate occasions and reasons for this action. No-one *just* walks in and out. Entry into and exit from the classroom are rule-governed affairs and these rules are in large part enforced and interpreted by the teacher (Hargreaves, Hester and Mellor, 1975). The absence of such rules, therefore, entails the suspension of normal teacher-pupil relationships. What Mr. Stones did was to draw on those shared interpretative schemes concerning alternative practices which normally enabled staff to interpret contrastive rhetoric when it was employed by others but which, given his incidental and somewhat second-hand experience of Countesthorpe, also enabled him to produce contrastive rhetoric of his own on this one occasion. What analysis of this initially discrepant case reveals, therefore, is that the routine responses of the staff to contrastive rhetoric and Mr. Stones' own production of it are each the product of their drawing on a dual repertoire; of professional experience on the one hand, and of a shared interpretative scheme concerning educational alternatives on the other[10]

Having examined the reasons why Mr. Stones' contribution to the discussion was in certain respects different from the usual staff responses to contrastive rhetoric, what I have yet to do is explain what distinguishes the contributions of the headteacher and his deputy from the rest of the staff. Why was it that the head and his deputy produced contrastive rhetoric when the rest of the staff, with one exception, did not? It is my contention that the reason once more has to do with the different nature of their experience, except that, in this case, those experiences are systematically and unequally distributed between ordinary and senior staff.

In the main the teachers have little continuing access to educational theory or detailed comparative knowledge of other schools and practices; the head and his deputy, on the other hand, while not necessarily possessing sophisticated knowledge of educational theory or detailed familiarity with the administration of the schooling system, do move more widely in these circles than the teachers. This differential access to the cultural resources underlying decision-making, therefore, means that the head and deputy hold not only *de jure* institutional power, but also tend to possess *de facto* interactional power. It is they who have the necessary familiarity with educational alternatives such that they can introduce them in an extreme way that resonates suitably with teachers' own conceptions of present practice and its enemies.

The maintenance of the boundaries of permissible practice is therefore achieved as a result of an intersection between head and deputy headteacher strategy, the cultural resources which teachers of all kinds bring to the interaction (these consist of professional experiences and shared interpretative schemes), and the influences of the dominant hegemony and the institutional distribution of power on the content of those resources. While I cannot honestly say that these conclusions amount to absolute confirmation or refutation of the hegemony thesis (much more research would be needed before that degree of certainty could be approached), what I can say is that no elements of the critical test I have presented constitute a *disconfirmation* of that thesis: on the contrary, there appears to be considerable, if less than definitive, support for it.

Extremist Talk

Having drawn these conclusions concerning the influence of the dominant hegemony on teacher thinking, it is as well to remember that the influence of hegemony is never total: it cannot be equated with unrelieved brainwashing. The hegemonic process is neither monolithic nor is it immune from forces of resistance and protest which contain the potential for the creation of counter-hegemony and for pushing out rather than drawing in the boundaries of existing practice. Close scrutiny of the data revealed the presence of such forces within the fine details of staff discussion.

As the data were analyzed a discrepancy became apparent—that educational alternatives were sometimes introduced into discussion by people other than the head and deputy. However, it was also evident that the staff couched these alternatives in a form quite unlike that of contrastive rhetoric. I shall refer to this second process by which the ordinary teaching staff introduced alternative conceptions of educational practice as one of *extremist talk*. [. . .]

[. . .] Among the ordinary staff, extremist talk was regularly used by two teachers. The first, Mr. Button, was a young, non-graduate teacher who had moved to Riverdale from a secondary modern school in order to take a Scale 2 post. [. . .] At the time of the research he was studying for an Open University degree which [. . .] entailed his taking a course in the sociology of education. His espousal of a range of educational opinions in discussion seemed to owe much to this course of study. Thus, Mr. Button could be heard to expound arguments which contained elements of deschooling, or Marxism, or soical phenomenology, or even a mixture of all these things. This does not mean that he succeeded in transforming staff discussion into a weighty sociological seminar, nor even that he engaged in a one-sided attempt to do so. The influence of experience as virtually the only acceptable and legitimate basis of teacher accounts in staff discussions was sufficient to prevent him from quoting educational theorists chapter and verse, or pulling out protracted threads of sociological argument. Yet the residues of his recent acquaintance, albeit a fleeting one, with some sociology of education were undoubtedly present in his terse and sometimes caustic remarks about schooling and its relationship to society. These could be seen in some of his contributions to the very first meeting, where he began with a loose exposition of the culture conflict thesis intermingled with an application of the interactionist concept, 'definition of the situation'.

Mr. Button: Don't children in many ways regard these [moral] aims really as being outside the scope of the teacher, because many children define the teaching situation as what happens in the classroom? A lot of children define the situation as being what they are taught and not such things as manners. There is enough conflict in the teaching situation as it is. The more of these we introduce, the more conflict we introduce into this job. You're gonna spend a lot of your time continually checking children in that situation.

Mr. Driver: Do you necessarily have to do it by checking children, or can you do it by somehow persuading them?

Mr. Button: Well, no matter what way you do it, there's gonna be some children who naturally resent the change.

Mrs. Fletcher: Well, don't you consider yourself *in loco parentis* when you have children in your care?

Mr. Button: Well, this is slightly different, Elizabeth, because what we're doing, we're changing them to aims which we think are desirable or not. And the child's own social background may not ... his parents may not demand this sort of behaviour from the child. So there's gonna be conflict when he comes to school with what he does at home.

Others: Yes/No [vociferously]

Mrs. Fletcher: It *is* possible. Well, perhaps many parents teach their kids 'Well, if somebody hits you, you jolly well see you hit them back' and many teachers perhaps think that it's a very negative attitude and that it's much more positive to say 'Well keep away from people you can't get on with and don't use your fists'.

Mr. Button: Well, whether the child fits into the school system, you've got to make the value judgement whether it's more important that he does not become alienated from his parents. Well, I mean it's like the working class child who goes to grammar school.

The discussion then moved on to a consideration of children's rights and the legitimacy of their perspective. This gave Mr. Button the opportunity to take up a libertarian position, though the conclusions he reached would probably evoke more sympathy from Rhodes Boyson than Ivan Illich.

Mr. Button: ... What I'm saying is that you want to minimize the amount of conflict that you've got in the situa ... institution by cutting out a lot of some of these aims which I would say are peripheral. A lot of these aims, although they're very desirable from our point of view, I would say they're not the main aims. I would say the main aim on the whole thing was literacy and numeracy. It's what the kids expect. It's what the parents expect.

Mr. Driver: I don't agree with you.

Mrs. Fletcher: I don't. Our job is to help to open kids' eyes. Now if they come ... come to school and they don't see everything clearly, it's because they are a child.

Mr. Button: Yeah! They are a child and we've got to not try to put adult concepts on to things that we think are desirable. I mean, children don't consider sympathy as desirable.

Mr. Driver: [Aghast] Ooh!

Mr. Button: I mean, you have to look at some of 'em to understand that.

Mrs. Fletcher: But Alan, we might just as well say that the children themselves should set ... should be able to set up all these objectives and really, children haven't got a clear perception of what ...

Mr. Button:	But they can't. As far as we're concerned, because they have to come to school, because the law says so, they are the lower level of this institution.
Mrs. Fletcher:	But are we thinking about having to come to school, or are we thinking about education?
Mr. Button:	Well, it's the same thing as far as children are concerned.
Mr. Kitchen:	[Head] But not as far as we're concerned!
Others:	[Together] No! No! No!

This outburst of libertarianism was by no means an isolated occurrence. Later, for instance, he described education as 'just an assault upon a child to make him conform with set aims that you've already put down'. At other points, however, Mr. Button's critique of the educational system seemed to have more affinity with Marxist economic determinism. In a discussion of the problems of failure, for example, he argued that 'Unfortunately, one of the jobs at school is the screening process. Whether we like it or not, the purpose of education in society is to provide workers. Failure is an inevitable part of it'.

There is no evidence that Mr. Button was a consistent and hard line libertarian, Marxist, phenomenologist or whatever. What he does appear to have done is weld parts of these divergent traditions into a somewhat brittle alloy of anti-liberalism which cut through the boundaries of normal debate about education.[11] Occasionally, this object of his observations and criticisms was made crystal clear as when he retorted: 'That is the liberal dichotomy that you've said, "Right, you can do what you like as long as I tell you what you do"'.

Extremist talk was not always 'left-wing' talk, though. While the seeds of counter-hegemony may well be contained in extremist talk, the varied content of that talk should serve as a reminder that, as Gramsci (1971) himself understood counter-hegemony need not take any particular form: it may for example lead to fascist outcomes just as easily as to socialist ones. In this sense, an interesting contrast to Mr. Button's extremist talk is that of Mrs. Speaker. A mature entrant to teaching with a previous background in journalism, secretarial work and as a housewife and mother, she was strongly committed to teaching English as a subject where, she felt, her greatest strengths and sources of enjoyment lay. On the surface, her standpoint did at times seem to converge with Mr. Button's, thus giving the appearance of an unholy alliance, as when she specified one of her aims of education—that children 'should be literate and numerate—to throw in two old fashioned ideas'. But beneath this unlikely correspondence with Mr. Button's radicalism on the question of 'basic skills' lay a deep seated and entrenched conservatism. In this respect, Mrs. Speaker's position held much in common with the classical functionalism of sociologists like Talcott Parsons (1959) and their view that schooling socializes children into the common value system of society. As Mrs. Speaker put it.

I think that it's part of our job to see that a child is as socially acceptable as possible. It is part of our job to see that they can be assimilated into a community.

This suggestion that education ought to integrate the young into the social order was given an additional twist when she continued: 'I think their whole development is vital too—their attitude, their ideas, their thinking, their creativity, their reasoning'.

For Mrs. Speaker the individual and social aspects of education were compatible [. . .] whereas for Mr. Button like Marxists and libertarians they were not. Thus, when Miss Rogers expressed her disagreement with Mrs. Speaker over 'the social conformity thing' and stated that, 'you're not going to make them start off being all child-centred and end up with them being round pegs for round holes', Mr. Button interjected, 'Yeah, but it's just unfortunate that it happens to work out that way in most schools, doesn't it?'.

What do these examples tell us about extremist talk and its differences from contrastive rhetoric (see Table 18.1)? First, whereas contrastive rhetoric is introduced by institutionally and/or interactionally dominant individuals or groups (in this case, the head and deputy), extremist talk is part of the repertoire of subordinate figures (in this case, a Scale 1 and a Scale 2 teacher). In participatory decision-making contexts, extremist talk appears to be a strategy of those beneath the highest levels of the school hierarchy, presumably because its employment by the institutionally powerful would constitute an ostensible and embarrassing breach of the formal principles of democratic decision-making[12]

Second, whereas contrastive rhetoric comprises stylized and trivialized accounts of actual, through frequently anonymized, cases of alternative educational practice, extremist talk consists of alternative conceptions of existing mainstream practice—these are not trivialized but stated in a matter-of-fact way as a generalized commentary on the nature of schooling, the educational system etc. Extremist talk therefore consists of a *critique of what is*, whereas contrastive rhetoric amounts to a *defence of what is* by virtue of its unfavourable treatment of those things that threaten existing practice.

Third, extremist talk involves high levels of commitment on the part of the speaker to his/her observations on, and critiques of, the workings of the educational system. Because of that commitment, extremist talk is, for any speaker, addressed to *one* end of the value spectrum only. Contrastive rhetoric, however, involves little commitment to the mentioned alternatives. Any positive commitments to the essentials of existing practice are present by implication only; they are the obverse of the speakers' cloaked damnation of educational alternatives. Since the implied virtues of the present system stand out just as well against archaic traditionalism as against extreme progressivism/radicalism, and even better against

Table 18.1 *Differences between contrastive rhetoric and extremist talk*

CONTRASTIVE RHETORIC	EXTREMIST TALK
Introduced by institutionally and/or interactionally dominant individuals or groups—(in this case the head and deputy)	Introduced by institutionally and/or internationally subordinate individuals or groups—(in this case members of the ordinary teaching staff)
Contains trivialized conceptions of actual alternative educational practices	Contains generalized alternative conceptions of existing educational practices
References made to *both* ends of the educational spectrum	References made to *one* end of the educational spectrum only
Low level of commitment to mentioned alternatives	High level of commitment to alternative interpretations
Leads to agreement	Normally leads to disagreement, but not always
Centripetal effect—drawing in the boundaries of existing practice and consolidating them	Centrifugal effect—acting as a force for extending the boundaries of existing practice

them both, contrastive rhetoric therefore refers over time to *both* ends of the educational value spectrum.

Fourth, whereas contrastive rhetoric leads to agreement (tacit or explicit) with the views expounded and, therefore, to an implied endorsement of the educational *status quo*, extremist talk is commonly followed by emphatic *dis*agreement. (This is partly because of the nature of the values communicated, but also because extremist talk is articulated at the level of generalized speculation, assertion and theorizing—and therefore open to counter assertion. Contrastive rhetoric, meanwhile, is articulated at the level of particular cases to which teachers have no independent access and, therefore no independent grounds for confirmation or repudiation.) There is one crucial proviso to be made here, though: whilst disagreement with extremist talk is usual, it can never be guaranteed. The normal response may well be a chorus of 'No's' or its equivalent, but just occasionally, a cacophony of 'No's' and 'Yesses' may ensue instead.

The implication of all this is that the inherent dynamic of extremist talk is centrifugal; it is a force which exerts constant pressure to push the boundaries of existing practice and debate outwards. In practice, of course, given the generalized mode of discourse in which such talk is cast, other teachers are usually able to resist that centrifugal tendency by counter-assertion and counter-argument. That is to say, the disagreement that extremist talk engenders normally acts only to confirm teachers' customary conceptions of educational practice. But it is as well to remember, nonetheless, as the data indicate, that such disagreement is never total and that important spaces remain where the boundaries of existing practice can be and occasionally are negotiated.

Contrastive rhetoric meanwhile, contains few such potentials, its internal dynamic being strongly centripetal: that is to say, it serves to draw in and consolidate the boundaries of permissible practice. Even here, however, there is always a remote possibility that resistance may occur—though this is contingent upon the not impossible, but certainly very unlikely event that particular teachers have, within their experience, come across any of the educational alternatives that are introduced into discussion, and that their experience has led them to view these in a favourable light. In this sense, from the standpoint of control, although rhetoric is a risk, it is not a substantial one. If we wish to look for sources of change in current educational practice, extremist talk would appear to be a better bet. [. . .]

Notes

[1] Actually, Keddie seems to employ at least two different definitions of the educationist context. At some points, the nature of 'context' seems to refer to the kind of people involved in discussion and the object of discussion: this is the meaning of 'the actual context of school politics', for example. On other occasions, the educationist context is something borne-in-mind that can be introduced into any kind of discussion as appropriate: this is the meaning of 'the educationist context may be called into being by the presence of an outsider to whom explanations . . . must be given'. In practice, it is the former usage that predominates in Keddie's work, and that is the one I employ here.

[2] In the case of my own work, see Hargreaves, A. (1978, 1979) for examples.

[3] The literature on the relationship between headteachers and teachers is scant, and hardly any of this focuses on the details of headteacher-teacher encounters. For a review see Ross, J.A. (1980). One notable exception is Hunter's (1980) important study of decision-making in a comprehensive school, though his analysis of the interaction between head and staff forms only one small part of his paper.

[4] This is documented in Hargreaves, A. (in process).

[5] On typical cases versus critical cases in school ethnography, see Hammersley (1980b). To

be more precise, this study of curriculum decision-making at Riverdale is a *limiting* case, where one would *least* expect a hypothesis (in this instance concerning the influence of hegemony) to be confirmed, such that if it *is* confirmed, it can legitimately be considered to be extensible to other parts of the educational system.

6 The concept therefore arises from a dual concern with theory generation *and* theory testing.

7 On the interchangeability of standpoints see the work of Schutz (1973), Garfinkel (1967) and Cicourel (1971).

8 This is one significant point on which contrastive rhetoric diverges from forms of rhetoric that researchers have identified in other occupational settings. In these settings, rhetoric is elaborated by all participants as a way of forging a collective occupational identity against intrusions by and confusions with other occupations. As Dingwall (1977) argues in the case of atrocity stories, they 'play an important part in defining the colleague group ... They allow for the assertion of the tellers' social theories and for mutual support in redressing the illegitimate actions of others'. (p. 325). Reviewing research in this area, Dingwall states that atrocity stories are conventionally the preserve of the powerless, though not exclusively so. However, even where he notes their use by the powerful (e.g. by doctors about patients) this is in terms of what powerful groups have to say about powerless ones. He makes no mention of the use of atrocity stories or similar strategies in interactional contexts where powerful and powerless groups meet; i.e. where they talk *to*, not *about* one another.

9 This also was the force of his concluding remark about handing things 'right over to the kids'.

10 By interpretative schemes I mean something very different from what ethnomethodologists have called interpretive procedures and interpretive abilities. These latter refer to *universal* abilities which make the conduct of social interaction possible, whereas interpretative schemes refer to specific sets of coding procedures used by *particular* cultural or occupational groupings.

11 It should be noted here that there is no necessary correspondence between the position advanced in any speaker's extremist talk and the nature of his/her classroom practice. Thus, while Mr. Button's talk was broadly radical, his classroom practice was perceived by many of the other staff as that of a conventional, traditional secondary teacher.

12 However, I suspect that this element is probably the *least* essential one that distinguishes contrastive rhetoric from extremist talk. A good way to test this proposition in further research might be to investigate the decision-making process where a very radical head attempts to spearhead a programme of innovation against the wishes of an entrenched, conservative staff—will they then be the users of contrastive rhetoric and the head the exponent of extremist talk? This test might enable us to disentangle institutional constraints from hegemonic ones.

References

Althusser, L. (1971) 'Ideology and ideological state apparatuses', in *Lenin and Philosophy and other Essays*, New Left Books, London.

Apple, M. (1979) *Ideology and Curriculum*, Routledge and Kegan Paul, London.

Cicourel, A.V. (1971) 'Interpretive procedures and normative rules in the negotiation of status and role' in *Cognitive Sociology*, Penguin, Harmondsworth.

Cohen, S. (1973) *Folk Devils and Moral Panics*, Paladin, St. Albans.

Dale, R. (1977) 'The structural context of teaching', E202 *Schooling and Society*, Unit 5, The Open University Press, Milton Keynes.

Dingwall, R. (1977) '"Atrocity stories" and professional relationships' *Sociology of Work and Occupations*, Vol. 4, No. 4.

Durkheim, E. (1964) *The Rules of Sociological Method* Free Press, New York.

Edwards, A. and Furlong, V.J. (1978) *The Language of Teaching*, Heinemann, London.

Erikson, K. (1964) 'Notes on the sociology of deviance', in Becker, H. S. (Ed.) *The Other Side*, Free Press, New York.

Garfinkel, H. (1967) *Studies in Ethnomethodology*, Prentice-Hall, New Jersey.

Gazdar, G. (1977) 'Conversational analysis and conventional sociolinguistics', *Analytic Sociology*, Vol. 1.

Glaser, B. and Strauss. A.L. (1968) *The Discovery of Grounded Theory*, Weidenfeld and Nicolson, London.

Gramsci, A. (1971) *Selections from the Prison Notebooks*, Lawrence and Wishart, London.

Hammersley, M. (1980a) A peculiar world?—Teaching and learning in an inner-City school. Unpublished Ph.D. thesis, University of Manchester.

Hammersley, M. (1980b) 'Classroom ethnography' *Educational Analysis* Vol. 2, No 2.

Hammersley, M. (1981) 'Ideology in the staffroom', in. Barton, L. and Walker, S. *School Teacher and Teaching*, Falmer Press, Brighton.

Hargreaves, A. (1978) 'The significance of classroom coping strategies', in Barton, L. and Meighan, R. *Sociological Interpretations of Schooling and Classrooms: A Re-appraisal*, Nafferton Books, Driffield.

Hargreaves, A. (1979) 'Strategies, decisions and control: interaction in a middle school classroom', in Eggleston, J. (ed.) *Teacher Decision-Making in the Classroom*, Routledge and Kegan Paul, London.

Hargreaves, A. (in process) *The Sociology of Educational Policy and Practice* Routledge and Kegan Paul, London.

Hargreaves, D.H. (1979) 'Durkheim, deviance and education', in Barton, L. and Meighan, R. *Schools, Pupils and Deviance*, Nafferton Books, Driffield.

Hargreaves, D.H., Hester, S.K. and Mellor, F.J. (1975) *Deviance in Classrooms*, Routledge and Kegan Paul, London.

Hunter, C. (1980) 'The politics of participation—with special reference to teacher–pupil relationships', in Woods, P. (ed.) *Teacher Strategies*, Croom Helm, London.

Keddie, N. (1971) 'Classroom knowledge' in Young, M.F.D. (ed.) *Knowledge and Control*, Collier-Macmillan, London.

Parsons, T. (1959) 'The school class as a social system', *Harvard Educational Review*, Fall. 1959.

Ross, J.A. (1980) 'The influence of the principal on the curriculum decisions of teachers' *Journal of Curriculum Studies*, Vol. 12, No. 3.

Sacks, H. (1972) 'On the analyzability of stories by children', in Gumperz, J.J. and Hymes, D. (eds) *Directions in Sociolinguistics: The Ethnography of Communication*, Holt, Rinehart and Winston, New York.

Schegloff, E. (1971) 'Notes on a conversational practice: formulating place' in Sudnow, D. (ed.) *Studies in Social Interaction*, Free Press, New York.

Schutz, A. (1973) *Collected Papers Vol. I*, Martinus Nijhoff, The Hague.

Smith, D. (1978) '"K is mentally ill": The anatomy of a factual account' *Sociology*, Vol. 22, No. 3.

Strauss, A.L. *et al.* (1964) *Psychiatric Ideologies and Institutions*, Collier-Macmillan, London.

Taylor, I., Walton, P. and Young, J. (1973) *The New Criminology*, Routledge and Kegan Paul, London.

Williams, R. (1973) 'Base and superstructure in Marxist cultural theory' *New Left Review*, Vol. 82, December.

Williams, R. (1977) *Marxism and Literature* Oxford, Oxford University Press.

Woods, P. (1979) *The Divided School*, Routledge and Kegan Paul, London.

Young, M.F.D. (ed.) (1971) *Knowledge and Control*, Collier-Macmillan, London.

17   Subject Disciplines as the Opportunity for Group Action: A Measured Critique of Subject Sub-cultures

S.J. BALL AND C. LACEY

Within the overall occupational culture of teaching, there are a number of different staff sub-cultures. One of the most important determinants of staff sub-culture in secondary schools is that of the teacher's subject. In this article, based on an analysis of four comprehensive school English departments, Ball and Lacey illustrate how the different departments use their strength and influence at the level of school policy. In addition, they analyse the basis of a subject sub-culture's strength in a school in terms of factors such as the cohesion of its members' views on the subject's content and teaching methods.

[...]
Subject Departments in Schools

The material to be presented derives from case studies of four English departments in four comprehensive schools.[1] The schools, which shall be referred to as Oak Farm, Furzedown, Handworth and Beachside, respectively, will each be described briefly and material taken from interviews with members of their English departments presented.

We intend to employ two concepts in particular in the analysis and discussion of the case studies and it will be useful to define these concepts clearly in advance. They are *subject paradigm* and *subject pedagogy*; the former *subject paradigm* refers to the views of English as a subject held by English teachers in terms of the appropriate content. The latter *subject pedagogy* refers to the system of ideas and procedures for the organisation of learning in the classroom under specific institutional conditions, that is appropriate method rather than appropriate content.

Oak Farm
Oak Farm is an 11–16 mixed comprehensive with 1,250 pupils in a small commuter town, its major features are aptly summarised in the following comment by the Head of English:

> Mr P: The school as such has good standing academically I think, we do manage quite well, it's a rather curious school in the sense that we certainly have a very good area, we draw children from very much a commuter area, bank managers and professional people, children of that type of person. And we also have a large council estate right near us from which we draw quite a number of other people.

And I'm afraid we tend to go in for image building you know, and exam results are important from the point of view of quite a few of the parents. So therefore, I'm afraid we concentrate rather too much on that.

The composition of the English department of Oak Farm is perhaps the most diverse of all the schools represented here.

> Mr P: We have three full-time English teachers including myself, Mr L., who has been at the school a couple of years and Mrs P. So that we have at the moment ten people who are teaching partly in the department or wholly. I've been fighting for more full-time English specialists since I've been here. We ranged from 22 teaching English, for a while it was 17, now it's ten. And I am hoping that whoever will take over from me will have a number of full-time specialists to work with.

This situation of having few full-time English specialists and the necessity, as a result, of having to make use of staff who have commitments elsewhere in the school, appears to adversely affect the status of English as a discipline and the English department in the school.

> SB: When over the years you've been able to reduce the number of people teaching English did this involve a process of negotiation, was it a very difficult thing to do?
>
> Mr P: Well it involved one trying to bring as much pressure as possible to bear on the Head and Deputy Head and other influential people in the school to make them see that English was being too much fragmented. And *the* most important subject, at least I consider it so, in the school, a basic subject and it's one that does demand specialists I think. I know that every teacher is a teacher of English, the old tag, but it doesn't work out that way. Even among the part-time English teachers, quite often I see English being used by teachers which is not a very good example for the children. I think it's not their fault, it's that they haven't been specially trained for this and therefore it's for the good of everybody to see that we get as few as possible and they are specialists.
>
> SB: Is that view of English, as the most important subject, recognised in the school generally?
>
> Mr P   I think that there is a more or less reluctant admission that we may have a case. And it so largely depends on the backgrounds and previous careers of headmasters. My present headmaster has done quite a lot since he's been here for the Science department; which is a good thing. But I feel that English is not recognised as firmly and as widely as it ought to be.

The question of the attitude and support from the headmaster, noted here, will be returned to in the later case studies.

This lack of 'recognition' apparently has its ramifications in terms of the way in which resources are distributed between the different subjects in the school.

> SB: Does that affect you in the competition for resources at all?
>
> Mr P: It does. It's only for three years that I've had a second in charge. It was thought that there were other priorities. And also physical things like an office. Which is quite a sore point, it hasn't been recognised in that way. But this was determined not so much by a positive opposition but by the circumstances which prevail in the school which make it difficult. I asked just in this last financial year that some provision be made whereby I could get a base to work from, but although it appeared on the list of requests, when it was sorted out into priorities, it missed the first priorities and was shelved again. It's not active opposition but nevertheless there isn't that positive urge that I would like to see.

However the weak position of the English department does not only have implications in terms of access to resources. The Head of English also finds himself at a disadvantage when his personal philosophy of education comes into conflict with the dominant ethos of academic success in the school. (The lack of success in this respect may be contrasted with that of the Head of English at Beachside which is presented later.) Three examples illustrate this. The first relates to the school's emphasis on examination attainment.

> Mr P: The Head obviously sets the tone so far as the school is concerned and I think there is rather too much stress on pure academic English, with a view to passing the public exams, than the sort of English which is more suitable I think to the majority of children in the school ... There is quite a lot of emphasis, too much I think, on examinations, in the set up here at the moment, public exams that is, and personally I'd like to see a bit of reorganisation from that point of view so that we cater for more of the 80 per cent of the people who need special treatment as far as English is concerned.

The second is the role of drama in the English department.

> Mr P: As far as Drama is concerned there are two ideas; one, prestige performances bringing in parents and a few chosen children displaying themselves, whereas I instituted English evenings where each of the teaching groups produces something that arises from drama in the classroom and we've had some very successful evenings with some 300 or more children taking part. But this year we are not having a prestige performance, but a musical, our Head of Music is keen on Drama too and is producing 'The King and I'.

The third is the question of Integrated Studies.

> Mr P: In the first year in the school we do an Integrated Studies scheme which consists of eleven periods a week, which are split up, five periods of English, three of History and three of Geography, but not strictly in that way. And a certain amount of team teaching goes on and they have themes around which they build. It's quite a thriving thing in the school and we keep a close liaison with the English. And personally I would be in favour of extending this into the second year, it's a very good basis on which to build later and it widens interest and makes them see English as an integrating force. But there's been again quite a lot of opposition to it, there's the feeling that, right from the word go, children should start preparing for public exams with set syllabuses, so therefore after the first year we fall into department subjects.

It seems reasonable to suggest that these problems of the English department at Oak Farm both in terms of giving access to scarce resources; specialist teachers, a departmental room, a second-in-charge, and in terms of asserting departmental policy over the questions of too much emphasis on examination English, the role of drama and extending Integrated Studies, are closely related. The diversity of those involved in teaching English prevents the development of a coherent department which can demand support and allegiance from its members, most of whom have major commitments elsewhere. (Head of Integrated Studies, Head of Remedial Department; Responsible for Curriculum Development, Head of Social Studies.) The department exists solely as an administrative, rather than a social, unit. The department functions, as the Head of Department sees it, through the medium of departmental meetings.

> I have departmental meetings you know. They are not so regular but they become necessary for special points and I do try to have meetings a couple of times during the course of a half term.

This diversity of its teachers also contributes further to the weakness of English in the school, as a subject department. This then creates a most difficult situation for the Head of English, for how can the department improve its status and strengthen its demands for more specialist teachers without the coherence, loyalty and support of specialist teachers to press its case. This problem will be returned to in the other case studies.

Finally with regard to Oak Farm we want to look briefly at the nature of English as a subject. The approach to the teaching of English at Oak Farm is represented in an outline syllabus written when the present Head of Department arrived at the school in 1968.

SB: What sort of English do you emphasise, what would be your philosophy?

Mr P: I think perhaps this is my scheme of working, which I brought out when I was first here, it's become a little outdated, in fact it's in the process of being refurbished. That's my philosophy, if there is such a thing, as far as English is concerned.

The rider added here 'if there is such a thing' is apparently well made.

SB: Apart from the drama and also the literature, you are also very clear in your document on the importance of basic skills and grammar.

Mr P: Yes, indeed yes.

SB: Presumably that again has been enforced across the whole department.

Mr P: Yes, well it varies from section to section, for instance we have children of a better academic level obviously who are going to want to take GCEs and go on to HE. And also in conjunction with the Languages Department where there is a need for them to know grammar, to be able to apply it in French and German and so on. We do a certain amount of formal grammar teaching in the higher streams, a lot more less formal in the lower stream. The nomenclature of parts of speech, clause analysis, etc., this is something that is necessary for some but not for others ... I look at English as a two-fold subject in as far as you are teaching English, a communicational, situational, secretarial English if you like, as a skill, as a tool to be used; but also there is what I consider the more creative, more important part of English, which is the creative using of it as an art. Where people compose with words. And these two strands we try to weave together. This fits in very well with the public exams because we do the Oxford board where they do test both these sides of English, and they, like myself, thankfully regard the creative side as a little more important than the other and it gets weighted in this way.

The discipline of English is defined differently here relative to different pupils. Different forms of English, grammar, communication and creative English, are appropriate to different kinds of pupils. But English in itself is seen to comprise language skills and creativity. It may be useful to refer to this view as a 'mixed paradigm'.

Furzedown School

Furzedown School is an 11–18 mixed comprehensive school with 1,500 pupils, set on the periphery of a large south coast seaside town. Its intake is socially mixed but dominated by two large municipal council estates. The school is in the process of recovering from a stressful amalgamation of grammar school and secondary modern school in which staff and parents of the grammar school fought against the amalgamation. As at Oak Farm the English department at Furzedown finds itself without a full complement of English specialists. (The Head of English at Furzedown was away ill during the greater part of the fieldwork period and most of the comment here comes from discussion with the second in charge (S in C).)

SB: In the school generally does the English department have a particular approach to English that identifies it?

S in C: I think we're still trying to find out ... we've had a large number of changes in the department over the last two years. We've had a number of ... or we've found ourselves in one way or another with two or three teachers who are not English specialists in the department teaching full-time.

This situation has implications for the way English is taught in the school, in that the non-English specialists

S in C: ... find English teaching in itself difficult. I think if anything there's been a recent rather disturbing tendency back towards a reliance on textbooks with exercises. Simply because they were the most obvious sort of lifesaver for the non-English specialist.

Again as at Oak Farm the presence of the non-English specialists has tended to affect adversely the coherence of the English department

S in C: ... because of those kind of people in the department and the turnover of staff, it's been very difficult to get any form of English policy ... [the Head of Department—H of D] has certainly got an instrument of policy which we have begun to fill out. But I think it would be wrong to say that it is uniformly accepted and worked, for the reasons I have given.

Once again the allegiance and loyalty of the non-English specialists are in doubt here, although in contrast to Oak Farm these non-specialists are full-time members of the department. This feeling of lack of coherence stemming from the presence of non-specialists is reinforced by the deputy head's opinion that 'I think generally speaking there's agreement among the *English specialists* about the way the department ought to be going' (emphasis added). Once again there are resource implications.

SB: Does that lack of consensus weaken the department's bargaining power in the school?

S in C: I think in some senses it must do ... ah ... It's certainly made our English adviser ... quite worried about us, he has devoted quite a lot of time to trying to help us sort out our problems. We've tended to find ourselves, and I hope it won't happen again, with awkward situations like classes on the timetable that can only be covered for English by splitting them between two or three different teachers. And obviously that's all right if you've got an agreed plan for team teaching but too often it just tends to be making sure that there's one person standing in front of the class at any given time during the day.

Once again this has led to conflict.

S in C: I'm sure that John [the Head of Department] has protested about it and I know that the English adviser has protested about it as well. I think that's one reason it's become clear that we need English specialists in the department.

Another aspect of resource deprivation for the English department is the question of remedial support.

I think one problem we face here is not having enough, many of us feel not enough, staff to deal with those who need remedial help. It more or less peters out by the time the kids get into the fourth year because there are two full-time remedial teachers and a third who splits with another department. That makes it possible to cover most of these normal classes for some time during the week to give them special attention. But that help usually stops by the the time they get into the fourth year, and that in a sense makes the kind of examination work that starts in the fourth year very difficult because you are likely to be faced with a class of very mixed-ability kids in the CSE range.

But the future for the English department at Furzedown looks rosy when compared with the situation at Oak Farm, both with respect to the non-specialists and remedial teaching.

H of D: Hopefully from next year onwards things will begin to settle down. With a large number of appointments to be made, I think three people ought to be appointed at the end of this term. Hopefully they will be English specialists and one of them at least will be an experienced English teacher.

S in C: The idea that's being worked, I think from next year onwards is that in the fourth and fifth years there will be special classes hopefully with special courses for the lowest ability kids.

The English policy of the department, referred to above, was clearly portrayed as oriented towards a single dominant paradigmatic view of teaching English. Although the non-specialists in the department are not committed to it, the specialists teachers are.

SB: Are there differences of view about English among the English specialists also?

S   I think probably very few really. No, I think there's general agreement about some kind of balance between the importance of what needs emphasising again and again to the children. You know, the basic skills of writing and so on, *but that the emphasis in the last analysis must probably be on the children's creative writing and self-expression* [emphasis added]

Several points may be drawn from this brief exploration of the Furzedown department. Firstly, once again, we would want to draw attention to the relationship between the lack of consensus among the members of the department and the access to resources (timetabling benefits, remedial support), although it would certainly seem that the English department at Furzedown is in a stronger political position than that at Oak Farm. However, it is recognised that the presence of non-specialist English teachers inhibits both the development of a formal instrument of 'policy' and the implementation of pedagogies like team-teaching, leading instead to what is regarded as an unproductive over-dependence upon the use of textbooks. This reliance on textbook exercises is obviously in contradiction with the view of English teaching held in common by the specialist teachers, which stresses the importance of the creative use of language by the children towards the development of the abilities of self-expression, which is differentiated from a 'basic-skills' approach.

An indication of the extent of this kind of pedagogic variation within different subjects, including English, is given in a study by Barnes and Shemilt (1974) which investigated teachers' assumptions about classroom communication. From a factor analysis of items relating to the uses of writing in the classroom the authors discovered consistent variations between subjects and notable differences within subjects and in addition they found differences in the range of views held by teachers of different subjects. As it turned out, Biology and Physics teachers were most homogeneous in their views.

There was a wider range among teachers of Languages and of Chemistry. Geography teachers were the least homogeneous, but teachers of History, RE and English showed almost as wide a scatter. Thus we have here a measure of the extent to which different subjects tend to constrain teachers' views: the Sciences and Languages place stronger constraints upon their teachers than do most arts subjects.

This suggests then that English may not be an exceptional case in the extent of disagreement that may exist, even in one school, over appropriate methods of teaching a subject or over the constitution of a subject.

Handworth
Our third school, Handworth, is an 11–18 mixed comprehensive with 1,000 pupils. It is situated in a large 'new town' but as a Church of England school with a good academic reputation it tends to attract pupils from predominantly middle-class homes from a large catchment area beyond the limits of the town itself.[2]

In contrast to the previous two schools all the English staff at Handworth are English specialists, five full-time and two part-time members. Also in contrast with the previous two schools the department is able, for a number of reasons, to present itself to the rest of the staff as a coherent entity. This coherence, which in certain respects may be seen to be deliberately fostered by the Head of Department in his dealings with others outside the department, derives from consensus among the members of department about what is an appropriate pedagogy for English teaching which tends to override paradigmatic differences among them concerning English as a discipline. But this pedagogic consensus also serves to separate off the English department from the rest of the school.

CD: The espoused theory of the English department is to, first of all, treat the pupils as individuals on a personal level. That's a very strong part of their underlying philosophy and it is demonstrated in the way in which they approach pupils in the classroom. The way in which they, for example, allow pupils to chew, wear boots, football scarves. Where the school rules says that they shall not, and the way in which they encourage people to … talk freely, and express their opinions honestly. All this is a part of the ethos of the English department which they do not regard as a part of the ethos of the school.

SB: Does this relate to their view of English as a discipline?

CD: Their view of English as a discipline is split: for example the Head of Department would be characterised by two other members of the department as giving much more concern to sociology and interpersonal relationships than he does to the literary elements of the English course, which they think is being underplayed— that is literature.

  What struck me in watching the teachers in the English department is that apart from their emphasis upon interpersonal relations, the value they place on the personal qualities of the pupils, rather than academic or basic skill qualities … But over the $2\frac{1}{2}$ years I've been in the English department there has in fact been a change. Whereas in the first year people were buoyant and optimistic and though they felt isolated, were positive about it. And if you like there was a binding force between them. Because they are all in a ten-year age span from 21 to about 31.

  But at the end of the first year I was there, the second in the department left and he was widely regarded within the department as a lynch-pin and stabilising influence on the sociologically progressive nature of the Head of the department. And so with that stability, or what they perceived as that stability, going, plus the fact that he wasn't replaced with a similarly experienced teacher, their expectations of the heavy work load have proved to be true during this year. And in addition two or three members of the department have become unsettled, not just within the department within the school, because of the increased emphasis placed by the school on discipline, both in outside the classroom, and cut-backs. Typical of the loss of optimisim of secondary school teachers.

SB: Is the incipient split within the department apparent to the rest of the school?

CD: No, it isn't.
SB: So that hasn't affected the department's access to resources?
CD: No, it hasn't. The thing about it is, they are personal friends ...

Here then is a situation in which the boundaries of the department are clearly drawn, all the members are English specialists and all share in a common view of teaching method. This provides for *and* highlights the differences between the English department and the rest of the school and as a consequence produces a situation in which the members feel isolated.

H of D: ... in a sense everything one does is in isolation, and the kids come to it and it may well be a wholly separate experience which they have to adjust to each time. The values are different, the aims are different, the objectives are different, and *they* have to adjust each time, so that you're having to clamber over the obstacles which have been placed by other people ... before you begin to make any kind of progress yourself. And nobody seems to see this. It appals me that we can have a Heads of department meeting and we can talk about exams as being the only motivation for our kids within the curriculum they follow ...

Clearly while there are paradigmatic differences within the one department, in terms of what should constitute the content of an English syllabus, these differences are of secondary importance to their commitment to a pedagogy. This sense of commonality may be encouraged and reinforced within the department by the similarity in ages of the members and the social bonds of personal friendship which exist. Nevertheless, paradigm conflicts are not unimportant.

CD: The strongest personality is someone who worked full-time while I was there in the first year and then converted to part-time, but who still very much influences a couple of full-time members of the department and who is very dissatisfied with the way the department is being run. Great personal friends with the Head of department, but she is a 'literature' lady and feels strongly that this should have a greater part to play.

At Handworth, then, the *literary* paradigm is contrasted with a sociological–interpersonal relationship paradigm, the former stressing the role of works of literature as a basis for English teaching, the latter stressing the importance of pupils talking freely and expressing their opinions honestly and de-emphasising aspects of discipline held to in the rest of the school.

H of D: Learning about relationship is the most fundamental aspect of education ... I want the department to adopt teaching techniques which are varied, but which ultimately place the responsibility for learning in the widest sense with the student; that we are people who open doors, and offer alternatives, and not keep saying, 'This is what you must learn, these are the answers to these questions' ... I don't think class teaching is the evil I used to think it was, but I think it mitigates against the possibility of presenting alternatives to kids of giving *them* the chance to evaluate ... analyse ... draw conclusions ...

This approach is embodied in a Mode 3 CSE course run in the fourth and fifth years which makes use of material drawn from the pupils' involvement in the pop-media and mass-media cultures. However, this paradigm conflict within the department is complemented by an inter-departmental paradigm conflict. The Languages department has attempted to put pressure on English to increase the amount of grammar work in the school, the lack of which they feel inhibits their language teaching.

CD: There are constraints that they normally feel and normally cope with, of feeling that other departments are getting at them. For example Modern Languages, who have been known to say to children—and this is from the children—that 'the English department ought to be teaching you grammar. It's not our job to teach you grammar . . .' They feel under pressure and this year under considerable pressue because of the increased work load.

This conflict between the *sociological–interpersonal relationships* paradigm of the English staff and the *grammarian* paradigm of the Languages department can be related back:

(a) to the differing views of English teaching apparent among the student teachers discussed elsewhere (i.e. in full original article); and
(b) to the evident co-operation, on exactly this second aspect of English teaching, between the English department and Languages department at Oak Farm.

Thus paradigm decisions or allegiances may have their consequences for political alliances both between as well as within departments.

Another contrast between Handworth and Oak Farm seems to be in terms of the rate of change in perspectives and methods; while the Oak Farm English department were about to 'refurbish' their policy document after ten years' service, Handworth was characterised as 'constantly questioning what they are doing and that's the kind of atmosphere'. It may be then that there is a further relationship between the degree of coherence and commitment within a department and the rate of change in the attitudes and practices of its members. At Handworth, change, innovation and independence are all associated with 'stability, or what they perceived to be as stability'; furthermore, while at Oak Farm the Head of English's aspirations for English and English teaching, a less academic syllabus, drama and integrated studies, are constantly frustrated, the English department at Handworth are able to go very much their own way and withstand, at least until now, the pressures from other departments in the school, for more grammar, more discipline or whatever.

Beachside

Beachside is an 11–18 mixed comprehensive with 1,400 pupils in a small south coast community. Its intake is predominantly made up of pupils of lower middle class and skilled manual parents. The English department is, with Mathematics, the joint largest in the school, there are 11 full-time English specialists and one of the remedial staff also contributes to the teaching of the department part-time. The role of the English department in the school is clearly defined and clearly articulated by the Head of Department.

SB: Would you say that you had a particular philosophy of English teaching within the department, that denoted your department in a particular way?
DL: Yes. Basically, within the context of a secondary school, we are interested in the creative aspects of language work. So bearing in mind that all of the kids are doing language work in all areas of the school curriculum, we could see our particular responsibility as for the expressive and creative, or expressive to poetic use of language and linking in with that we would therefore concentrate attention on literature, and what is sometimes called creative writing and that I suppose is the basic thing that holds us altogether in the department.

This *expressive/creative* paradigm is, the Head of department argues, shared unanimously by all the other members in the department. This is ensured in part by the careful selection of new members of staff.

SB: Is that approach, conception, shared by all the members of the department?
DL: Yes. Most of the members of the department; the majority of the department have been appointed in fact since I've been Head of the department and this is one of the things that I'm looking for when I'm wondering whether somebody's going to fit in. And the people that were here before me, we have a couple of older members of the department who are very happy about my view of what English should be and they share it.

Here then is a case where the department is apparently connoted by both a paradigm consensus and a full complement of fully committed full-time English specialists. If our analysis so far has any validity then there should be some relationship between this state of affairs and the influence accruing to the department in terms of such things as access to resources. But, as we shall see, the story is not that simple, we first of all have to return to the attitude and policy of the Headmaster. As the Head of department explains

DL: In my experience what you get within the department, to do with resources and timetable time and the lot, fundamentally here, relies on one's relationship with the Head. I think that's the central thing. We don't have a sort of open competitive market system, all sitting round in a circle haggling. Resources are allocated via the Headmaster. He sees each of the Heads of department and gets their views about what is required; money, staffing, timetable time or whatever. And really, as the Head, he is the one who will do what he thinks is right. I can't see how the strength of a department is going to influence that. It's not the strength of the Head of the department, but is much more to do with the relationship between the Head of department and the Head.

This, then, suggests an alternative model to account for the 'strength' and access to resources of different departments. As we saw earlier, at Oak Farm the Head of English feels that he does not have the ear of the Headmaster and that instead the Science department has reaped the benefits of a special relationship. But then the question remains as to what factors enter into the Headmaster's evaluation of the importance of one department over another. The Head of English at Oak Farm suggests the Headmaster's 'background', his own subject specialism perhaps. What else? The Head of English at Beachside suggests the following:

DL: Different Heads obviously must have different views of the sort of hierarchy of academic subjects. Typically, from my experience of other schools, English and Maths are traditionally considered the central departments in a large secondary school. That's certainly the case in our school ... And I'm sure our Head sees the various departments partly in terms of their examination successes. There are some departments that are more cohesive and coherent in general. People stay in some departments longer and leave more often in others. Some departments have a feeling of togetherness and unity and all the rest of it and this he values. He sees this.

So there are other factors, but the unity and coherence of departments does emerge again as a matter of some importance.

As far as English is concerned the beneficence of the Headmaster, the relative success of the department in achieving public examination passes and the coherence and consensus of the department in terms of what English to teach and how to teach it (see below) all contribute to the department being in a relatively advantageous position in terms of staffing, timetabling, etc. But beyond this the strength of the department is reflected in their stand on the role of specialist English teaching. They do not see themselves as having any special responsibility for 'language work' in the school.

> DL: I don't see an English department as centrally responsible for the English language in a school . . .

The department at Beachside had pre-empted any possibility of pressures from Modern Languages or other departments to teach 'grammar', as at Oak Farm and Handworth. Indeed the English department's position of strength at Beachside enabled them to put the Languages department under pressure with regard to mixed-ability grouping.

The members of the English department at Beachside were outspoken advocates of mixed-ability grouping and played an important part in convincing many of the rest of the staff of the school of its desirability and practicability. As the Headmaster explained:

> the English department has had a seminal role in this . . . it was the English department who pioneered the actual mixed ability; it's very important in innovation to show people that it can be done.

In a staff meeting, in response to the opposition of members of the Languages and Mathematics departments, the Head of English was able to assert that:

> Comprehensive means mixed ability, if it does not then this is not the kind of school I would want to be concerned with.

As a result of this debate mixed ability was accepted, by a majority vote of all staff, across all subjects in the first year, but Languages and Mathematics were allowed to 'set' in the second. Nonetheless both these departments, Languages in particular, were placed on the defensive, while the English department went on to extend mixed-ability grouping into the fourth and fifth years.

Finally we should look again at dominant subject and pedagogic paradigms in the English department at Beachside. The Head of department identified their approach as creative and expressive, 'what is sometimes called creative writing'. The boundaries of this approach and some insight into its pedagogy are evident in the Head of department's comments on appointing new staff. He says

> There are new ideas and new ideas. I mean if somebody came to my department and wanted to teach formal grammar all of the time, or wanted to do funny exercises from a course book, and thought that this was the way to improve language work. Or wanted to use those 'English in Use' things. I think obviously they wouldn't fit in. But you find that out at interview.

Thus once again the *creative/expressive* paradigm is differentiated from the *grammarian*, and the grammarian paradigm is pedagogically identified once again with the use of course books and the doing of exercises.

Summary

Obviously it is difficult to begin to draw firm conclusions from the data presented here. The work done so far is an exploratory incursion into what is clearly a promising but complex area. Nonetheless the data available here do suggest certain issues and directions for further consideration and investigation.

Firstly there is the question with which we began, that is the extent of unity and communality within subjects in terms of their paradigms and pedagogies. In the case of English the assertion of communality and consensus is clearly problematic both in terms of what should be taught and how to teach it. Several different paradigms are indicated from the case studies, three in particular emerge as distinct from and opposed to one another. However this classification may still be oversimplistic and certainly requires more exploration. The major dimensions of the three paradigms identified here are outlined in Table 17.1 [. . .]

The interviews suggest that there is some degree of covariation between paradigm and pedagogy, but this is relatively unexplored, and at Handworth there is a situation where there is a pedagogic consensus and paradigm dissensus. Both paradigms and pedagogies are associated with institutional locales and particular schools can be characterised as representing particular dominant paradigms and pedagogies. Our data suggest that schools are both selective and productive in terms of paradigms and pedagogies. They are selective in two senses:

1 in terms of the recruitment of personnel; and
2 in that only certain types of paradigm or pedagogy can be tolerated or implemented within the limits set by an institutional environment (c.f. Lacey, 1974).

A second area for further consideration must be the relationship of department 'strength' to resource allocation and influence over policy. We have identified a number of factors as contributing to department 'strength', mainly in terms of coherence and consensus. The four case study departments may be compared in terms of the absence or presence of these various factors (see Table 17.2).

These factors certainly provide a way of looking at department 'strength' but must not be interpreted mechanically. Two caveats are needed. First, it is possible that a degree of dissensus and disunity within a department can be adequately contained and managed so that the department appears as cohesive and unified to others, as was the case at Handworth. In the public arena of the staffroom or staff meeting the subject department may be considered, in Goffman's (1959) sense, *a performance team*.

> While a team performance is in progress, any member of the team has the power to give the show away or to disrupt it by inappropriate conduct. Each team-mate is forced to rely on the good conduct and behaviour of his fellows, and they, in turn, are forced to rely on him.

Table 17.1 Subject paradigms

Creative/Expressive	Grammarian	Sociological
Emphasises		
creating writing	functional use of	personal relationships
the self expression	language, communication	children's own culture
of pupils	and syntax	and free expression
		opinions
Uses		
poetry and literature	course books and	magazines and
	exercises	newspapers, etc.
Key words		
stimulus and excitement	basic skills	pupils as individuals

Table 17.2 Direction of increasing cohesion and 'strength'

	Oak Farm	Furzedown	Handworth	Beachside
Subject paradigm consensus	Not clear	—	—	Yes
Subject pedagogy consensus	—	—	Yes	Yes
All teachers are English specialists	—	—	Yes	Yes
All teachers have major teaching commitment to department	—	Yes	Yes	Yes
Specific contextual factors Headmaster views subject as important	—	—	Not clear	Yes
Other support (from subject advisor)	—	Yes	—	—
Social bond/similarity of ages of members of the department	—	—	Yes	Not clear

Second, in the case of what may be regarded as a 'strong' department, the use of this 'strength' to assert an independent subject policy or influence policy-making in the school generally, is best considered as a potential. It will not necessarily be used or brought to bear in every case. [. . .]

Notes

[1] The case study data presented here represents what is essentially an exploratory stage in our investigation. In each case only one informant was interviewed and in each case he was chosen for convenience rather than on the basis of any kind of sampling. At Oak Farm and Beachside the Head of department was interviewed, at Furzedown the deputy head and at Handworth a research student, ex-LEA advisor who is engaged in research into English teaching. If we are able to pursue the analysis we envisage a much more intensive and comprehensive methodology. In each case all the members of a department would be interviewed, perhaps also other members of staff outside the department. Also observation of departmental meetings would be important.

[2] We are indebted to Chris Day, a research student at the University of Sussex, for his help in constructing this case study and his willingness to allow us access to his own data.

References

Barnes, D. and Shemilt, D. (1974) 'Transmission and interpretation', *Education Review*, Vol. 26: No. 3.

Goffman, E. (1959) *The Presentation of Self in Everyday Life*, Penguin, Harmondsworth.

Lacey, C. (1974) 'Destreaming in a pressure academic environment', in Eggleston, J. (ed.) *Contemporary Research in the Sociology of Education*, Methuen, London.

18 Teacher Careers and Comprehensive Schooling: An Empirical Study

G.F. RISEBOROUGH

For some teachers, the re-organization of secondary education in Britain seemed to offer the prospect of new career opportunities and enhanced rewards. In the following case-study of teacher relationships in one re-organized comprehensive school, George Riseborough shows how, for one group of ex-secondary modern school teachers, quite the opposite occurred. We see here, in a curious parallel with pupils, how teachers can develop a counter-culture within the staff when their careers are 'spoiled' and basic work satisfactions are denied them.

The area, the school and the teachers

'Woodend'[1] (population 30,000) is a town on the periphery of a major conurbation. The social classes are not equally represented, there being a slight numerical preponderance of non-manual groups. Housing is predominantly owner-occupied but there are also two council estates. The middle class working population tends to commute to the centre of the conurbation and the working class working population tends to be employed in local motor and light industries.

There are now no state selective schools within Woodend, secondary education being reorganized on all-through 11–18 comprehensive lines as from September 1968. In that year 'The Ashes Mixed Secondary Modern School' was designated 'Phoenix Comprehensive School' and the first-year pupil intake was fully comprehensive. Thus the school was fully comprehensive by 1975. During 1969–75 the pupil population grew from 760 to 1,300. With designation the head- and deputy-headships were subject to reappointment and consequently advertised. The head and deputy head of the secondary modern school applied but a new head and deputy head were appointed. The 'old' head and the majority of the existing teaching staff continued to serve in the new comprehensive school, although the deputy head and several teachers left.

This study is primarily concerned with the male staff of the secondary modern school and their experience of reorganization. They total 17 in number. They are referred to as the 'old' staff, which is how they were generally referred to in the school, in order to distinguish them from the 'new' staff who were appointed during and after reorganization. All were non-graduates except one who had a general degree. The majority had been two-year trained in Training Colleges, but four had been emergency trained. All had been teaching for considerable periods, the minimum length of service was five years prior to comprehensivization, and had taught only in secondary modern schools.

Before comprehensivization

All the 'old' staff had a keen sense of seniority, on the basis of their experience they perceived that there was and there ought to continue to be a necessary relationship between length of service and career rewards. They saw themselves as held in esteem [. . .]. For example, one was a senior master, others were heads of departments or held lesser posts. Relations between the 'old' staff and the 'old' head were generally equable, the school was characterized by an 'indulgency pattern'.[2] All thought that the 'old' head considered them to be good teachers.

> He was a stickler. He had his standards. He always made the big decisions. He always consulted his team. He told me once he didn't want to lose a teacher as good as me. I was flattered but I knew he meant it so I agreed to stay. (Age 34)

They were professionally socialized into secondary modern school teaching. Over the years they had formed stable definitions of themselves as teachers and acquired a range of teaching skills considered necessary for secondary modern schools.

> There was this group of us who had been here a long time and we were the school. We really did set the tone and the kids knew it. You realize one morning that you are unassailable, that you can never be beaten. You cease to have problems and you get on with the job. In the old days teaching counted for something, you were consulted, you were asked advice and you gave help. (Age 48)

Teaching in the secondary modern school was very satisfying for the 'old' staff. All saw their experience there as the halcyon days of their career when status, commitment to teaching and job satisfaction were at their zenith.

> I was highly committed at this time. The school was a community. You knew everyone, you belonged. You were wrapped up in your work. We were very contented. We had security. We were doing a good job. We'd built up something from nothing. It'd started up as a tiny school. The school had grown up and we'd grown up with it. (Age 46)

The new head

The new head was 35 years of age, having an honours degree in history, a higher degree and a Diploma in Management (Education). He had been the deputy head of a Midlands comprehensive school. He defined his role as 'a pioneering one' and was concerned about 'the public image' of comprehensive schools.

> You see the sad thing about comprehensive schools is that one bad comprehensive school is picked upon by the press or politicians and the system is hammered. A lot of people are gleeful about that. I feel we've got to make sure our image is good. I'm very conscious of the adverse opinions of the public towards comprehensives. I think successful ones have to carry the burden of others less successful. We've great advantages here and the onus is on us to show what can be done.

He described himself as 'a social democrat and evolutionary'. His view was that historically the education system had denied equality of opportunity by which he meant it denied equality of access, particularly by the operation of what he considered 'the universally agreed, inequitous eleven-plus examination'. His school was to redress this traditional inequality, ending sponsorship to élite social positions by substituting a fairer, more open, competitive system. The school would redress social inequalities and social divisions by enabling the able but lowly to rise up and the unable but highly placed to sink down the social ladder. For him, comprehensive education was to provide efficient equal access for all to become unequal on the basis of merit rather than social position.

> We've failed if we produce an homogeneous product. I think the aim of a comprehensive school is to allow children to be different and to make a contribution to our society, not just to produce followers but produce leaders. We can't all be leaders but if comprehensive schools only produce followers we're in a mess. What worries me are societies like Sweden where they've abolished competition completely. If you don't give children some kind of goal that they can understand and approve of and compete for you are destroying the fibre of very good people and this concerns me. You've got to allow people to compete for what they want.

The prize for the winners of the open contest was defined by the head as academic achievement as traditionally defined and given, which would provide, for the able pupils, entry to universities and professions. Thus, the public examination system and success in it were given prominence. The desired, structural embodiment of his ideology, outlined by the head, can best be described as a 'postponed' ' "pressured" academic environment';[3] 'postponed' in the sense that it was not fully institutionalized until the third year thus 'suspending early, dangerous decisions'.

> We're under pressure to produce results. There is immense pressure from parents. I think it is quite tremendous. They're used as a measure of a school. The eleven plus has gone, but we have a sixteen plus and an eighteen plus now and I have to accept that. My credibility as a head depends on results. Social pressures want you to say how many 'O' levels and 'A' levels and university places you have. There is no doubt that the validity of everything I do here is dependent to a considerable extent on results. You see exam results gives confidence to the school. They give confidence to the kids. What I'm saying is I can do what is educationally important but sometimes you have to blow up specific areas for the approval of certain sections of the public. So certain areas of the school become illuminated and the most important is the results area.
>
> A good comprehensive school is one that has all kinds of pupil in it, whatever background they come from. If you're losing out on any of these backgrounds you're not a real comprehensive school. Right, O.K. now to win your middle class you have to turn in your results which we do. I want them in this school. Let's have no illusions about it. I'm not interested in a one class school. I'm sorry that's unfortunate, I am interested in a one class school but not from one section of the community.
>
> We live in a society where entry to the occupations depends on exam results. We would deprive children if we didn't give it to them, I'm not interested in turning out deprived children. I am very aware that this school is having to prepare children for a competitive society. Youngsters are going out from here and we would be foolish if we didn't prepare them adequately results-wise and socially as well I think. We can't get away from 'O' levels, short of everyone scrapping it. I'm afraid we live with the system or we penalize the children and I'm not prepared to penalize anybody's child.

Thus for the head comprehensive education was to improve *access*. At no time, in staff meetings, head of department's meetings etc. was the *content* of education ever, critically, considered. Curricular provision, as traditionally defined, was merely taken as given.

Comprehensivization

When the 'old' staff were informed that the school would become comprehensive and a new head appointed, feelings were highly ambivalent. They did not relish a change of head for they knew it could upset the existing pattern of career concerns and rewards. Amongst themselves they questioned the legitimacy of the head's appointment; particularly his age, experience, educational background, imputed teaching ability and administrative competence.

> We were rabidly against comprehensives. I had a fear that the putting together of grammar school children with secondary modern children might not be everything that everyone said it was going to be. (Age 53)

However, most of the 'old' staff had experienced the historical development of the official career structure. These changes, increasingly stratifying and differentiating the profession had provided them with previously denied opportunities to develop their careers 'vertically' and 'horizontally' (Becker, 1952a, p. 75). They saw comprehensivization as offering a further extension of career opportunities and they hoped, particularly, to negotiate further vertical promotion. Thus, career aspirations were fired during comprehensivization and the 'old' staff thought, on the basis of their prior teaching record, these aspirations would and could be realistically fulfilled. Much staffroom conversation was concerned with potential career advancement. What specific jobs would there be? What kinds and sizes of posts of responsibility would be made available? How would appointments be made? Who was going to get what? What criteria would be used in appointments?

> We were prepared to go along, besides there was nothing we could do about it. We realized that there were career prospects. There was going to be more posts of responsibility. Right, we said, this is for us. Comprehensives here we come. (Age 37)

> We saw the comprehensive school as a real prospect for improving our careers. I had contributed a lot in the secondary modern. One doesn't like change but we all expected to command respect and responsibilities. It's only natural. (Age 48)

When the new head took up his appointment, the 'old' staff mindful that he was the mediator of their new comprehensive school careers, used a variety of ingratiation, bargaining and impression management techniques. In short, they enacted 'the laws of pleasing headteacher' (Hargreaves, 1972, pp. 411–14).

> No question of anybody not wanting to help. He seemed at first to be very sympathetic, I thought he was going to be great to work with. He assured us no-one would suffer. No doubt about it, we were jockeying for positions. We sucked around an awful lot. It really was like 'Oh! What a Lovely War!', a question of 'One staff officer jumping right over the other staff officer's back'. (Age 36)

In this overall ambivalent situation of career uncertainty and career expectation, conflict between the new head and the 'old' staff was predictable if the head did not meet these career expectations. In a series of staff meetings the head elaborated his 'philosophy'. He made it increasingly clear to the 'old' staff, implicitly and explicitly that he considered them 'bad' teachers, 'ascribed rule-breakers' (Mankoff, 1971, pp. 206–7), vis à vis his organizational goal of a '"pressured" academic environment'. This was made particularly explicit to the 'old' staff when posts of responsibility, which were subject to reappointment were distributed. Several of the 'old' staff were taken off the 'establishment' of the school and given 'protected' salaries. The reasons given, or deduced, were inferior academic qualifications, limited experience of and incompetence in public examinations. This vertical demotion of some was interpreted by all the 'old' staff as a reflection of the head's assessment of their professional worth and they knew that they had been allocated roles of low esteem and priority in the new comprehensive school.

> We didn't wake up until we found our jobs attacked and then all hell broke loose. Posts weren't given out and people realized they weren't going to be what they thought they were going to be. I suddenly found I wasn't on establishment at all. In fact a number of us weren't. The head never saw this as important. His attitude was we weren't losing money thus we weren't affected. (Age 53)

> I can remember pointing out at a Union meeting that people would be affected in terms of their status. When it happened here the leader of the Union came down. I had written to him pointing out the facts to him, discussing status at length. He'd written to me and told me I ought to be content with the fact that I was receiving the same pay. We had a chat before he started the speech and I harped on how important status was to a man. You know, if you take this away, not all the money in the world will make him feel content with his job, and this is what teaching is all about. You've got to feel right. He'll remember the bloke who told him his ideas were wrong. I ended up by being nasty and saying how would he feel if he was no longer the General Secretary of the Union but Assistant, still having the same pay but no longer being the controlling interest in the Union. Would he feel that because he was receiving the same pay that everything was alright? How would he feel when somebody said he was no longer the right type for the job? I said the same thing was happening to us. We thought we could cope with the job in the comprehensive. Looking back and seeing the people who came in, this is too fantastic. It's hardly surprising, is it, that relations became so vitriolic? (Age 43)

That they were considered 'bad' teachers was further confirmed for the 'old' staff when the head appointed in the developing comprehensive situation teachers having good honours degrees, and a record of public examination success in other schools. Many were promoted to 'established' posts of responsibility higher than those once held by the 'old' teachers.

> It was a very difficult situation. I was aware that it was an area of high parental aspiration and expectation. It was also a school of low first choice. Most of the children were drafted into the secondary modern school. Neighbourhood confidence was low, I had to restore confidence. Also, I had to expand the staff rapidly. The staff had got out of balance. We've been successful. We're now oversubscribed. This reflects the new confidence parents have but it would not have been achieved without the infusion of new blood. (New Head)

> I got angry about seeing these people getting the plums we were considered not good enough for. All the teachers he appointed were youngish with bloody degrees. People realized they were absolutely stopped and this is a terrible thing to realize. (Age 39)

> The head's idea of a good teacher is everything I'm not. Just look at the ones he's appointed. That's what he thinks a good teacher is. The rating really is on academic qualifications and examination record. This man has a tremendous fear that he has to show results. From the beginning I realized the writing was on the wall. He'd looked up my record and saw someone who'd matriculated at sixteen, been emergency trained etc. He told me in an argument once that I was more a schoolteacher than master. He meant that I could cope with children much better than I teach, I suppose. He once said to me that I was teaching beyond my capacity, which I resented. You can no longer prove that you've got ability although you may be able. (Age 56)

Mixed ability groups and integrated schemes of study were developed at Phoenix School, instigated by the head. Indeed, such innovations gave to the head and school a gloss of progressivism but they represented no challenge to his primary goal of a 'postponed' '"pressured" academic environment'. Such innovations were primarily implemented in the lower school, or in 'non-academic' subject areas, or for 'less able' children. As such, they constituted no threat to the assumptions of the worthwhileness of the academic goal.

By the third year children were tracked into 'streamed sets' (Lacey, 1974, p. 149) for most of their time in school, being offered a stratified 'curriculum for inequality' (Shipman, 1971, pp. 101–6); characterized by differentiated courses leading to GCE, CSE or no examination. This consideration of pupil grouping practices and curricular provision has been made to stress the point that not only did the 'old' staff suffer in the distribution of vertical promotions but also in the distribution of 'horizontal' promotion. Analysis of teacher timetables at Phoenix School yielded evidence not dissimilar to Allen's (1971, pp 17–21) and clearly showed that the 'old' staff were allocated lower stream pupils (see Table 18.1). No 'old' member of staff had a timetable in which he spent the majority of his time with 'top' sets. Very few had examination classes and when they did they were with the lower sets entered for CSE. No-one had GCE examination classes except for teachers of 'non-academic' subjects. Commonsensically, the old staff knew they were streamed.

> It's a question of horses for courses, isn't it? Certain teachers are better at certain things. You can't give good classes to bad teachers can you? Or they won't be good classes very long! Some teachers have to teach where they can do no harm. (Deputy Head, age 43)

> In science the high quality kids have heads of department. They work down to us. That's all Harry and I get all the time, the lower streams. General science only for us lot. We have the grubby labs. We're not allowed in the new block. I've been written off. I'm allocated the lower streams. I've been pushed out of the better streams. (Age 38)

This horizontal demotion (additional to their vertical demotion) was not without consequences for the 'old' staff. It was interpreted as a further public manifestation of their professional degradation and contributed to a feeling of utter hostility and alienation from the head and the school. They realized they had been allocated to the role of school 'dirty worker' (Hughes, 1958, pp. 23–36; Woollacott, 1976, pp. 91–123); they knew they had been allocated teaching responsibilities which the head and all the staff found morally repugnant and degrading, teaching

TABLE 18.1 *Percentage of weekly teaching time three groups of teachers spent with various pupil sets in 1974*

Catagories of staff[4]	Top Sets	Middle Sets	Bottom Sets	Unstreamed
'Old' Staff	11%	25%	50%	14%
(n = 17)	(64)[5]	(140)	(283)	(81)
Heads of Departments[6]	67%	23%	7%	3%
(n = 8)	(177)	(61)	(19)	(8)
Other Graduates[7]	59%	24%	11%	6%
(n = 12)	(241)	(98)	(45)	(24)

$(x^2 = 419.59,\ df = 6,\ p < 0.001)$

low status children judged to be destined for low status social positions (Becker, 1952b, pp. 119–25; Dale, 1976, p. 86).

> It's suddenly thought I'm better with this kind of child. I'm the teacher capable of teaching the bad child. I'm supposed to have the greater skill. This isn't done for a good reason. The head and his cronies thought, 'We don't want you teaching more able kids. It doesn't matter what you do with them. Just look after them'. He's absolutely no interest in what I teach. He's not interested. I've no incentive. I must have incentive but my employer has no interest in anything I am offering. (Age 48)

> It's like working at Fords. I feel like any other bloke who does a labouring job. I get so little satisfaction from the kids. I've got the riffraff, there's no point. I saw a film about policemen last night on telly. One of them said his job was like shovelling shit against the tide. That's how I feel. No matter how hard you try it makes no difference. There's no challenge there at all in my teaching. (Age 42)

This vertical and horizontal demotion set a self-fulfilling prophecy in motion. Wilkins (1964, pp. 219–25) has defined such a process as 'deviance amplification'. The head defined the 'old' staff as 'bad' teachers differing and deserving of special treatment, that is penalizing them horizontally and vertically career-wise. The 'old' staff reacted antagonistically, isolating and alienating themselves from the head and his 'good' teachers still further. In this situation of isolation and alienation they developed inverted norms and values which the head perceived as even more deviant than before. The head reacted further, resulting in his assumptions becoming 'actualities' and a deviant orientation to work being established amongst the 'old' staff. In short, the 'old' staff took on a stigmatized, spoilt, professional identity and now deny any legitimacy to the promulgations of the head and new staff in hierarchical positions.

> Things got worse and worse. We were in rebellion. Every suggestion he made we jettisoned for the hell of it. We took issue with him on every change. It's stupid that there should have been a rumpus over so many trivial things but that's how things got. (Age 37)

> We had to get out of the staffroom and talk about the latest incident. We'd get our heads together. We'd plot. We're all facing similar problems and we'd talk about them. If I'd been alone I'd have gone mad. I can't offer him loyalty. There can be no agreement between us, we agree to differ. I don't mind in the least backstabbing now. Once you would never have got me to have an interview like this because it was disloyal. I don't like to talk to him. When I see him I walk in the other direction or I don't see him, if you know what I mean. Everything he does and says now as far as I'm concerned is stillborn. We've reached a position where we can't discuss anything. We're poles apart. I can't accept anything this man puts forward. Comprehensives are rubbish. If it was announced that we were going back to what it was there would be no groans here. As far as I'm concerned it has been shown not to work. (Age 46)

The 'old' staff are now utterly antagonistic to the 'new' 'normal' teachers who appear to conform to the head's definition of the ideal teacher role. They could tell endlessly of confrontations and conflicts. Characteristically, they critically disavow amongst themselves through sarcasm, irony and cynicism the head's values, the workings of the school, the activity of children and successful new members of staff.

> No, the new and old staff don't mix. I don't even know their names. I've nothing in common with them. We never meet. It needs some years to learn the profession.

So many of them expect and get promotion too soon. They amaze me, they're running and they can't really walk. What really annoys me, continuing the analogy, is that they think I'm some kind of cripple. (Age 56)

Thus, the staff at Phoenix School were differentiated and became increasingly polarized. Distinct segments emerged (Bucher and Strauss, 1967, p. 79). The 'old', 'bad' teachers emerged as a 'clique'.[8] Membership of this clique represented an accommodation to official failure as a teacher; an organized retreat from role; a desire for a stabilization of the situation and for the return of the 'old indulgency pattern'.

I believe in career teachers. I feel teachers should be paid for longevity of service. If a man is forty he should be paid more than one who is thirty. There wouldn't be this bitchiness, this manoeuvering, the manipulation that goes on. There will never be peace in the setup there is now. It lends itself to the head, he has this tremendous power to control your salary. A youngster has got to conform, he has got to give loyalty no matter what kind of head he is. A man can't maintain his dignity, some semblance of his own ideas. He can't go counter to those in authority. Get rid of this payment by results and that's what it is, make no mistake. (Age 51)

The orientation to work of this emergent clique was an inversion of the head's ideological orientation and can be characterized as one of ultra 'militant conservatism' (Marcus 1971; pp. 191–226). They were caricatured by the new staff and the head as irrational diehards, educational backwoodsmen because of their calls for returns to traditional standards of morality and order; their indifference to organizational change; their belief that small is beautiful; their stress on didactic teaching; their support for selective schools; and the end of all 'trendiness' in educational ideas.

In the old days you see, the discipline was pretty good. The head used the cane and didn't mind them being punished. The children knew where they stood. Now because of this head, all this equality and freedom business, discipline has gone downhill. My authority within the school has been eroded. When you knew all the children, they also knew you. Now a large number think I'm a caretaker or something. Mind you he doesn't help. He doesn't want to know. It's such a wonderful school, as far as he's concerned. How can there be discipline problems? (Age 46)

The thing that's wrong is the sixth form. He begs them to stay on so he can boast how it's grown and to get extra points. So we've got a lot of wasters and it's. 'They're young persons, they're here voluntarily, we've got to be flexible, we shouldn't worry too much about standards'. (Age 51)

It's all this counselling business that's the trouble. The best bit of counselling I know is a bit of stick. It never does anyone any harm. (Age 45)

This non-streaming in the first year, I've never heard anything so stupid. It does nothing but make the good ones unhappy because they're held back and the poor ones unhappy because they know they are poor. All this rubbish about men cooperating, it doesn't work. (Age 37)

Teaching is chalk and talk, no matter how you choose to ignore it. How can you teach unless children sit down, shut up and are made to listen, unless they're under firm control. All this wandering around the classroom, film shows, modern methods, that's why there's discipline problems. (Age 46)

Education is not an adventure, it's hard graft. Children have to be forced to learn. You can't ask them because more often than not they don't want to learn. Look at this integrated studies I teach. It's terrible. It's a hotchpotch. It means children pick up a bit here and a bit there. This team teaching, it doesn't work here. How can it? Teachers have to be independent, be responsible for their own work. I learned a long time ago that I don't belong here any more. It's all chaotic. So all I do is make sure that everything is O.K. in my room. If all's well there I don't care. What I do in my room is my business. I don't care about anything now that goes on outside of it. (Age 39)

The 'old' staff's orientation to work is thus centred round an utter personal antipathy to the head; to teaching and to the school as defined by him; and to any kind of conception of comprehensive education. They define their role in opposition to the head's expectations. They are embittered about teaching and interpret it now as a menial job rather than a vocation and career. They feel proletarianized.

What's happened must affect the teaching. You can't go into the classroom and forget about what's happening to you. I don't work as hard as I used to. I don't think about the job anything like I used to. I just make sure I'm not snowed under by kids. I've become quite mechanical. They took away what was important, the job I could do. You lose interest. You meet a level which gets you by. You're always wondering whether some parent or other will turn around and say what the hell is he doing with my kid. I'm getting money for nothing. My skills are certainly not used by me, they are used to make the kids give me a peaceful life if I'm honest. Before comprehensivization I was a very tired man because I gave everything. Now I'm as fresh as a daisy. I'm never ever at full stretch. (age 51)

Because the 'old' staff are unable to gain any sense of equality of professional worth within the school, career aspirations have been cooled out and motivational investment in their role withdrawn. They are role retreatists, using typically a 'domination' mode of adaptation in the classroom (Hargreaves, 1967, p. 104).

The amount of help I give pupils is minimal really. I mark out time. Just give the kids some work. The drive has gone out of my teaching. It's hard to teach a class now. Many times, too many, I don't teach at all. I just stand and ruminate and give some work out, waiting for the bell. I haven't felt fit to teach. I've actually stopped teaching if I'm honest. I can't remember when I did a good day's teaching last. It's a long time ago. Now they're all grot, every day is grotty. Most of my lessons turn out to be a bit of a circus. Some are utter washouts I suppose I see the kids are bored stiff. This is why they are bad, they are makeshifts. I'm using my skills to get on by now. I think they're grot. By my standards I think they're terrible. They terrify me. I can't do anything abut it now. I exist from nine 'til four and live from four 'til nine. Now once I'm out of the school gate that's it. Money is more important now. What else is there? I have good relations with certain colleagues. (Age 45)

For example, all my marking, if I do any, is done in the classroom now. The same with lesson preparation, I don't put half the preparation into it. I don't set homework. I tell children if they want homework to come and see me, just to cover myself, knowing damn well they won't. Every job extra to teaching gets done in lessons or it doesn't get done at all. When the bell goes that's it. I don't plan anything now. Very often I don't know what I'm doing with children until I've done it. I'm strangely indifferent. (Age 54)

Put it this way, If I had children of my own at school I would be very, very worried if they had a teacher like me. I'm purely a time filler, a babysitter. You know I sit in my stockroom half the day with my electric kettle and a fag and a cup of coffee. And I don't care now that everybody else knows. (Age 43)

The head has now little or no control over the 'old' staff for they deny control of themselves; they happily ignore or invert his policy recommendations and 'do their own thing' irrespective of his desires. Staffroom graffiti declares 'Down in the gutter but free'. They are an assertive coalition, a persistent source of subversion for the head and the new staff.

> It's not in my nature to bury the hatchet. At least not on his terms. Besides, I now like to see how far it is possible to push the establishment. I'm not willing to conform. I couldn't change my ideas now on how the school should be run. I've become old as a result of disputing things. But I feel better when I stake my claims. Whatever happens I've not lost. I'm still able to oppose. I don't enjoy opposition but having done it again I feel I am still in my prime, am not counted out yet. I'm not worried that the head thinks he's won, he won a long time ago, but I'd hate him to think that not only has he won but he has beaten me as well. He'll never beat me. The bigger the thorn I am in his side, the happier I am. I know he'd like me to leave, but I wouldn't give him the satisfaction. (Sam, Ex-Senior Master, Clique Spokesman, Age 53)

> They fought back. It's very sad to see what it has done to them. The person who is most sad is Sam. Now for Sam life is ruined. He has let everything get under his skin, because he is an emotional man. Literally one wonders what is going to happen to him. Some of us get really worried about him because sometimes he is almost on the edge of some kind of collapse. He is a man of principle but of too much emotion. I've seen him nearly in tears. Sam's a nice person. I hate to think the head can do this to a person. I wish he'd got the ability to get out of it, start afresh. Certainly to get away, because the head regards Sam as some kind of snapping dog at his heels, a dog he can always beat. He's changed quite visibly. The spring's gone out of him. Sam has now got the reputation of a rabid dog. It's eroded him. It's done terrible things to him. He's an alltime loser. It's a tragedy because of course Sam's not the only one. (Colleague of 'Old' Staff)

Thus, experience of comprehensive reorganization reconstituted the 'old' staff's professional identities; gave a distinctive orientation to work and educational ideology. This provided the basis for a distinctive pedagogical style and hidden curriculum. Their reconstituted professional selves and emergent subculture provided a 'latent identity' and 'latent culture' (Becker and Geer, 1960, pp. 56–60) in their interactions with pupils in the classroom. They now defined their role as primarily custodial; the enforcement of obedience and conformity.

> Education is now a paperchase. I've reached a stage where I suspect any inculcation of knowledge with the kids I teach. It's overdone. Character and skills, that's all that's required. When you look at people here, who have been successful, got their 'O' and 'A' levels and degrees, you realize how stupid such a thing is. By what criteria can you say they are better? I'm not impressed when people are measured by exam results and paper qualifications. You've only got to look around here to realize how absurd that is. (Age 51)

The 'old' staff found themselves in a situation where career aspirations outstripped career realities. Their market and status situation had deteriorated in the new work situation of the comprehensive school. They experienced a truncation of their careers, a situation where they came to realize that there was no longer any possibility of vertical and horizontal career development within the school or wider education system. Their status within the school, conceived by them as the combination of vertical and horizontal positions had declined *vis à vis* new members of staff. In its more severely experienced form status decline was not merely remaining stationary on the career ladders and declining relative to others, but actually falling down. The 'old' staff were 'skidders' (Wilensky and Edwards, 1959), they could not see any future possibility of movement up the career ladders and no way out of their career impasse. They perceived their careers to be at an end. Such realizations of truncated careers and status decline had profound implications for perception of self and role performance. During comprehensivization at Phoenix School there was a shift in their framework of imagery for judging themselves, colleagues and pupils. Their official careers were characterized by a decline in status and their moral careers had correspondingly shifted too.

Our status is demeaned. People have been made redundant. It's a different kind of redundancy. Because a job is secure you think you can't be made redundant but you are. You're finished, you're due for the dustbin sort of thing. Oh yes, I got used to the idea you're not going forward any more, that you can only go backwards. You find yourself taking instructions that at one time you were giving and you find someone doing a job you did. Others are promoted over you. I'm left with a profound sense of failure. The fruits of a lifetime's work is lost. How else can I look at it? The only comfort is that I'm not alone. I often think of applying for jobs but realistically I can't go. Who's going to appoint me in or out of teaching? This head would never appoint anyone like me so why should other schools be different? Anyway I was here before him. (age 51)

Some of the men saw their work devalued and themselves devalued and are very disgruntled. Even children in discussion say 'There shouldn't be any old teachers Miss, they seem to be very grumpy the old teachers'. They thought they were of proven worth. They didn't see what the head coming in was. Some of them found their careers were stopped. They'd worked hard. The whole basis of their life had been stopped. They scratched their way up some sort of ladder and then quite suddenly their professional lives were over. These men are tragic. There is no other way to describe them because they are so unhappy, so disgruntled, so stuck. There is no way out for them. Now I suppose financially they are well off. They have bought houses here cheaply. But there is nothing there, no job satisfaction. Their lives are lived in some other place. Look at Ted Taylor who says that he had more dignity as a human being when he was a German prisoner-of-war than as a teacher now. They are totally devalued, almost disenfranchised as teachers. Some sort of sparkle is missing. It must be. Most are just waiting for the day they retire and are getting more and more embittered about the whole thing. They're a group without power, a grumble-group who sit in a corner moaning away. They've been excluded from the school. These men have had to accept a defeat and it has become part of them. (Colleague of 'Old' Staff)

In conclusion, of course such an overall 'negotiated order' (Strauss, Schatzman, Ehrlich, Bucher and Sabshin, 1963, pp. 301–20) was a negation of aspects of the head's professed ideology. However the head was publicly unperturbed, seeing it as a short-term management problem, for as far as dominant local publics were concerned Phoenix School was thought to be excellent. Given the public manifest-ations (i.e. examination results) of the 'postponed' '"pressured" academic environment', the head accounted fully for his mandate. This was much to the chagrin of the 'old' staff.

What we have here is a watered-down grammar school and a watered-down secondary modern under one roof. Comprehensives are the biggest mistake they've made, a wishy-washy mess. It really irks me. Look at the scrapbook in the library. Every week the school is in the press. How it's doing this and doing that. Parents are really impressed, they're queuing up to get their children in here. I met the Chairman of the Education Committee once, nothing to do with school. He said to me, 'What do you do?' I said, 'I teach at Phoenix School'. He said, 'That's really a great comprehensive school isn't it? A very good head. A lot of exciting things going on'. How could I begin to tell him what a shambles I think it really is. Nobody would believe me. Sometimes I think I'm going quite mad. (Age 48)

The 'good' teachers; an omission

The weakness of this study is that, it has concentrated on one group of teachers who now constitute a minority of the total school staff. It is important to stress the head is an amplifier of teacher 'normality' as well as teacher 'deviancy', but such processes have been ignored. Through the head's selective recruitment, promotion and deployment of 'good', new teachers, a 'cabal'[9] was formed from their ranks. Members of this cabal comprised those who had gained career-wise from the reorganization and hoped to continue to do so into the future. This cabal constitutes the school's 'dominant coalition' of 'decision makers' (Child, 1972, pp. 101–2), with a high commitment to individualistic, achievement values; to the official career structure; to a professional version of the Protestant Ethnic. This ideology informs their classroom pedagogy and is the basis of a hidden curriculum.

Cabal members identify with the head's norms and values since loyalty to these guarantees future career success in and out of the school. Many aspire and expect one day to become heads of other comprehensive schools. They share the head's ideology, are morally involved in teaching, and with the school as the head defines it. In their own terms they teach well and obtain a great deal of intrinsic satisfaction; work is experienced as pleasant and rewarding. Their orientation to work fits more the image of professionalism and role performance presented and taken for granted within the normative paradigm. The head has considerable influence over his 'good', new staff. They can be reliably involved in decision making processes and left to perform at their own discretion what needs to be done within agreed policy guidelines. For example, they can be deputed to make or advise upon lower level teacher appointments; and if a head of department, to allocate teacher resources 'in the right way' within the timetable.

As the school's 'clean workers' they have faced the dilemma 'that there is little prestige to be derived from serving groups which . . . are defined as lacking in moral vitue, ambition, self-dependence etc.' and solved it by 'the shedding of "dirty work" in an attempt to devote one's time—and to be seen as devoting one's time—to "more professional" activities' (McKinlay, 1972, p. 363). As such they can be relied on to deliver annually increasing numbers of public examination successes and higher education places. This is simply interpreted by the head, the cabal and lay audience alike; that numerically more this year is better than numerically less last year and means the school is getting better and better. [. . .]

Notes

[1] These names are, of course, fictitious.

[2] I have borrowed this concept from A. Gouldner, discussed by Silverman (1970, p. 155).

[3] 'A' "pressured" academic environment is one in which great emphasis is placed on academic achievement in a traditional sense. Examination sucess is given great prominence and the school's resources are allocated to produce the highest possible achievement for the best pupils' (Lacey, 1974, p. 150).

[4] The categories are the author's.

[5] Figures in brackets are the numbers of actual lessons taught.

[6] The departments of Mathematics, English, History, Geography, Sciences and Modern Languages.

[7] In the same departments as (ref. 6), above.

[8] Burns (1955, p. 474) writes ' . . . the role that involves clique membership is one that accomodates to a degree of failure in the status. The clique . . . appears as an organized retreat from occupational status'.

[9] Burns (1955, p. 480) writes 'The essential points distinguishing cabals from cliques are: (1) there are real status distinctions involved between cabal members. Leadership is important and proximity to the leader is important; (2) the function of cabal membership is neither to redress occupational failure, nor to gain reassurance, but to promote further occupational success outside the cabal; (3) the relationship of the cabal to the outer milieu is not one of withdrawal or rejection, but of power, in which the cabal attempts to restructure situations and values in the interests of its members.'

References

Allen, A. (1971) 'Are teachers streamed?' *Where?* No. 53, pp. 17–20.

Becker, H.S. (1952a) 'The career of the Chicago public schoolteacher', in Hammersley, M. and Woods, P. (eds) *The Process of Schooling*, Routledge and Kegan Paul, London.

Becker, H.S. (1952b) 'Social-class variations in the teacher–pupil relationship', in Cosin, B. *et al.* (eds) *School and Society: A Sociological Reader*, Routledge and Kegan Paul, London.

Becker, H.S. and Geer, B. (1960) 'Latent culture', in Cosin, B. *et al.* (eds), *School and Society: A Sociological Reader*, Routledge and Kegan Paul, London.

Bucher, R. and Strauss, A. (1961). 'Professions in process', in Hammersley, M. and Woods, P. (eds), *The Process of Schooling*, Routledge and Kegan Paul, London.

Burns, T. (1955). 'The reference of conduct in small groups; cliques and cabals in occupational milieux', *Human Relations*, Vol. 8, pp. 467–86.

Child, J. (1972). 'Organizational structure, environment and performance: the role of strategic choice', in Salaman, G. and Thompson, K. (eds), *People and Organizations*, Longman /Open University Press, London.

Dale, R. (1976) 'Work, career and the self', in *Occupational Categories and Cultures I*, The Open University Press, Milton Keynes.

Gouldner, A. W. (1968) 'The sociologist as partisan: sociology in the welfare state', *American Sociologist*, Vol. 3, pp. 103–16.

Hargreaves, D.H. (1967) *Social Relations in a Secondary School*, Routledge and Kegan Paul, London.

Hargreaves, D.H. (1972) *Interpersonal Relations and Education*, Routledge and Kegan Paul, London.

Hughes, E.C. (1958) *Men and their Work*, Free Press, New York.

Lacey, C. (1974) 'Destreaming in a "pressured" academic environment', in Eggleston, J. (ed.), *Contemporary Research in the Sociology of Education*, Methuen, London.

Mankoff, M. (1971) 'Societal reaction and career deviance: A critical analysis', *Sociological Quarterly* Vol. 12, pp. 204–18.

Marcus, E.M. (1971). 'Schoolteachers and Militant Conservatism', in Friedson, E. (ed.), *The Professions and their Prospects*, London: Sage Publications.

McKinlay, J.B. (1972). 'Clients and organizations', in McKinlay, J.B. (ed), *Processing People: Case Studies in Organizational Behaviour*, Holt, Rinehart and Winston, New York.

Shipman, M. (1973). 'Bias in the sociology of education', *Educational Review* Vol. 25, pp. 190–200.

Silverman, D. (1970). *The Theory of Organizations*, Heinemann, London.

Strauss, A., Schatzman, L., Ehrlich, E., Bucher, R. and Sabshin, M. (1963). 'The hospital and its negotiated order', in Salaman, G. and Thompson, K. (eds), *People and Organizations*, Longman, Harlow.

Wilensky, H.L. and Edwards, H. (1959). 'The skidders: ideological adjustments of downward mobile workers', *American Sociological Review*, Vol. 24, pp. 215–31.

Wilkins, L. (1964). 'The Deviance Amplifying System', in Carson, W.G. and Wiles, P. (eds.), *Crime and Delinquency in Britain*, Robertson: London.

Woollacott, J. (1976). 'Dirty and deviant work', in *Occupational Categories and Cultures I*, The Open University Press, Milton Keynes.

Index